The Challenge of
American Foreign Policy

JOHN P. LOVELL

INDIANA UNIVERSITY

The Challenge of American Foreign Policy

Purpose and Adaptation

∽

MACMILLAN PUBLISHING COMPANY, INC.

NEW YORK

Collier Macmillan Publishers

LONDON

PRINTED IN THE UNITED STATES OF AMERICA

Macmillan Publishing Company
866 Third Avenue, New York, New York 10022

Collier Macmillan Canada, Inc.

Library of Congress Cataloging in Publication Data

Lovell, John P.   (date)
    The challenge of American foreign policy.

    Bibliography: p.
    Includes index.
    1. United States—Foreign relations administration.
2. United States—Foreign relations—1945-
I. Title.
JX1706.L68   1985   353.0089   84-15421
ISBN 0-02-371800-5
PRINTING: 1   2   3   4   5   6   7   8   YEAR: 5   6   7   8   9   0   1   2   3

ISBN 0-02-371800-5

To William Metcalf Lovell
and the memory of
our brother, D. J.

Preface

For some years I have had the nagging feeling that Walt Kelly's cartoon character, Pogo, may have been right. Returning from the swampy field of battle, Pogo observed, "We have met the enemy, and they is us" [sic].

The observation, I fear, has applicability to American foreign policy in at least two respects. First, too many times in recent decades American policy makers have compounded rather than alleviated policy problems by their inability or failure to address root causes and by their failure to make adjustments in policy appropriate to changing circumstances. Second, the inadequacies of policy too often have been overlooked or dismissed by those of us who purport to be specialists in the study of foreign policy, reflecting serious deficiencies in the paradigms that we ourselves have employed in interpreting world affairs. Quite simply, often we have asked the wrong questions and therefore have arrived at conclusions that are misleading or irrelevant, and that—to the extent that such paradigms become assimilated into the policy process—make appropriate policy responses to future challenges less probable rather than more probable.

The theme of purposeful adaptation as the central imperative of foreign policy, as developed in this book, is designed to highlight questions that increasingly I have come to see as important—but too often neglected. My uneasiness about the prevailing assumptions and beliefs that have dominated the study and the practice of

American foreign policy goes back many years. Particularly in the era of growing American involvement in Vietnam it seemed to me that a sensitivity to the underlying dynamics of social and political change in Southeast Asia was almost totally missing from the calculations of American policy makers. The 1970s provided an added urgency to the need for policy and paradigmatic reappraisal and readjustment, occasioned, for example, by a world monetary crisis and an energy crisis.

Some readers will find it curious that it was during a year in Carlisle Barracks, Pennsylvania, at the Army War College as a civilian visiting professor that thoughts for the book began to crystallize. The milieu of a military organization is not often thought to be conducive to intellectual creativity and reflection. But in 1978–1979, when I was in Carlisle, the Army itself was in the throes of institutional self-examination in the aftermath of Vietnam, which was reflected also in an openness to critical inquiry more generally about policy matters. The War College was fortunate to have as its commandant an exceptionally articulate and enlightened Army officer, Lieutenant General DeWitt Smith, who was committed to preparing students at the college adequately for future high-level policy responsibilities and thus for fostering an atmosphere in which such preparation was encouraged.

I shared an office with another civilian visiting professor. Eugene Rosi proved to be a kindred spirit in his outlook on foreign policy issues, which we discussed endlessly. From those discussions emerged an outline for this book, which was to have been co-authored. Gene was forced to leave behind those writing plans in order to assume new responsibilities as vice president for academic affairs at Monmouth College, New Jersey, but the book reflects many of the ideas that emerged from our dialogue.

Our mutual concern about the American policy response to the challenges of an era of change was underscored almost weekly if not daily in 1978–1979 by events and actions at home and abroad. For example, among the issues that commanded our attention as well as that of American policy makers in approximately an eighteen-month period beginning in the summer of 1978 were the following. Martial law was declared in Nicaragua in an effort by the Somoza regime to quell a widespread rebellion led by Sandinista forces; ultimately the Sandinistas prevailed and Somoza was forced into exile. Egyptian leader Anwar Sadat and Israeli leader

Menachim Begin met with President Jimmy Carter at Camp David to sign a peace accord, over the heated protests of other Middle Eastern Arab states. American Congressman Leo Ryan and four others were killed in Guyana investigating the activities of a religious cult in Jonestown; shortly thereafter the Reverend Jim Jones and over 900 of his followers had either committed suicide or were murdered. Pope Paul VI died, and within five weeks his successor, Pope John Paul I, also had died and was succeeded by the first Polish Pope, John Paul II.

China reestablished formal diplomatic relations with the United States for the first time since they were broken at the outset of the 1949 Communist victory in the Chinese civil war. Vietnam invaded Kampuchea (Cambodia), and China in turn invaded Vietnam. Somalia, where the United States had established a military base, and Ethiopia, which was supported by a large contingent of Soviet and Cuban military advisors, went to war with one another. Several thousand Angolan-based rebels invaded Shaba province in Zaire. A presidential commission on Latin America chaired by Sol Linowitz, citing evidence from Uruguay, Argentina, Brazil, Guatemala, El Salvador, and elsewhere, reported that "Latin America is suffering a plague of repression." In the face of widespread internal revolutionary opposition and American pressure, the Shah of Iran went into exile, and revolutionary leader Ayotollah Khomeini returned to Iran from exile in Paris. After months of Iranian turmoil, the American embassy in Teheran was seized and some sixty Americans were held hostage. The American ambassador to Afghanistan was assassinated; several months later a coup d'etat occurred, triggering a Soviet invasion to restore a government sympathetic to the Soviet Union. Alarmed by the buildup of Soviet nuclear missiles targeted at West Europe, the NATO defense ministers decided to install nuclear-armed cruise missiles and intermediate-range ballistic missiles in Europe. In South Korea, President Park Chung Hee was assassinated by his intelligence chief; a power struggle ensued that culminated in the imposition of another military-dominated regime.

The Organization of Petroleum Exporting Countries (OPEC) announced two major price increases. Pennsylvania, among other states in the United States, partially rationed gasoline by limiting purchases to odd- or even-numbered days of the month, depending on the final digit on one's auto license plate. Finally, the threat of disaster was posed by an accident at the Three-Mile Island nuclear reactor site, less than an hour from Carlisle.

These and other events provided the focal point for policy discussions. Typically, Gene Rosi and I would meet with several military faculty colleagues in the coffee shop first thing in the morning to explore the issues at hand, to ruminate on policy trends, to marvel at our colleagues' accounts of the inner workings of curious institutions such as the Pentagon, and—if no other topic generated spirited debate—to reargue American policies in Vietnam. The composition of this floating seminar varied somewhat from one day to the next. At the risk of failing to mention some of the key participants, I do want to acknowledge that the following Army colonels (all with advanced academic degrees in the social sciences, history, or the law) were among those who endeavored—sometimes successfully—to help me to sharpen my foreign policy views: Norm Smith, Zane Finkelstein, George Joulwan, Don Shaw, Dave Blackledge, Dick Rodney, George Shevlin, Jim Cullen, Dwight "Hooper" Adams.

Over a period of two decades, I have profited intellectually from exchanging foreign policy ideas with my colleagues at Indiana University. Harvey Starr, Bernard Morris, Edward Buehrig, and Alfred Diamant are among those whose ideas I have tapped with some regularity in recent years. Elinor Ostrom chaired the department of political science during the writing of the book: I appreciate her encouragement and the efforts that she has made to facilitate the work. I am also grateful to my students, undergraduate as well as graduate, with whom I have shared my ideas and whose questions and comments have pushed me to refine my analyses.

Larry Elowitz, John Fitzgerald, Betty Glad, and James Harf critiqued the entire manuscript for the publisher, who forwarded their comments to me. Lisa Condit, Glenn Hastedt, Harvey Starr, Susan Stoudinger, and Barry Zulauf provided comments on one or more chapters.

Bernadine Psaty and Barbara Hopkins helped with the typing, and Fern Anderson and Steve Flinn helped to initiate me to the wonders of the word processor.

I am grateful to the *Air University Review* for permission to incorporate into Chapter 5 portions of my article, "From Defense Policy to National Security Policy," which appeared in the *AUR* 32 (May–June 1981); and to the *Journal of Political and Military Sociology* for permission to reprint, with modification, portions of my article, "The Idiom of National Security," from the *JPMS* 11 (Spring 1983). Also incorporated into various chapters are excerpts from my *Foreign Policy in Perspective* (New York: Holt, Rinehart and Winston, 1970), to which I hold rights.

Tolerance of the intrusion of the author's research and writing habits upon family activities has been provided by my wife, Joanne, and our college-aged children, Sara and David. I love them for that, but mostly for other reasons.

The book is dedicated to two others to whom I have been close for an even longer time—my brothers Bill and D.J.

J.P.L.

Contents

PART FOUR   Conclusions   297

CHAPTER 9   Meeting the Challenges of the 1980s and 1990s: Purpose and Adaptation   299

PART ONE

Foreign Policy: The Nature of the Challenge

CHAPTER 1

་〜

The Study of Foreign Policy

Americans look to their foreign-policy makers in the 1980s to help them meet enormous challenges. The risks of miscalculation and error have never been greater. Of particular concern is the danger of nuclear war in an era of strained relations between superpowers. Related concerns include the failure to secure a workable comprehensive arms control agreement among the superpowers, the continuing frailty of global mechanisms to contain or eliminating armed conflicts which carry the risk of escalation, and the prospect of nuclear-armed terrorists.

However, the challenges of the 1980s and 1990s are not limited to those of avoiding a nuclear holocaust. The world is experiencing profound economic, social, political, technological, and environmental changes—each of which has implications for the United States and for the well being of its people. The challenges of foreign policy therefore include defining and pursuing the national purpose in terms that are consonant with the diverse and changing needs of the American people, and adapting policies and policy institutions to a world environment in flux.

A major objective of this book is to increase the sensitivity of the reader to the imperatives of purpose and adaptation in American foreign policy. Supplementary objectives include familiarizing the reader with the foreign policy process, with the structures and institutions that are most centrally involved in the process at various stages, and with the instruments of foreign policy.

Recent foreign policy experience is cited frequently in order to illustrate the workings of the policy process. More so than in many foreign policy texts, however, the analysis draws upon key transitional epochs in earlier American historical experience. Such experience not only helps to reveal, in many instances, the roots of ideas and attitudes that continue to influence the American approach to world affairs, but also provides insight into the nature and requisites of foreign-policy adaptation in periods of profound change. Hopefully, awareness of how and why American policy makers have met or failed to meet the adaptive demands of the past will improve the capacity of those who gain such awareness to contribute to the solution of the perplexing foreign-policy problems that confront the nation in the years ahead.

The goal of the present chapter is to describe some of the distinctive analytical demands that the student of foreign policy must confront, and to provide an overview of how subsequent chapters will help the reader to meet those demands. A starting point for meeting such demands lies in a recognition of the relevance of foreign policy actions and decisions for all of us as individuals, often in very personal ways.

AMERICANS AND THE WORLD: LINKAGES AND ADAPTATION

The will-o'-the-wisp of American isolationism ended with World War II. The deep involvement in world affairs that followed has had a pervasive influence on the everyday lives of Americans in all parts of the country.

- In Baltimore, an elementary school teacher weeps with a mixture of relief and anguish upon learning that her youngest son, a United States Marine stationed in Lebanon, has survived a terrorist attack that killed or wounded some 300 Americans. Her oldest son died in Vietnam twelve years earlier.
- In the heart of the Midwest, once the bedrock of American isolationism, an Iowa farmer listens carefully to the news announcing the end of an embargo of grain shipments to the Soviet Union. He then calculates the probable effects of the policy change on sales of his wheat crop for the coming year.

- A television sportscaster in Seattle withdraws $2,000 from his bank savings account with the intention of investing in gold. Friends at the television station, however, convince him that such an investment would represent support of South African racism, so he opens up an account in silver in a Swiss bank.
- The valedictorian of a high school graduating class in Omaha enters the Air Force Academy in Colorado. Partly her decision is prompted by a strong sense of patriotism, but partly she is motivated by the thought that an Air Force career may take her back to Brussels and London, where she grew up while her father was serving in these cities as an American Air Force officer.
- A seaside resort in South Carolina is thriving to the point that expansion of facilities is warranted. The manager describes the pattern of profit and the need for expansion in a long letter to the resort owner, a Kuwaiti.
- In Philadelphia, an insurance salesman goes to his local parish church for an evening meeting devoted to a discussion of the devastation wrought by an earthquake in southern Italy, which demolished nearly 400 villages and killed thousands of people. In the end he is persuaded that American governmental relief efforts are meagre and he should contribute to the Catholic Relief Services, which in conjunction with many other private organizations is sending additional aid.
- An automotive engineer sells his home in a Detroit suburb and removes the "Buy American" sticker from the bumper of his car. He is moving to Los Angeles where he will take a job with a company owned by Datsun.
- The president of a department store chain in east Texas becomes concerned about the difficulties that salesclerks are experiencing in communicating with customers, increasing numbers of whom are recent immigrants from Mexico and the Caribbean. Thus, she asks a vice president who is bilingual to launch a program to train all sales personnel so they will have at least minimal proficiency in Spanish.

As events abroad have gained in salience for Americans, so also the actions even of private American citizens can have an important impact on the lives of peoples elsewhere and on the policies of their governments. American businessmen and bankers trade and invest in countries from Europe (East and West) to the Orient.

Tourists from Honolulu and Boston ski on the slopes of the Alps, sip wine in sidewalk cafes in Paris or Mexico City, gaze at the ancient monuments of Athens, and bargain in the shops of Hong Kong. American athletes compete in foreign games.[1] Scholars participate in international conferences; and artists and entertainers perform on world tours. Satellites beam American telecasts to audiences in Rio de Janeiro, Belgrade, Helsinki, and New Delhi.

Often more evident than the effects abroad of the actions of American private citizens has been the impact on other parts of the world of American governmental actions and policies. American soldiers, sailors, airmen, and Marines were dispatched to fight in Korea and Vietnam; more recently, Marines have given their lives as members of a peacekeeping force in Lebanon. Agents of the Central Intelligence Agency helped to topple regimes in Iran and Guatemala in the 1950s and have supported rebel groups seeking to overthrow the Sandinista regime in Nicaragua in the 1980s. Governmental economists and financial experts flew to European capitals and to Tokyo to discuss the devaluation of the dollar in the early 1970s and have met with their foreign counterparts in the 1980s to seek solutions to a world recession compounded by widespread indebtedness (especially evident in countries such as Mexico, Poland, Argentina, and Brazil). In the late 1970s and early 1980s, top-level American diplomats shuttled between Israel and Saudi Arabia to negotiate the terms of the sale of American jet fighter aircraft and AWACS (airborne warning and control system) airplanes to the rival governments. And as demonstrators jammed the streets of Bonn late in 1983 to protest the pending installation of Pershing II intermediate-range nuclear missiles in Germany, American and Soviet representatives met in Geneva to discuss their conflicting views of how the nuclear arms race might be ended and nuclear disarmament initiated.

These are merely among the more highly publicized examples of the impact of an official American presence abroad. At a less dramatic level, the daily activities of the thousands of individuals working for the American government abroad also have their impact. Since World War II, the number of American governmental personnel abroad has risen sharply. As of 1980, the State Department alone had nearly 6,000 of its personnel stationed in some 133 embassies and consular posts abroad, in contrast to 840 State Department personnel stationed in 58 overseas posts in 1940. The

Pentagon, in turn, had half a million military personnel stationed overseas in 1980, from Western Europe to Korea (with an additional 370,000 accompanying them as dependents). Other departments and agencies—Treasury, Commerce, Agriculture, Energy, Labor, CIA—also have hundreds of personnel stationed overseas.

Such personnel abroad, together with their associates in the federal government in Washington, help to formulate and to execute the foreign policies of the United States. Foreign policies are the governing principles that provide the basis for the relations between the United States and other actors on the world stage—other nation-states, international institutions such as the United Nations and the World Bank, multinational corporations, and other groups and institutions. To an important extent, the world environment represents a series of ongoing demands that foreign policies are designed to meet—threats to needed oil supplies, the seizure of diplomatic hostages, propaganda attacks to be countered in the United Nations, a coup d'etat toppling a once-friendly regime. Yet in part the world environment also represents a series of opportunities, which, if pursued successfully, can enhance American interests—beneficial trade agreements to be negotiated, once-hostile governments to be wooed back into friendship, alliances to be secured.

The world, of course, is constantly in flux, and so also are the needs and interests of Americans. Foreign policy makers therefore must learn to adapt to an ever-changing pattern of demands and opportunities. Yet adaptation, in the sense of identifying and responding to change, is a necessary but not a sufficient condition of successful policy. Policy goals must be formulated and priorities among goals must be established that are responsive to national needs and purposes. Policy "success" implies performance that realizes such goals; in the process, it may become necessary to resist some demands from the environment, even as it is important to meet other demands. Moreover, changes that might be required in response to a changing environment or to changing domestic priorities must be anticipated at least in part, lest the resulting shifts of policy be chaotic and disruptive of goal attainment. In short, the foreign policy imperative can be understood as that of *purposeful adaptation*—that is, the need to develop and pursue foreign policy goals that are sensitive to national needs and aspirations and to the realities of a changing world environment.

To describe foreign policy in terms of the adaptive challenge, however, still does not fully capture the complexity of the task. Foreign policy making is centrally involved with keeping abreast of fundamental fluctuations in the global system but it is also more than that. Policy makers must make hundreds if not thousands of decisions daily, the vast majority of which represent responses to immediate problems or routine actions of a preprogrammed nature. Moreover, policy makers sometimes take new initiatives, shift ground, or reconsider policy moves not on the basis of a long-range assessment of adaptive requirements but rather in response to the immediate challenge of an adversary or in order to gain an advantage in an international bargaining situation.

Domestic politics also has its effects upon foreign policy, not merely in the form of pressures that policy makers feel from advocates of "pet" programs or actions but also in the form of parochial concerns pursued at the expense of policy coherence by various organizational elements of the governmental bureaucracy. The turbulence of the domestic and global policy environments and the complexity of the problems and demands to which the makers of foreign policy must respond pose challenges not only for the practitioner but also for the student of foreign policy. It is appropriate for the student as well as the practitioner to attempt to identify fully the nature of the challenges without (in either case) becoming overwhelmed by them.

"LEAVING IT TO THE EXPERTS" AND RELATED HAZARDS

"If you can't stand the heat, stay out of the kitchen," Harry Truman used to say to those who shied away from confronting the tough choices to be made in government. Expecially in the realm of foreign policy, decisions must be made with imperfect information amidst conflicting interpretations of events and competing recommendations regarding preferred courses of action.

The foreign policy agenda with which Harry Truman had to deal in the closing stages of World War II and in the years immediately thereafter was one crowded with difficult and urgent problems demanding attention. Yet the world today in many respects is even more complicated than it was then, and the ability of the United

States to control its geopolitical environment is more limited. Each of us is likely to have been baffled and frustrated at various situations that have arisen in recent years on the world scene—an American embassy is stormed and hostages are seized in Iran; Soviet troops invade Afghanistan and the Soviet government seems oblivious to angry demands by the United States and other governments that they withdraw; the government of South Africa refuses to accept proposals backed by the United States and other governments for elections in Namibia, over which South Africa continues to maintain control despite a World Court ruling declaring such control illegal; insurgencies in Central America lead to bloody strife, with American nuns and journalists among the victims; American Marines, seemingly paralyzed by the limitations of their peacekeeping role in Lebanon, are the object of repeated guerrilla harassment and ultimately of a suicidal terrorist assault.

Yet despite the complexity of global patterns and the irradicable element of uncertainty regarding cause and effect, few events occur about which one does not hear or read interpretations or critiques the tone of which is definitive. "The *real* reason that the OPEC countries raised oil prices so high is as follows . . ." one pundit will tell us. "The Chinese fully expect to go to war with the Soviet Union within five years," another tells us. "President Reagan really is taking his cues now on foreign policy and defense matters from Secretary of State George Shultz rather than from Secretary of Defense Caspar Weinberger," a Washington-based correspondent informs us. Or is it really Presidential assistant James Baker who is the "power behind the scenes"?

Assertions such as these often gain a special aura of authenticity by virtue of the special access to "inside information" that is claimed, explicitly or implicitly. For example, a governmental official defends the actions of the Administration in deploying cruise missiles and Pershing II intermediate-range nuclear missiles in Europe as being essential to the defense of the NATO alliance. When asked about the circumstances under which the missiles would actually be used in the event of a crisis with the Soviet Union, the official declines to answer on the grounds that contingency plans for such use are highly classified. Or a journalist provides what appears to be a devastating exposé of CIA activity in Latin America, based on an interview with a former CIA operative who prefers to remain anonymous.

9

Especially when events seem otherwise impossibly confusing and complicated, such seemingly definitive and simplifying interpretations can be appealing. Why not "leave foreign policy to the experts," the ordinary citizen may be incline to feel. For some persons "leaving it to the experts" provides a rationale for ignoring foreign policy issues completely, in the hope and perhaps the belief that "experts" will keep problems from intruding too extensively into the lives of individual Americans. For others, "leaving it to the experts" can serve as a crutch to prop up preexisting biases and beliefs without the requirement of critical independent thought. If one is predisposed to believe that the current Administration is wise and virtuous, one can be sure of sustaining that belief by treating Administration policy pronouncements as unchallengeable. If, on the other hand, one is inclined to believe that the Administration is filled with knaves and fools, exclusive and uncritical reliance for interpretation of events on sources hostile to the administration will reinforce one's bias.

Although each of us may succumb to one or another of the "leave it to the experts" impulses upon occasion, the impulse is fundamentally contrary to the democratic temperament that most of us share. Instinctively, we recognize that no set of "experts" is infallible. Moreover, we sense that determining which among various foreign policy options is best is in part a matter of making value judgments and only partly a matter to be decided on the basis of resolving questions of fact. In our effort to cope intellectually with the complexities of foreign policy, we profit by consulting the studies and interpretations of persons with special expertise regarding the issues at hand. Yet in so doing we recognize that it is finally we who must sift and winnow the available facts and competing interpretations in our search for understanding. And it is finally we who must apply our own value preferences in reaching conclusions about which of various policy alternatives is "best" or in making judgments regarding the desirability or undesirability of actions that particular policy makers have taken.

To accept responsibility for making one's own judgments about foreign policy is not to ignore the obstacles that may sometimes make it difficult to gather the requisite information for formulating informed opinions. Nor is it to deny that the observer who is not directly privy to policy discussions at top levels has some disadvantages in comparison to the policy "insider." It is useful to be explicit about some of these disadvantages, but it is also important to note that the obstacles to be overcome need not prove to be insurmountable.

DECLARATORY POLICY AND ACTION POLICY

The observer frequently is confronted with nagging doubts about the accuracy of official statements describing policy commitments and intentions. The President or the Secretary of State may "talk tough" in describing American policies toward the Soviet Union, for instance, but how much of the talk is mere rhetoric and how much an accurate description of policy intent? And how can we who are not privy to top-level policy planning sessions know?

The outsider cannot know, for sure.[2] But a starting point on the road to reliable analysis of foreign policy is to accept the possibility of a distinction between what is said (declaratory policy) and the policy commitments or acts that actually are intended (action policy). Almost invariably such a distinction is useful, and it is useful for reasons that go well beyond evasiveness or chronic deceit on the part of politicians.

Declaratory policy is what the government would like potential adversaries, allies, or the domestic public to believe are the government's intentions. Oftentimes, declaratory policy is a reasonably accurate reflection of the government's intentions; many times it is not. Governments often feel that they must disguise their actual intentions.

By appearing belligerent and willing to risk war in defense of particular interests, for example, a government may believe that it can extract concessions from an adversary that would not be forthcoming if a more conciliatory posture were adopted. The hard line that the Kennedy administration adopted in order to get Khrushchev to withdraw missiles from Cuba in 1962 is an example. It appears that the President was prepared to launch an air strike against missile installations if Khrushchev had refused to withdraw the missiles, but how much farther he really was prepared to go in risking war remains unclear.

Under other circumstances, an administration has adopted a declaratory policy that was more conciliatory than the action policy, in order to placate foreign and domestic critics. The use by President Johnson of bombing halts as a prelude to further escalation of the fighting in Vietnam at the end of 1965 and again in early 1967 is illustrative. In each instance, the cessation of bombing of targets in North Vietnam was accompanied by announcements from the White House of offers to the North Vietnamese of peace (on terms which the administration had reason to know were unacceptable). The Johnson declaratory policy had the effect of reassuring the American public that the President was a man of peace, who had resorted to force only because a warlike adversary had been unwilling to respond to reason. Although the majority of the public found the Johnson rhetoric persuasive (at least from 1964-67), it is important to note that many careful observers, even without access to documents and conversations from inside the government, were able to recognize the contrast between the Johnson declaratory policy and action policy from the earliest stages of the escalation of American involvement.[3]

When changing circumstances in world affairs lead to a critical reexamination of American policies, the administration often will maintain a declaratory policy that denies that changes are anticipated. The declaratory policy in such instances is seen as a device for buying time and for providing reassurances to those to whom previous commitments have been made until the administration is fully ready to accept the consequences of abandoning the commitments. A case in point is the Carter administration's rather unenthusiastic expression of continuing support for the Somoza regime in Nicaragua in 1979 even when it appeared clear that the insurgency would succeed in toppling the regime.

Variations on the theme are too numerous to recite here. The point to be emphasized is that the student of foreign policy seldom will have great difficulty identifying declaratory policy. The problem is to determine the extent to which declaratory policy accurately reflects action policy. If a gap exists, the challenge is to try to identify the latter.

The challenge is seldom beyond the reach of the perceptive observer. Actions do speak louder than words, and, over time at least, actions are likely to reveal a pattern of intent. Thus, the observer may remain in doubt regarding immediate, short-range policy plans, but longer-range goals and strategies are likely to be discernible.

PROBLEMS OF ACCESS TO TECHNICAL DATA

Another obstacle that confronts the ordinary citizen in his or her efforts to gain knowledge about foreign policy is lack of access to relevant technical data. Details of the construction and capabililties of American and foreign weapons systems are of this sort. Many such details are made public in popular magazines or professional journals, but much of this type of information is classified and therefore not generally available. One might also properly regard as technical details such information as the number of Soviet military personnel stationed in Afghanistan or the number of Cuban advisors in Angola. For that matter, the size and disposition of specially trained counterterrorist units that are maintained by the United States and its allies are secret—technical details not deemed appropriate for public disclosure. Although details such as those in the examples cited sometimes "leak" from official sources or are uncovered by the probes of unofficial investigators, often they remain available only to a relatively small number of persons.

However, lack of access to secret documents and to policy discussions that are carried on behind closed doors is less debilitating than it might seem to the outsider who is trying to gain an understanding of foreign policy. Crucial policy choices seldom are made primarily on the basis of quantified secrets and technical details. The ordinary citizen may not know precisely the numbers and dispositions of nuclear-equipped weapons possessed by the United States and the Soviet Union in various parts of the world, for instance, but that should not inhibit him or her from arriving at intelligent judgments regarding the desirability or undesirability of various alternative proposals for control of nuclear arms.

Similarly, the policy maker may have more complete access than does the ordinary citizen to details such as the numbers and locations of troops being deployed by the Soviet Union along the Polish or Chinese border, the web of interconnections among international terrorist groups, or the ability of military personnel in certain third-world countries to utilize the American equipment supplied to them effectively. The intelligent student of foreign policy as well as the policy maker, however, is able to gain an understanding of the political, economic, and military contexts within which such details have meaning—to discern the nature of the Sino-Soviet dispute,

13

for instance, or the pattern of recent frictions between Poland and the Soviet Union; to grasp the goals of various international terrorist groups and the risks and promises of alternative strategies for countering them; and to formulate informed judgments about the costs and benefits of supplying military technology and hardware to various third-world regimes.

After all, facts take on significance as guides to policy only as they are interpreted, and the biases and predispositions of "insiders" in the policy process often have neutralized whatever apparent advantage they might have over "outsiders" in the ability to reach sound judgments in making choices among policy options. Occasions in which the public has gained access to hitherto secret governmental documents, such as that provided by the unauthorized publication of the Pentagon papers in 1971 by the *New York Times* and other newspapers, have revealed the frailty of the claim of "insiders" to superior judgment. As Senator Mike Gravel observed in the introduction to a collection of *The Pentagon Papers*, "it is the leaders who have been found lacking, not the people. It is the leaders who have systematically misled, misunderstood, and, most of all, ignored the people in pursuit of a reckless foreign policy which the people never sanctioned."[4] The Pentagon papers traced the sometimes successful efforts of the American government to withhold or misrepresent pertinent facts about the war in Vietnam. Yet a comparison of the judgments made by policy makers with those made by policy critics reflects favorably upon the latter, even though the judgments of perceptive "outsiders" typically were based only on information in the public domain.

The importance of classified information thus should not be overemphasized. Governmental intelligence about day-to-day activities in most parts of the world is derived heavily from sources that are also available to enterprising laypersons. Moreover, the "outsider" has resources available that compare very favorably with those of the policy maker that allow making informed judgments about general trends in world affairs and the fundamental interests and commitments that underlie the foreign policies of nation-states. There is no reason why the intelligent citizen cannot become informed about trends in world energy production and consumption, for example, and thereby draw conclusions about the foreign policy implications of these trends. The same citizen can formulate informed opinions about the future of NATO, about the roots and directions of radical change in Central America and their implications for the United States, and about the depth and probable future direction of the Sino-Soviet dispute.

In other words, the intelligent student of foreign affairs as well as the practitioner can interpret patterns by which interrelated events acquire particular significance. The student can learn to ask the right questions about ongoing world events and policy developments, even though the answers that are formulated to the questions always must remain subject to modification through further inquiry.

THE PROBLEM OF BIAS AND MISPERCEPTION: THE INTERPLAY OF VALUES AND BELIEFS

Although the student of foreign policy can overcome disadvantages that he or she has relative to the "insider" with privileged access to relevant data, other obstacles remain. The observer no less than the policy maker is susceptible to various preconceived biases and faulty assumptions that blur or distort the perception of reality, and that susceptibility may lead to imprudent if not erroneous policy judgments and assessments.

The belief (cognitive) and evaluative (affective) components of the perception and interpretation of reality are closely intertwined. In the first place, our beliefs influence our likes and dislikes. Advertisers, of course, rely on such influences when they market products, and governments employ analogous techniques to promote their policies. Especially in wartime, adversaries are depicted as immoral, allies as virtuous and courageous, and government officials as wise, selfless, and tireless.

Of course attempts to persuade may be factual as well as fabricated; the point to be made, however, is that our beliefs, whether well-founded or not, influence our value preferences. Whether the war in Vietnam arouses in us anger, sorrow, or pride depends largely upon our beliefs about the events that occurred and decisions that were made during the war.

Perhaps more interesting and significant than the influence of beliefs upon value preferences, however, is the influence that value preferences have upon beliefs. The average individual's level of information about most issues of American foreign policy is low rather than high, yet he or she often formulates opinions even in the absence of factual information. Numerous national opinion polls have shown that on any given foreign policy issue, most people who are polled are likely to express their opinions (even though across all issues included in the poll there is likely to be a sizeable group of respondents who have expressed "no opinion" on one or more issues). In those cases in which polling has been accompanied by more extensive interviewing, it has been apparent that opinions are often based on minimal amounts of information.

For instance, individuals took sides on the issue of whether President Truman or General MacArthur was right during the Korean War controversy without knowing in any detail the policy positions of the two men. Individuals express opinions about whether or not the United States government should encourage or permit trade with East European countries without knowing the current legislative restrictions on trade and without any idea of what the economic effects of broadened trade would be. They shout agreement or disagreement with a political candidate who argues that aid to Latin American nations should be terminated, although they lack knowledge of how much aid Latin American nations receive, how the aid is used, and what consequences could be anticipated if aid were reduced or eliminated.[5]

In the absence of factual information, preexisting values and beliefs about other phenomena provide cues to which individuals respond in filling out their belief system. Stereotyping is one familiar device to which people resort in constructing beliefs that conform to existing values and biases. A pertinent example is the research findings of a social psychologist who has compared the views that Americans have of citizens of the Soviet Union with those that Soviet citizens have of Americans. Speaking both Russian and English fluently, he was able to interview a large number of Soviet citizens and a large number of Americans, and his interviews revealed a fascinating pattern of beliefs. The views that citizens of the Soviet Union had of Americans were essentially a mirror image of the views that Americans had of the Soviets. The pattern was one of mutual suspicion and distrust, generating a series of similar beliefs such as the following: the Soviets (Americans) are aggressors; the Soviet (American) people have no real emotional commitment to their government; the Soviet (American) policies are unrealistic and irresponsible.[6]

Granted that the average person falls into a variety of intellectual traps such as stereotyping; what about the person who is above-average in various ways? For instance, what about the individual who is involved more deeply than the average person in foreign affairs or who is better educated? What about the individual who has traveled more than the average person? Do such individuals possess a capacity for objectivity in the perception and interpretation of foreign policy that the average person lacks? Are their opinions based solidly on the facts, uncontaminated by bias or preconceived images or reality?

In the first place, the probability of a person having any opinion on a foreign policy issue is higher among those with a college education than it is among those with only a high-school education. Among those with only a grammar-school education, still fewer are likely to have opinions on foreign policy issues. It is also known that the more formal the education a person has received, the more likely he or she is to express opinions in ways that have an impact on the policy process—writing letters to members of Congress, organizing citizens' groups on behalf of a particular candidate, writing letters to the local newspaper, and so forth.[7] More pertinent to the point at hand, both formal education and informal experiences that increase exposure to and familiarity with foreign policy issues are important bases for reducing a person's susceptibility to error.

Of course, formal education is no guarantee that individuals will utilize their intellectual faculties critically and objectively. It is instructive to note that at the outset of the Korean War and again during the early stages of the escalation of the American involvement in Vietnam, the "follower mentality" was especially pronounced among persons with considerable formal education. That is, in each conflict the President was better able to rely upon educated voters for immediate unquestioning support than he was uneducated voters.[8] Although pollster Daniel Yankelovich has suggested that this "president knows best" tendency among Americans diminished sharply in the post-Watergate era, his data and those of other pollsters obtained in the early 1980s show an increased yearning by voters of all educational levels for strong Presidential leadership.[9]

Other evidence reveals that even those with relatively extensive education and experience tend to look at the world through a filter colored by their value preferences and prior beliefs. American business executives, for example, display an interest in foreign policy issues and a level of knowledge that exceed those of the average citizen. Moreover, they consult news sources with greater regularity than the average citizen. Almost all the respondents included in a study of the foreign policy behavior of business executives indicated that they read at least one daily newspaper regularly, and in most cases, two or three newspapers regularly. Yet, the authors of the study found that even among executives with exposure to reading, discussion, and foreign travel that is much more frequent than is characteristic of the population at large, "exposure to rebutting evidence was much less than one might expect and . . . systematic forces worked to favor exposure to reinforcing information.[10]

This conclusion highlights a general human inclination to expose oneself to viewpoints that are comfortably familiar and to avoid or repress those that challenge one's values and beliefs. The person of conservative disposition, for instance, might well turn regularly to the editorial pages of the *Chicago Tribune* or the *Indianapolis Star* for commentary on current issues of foreign policy, but it is unlikely that he or she would also regularly consult the foreign affairs coverage in *The New York Review of Books*. Conversely, the self-proclaimed radical might well be a devotee of the writings of Herbert Marcuse; it would be rare, however, if the radical were also to follow closely the writings of William F. Buckley, Jr.

None of us, from the most conscientious and intelligent to the most illiterate or indifferent, can rightly make the claim of complete objectivity in continued observations of world affairs. But obviously the starting point for overcoming the distortions introduced by bias and misperception is awareness of their roots and attentiveness to diverse sources of policy interpretation and commentary.

THE ANALYTICAL FRAMEWORK

The obstacles to analysis that have been described will discourage only the fainthearted. For persons truly committed to improving their understanding of American foreign policy, recognition of the obstacles that exist will serve as a useful first step toward analytical competence. The continuing journey, although by no means effortless, is one that persons who value intellectual accomplishment will find rewarding. To those who are sensitive to the drama as well as the importance of current foreign policy issues, the journey is likely to prove to be not merely worthwhile but irresistible.

An understanding of foreign policy requires a sensitivity to the varied preoccupations and concerns of policy makers: coping with daily routines; "playing the game" of international politics with bargaining and the use of various "carrots" and "sticks"; engaging in domestic and bureaucratic politics; making ad hoc as well as carefully planned responses to contingencies as they arise. It is hoped that the chapters that follow will help to cultivate such a sensitivity, but within an analytical framework that highlights the importance of *purposeful adaptation* as the most fundamental function that foreign policy can be made to perform on behalf of the nation-state. The framework is one that permits the description of other activities (presidential decisions, diplomatic maneuvers, bureaucratic politicking, congressional debates) in terms of their effects, for better or worse, on the capacity of the political system to adapt to a complex and ever-changing world environment.

The process by which demands and opportunities are identified, goals and priorities are formulated, policy options are explored and assessed, choices are made, and actions are taken to carry out policy decisions sometimes is nearly as disorderly and intractable as the world to which policy makers must respond. For purposes of clarifying what is involved, however, the various tasks to be performed can be described in terms of stages in the policy process and the logical requisites of optimal performance at each stage can be specified. It takes but a slight leap of the imagination in this age of high-powered computers to conjure up an image of an exotic machine that might be programmed to carry out these various tasks. In Rube Goldberg-style, Chapter 2 outlines such a contraption, an Imaginary Ideal Machine for Making Policy, termed the IIMMP.

The various idealized standards of performance that are assigned to the IIMMP provide a basis for highlighting by contrast the characteristics of the actual policy process. In Chapters 3 through 8 policy making is described as inexorably a political process, and thereby shows how, why and with what consequences the process operates in a fashion that departs from abstract notions of perfect rationality.

The experience of the United States from independence into the early nineteenth century provided the basis for assumptions, images, and goals that served as guideposts for American foreign policy throughout most of the remainder of the nineteenth century. Although challenged at the turn of the century, the traditional foreign policy orientation continued to command respect at least until

World War II. The early foreign policy experience, which is examined in Chapter 3, is important not only because it helps explain the origins of ideas that continue to receive attention into the present, but also because it illustrates vividly the process of purposeful adaptation to a world environment that was changing.

Although America had most of the credentials of a world power at least by the time of World War I, the United States assumed the responsibilities of a world power only beginning with World War II. The challenges of the post-World War II period were formidable, ranging from the urgent need to develop a system of global peace in an era in which weapons of mass destruction had attained unimagined capabilities to the exigencies of postwar economic relief and recovery. An understanding of how the American political system responded to these challenges, and why, is vital as a background to subsequent foreign policy developments, including those of the 1980s. The policies formulated in each of the various postwar issue areas are discussed in Chapter 4, with particular attention to the tendency of the emerging Cold War struggle with the Soviet Union to dominate the policy agenda.

A consensus in support of the foreign policy of containment of Communism emerged in the late 1940s and early 1950s. It was, however, a consensus purchased at some cost in terms of policy flexibility; and it was a consensus that proved incapable of enduring a succession of crises in the late 1960s and early 1970s, including an energy crisis, a monetary crisis, and the agonizing involvement of American forces in Vietnam. These developments are examined in Chapter 5, as are the efforts of subsequent administrations (Nixon, Ford, Carter, Reagan) to forge a new foreign policy consensus. Chapter 5 includes a consideration of the role in the foreign policy process of mass and attentive publics on the one hand and of political elites on the other hand. As the discussion in Chapter 5 explains, the idiom in which foreign policy debates occur is likely to reveal the pattern of political influence that will determine policy outcomes.

Presidential leadership is central not only to consensus building but more fundamentally to the process of adaptation to a changing global and domestic environment. Leadership, however, is a complex phenomenon, involving not merely the personal qualities of the President but also the organizational capabilities of the bureaucracy and other elements of the foreign policy structure. The evolution of the modern foreign policy bureaucracy is traced in Chapter 6, with emphasis on the emergence of national security concerns in the post-World War II era, and on distinctive attitudes and values that have shaped the organizational subcultures of the State Department, the Pentagon, and the Central Intelligence Agency. The efforts of the President and his advisors to devise procedures and organize the bureaucracy in a manner that will be optimal for foreign policy effectiveness and efficiency are examined in Chapter 7, with particular attention to a number of vexing dilemmas that complicate these efforts.

The President, as the nation's chief diplomat and as commander-in-chief of the armed forces, stands at the apex of authority for the formulation and execution of foreign policy. Throughout much of the Cold War era, the Congress gave the President a virtual "blank check" for charting the course of foreign policy. Beginning in the late 1960s, the Congress became more assertive, making demands for extensive involvement in defining the direction if not the content of foreign policy that continued into the 1970s. Although Ronald Reagan interpreted his election to the presidency in 1980 and his reelection in 1984 as a mandate for strong presidential leadership and expected that Congress would follow the presidential lead, control of the lower house of Congress was retained by the opposition party and on many foreign policy issues the President has continued to encounter a feisty Congress. The political interplay between the President and the Congress on foreign policy issues, their respective styles and approaches to the issues, and their strengths and limitations as key participants in the policy process are examined in Chapter 8.

The book turns in Chapter 9 to a consideration of the global challenges facing the United States as we approach the final decade of the twentieth century. The chapter concludes with a critical assessment of the doctrines and assumptions that to date have provided the conceptual underpinning for the American foreign policy response to those challenges.

NOTES

1. Or, as in the case of the 1980 Olympic Summer Games in Moscow, fail to do so, with consequences for the policies of foreign governments as well.
2. Indeed, sometimes even the close associates and advisers of a President or a top policy

official cannot be totally confident that a public statement fully and accurately reflects policy intent.

3. See Theodore Draper, "Vietnam: How Not to Negotiate," *New York Review of Books* (May 4, 1967), special supplement pp. 17–29. Also Franz Schurmann, Peter D. Scott, and Reginald Zelnik, *The Politics of Escalation in Vietnam*, paperback edition (New York: Fawcett, 1966).

4. *The Pentagon Papers, The Defense Department History of United States Decisionmaking on Vietnam*, Senator Gravel edition, 4 vols. (Boston: Beacon press, 1971), 1: x.

5. A national poll conducted in 1981 found that half of the American people had no idea of the location of El Salvador, but nearly three fourths of the respondents expressed the view that it would be unwise for the United States to become involved in that country.

6. Urie Bronfenbrenner, "The Mirror Image in Soviet-American Relations: A Social Psychologist's Report," *Journal of Social Issues* 17 (1961): 45–46.

7. The relationship between education and public opinion is discussed in Bernard Hennessy, *Public Opinion*, 4th ed. (Monterrey, Calif: Brooks/Cole, 1981), Ch. 11; also V. O. Key, Jr., *Public Opinion and American Democracy* (New York: Alfred A. Knopf, 1961), pp. 315–343.

8. John E. Mueller, *War, Presidents and Public Opinion* (New York: John Wiley & Sons, 1973), chap. 5.

9. Daniel Yankelovich, "Farewell to 'President Knows Best'," in *America and the World 1978*, ed. William P. Bundy (New York: Pergamon Press and Council on Foreign Relations, 1979), pp. 670–693: also Daniel Yankelovich and Larry Kaagan, "Assertive America," in *America and the World 1980*, ed. William P. Bundy (New York: Pergamon Press and Council on Foreign Relations, 1981), pp. 696–713.

10. Raymond A. Bauer, Ithiel de Sola Pool, and Lewis A. Dexter, *American Business and Public Policy* (New York: Atherton, 1963), p. 241. Nearly half read the *Wall Street Journal* daily and roughly a third read *The New York Times* regularly.

SUGGESTED ADDITIONAL READING

AMBROSE, STEPHEN E. *Rise to Globalism: American Foreign Policy Since 1938.* 3d rev. ed. New York: Penguin, 1983.

BERKOWITZ, MORTON; BOCK, P. G.; and FUCCILO, VINCENT J., eds. *The Politics of American Foreign Policy.* Englewood Cliffs, NJ: Prentice-Hall, 1977.

BROWN, SEYOM. *On the Front Burner: Issues in U.S. Foreign Policy.* Boston: Little, Brown, 1984.

GRAY, ROBERT C. and MICHALAK, STANLEY J., JR., eds. *American Foreign Policy Since Detente.* New York: Harper & Row, 1984.

HOFFMANN, STANLEY. *Primacy or World Order: American Foreign Policy Since the Cold War.* New York: McGraw-Hill, 1978.

KEGLEY, CHARLES W., JR. and WITTKOPF, EUGENE R., eds. *Perspectives on American Foreign Policy: Selected Readings.* New York: St. Martin's, 1983.

NATHAN, JAMES A. and OLIVER, JAMES K. *United States Foreign Policy and World Order.* 2d ed. Boston: Little, Brown, 1981.

OYE, KENNETH A.; LIEBER, ROBERT J.; and ROTHCHILD, DONALD, eds. *Eagle Defiant: United States Foreign Policy in the 1980s.* Boston: Little, Brown, 1983.

ROSENAU, JAMES N. *The Study of Political Adaptation.* New York: Nichols, 1981.

SMITH, STEVEN M. *Foreign Policy Adaptation.* New York: Nichols, 1981.

SPANIER, JOHN. *American Foreign Policy Since World War II.* 8th ed. New York: Holt, Rinehart and Winston, 1980.

SPROUT, HAROLD and MARGARET. *The Ecological Perspective on Human Affairs: With Special Reference to International Politics.* Princeton, NJ: Princeton University Press, 1974.

VOCKE, WILLIAM C., ed. *American Foreign Policy: An Analytical Approach.* New York: Free Press, 1976.

CHAPTER 2

⌒

The Structure and Process of Foreign Policy in the Computer Age: Imaginary Ideals and Real Requirements

"The goal of the new intellectual technology is, neither more nor less, to realize a social alchemist's dream: the dream of 'ordering' the mass society. . . . The aggregate patterns [of billions of decisions which individuals make daily] could be charted as neatly as the geometer triangulates the height and the horizon. If the computer is the tool, then decision theory is its master."

—Daniel Bell, author of *The Coming of the Post-Industrial Society*

". . . The making of national decisions is not a problem for the efficiency expert, or of assembling different pieces of policy logically as if the product were an automobile. Policy faces inward as much as outward, seeking to reconcile conflicting goals, to adjust aspirations to available means, and to accommodate the different advocates of these competing goals and aspirations to one another. It is here that the essence of policy-making seems to lie, in a process that is in its deepest sense political."

—Roger Hilsman, former advisor to Presidents John F. Kennedy and Lyndon B. Johnson

In 1982 *Time* magazine's choice for "Man of the Year" was a computer. The selection symbolized an increasing popular awareness of the revolution in computer technology that has been transforming

modern business practices, educational techniques, and even entertainment patterns.

The realm of foreign policy, too, has felt the impact of computer
technology—illustrated, for instance, by the incident in September
1983 in which a South Korean airliner was shot down over Soviet
territory with a loss of 269 lives. It was through the use of computerized electronic detection equipment that the American, South
Korean, and Japanese governments were able to track both the
flight of the Korean airliner and the Soviet jet aircraft that pursued
and ultimately destroyed it; it was on the basis of such information
that the Reagan administration and its allies decided on a set of
policy sanctions to be imposed against the Soviets.

The computer has become such an integral component of information processing that it is fair to say that without such a capability,
a government in the modern age would be at a competitive disadvantage relative to its computer-aided rivals. This disadvantage
would be comparable to a horse and buggy competing with the
frontrunners in the Indianapolis 500 auto race.

Given the revolution in computer technology, it is tempting to
speculate wishfully about a vastly expanded application of such
capabilities for dealing with the challenges of foreign policy. In
this chapter, you are asked to engage in such speculation and
visualize foreign policy being formulated and executed by an imaginary computer. In indulging in such speculation, the flight of fancy
should be recognized for what it is. The image is designed to
highlight the essential tasks that must be performed in the foreign
policy process. Idealized standards for the performance of these tasks
are postulated early in the chapter not because it is to these standards that policy makers should be held, but, on the contrary,
because these standards provide insight into the limitations of performance that prevail in the real world of policy making.

IMAGINARY IDEAL MACHINE
FOR MAKING POLICY

Although it was common even before the computer age to refer
to "the machinery of government" that makes foreign policy, let
us consider the seemingly infinite capabilities of the modern computer and push the machinery metaphor to its extreme. Let us
suppose that we were able to prevail upon some modern-day Rube

Goldberg, assisted perhaps by a few computer programmers from the University of Michigan, the University of California, and Harvard and a crew of engineers from the Massachusetts Institute of Technology, Georgia Tech, and Purdue, to construct a miraculously sophisticated computerized machine that could accomplish all the functions associated with the foreign policy process. Let us dub such a fanciful creation the Imaginary Ideal Machine for Making Policy (the IIMMP).

What tasks should such a machine be capable of performing? What performance criteria should it meet in order that the machine could be described as ideal?

The essential tasks to be performed in the foreign policy process can be conceptualized as a series of sequential steps (Fig. 2-1). General goals are formulated; intelligence regarding developments in world affairs that might bear on goal attainment is gathered and analyzed; policy options are formulated and weighed; policy plans, programs, and actions are developed; appropriate official policy pronouncements are made; the implementation of policy is monitored and appraised. At each stage, policy makers draw upon their own previous experience and that of the institutions with which they are associated (represented in Figure 2-1 by memory storage and recall); in turn, their decisions and actions contribute to the body of experience upon which they or their successors will draw. Finally,

FIGURE 2-1   **THE FOREIGN POLICY PROCESS**

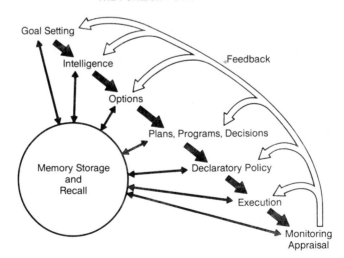

a feedback loop suggests that as policies are formulated, implemented, and appraised, these actions in turn "feed back" to the first steps of the process, leading perhaps to modification of goals, new intelligence estimates, and new policy options. The capabilities that the designers of the IIMMP must incorporate for the performance of each of the requisite tasks are outlined in Table 2-1.

Logically, the first of the tasks to be performed in the foreign policy process is goal setting. The central challenge of foreign policy has been described as being that of purposeful adaptation to an ever-changing world environment. Policies must be developed not merely in response to problems that are posed by the actions of others in the global arena, but first and foremost in pursuit of objectives that will meet national needs and promote and protect national interests. Thus, the first requirement that the designers must meet in building the IIMMP would be that the machine have

TABLE 2-1   Capabilities of an Imaginary Ideal Machine for Making Policy

TASK	CAPABILITY
Goal Setting	Identification of national needs, interests, and priorities
Intelligence	Thorough, rapid, accurate gathering, interpreting, and reporting
Option Formulation	Comprehensive search for options; tallying of probable costs and benefits of each
Plans, Programs, Decisions	Selection of option most likely to provide optimal ratio of gains to costs
Declaratory Policy	Effective articulation of policy and rationale, so as to enlist domestic and foreign support
Execution	Allocation of resources in a manner to ensure effectiveness of each action element and minimize waste; clear coordination and control of all action elements; decisive
Monitoring and Appraisal	Thorough and continuous assessment of the effects of policy actions and commitments; flexibility in correcting for error and adjusting to changing circumstances
Memory Storage and Recall	Learning from experience; quick and accurate recall

the capability to identify national needs and interests and formulate goals, in order of priority, that would satisfy these interests and needs.

The next task is that of intelligence, that is, the gathering, analyzing, and reporting of information about world affairs. The designers of the IIMMP would need to provide the IIMMP with a capability analogous to a super-radar, which could constantly scan the geopolitical world environment in order to determine which of the hundreds of thousands of actions and events that are occurring at any given moment are of potential relevance to policy. Rumors would need to be sorted out from "hard" facts. The actions and events that are observed would need to be given meaning within the cultural, political, and historical contexts in which they occur. Patterns and trends among events would need to be identified and their policy significance assessed. Moreover, the IIMMP would need to be able not only to gather and interpret intelligence data but also to make it rapidly available in usable form for purposes of formulating and evaluating policy options.

The intelligence that is gathered in the policy process is linked to goals that have been established as the IIMMP illuminates alternative courses of action that are available. Recognition of available options and an ability to differentiate among them clearly are crucial to policy success. What alternative courses of action are available and what would be the consequences of pursuing each of the various alternatives, given an ever-changing pattern of demands and opportunities in a complex world environment?

An IIMMP would need to be able to process an enormous number of variables at once, analyzing the most complex relationships among these variables. In other words, the IIMMP must have the capability of the most advanced computer in contrast, for instance, to the capability of early models of the cash register or desk calculator, which can perform only a few simple operations involving a small number of variables. Moreover, the IIMMP would need to be able to predict the probable costs and benefits of alternative courses of action—in terms of immediate consequences and in terms of the longer-range adaptive challenge. Therefore, an additional IIMMP performance requirement would be that of formulating policy options in terms that make explicit the risks and potential rewards that are associated with each.

Having developed an array of policy alternatives, with the potential consequences of each clearly identified, the IIMMP would need to translate preferred alternatives into plans, programs, and actions and to formulate declaratory policies appropriate to each of the action policies. As explained in Chapter 1, the tasks of formulating "action" policies and formulating "declaratory" policy are distinct. Action policies in the foreign policy realm consist of plans for what the government actually will do in the future or would do if particular contingencies were to arise. They consist also of the allocation of resources to particular programs, such as bilateral trade agreements or defense pacts, and of actions, such as the imposition of a trade embargo or the dispatch of a military advisory team to a foreign country.

Declaratory policies are threats, promises, proposals, proclamations, or official descriptions of policy that are announced by the government or suggested by governmental officials in press briefings, public presentations, meetings with foreign officials, and the like. Declaratory policy is what the government would like the target audience—the domestic public, allies, or adversaries—to believe are the policy intentions of the government.

The challenge that the designers of the IIMMP must meet is to develop a capability for formulating plans, programs, and courses of action that are optimal, given available options, and for designing declaratory policies that would enhance the chances of success for the execution of action policies by enlisting support at home and abroad.

Policy takes effect not simply when it is designed or articulated, but when it is implemented. Thus, a vital additional task element to be included in the IIMMP is that of policy execution. Resources must be allocated among the various agencies and elements of the government that are needed to carry out policy programs and actions. An IIMMP would meet our standards of perfection only to the extent that such allocation provided all action elements with sufficient resources to carry out assigned tasks effectively; at the same time, however, no resources should be committed that are not needed for the task at hand. The IIMMP would be expected to develop clear lines of authority for execution of policy and to ensure the coordination of the activities of all action elements. Implementation would be decisive, without hesitation or delay.

Successful foreign policy is more than a matter of making wise choices in the design and execution of policy. It also requires thoroughness in monitoring policy actions and commitments and evaluating their effects and flexibility in making adjustments to correct for initial errors or for changing circumstances. The process of monitoring and appraisal would provide feedback on a continuing basis into intelligence estimates, into the formulation and assessment of policy options, and into the storage and recall that are associated with policy learning.

Finally, if the IIMMP truly were to enable the nation to realize its goals in a complex and dynamic world environment, it must have a capability for learning from experience and for making available in the future the lessons of the past. The IIMMP designers, therefore, must develop a machine with an unlimited memory and a capacity for instant and accurate recall whenever the need arises.

THE IIMMP AS AN ILLUSORY STANDARD

The notion of assigning all essential tasks of foreign policy to a machine with unlimited capabilities is one that in the computer age may have some appeal. Perhaps with an IIMMP success in the development and execution of foreign policy might be assured. The machinery of American foreign policy at last would be freed of costly blunders, setbacks, and frustrations.

Such yearning for perfection, however, must be recognized as illusory. The Rube Goldberg-like device described here is not, in fact, the embodiment of performance capabilities to be approximated in the actual foreign policy system. Rather, as the name of the machine suggests, imaginary ideals were described. The most obvious reason that policy making in the real world resembles an IIMMP only in tasks that are undertaken and not in performance is that the requisite functions are performed by fallible human beings operating within the context of human organizations and political pressures.

The second reason why the performance capabilities attributed to an IIMMP are but imaginary ideals is less obvious: even if an IIMMP with the characteristics described could be created, success in the formulation and execution of foreign policy could not be assured because the requisites of "success" itself are matters of value judgment to be determined through the political process—not through "programming," as would be the case with a computer.

The making and execution of foreign policy invariably involve tradeoffs among competing values. Even when agreement among key parties can be reached regarding what performance criteria such as "effectiveness," "efficiency," or "accountability" mean, the process itself requires at least the partial sacrifice of some of these values in the pursuit of others. Moreover, short-term "success" in satisfying some values may represent failure to make the hard choices necessary to preserve these and other values in the long term, which is the adaptive challenge.

In short, the policy process is political, and politics cannot be reduced to the functions of even a marvelously ingenious machine. In the final portion of the chapter, the nature of some of the important tradeoffs that are made in the foreign policy process is explored.

HUMAN FALLIBILITY AND
THE FOREIGN POLICY PROCESS

There is logic in the process by which American foreign policies are made and executed in the real world, but it is the tumultuous logic of human beings attempting to cope under competing political pressures with the demands of an ever-changing environment. At times, the pattern has been one of vision and courage in the face of complex challenges and adversity. At other times, however, experience has provided support for Gunnar Myrdal's judgment that "the foolishness of foreign policies may, on balance, be even greater today . . . [than they were three hundred years ago, when the Swedish Chancellor reflected], 'My son, my son, if you knew with what little wisdom the world is ruled.' "[1]

The remainder of this book is devoted to a detailed examination of how the American political system functions in the performance of the essential tasks of making and executing foreign policy. At this point, some of the important limitations that are experienced because the tasks are performed by human beings operating within political and organizational contexts in response to an enormously complex world environment are highlighted. The limitations are summarized in Table 2-2.

NATIONAL INTERESTS AND GOALS   Of course, at the very outset of the design of the fictitious IIMMP, a problem crucial to

31

TABLE 2-2   Foreign Policy "Machinery" in Practice:
            Characteristic Limitations

TASK	CAPABILITY
Goal Setting	"National interests" are the object of competing claims; goals are established through political struggle
Intelligence	Always incomplete; system susceptible to overload; delays and distortions in reporting; biases and ambiguities in interpretion
Option Formulation	Limited search for options; comparisons are made in general terms according to predispositions rather than according to specific cost-benefit items
Plans, Programs, Decisions	Choices are made in accordance with prevailing mind-sets, influenced by "groupthink" and political considerations
Declaratory Policy	Multiple voices, contradictions and confusion; self-serving concern for personal image and feeding the appetite of the media
Execution	Breakdowns in communication; fuzzy lines of authority; organizational parochialism; bureaucratic politics; delays
Monitoring and Appraisal	Gaps; vague standards; rigidities in adaptation; feedback failures
Memory Storage and Recall	Spotty and unreliable; "lessons" from experience are remembered selectively and applied imprecisely

real-world policy making was arbitrarily wished away. Its designers were to make sure that the IIMMP had "a capability of identifying national needs and interests, and of formulating goals, in order of priority, that would satisfy these interests and needs." But how are "national needs and interests" to be identified? And how can we be sure that goals and priorities that are established by any given administration in fact satisfy national needs and interests?

It is comfortable to be told, as we frequently are by governmental officials, that a given policy has been adopted because it "meets national needs" and is "in the national interest." It is emotionally disquieting to hear, as we often do from critics of particular policies, that national needs and the national interest have been ignored or compromised. But for reasons that shall be elaborated in Chapters 3 through 5, "national needs" and "the national interest" are identifiable only through the give and take of the political process, not through an abstract process of deduction from "the facts." We Americans are urban and rural; rich and poor; female and male; black, white, yellow, and red. Our needs and interests vary not only with these differences but also with others, such as occupation and the regions in which we live. "The national interest" is the object of competing claims; so also are the generalized foreign policy goals and priorities that are deemed to be "in the national interest." The challenge of foreign policy leadership, therefore, is less that of "discovering the national interest" (as an archaeologist might discover an early Roman artifact) than it is that of mobilizing a national consensus on behalf of a set of goals and priorities that reflect a compromise among competing claims.

THE GATHERING AND ANALYSIS OF INFORMATION   In recent decades, the challenge of mobilizing a national consensus has proved to be one that has eluded presidents much of the time. The contrast between the real world and that of the IIMMP, moreover, is evident when the problem of information-gathering and analysis, that is, intelligence, is considered. Hundreds of thousands of events are occurring hourly in the global environment. In contrast to the fictitious IIMMP, no political system can possibly keep abreast of all these occurrences, much less respond to them all.

The magnitude of the problem of managing the flow of information can be appreciated with the help of a mental image. Imagine a huge map of the world, large enough to cover the entire wall of a large auditorium. Suppose that on the map were plotted the locations of every American diplomat, intelligence agent, and other individual who had a responsibility for feeding information about occurrences in the world into the foreign policy system. The plot would result in thousands of dots reaching nearly every land mass on the map, as well as several locations at sea.[2]

Imagine further that for every location of an intelligence source, there is a small light bulb, and that wires lead from each of the bulbs back to data processing and analysis locations (for example, several of the major capitals of the world and geographic crossroads such as Honolulu) and to the governmental "nerve center" in

Washington. Imagine now that for every impulse received in the form of information about some event by an intelligence source, the bulb at the source would light up.[3]

Also imagine that every time information is transmitted from a source to data processing locations and to the nerve center in Washington, the wire between the points would also light up. The picture that would be created would resemble an enormous nervous system. At any given instant, hundreds of bulbs on the map would be flashing and an intricate web of illumination would describe the pattern of signals being sent.

Charles Thayer, retired American diplomat, has accurately described an American embassy as being "in a very real sense a switchboard for messages between Washington and a foreign government. It is duplicated by another switchboard in the host nation's embassy in Washington."[4] It must be added, however, that "switchboards" sometimes become overloaded in the world of diplomacy. Moreover, the "switchboard operators" of the foreign policy process get lines crossed or fall behind in processing calls. Some messages never get sent; others become garbled or distorted in transmission or cannot be understood because of the "noise" in the system created by competing signals and events. Furthermore, those in Washington or in other communications centers who have responsibility for receiving and analyzing information may misinterpret the messages that are sent. Even the brightest and most objective of policy makers bring to their roles their own predispositions, values, and operating assumptions, and therein lie the bases for bias and distortion.

FORMULATION OF OPTIONS AND INITIATION OF ACTION

The contrast between the behavior of real human beings in the foreign policy process and the hypothetical capabilities of an IIMMP is also evident in the ways in which options are formulated and evaluated and actions initiated and executed. Whereas the designers of the IIMMP were asked to have the machine consider all policy alternatives that might be logically possible in any given situation, human beings tend to be far from comprehensive in their search for options. Rather, policy makers are likely to be predisposed toward consideration of two or three possibilities, ignoring choices that would force them to reexamine high priority goals or cherished operating assumptions.

Moreover, the information needed to make a totally thorough assessment of policy alternatives is likely never to be present. The costs in terms of time and energy required to obtain the information needed to make the search for and assessment of options more complete are likely to seem to outweigh probable benefits to be derived from the search. Abundant studies of behavior in governmental and nongovernmental organizations alike reveal that precise cost–benefit comparisons rarely are the basis for policy choices; rather, policy makers tend to make generalized comparisons among options, rejecting courses of action simply when they fall outside broad guidelines of acceptability.[5]

As noted by observers such as de Rivera, Yergin, and Janis, the choices that are made tend to be influenced by prevailing "mindsets"—the "commanding ideas" of an era—and by the tendencies toward "groupthink" that operate especially in groups sharing a common sense of loyalty and commitment and operating under pressure.[6] With the IIMMP, as courses of action are formulated, declaratory policies are developed that would support the action policies, increasing the probability that such policies would be implemented successfully. In actual practice, however, the complementarity of declaratory and action policies cannot be assumed. First of all, declarations and seemingly official commentary on policy emerge from a variety of sources within the government, providing an array of descriptions and explanations of policy that may be notable primarily for its contradictory themes. During the 1982 war in Lebanon, for example, comments to the mass media on the American policy position were provided by President Reagan and his press secretary, by roving ambassador Philip Habib, by Defense Secretary Caspar Weinberger, by Secretary of State Alexander Haig (until he resigned and was replaced by a man seemingly less pro-Israeli, George Shultz, who offered his own comments) and even by a congressional delegation that met with Palestine Liberation Organization leader Yassir Arafat and made their own policy recommendations.

The mass media have an important role to play in a democracy. When played effectively, the role results in continuous challenges to public officials to justify their actions and to explain why policies that are being pursued are preferable to available alternatives. The counterpoint of the media challenge, however, is a tendency for those in public life to provide self-serving explanations of their actions and to become skillful in shrouding their policy statements in sufficient ambiguity to permit a shift of position if subsequent political demands should so dictate. Moreover, those whose careers as aides or staff members depend upon remaining in good favor with the President, the Secretary of State, or other top personnel, tend toward hyperbole in the claims they make for policies identified with their patrons and toward obfuscation in instances when particular policy commitments or actions might seem to reveal misjudgment or error.

The complexity of the governmental apparatus also helps to explain the discrepancy between real policy making and execution and abstract models of how the process ought to operate if it were totally "rational." On major foreign policy issues, the President's principal White House advisors, the secretaries of State and Defense and perhaps of other departments such as Treasury, all are likely to have important responsibilities for developing policy. Lines of authority in regard to the handling of such issues often are inexact and fluid, as periodic feuds between recent secretaries of State and Defense, and between the secretaries and White House advisors, suggest.

Coordination of major foreign policy undertakings can assume gargantuan proportions, given the vast network of agencies and personnel that is likely to be involved in policy roles. Delay is endemic, and a breakdown of communications among key participants is a contingency that must be anticipated periodically.

EXPERTISE AND RESPONSIBILITY   Expertise and responsibility are broadly distributed throughout the structures of foreign policy. Persons whose primary responsibility is that of keeping abreast of the United States–Soviet strategic competition and formulating doctrine appropriate to strategic requirements, for example, are unlikely to have primary responsibility for decisions regarding the allocation of the budget or for formulating arms control policies— even though all of these areas of concern are interrelated in important respects.

Budgetary experts in the Office of Management and Budget (OMB) may confer with strategic planners in the Pentagon as well as with arms control experts in the Arms Control and Disarmament Agency (ACDA). However, representatives of each of the various agencies and realms of expertise is likely to bring a distinctive perspective to bear on the problems at hand. The strategic planner, for instance, necessarily gives emphasis to threat assessment, often-times imposing "worst case" assumptions in a determination of what is required in order to preserve an American strategic advantage. The budget analyst is likely to address himself or herself to questions of cost-efficiency, weighing the merits of particular programs not only against alternative strategies that seem feasible and perhaps more cost-effective, but also against competing domestic programs. The arms control expert looks at the implications of strategic policy decisions for current arms control agreements and for bargaining positions in future negotiations. "Where you stand depends upon where you sit," as Miles's Law puts it. The result is bureaucratic politics, which is an important influence on the foreign policy process.

Even with the best of intentions, those who are charged with monitoring policy operations and providing the appraisals by which errors can be corrected and adjustments to changing circumstances can be made are unlikely to be able to provide continuous feedback. Military officers charged with overseeing a military assistance prog-ram in El Salvador, or Agency for International Development per-sonnel monitoring a program for economic development in Sierra Leone, for example, are likely to have their own ideas about the kinds of information that should be provided to Washington regard-ing the progress of these programs. It simply is not feasible for policy makers in Washington to anticipate fully the data that might be required of personnel in the field in order to provide an adequate basis for policy adjustments.

In practice, these means that gaps between what is needed and what is provided arise. Gaps arise from lapses in reporting and also from flaws in individual and organizational learning capabilities. The perception and retention abilities of human beings, unlike those of an IIMMP, are incomplete. Information or lessons from experience that might be vital to future needs are filtered out, forgotten, or distorted. Current desires, fears, and beliefs are likely to affect what is recalled and what is forgotten, and previous experi-ence may take on totally new form in order to be emotionally acceptable in the present.

Moreover, even when previous experience is remembered accu-rately, the "lessons of the past" may be applied inappropriately to the current context, as Ernest May's vivid examples from American historical experience remind us. Adjustments that ought to be made to changing circumstances are not made, either because feedback is inadequate or because the machinery of government has proved too cumbersome to respond to the signals calling for change. As the prolonged involvement of the United States in Vietnam painfully demonstrated, a powerful inertia can develop even in support of ill-conceived policies and even when reports from the field provide ample evidence of a need for change. Moreover, as Earl Ravenal has demonstrated in an analysis of foreign policy debate in the years since Vietnam, those who have shared a common experience may interpret what they have experienced in sharply divergent ways. Thus, rather than serving as an instrument for coping with a new environment, "lessons" imperfectly assimilated from previous experience may hinder the process of adaptation.[7]

VALUE TRADEOFFS
AND COMPROMISES IN THE
POLICY STRUCTURE AND PROCESS

The points made above about the contrast between the actual foreign policy process with the IIMMP emphasized the fallibility of human beings and the organizational and political pressures to which they are responsive in carrying out their responsibilities. These points go a long way toward answering the question posed early in the chapter: "What is it that we can reasonably expect of the foreign policy process and its institutions?" However, only as we recognize the competing values that are at stake in the formulation and execution of policy can we fully clarify our expectations regarding the operation of the policy process; only then can we deal adequately with another important question: "How do policy makers measure the success of the policy-making system and how do we concerned observers, in turn, determine if the institutions that are central to the foreign policy process are serving us well or serving us poorly?"

In postulating requirements for the design of an IIMMP, a variety of performance criteria were stipulated, ranging from responsiveness to national needs and interests to effectiveness in the performance of requisite tasks and efficiency in the utilization of resources. The implicit assumption that was made was that all of these desiderata were mutually compatible. That is, effectiveness could be attained (through the IIMMP) without sacrificing efficiency; efficiency could be gained without compromising the commitment of the system to being responsive to popular expressions of needs and interests, and so forth.

CHOICES AMONG COMPETING VALUES   One of the most important insights that can be gained into the challenge of foreign policy making in real political systems, however, is that the above assumption does not hold true. Rather, the foreign policy process invariably involves tradeoffs among competing value preferences. The general problem was indentified a century and a half ago by the perceptive French observer of American life and democratic institutions, Alexis de Tocqueville. In Tocqueville's view, a tradeoff that policy makers in a democracy invariably made was to sacrifice diplomatic finesse in order to remain responsive to popular demands. His reasoning, in part, was as follows:

> Foreign politics demand scarcely any of those qualities which a democracy possesses; and they require, on the contrary, the perfect use of almost all of those faculties in which it is deficient. . . . A democracy is unable to regulate the details of an important undertaking, to persevere in a design, and to work out its execution in the presence of serious obstacles. It cannot combine its measures with secrecy, and it will not await their consequences with patience. These are qualities which more expecially belong to an individual or to an aristocracy.[8]

Tocqueville's view that undemocratic systems are likely to be more skillful than democratic ones in the conduct of foreign policy may be disputed. A comparison of the foreign policy process in the Soviet Union with that in the United States, for instance, does not offer impressive substantiation of the proposition that undemocratic systems are more consistently adept in matters of diplomacy. Soviet foreign policies of the late Brezhnev period have been described by Seweryn Bialer, a prominent student of Soviet affairs, as "characterized by inconsistencies, ambiguities, and drift." Of course, one must not exaggerate the distinction in practice between constraints that American policy makers experience in a democratic system and the apparent absence of such constraints in a system like the Soviet Union. Bialer concluded that "despite the key role of the top leader, Brezhnev, in formulating Soviet foreign policy, the policymaking process has become more consensual than at any time in the past. An attempt is made to achieve unanimity in policymaking at the top level and to take into consideration the institutional interest of various elite groups."[9]

On the other hand, whether or not one accepts the applicability of Tocqueville's conclusions to current comparisons, his argument raises a provocative issue: can policy makers adhere fully to the requisites of democratic practice, such as responsiveness to the popular will, while also performing their job in a manner that will be optimal to the attainment of foreign policy success? The answer, in practice, is that they do not invariably satisfy both sets of requirements. Compromises of one set of values are made in situations when demands for the attainment of the other set of values are more pressing. In every major war, for instance, the American government has increased the secrecy of its procedures and has imposed severe restrictions on individual liberty. To the extent that the public has found such measures acceptable, in the name of strengthening the war effort, their acceptance represents an endorsement of the judgment of policy makers of the value tradeoffs that were required.

Policy makers, however, are confronted with similar choices among competing values all the time, and frequently in making the choices they risk incurring the wrath of important elements of the public. The experience of several presidencies in the years since World War II illustrates the dilemma.

EFFECTIVENESS AND EFFICIENCY   Given a multitude of foreign policy commitments and objectives to which resources must be committed and given finite limits in the availability of resources, every administration is confronted with balancing concerns for effectiveness (getting tasks accomplished successfully) with concerns for efficiency (minimizing waste of resources). Should more resources than might be necessary be committed to foreign policy objectives if there is doubt about the requisite resource commitment necessary to ensure success? Or should economy be a prime consideration in the commitment of human, material, and financial resources, even at some risk of failure?

The Truman administration provides an example of a shift in value priorities as circumstances changed. Upon assuming the presidency, Harry Truman displayed a firm commitment to keeping the federal budget balanced. Although concerned about the threat of Soviet expansion, Truman insisted that programs to meet American military needs be budgeted within ceilings of only 13 to 15 billion dollars. Critics, including his own senior military chiefs, complained that the ceilings were too low to ensure preparedness to meet foreseeable contingencies. Truman, however, was implicitly accepting the risk of insufficiency in military strength in order to avoid the severe strains on the economy that he was convinced would occur with an unbalanced budget. Truman changed his mind and the lid came off the defense budget with the outbreak of the Korean War in June 1950 (which followed only by a few months a report by the National Security Council staff urging greatly increased military spending). The exigencies of fighting a war took precedence over concern for economic frugality.

The tradeoff calculation between probable effectiveness and economy of resource usage does not necessarily take the form that it took for the Truman administration. The failure of the mission to rescue the American hostages in Iran in the spring of 1980, for instance, was attributed primarily to an insufficiency in the number of helicopters that had been committed to the mission. It had been estimated that a minimum of six were needed to carry out the mission effectively. Two additional helicopters were committed to make sure that at least six would make it to the rescue site; but when three were lost or disabled en route, the mission was cancelled. In this instance, it was not a case of the Carter administration being anxious to conserve resources, despite the risk that this posed to failure. Rather, as the President's national security advisor, Zbigniew Brzezinski, recalls: "A larger fleet of helicopters would have required more planes for refueling and created a mission more susceptible to detection by radar or visual observation."[10]

In other words, the risk of failure from committing too few helicopters seemed to be outweighed by the risk of failure from committing too many of them.

CONTROL AND CREATIVITY   Value tradeoffs occur not only as a result of having to choose from among alternative courses of action, but also as a result of the value biases inherent in organizational arrangement and processes that are utilized in policy making. Several dilemmas that characteristically confront a new administration in making organizational and procedural choices are

41

discussed in Chapters 6 and 7. A few examples will suffice here to emphasize that the way in which the machinery of policy making is organized and the operating procedures that are utilized reflect, at least implicity, choices which a President and his advisors have made among competing values.

The organization of the Defense Department under Secretary Robert S. McNamara during the Kennedy and Johnson administrations, and of the national security system under Henry Kissinger during the Nixon and Ford administration, illustrate a trend toward centralized control at the expense of initiative at lower levels of government.

Robert McNamara's immediate predecessor as Secretary of Defense, Thomas S. Gates, had been convinced that in order to manage the department effectively, "you must in the modern sense decentralize and hold people responsible, and then coordinate." But Gates acknowledged that "coordination in its true sense is a very difficult art for an American because he wants to run something."[11] Robert McNamara was the quintessential American in wanting "to run something." He had brought "active management" to the presidency of the Ford Motor Company and he proposed to do the same in the running of the Pentagon. Active direction from the top was essential, in McNamara's view, in order to impose order on the chaos that had developed from a tradition of separate and rival fiefdoms among the various armed services. Each of the latter had its own procedures, its own pet projects and protected domain, and even its own scenarios for how the next war would be fought. "The Army was preparing for one length of war, and the Air Force for another [McNamara observed]. . . . There had to be control at the top, total departmental control to resolve a conflict like that.[12]

Melvin Laird, who was appointed Secretary of Defense when Richard Nixon assumed the Presidency in 1969, retained many of the elements of the planning, programming, and budgeting system (PPBS) that McNamara had used as the primary instrument of managerial control. Laird's emphasis on "participatory management," however, restored a great deal of authority to the chiefs of the various armed services, and thereby endeared Laird to military professionals, many of whom had both feared and resented McNamara's approach.[13]

However, if the Pentagon under Laird was somewhat more decentralized in operation than it had been under McNamara, the national security system as a whole became more structured and centralized under Richard Nixon than it had been under either President Kennedy or President Johnson. As perceptive reporters of that era noted, Nixon had been appalled at the Johnson style, which had included policy improvisation at Tuesday lunches with his key advisors rather than reliance on the formal machinery of the National Security Council. "Nixon—anti-ad hoc, anticonsensus, at times even anti-lunch—wanted a leaner, leakproof NSC operation, with none of the freewheeling political give-and-take that characterized the Johnson-era NSC. . . . He wanted total control and a break with the Democratic past."[14]

The resulting system indeed gave the President control, through Henry Kissinger, in the sense that few important policy issues were resolved at lower levels. However, did better foreign policies result? Critics doubted it and pointed to numerous problems: a problem-solving overload on Kissinger and Nixon; a tendency to departments such as State and Defense to refrain from initiating in-depth studies on their own, since their analyses were likely to be superceded by ones prepared by Kissinger's personal staff; a conflict in roles for Kissinger, who was acting to shape the substance of policy even as he attempted to play the role of neutral facilitator and coordinator; and a tendency, within the highly formalized structure, for the President to be presented only with a narrow range of "sanitized" options for decision.[15]

In short, a highly formalized, rationalized structure for formulating and executing foreign policy can only foster the illusion that tradeoffs among key values that are desired will not be necessary; the reality invariably is otherwise. The point can be illustrated further by experience with crisis-management structures. In 1968, when an American intelligence ship, the USS *Pueblo*, was halted by North Korean vessels off the coast of North Korea, urgent messages from the *Pueblo* took up to two and a half hours to reach the National Military Command Center in Washington. No help arrived in time to prevent the *Pueblo* from being forced into a North Korean port, with its crew removed and held prisoners of the Communists for eleven months. Concern about this incident and a subsequent one in 1969, when messages from an American intelligence aircraft being intercepted by North Korean jets took upwards to three hours to be relayed to Washington, led to investigation and a revamping of crisis management procedures.

If the United States were to be able to respond to a threat to its interests effectively, it seemed obvious that a capability for rapid response was essential. Equally obvious was the need to obtain thorough and accurate information quickly. Yet if policy makers have come to regard both speed of response and completeness and accuracy of information as being essential to an effective response to crisis situations, in practice policy makers often have found it impossible to avoid compromising one "essential" in hopes of fully realizing the other.

In May 1975, for example, the Ford administration felt compelled to make such a compromise in its response to the *Mayaguez* seizure. Only two weeks after the last American forces had been evacuated from Vietnam with the fall of Saigon to Communist forces, an American-registered commercial container ship, the S.S. *Mayaguez,* with a 40-man crew, was stopped and boarded sixty miles off the coast of Cambodia by forces of the Khmer Rouge. Within less than 48 hours of receiving reports of the incident, President Ford authorized a military operation to rescue the ship and crew—even though intelligence available at this time was unable to provide confirmation of the location of the crew!

The President, however, felt obliged to compromise the need for complete information in order to satisfy the sense of urgency for action. The American government had seemed impotent after a humiliating withdrawal of American forces from Vietnam. The memory of the fate of the crew of the *Pueblo* was still fresh in the minds of the President and his advisors. It seemed imperative to act before the Cambodians had forced the crew to the Cambodian mainland, where a rescure operation would have been far more costly and difficult.[16] Thus, a military operation was launched, resulting in 91 Americans killed, wounded, or missing in action. A short time after the operation had been launched, it was learned that the crew of the *Mayaguez* had been released by the Cambodians—adding irony and anguish to the policy decision that had been made.

Irony, anguish, and frustration—for policy makers themselves and for concerned citizens as well—are not uncommon byproducts of the policy process and of the value tradeoffs that are required. Even in situaitons in which most people recognize that value tradeoffs are required, rarely can there be full agreement regarding the tradeoff that is best. Disagreement arises not only from differing value preferences, but also from differing calculations about the probable consequences of particular tradeoffs. Will acceptance of a high degree of secrecy in the policy-making process actually enhance the security of the nation against threats posed by foreign adversaries? Will committing more resources to military programs really make it more likely that the programs will be effective? Will imposing greater centralized control necessarily require a sacrifice of creativity and initiative at lower levels? Will accepting a delay in responding to a crisis situation ensure the acquisition of vitally needed additional information? Will a conciliatory gesture improve the prospects of a just and equitable settlement to a dispute with a tough-minded adversary or merely convey an image of weakness that makes the adversary more intransigent?

No IIMMP can be constructed that will tell which tradeoffs are justified under all circumstances. Reasonable men and women can—and do—differ with one another in the answers that are given when competing values are at stake. Thus, they will differ with one another also in their judgments about when the foreign policy system has been successful and when it has failed. All of which is simply to say that the process of making and executing foreign policy is political. So also is the process by which judgments about success or failure become translated into an endorsement of the system or into actions that produce changes in the system.

The politics of the processes may not assume partisan labels, such as Republican or Democrat. Invariably, however, the processes will involve the clash of diverse interests, of competing value priorities, and of differing opinions of what is required in order to advance those interests and values. Therefore, although the nature of the foreign policy process requires governments to attempt to articulate goals that embody the nation's sense of common purposes, in a complex society such as America, the quest for unity often eludes even the most dedicated leaders.

NOTES

1. Gunnar Myrdal, "With What Little Wisdom the World is Ruled," *New York Times Magazine*, July 18, 1965, p. 20.
2. In order to avoid confusing the imagery unduly, an important source of intelligence,

i.e., that gathered by electronic means through satellites and aircraft, has been left aside for the present.

3. Readers who have seen the simulation of the battles of Gettysburg or Waterloo on the illuminated map at either location will picture the scene clearly.

4. Charles W. Thayer, *Diplomat* (New York: Harper & Row, 1959), p. 82.

5. See for example John D. Steinbruner, *The Cybernetic Theory of Decision* (Princeton, NJ: Princeton University Press, 1974). See also Richard M. Cyert and James G. March, *A Behavioral Theory of the Firm* (Englewood Cliffs, NJ: Prentice-Hall, 1963).

6. Joseph H. de Rivera, *The Psychological Dimension of Foreign Policy* (Columbus, Ohio: Merrill, 1968); Daniel Yergin, *Shattered Peace: The Origins of the Cold War and the National Security State* (Boston: Houghton Mifflin, 1977); Irving L. Janis, *Groupthink: Psychological Studies of Policy Decisions and Fiascoes*, 2d ed. (Boston: Houghton Mifflin, 1982).

7. Ernest R. May, *"Lessons" of the Past: The Use and Misuse of History in American Foreign Policy* (New York: Oxford University Press, 1973). See also Earl C. Ravenal, *Never Again: Learning from America's Foreign Policy Failures* (Philadelphia: Temple University Press, 1978).

8. Alexis de Tocqueville, *Democracy in America*, trans. Henry Reeves, 2 vols. (New York: J. and H. G. Langley, 1841), 1: 254.

9. Seweryn Bialer, "Soviet Foreign Policy: Sources, Perceptions, Trends," in *The Domestic Context of Soviet Foreign Policy*, ed. Seweryn Bialer (Boulder, Co: Westview, 1981), chap. 15. See also one of the few detailed comparisons of the two systems, Zbigniew Brzezinski and Samuel P. Huntington, *Political Power: USA/USSR* (New York: Viking, 1964). The authors find strengths and weaknesses in each system. Another scholar strongly disputes Tocqueville's thesis in these terms: "It was long believed that America's democratic institutions would prevent her from behaving effectively and responsibly in the world. The judgment should be reversed. American institutions facilitate rather than discourage the quick identification of problems, the pragmatic quest for solutions, the ready confrontation of dangers, the willing expenditure of energies, and the open criticism of policies." Kenneth N. Waltz, *Foreign Policy and Democratic Politics* (Boston: Little, Brown, 1967), pp. 307–308.

10. Zbigniew Brzezinski, "The Failed Mission: The Inside Account of the Attempt to Free the Hostages in Iran," *New York Times Magazine*, April 18, 1982, p. 30.

11. Thomas S. Gates, quoted in James M. Roherty, *Decisions of Robert S. McNamara: A Study of the Role of the Secretary of Defense* (Coral Gables, Fla: University of Miami Press, 1970), pp. 44–45.

12. Robert S. McNamara, quoted by Brock Bower, "McNamara Seen Now, Full Length," *Life* 64 (May 10, 1968): 78.

13. For an overview of the evolution of relations between Secretary of Defense and the Joint Chiefs of Staff, see Lawrence J. Korb, *The Joint Chiefs of Staff: The First Twenty-Five Years* (Bloomington: Indiana University Press, 1976). See also Douglas Kinnard, *The Secretary of Defense* (Lexington: University Press of Kentucky, 1980).

14. Marvin Kalb and Bernard Kalb, *Kissinger*, paperback (New York: Dell, 1975; copyright Little, Brown, 1974), pp. 97–98.

15. A detailed critique is provided by Alexander L. George, *Presidential Decisionmaking in Foreign Policy: The Effective Use of Information and Advice* (Boulder, Co: Westview, 1980), see esp. chaps. 8 and 10.

16. A detailed description and analysis of decision making during the *Mayaguez* crisis is provided by Richard G. Head, Frisco W. Short, and Robert C. McFarlane, *Crisis Resolution: Presidential Decision Making in the Mayaguez and Korean Confrontations* (Boulder, Co: Westview, 1978).

SUGGESTED ADDITIONAL READING

COHEN BERNARD C. AND HARRIS, SCOTT A. "Foreign Policy". In *Policies and Policymaking*, ed. Fred I. Greenstein and Nelson W. Polsby. Vol 6, Handbook of Political Science. Reading, MA: Addison-Wesley, 1975.

DE RIVERA, JOSEPH H. *The Psychological Dimension of Foreign Policy*. Columbus, OH: Merrill, 1968.

DEUTSCH, KARL W. *The Nerves of Government: Models of Political Communication and Control*. Glencoe, IL: Free Press, 1963.

GEORGE, ALEXANDER L. *Presidential Decisionmaking in Foreign Policy: The Effective Use of Information and Advice*. Boulder, CO: Westview, 1980.

HILSMAN, ROGER. *To Move a Nation: The Politics of Foreign Policy in the Administration of John F. Kennedy*. New York: Doubleday, 1964.

JERVIS, ROBERT. *Perception and Misperception in International Politics*. Princeton, NJ: Princeton Univeristy Press, 1976.

MAY, ERNEST R. *"Lessons" of the Past: The Use and Misuses of History in American Foreign Policy*. New York: Oxford University Press, 1973.

ROSENAU, JAMES N. *The Scientific Study of Foreign Policy*. New York: Free Press, 1971.

STEINBRUNER, JOHN D. *The Cybernetic Theory of Decision: New Dimensions of Political Analysis*. Princeton, NJ: Princeton University Press, 1974.

WALTZ, KENNETH N. *Foreign Policy and Democratic Politics*. Boston: Little, Brown, 1967.

PART TWO

The Foreign Policy Process
and the Imperative
of Purposeful Adaptation:
Landmarks in the
American Experience

℘

CHAPTER 3

⟡

Guiding Assumptions, Images, and Goals: The Early American Foreign Policy Experience

"If we could first know where we are, and whither we are tending, we could better judge what to do, and how to do it."

—Abraham Lincoln, 1863

"The twentieth century looms before us big with the fate of many nations. If we stand idly by, if we seek merely swollen, slothful ease and ignoble peace, if we shrink from the hard contests where men must win at hazard of their lives and at the risk of all they hold dear, then the bolder and stronger peoples will pass us by, and will win for themselves the domination of the world."

—Theodore Roosevelt, 1899

". . . The year 1898 is a great landmark in the history of the United States. . . . Expansion and imperialism are at war with the best traditions, principles, and interests of the American people . . . and they will plunge us into a network of difficult problems and political perils, which we might have avoided, while they offer us no corresponding advantage in return. . . ."

—William Graham Sumner, 1899

The bedrock of the American foreign policy process is a set of assumptions that those in policy positions hold about who we Americans are as a people, where our fundamental interests lie, and, as

Lincoln put it, "whither we are tending." Upon such assumptions are constructed the generalized goals that provide a compass setting for navigating in the turbulent seas of world politics. It is not a setting that is invariant; when assumptions change, the navigational course must change. Moreover, sometimes the turbulent seas themselves impose the requirement for adjustments in policy direction.

Because almost all of the hallowed foreign policy assumptions had become the object of critical scrutiny and debate by the 1970s and 1980s, it is not surprising that the current era has been one in which the ship of state has wavered. Nor is it surprising that various pundits and politicans in recent years have called for or attempted to articulate a new or refurbished set of guiding principles around which the nation might rally.

In the present chapter, we seek two objectives: (1) It is useful to elaborate on the nature and significance of the task which in Chapter 2 we identified as being logically first in the foreign policy process: *defining the nation's interest and goals.* (2) A consideration of broad historical patterns of continuity and change in the images that policy makers have had of the nation's identity, interests, and capabilities, and in the visions that they have maintained of the nation's general goals and destiny, is important as a means of providing insight into the *dynamics of foreign policy adaptation to change* in the world environment.

Two important periods of transition in the American foreign policy experience are examined in the present chapter for the purpose of providing insight into the dynamics of policy adaptation to changing external and domestic demands and opportunities. The first of these is a period of several decades from the end of the Revolutionary War, when the overriding concern of policy makers was that of preserving national independence and unity. The early decades of American foreign policy experience not only were crucial ones in defining an orientation toward world affairs that prevailed throughout most of the nineteenth century, but more enduringly in establishing a record of action and interaction that would continue to influence relationships into the 1980s. For example, the student who would seek to understand the problems and perspectives that define United States relations with Cuba, Mexico, Central America and the Caribbean in the 1980s would be well advised to consider the lasting effects of several of the key events of the early to mid-nineteenth century—such as the Louisiana Purchase, the

Monroe Doctrine, the annexation of Texas, the war with Mexico, and the Gadsden Purchase.

A second important period of transition in American foreign policy began near the end of the nineteenth century and continued into the depression years of the 1930s.[1] Repercussions from American actions in this period also continue to be felt into the 1980s, despite the dramatic shift in foreign policy that was effected in the years during and shortly after World War II, and the further transformation that began in the early 1970s. Of particular continuing relevance, especially in American relations with the Third World, are the arguments that surfaced at the turn of the century between proponents of American expansion abroad and those who feared that imperialism would irreparably corrupt American ideals and institutions.

ORIENTATION TO THE WORLD ENVIRONMENT: GENERALIZED ASSUMPTIONS, IMAGES, AND GOALS

Viewed over a period of hours or days, American foreign policy can be seen as a pattern of responses to an incessant stream of communications and problems from every corner of the globe—decisions made or postponed, actions taken or cancelled, programs initiated or modified, plans formulated or scrapped. Over a period of decades or generations, however, foreign policy is discernible primarily in terms of broad patterns in the relationship of the nation-state to other world actors. The broad historical patterns that define the relationship are describable in terms of policy behavior—patterns of internal consolidation or of territorial expansion, for example; patterns of isolationism or of alliance-building; patterns of according primacy to European affairs or of shifting the emphasis to the Middle East, Asia, or Latin America. In effect, the patterns represent the ongoing efforts of policy makers to maintain American goals while adapting to a changing series of demands and opportunities.

Others have found it fruitful to pursue the analogy between the adaptation of a political system to its environment and the adaptation of biological systems to their environments.[2] The analogy is not pushed here, but it is mentioned only to suggest that if the term has utility it lies in its reference to a process of interaction between an organism and its environment over a period of time. Therefore, the term *policy adaptation* will not be used interchangeably with *policy response* (that is, "the United States *responded* to the Soviet Union's invasion of Afghanistan by boycotting the Moscow Olympics"; not "the United States *adapted* to the Soviet invasion of Afghanistan by boycotting the Olympic Games in Moscow").

Adaptation is a more complicated and continuous process than is the one implied by the term *response*. Moreover, foreign policy adaptation is more than simply a matter of solving particular problems or coping with particular difficulties or seizing upon particular opportunities, although problem-solving, coping, and opportunity-seizing might prove to be important elements in the process of adaptation.

A variety of adaptive challenges confronts the United States in the modern age—the challenge of maintaining peace in a nuclear era, of keeping abreast of technological change, of ensuring access to vital resources that on a global scale are being depleted, of communicating effectively with friends and with adversaries in a global milieu of cultural and ideological diversity, of maintaining security in the context of military threats and imbalances. Major policy decisions may have an important effect upon the capacity of the United States to meet any one or all of these challenges, but adaptation to a challenge such as resource depletion or technological change will be the product of a multitude of choices and actions over time, not of a "moment of truth" in which a policy decision is made that succeeds in meeting the challenge.

Even with the benefit of hindsight, a determination of the extent to which foreign policies have been adaptive or maladaptive is a matter of judgment about which intelligent observers can disagree. Still, as Rosenau notes in his study of political adaptation, "the concept itself is quite simple" (if lacking in empirically measurable precision).[3] It refers basically to a process by which a political system adjusts to a changing environment through modifications of politics, structures, and practices that enable it to keep the fundamental institutions of political, economic, and social life intact (not necessarily unchanged, but altered only within limits that preserve the integrity of the system).

In relation to this conceptualization, it is useful to reiterate that the imperative of foreign policy is purposeful adaptation. Policy making is purposeful activity. For that reason, the first of the various stages of the foreign policy process has been labelled "goal-setting." However, in order to understand the relationship of foreign policy behavior to the process of adaptation to the world environment, an important distinction must be made in discussing foreign policy "goals."

One must distinguish between the particular policy goals which are the object of day-to-day American foreign policy actions, and the more abstract underlying values and beliefs, which serve as the motivating force that shapes the orientation of the nation-state to its environment generally.

The general thesis to be described and supported with historical examples here is twofold: (1) the broad orientation of the United States toward its world environment is explicable primarily in terms of the images that prevail among policy makers of the nation's identity, vital interests, and capabilities, and in the prevailing assumptions regarding global trends; (2) continuity of foreign policy orientation is sustained by consensus among policy makers regarding these images and assumptions; major change occurs only after a breakdown in the policy consensus.

IMAGES OF THE NATIONAL IDENTITY

A sense of national identity, like a sense of personal identity, is established in relationship to others and to the environment, as well as in relationship to past experience, the present, and roles that are imaginable in the future. An individual's self-image, for example, is built upon the perception that the individual has of himself or herself in the present, interacting with others in a particular set of surroundings (environment); however, the image also is likely to draw heavily upon childhood experiences and the influence of parents, including in many instances strong images of an ancestral heritage. Moreover, almost always one's self-image includes one's aspirations for the future. Similarly, the sense of national identity that a people such as Americans develop includes not only their images of themselves under current circumstances compared to other peoples such as the Russians, the French, or the Japanese, but also images of a real or mythical national heritage.

Moreover, the sense of identity will include visions—realistic, utopian, or pessimistic—of the future destiny of the nation.

To recall a national heritage, often a people must recall extensive cultural borrowing from or even colonial subordination to another nation. The result may be ambivalent attitudes and behavior—emulation under some circumstances, exaggerated efforts to dissociate the people from the "mother country" under other circumstances—much as individuals in adolescence and young adulthood frequently display ambivalent attitudes toward their parents in an effort to define a unique identity. Intense nationalism may be interpreted as a collective effort of a people to assert their distinctive identity and self-worth. As demonstrated here, the foreign policy orientation of the United States at the time of the founding of the republic took form particularly in relationship to images that policy makers projected of the unique character and destiny of the new nation. At the turn of the century, the orientation shifted, not because of the rejection by policy makers of that era of the concept of national uniqueness, but rather because of their conviction that the American "manifest destiny" could be fulfilled only by some fundamental alterations of policy direction in order to meet changing circumstances.

IMAGES OF THE NATION'S
VITAL INTERESTS AND CAPABILITIES

Closely related to the policy maker's image of the national identity is the image that he or she maintains of the nation's vital interests and its capabilities to preserve or advance those interests in world affairs. Justification of particular policies on grounds that "they are in the national interest," or criticism of other policies on the grounds that they place "the national interest" in jeopardy, are themes with a long tradition in American politics. Like the public eulogy and similar practices, however, the perennial assertion of "the national interest" in tones that suggest that an authoritative discovery has been made, tells us more about politics than about eternal verities.

If reasonable men and women can—and do—disagree about where the vital interests of the nation lie and what is required to defend or promote them, what is important is the subjective images that policy makers have of the nation's vital interests and capabilities. Sometimes these images will be broadly shared among policy makers; after an early period of debate, such a consensus emerged among American policy makers in the decades after the founding of the republic. Often, however, the nation's vital interests and capabilities are the focal point of foreign policy debate; this came to be so, for instance, in the period of the turn of the century—partly because important value conflicts had arisen among national leaders, and partly because of profound disagreement among various political leaders in the assessment they made of trends in world affairs and of the implications of those trends for American ideals and interests.

ASSUMPTIONS ABOUT GLOBAL TRENDS

Foreign policy is influenced both by the realities of the world environment (for example, distances, geographic configurations, weather), and by the assumptions that undergird policy decisions regarding environmental conditions and trends. As demonstrated effectively by Harold and Margaret Sprout, the "operational milieu" of foreign policy (elements of the world environment that impinge upon the nation-state, whether or not they are recognized by policy makers) and the "psycho-milieu" (the environment as policy makers perceive it) both may affect policy outcomes.[4] A drunken man placed on a wild horse is likely to get thrown off whether or not he recognizes his predicament. Likewise, governments—even sober ones—may be toppled under circumstances that they fail to recognize. However, if the significance of the "operational milieu" lies primarily in the limits that it sets on what is possible in foreign policy, the significance of the "psycho-milieu" lies in what it makes probable. Over time, the assumptions that American policy makers have made about the world around them and about trends in world affairs have contributed to the distinctive orientation that American foreign policy has had in particular eras. Moreover, in periods in which significant disagreements have arisen regarding such assumptions, the basis for foreign policy consensus has been eroded.

THE POLICY CONSENSUS

In this and the following chapter, the emergence of a foreign policy consensus in the early decades after the founding of the republic, rooted in shared images among policy makers of the nation's identity, interests, and capabilities, and in general agreement about the salient features of world affairs is discussed. The dissolution of this consensus at the end of the nineteenth century, followed by a period of vacillation (intense involvement in world affairs alternating with isolationism) that ended only with World War II is also examined.

Paradoxically, the breakdown of a foreign policy consensus may be a sign of health and vitality in a political system rather than a sign of political paralysis or decay. Major adaptive challenges carry with them the requirement that old axioms and precepts be reexamined. In turn, the abandonment of a policy consensus that supported the old axioms and precepts may be evidence that the essential first adaptive steps are being taken, rather than signs that the society has proved incapable of mastering the challenges.

1783–1820's:
ORIGINS OF A
FOREIGN POLICY TRADITION

Throughout most of the nineteenth century, American foreign policy was guided by two fundamental precepts: avoid entangling alliances (most notably alliances with the European powers) and continue westward expansion on the North American continent. Although the continued applicability of the precepts became sharply challenged at the end of the century and the basic orientation of American foreign policy shifted in response to the altered views of policy makers, the traditional precepts continued to be invoked in policy debates, sometimes with decisive results on policy outcomes.

A review of the factors that contributed to the emergence, in the decades after the United States gained its independence, of a distinctive orientation toward world affairs, provides insight into the dynamics of foreign policy adaptation and into the core beliefs and values that helped to shape the distinctive approach.

The changes that were occurring in Europe and in the western hemisphere in the decades between the Treaty of Paris, which brought a formal end to the war for independence from England, and the 1820s presented the new republic not only with challenges but also with opportunities.

ENVIRONMENTAL CHALLENGES
AND OPPORTUNITIES

Most of the governments of Europe experienced, either directly or indirectly, profound social and political upheaval during the period. The great catalyst of change was of course the French Revolution, which, in its turn, had received impetus from the American Revolution. In fact, a prominent student of the circumstances that led to the French Revolution has called the American Revolutionary War "the principal direct cause of the French Revolution, both because in invoking the rights of man it stirred up great excitement in France, and because Louis XVI in supporting it got his finances into very bad condition."[5]

The ideals of the French Revolution were widely disseminated throughout Europe. Revolutionary demands for the rights of man and for expansion of popular voice in government were threatening the autocratic regimes that were then so prevalent. Even with the period of Thermidor—the reaction that represented the abandonment of many of the goals of the revolution—the government of Napoleon could delay, but not erase or indefinitely suppress, popular demands for an expanded voice in government. The subsequent installment of Louis XVIII, after the Congress of Vienna, may have temporarily satisfied French aristocrats that they had achieved the Bourbon Restoration, but Louis XVIII could not be Louis XVI; the days of the latter were gone forever.

The same trend was occurring elsewhere in Europe, however assiduously Metternich and others worked to forestall it in the days after the Congress of Vienna of 1814–1815. In current terminology, adopted to describe the changing outlook in recent decades of the peoples of "developing areas," the Europeans in the nineteenth century were experiencing a "revolution of rising expectations." Hegel, for one, recognized the profound transformation of attitudes and beliefs that was occurring when he wrote early in the nineteenth century of his fellow Germans: "The quiet contentment with what is, the despondency, the patient acceptance of an all-powerful fate has been transformed into expectancy, and into courage for something different."[6]

Changing expectations were not exclusively the product of ideology emanating from the French Revolution. European economies were becoming altered, and consequently, changes in social structure were also occurring. Industrialization and its twin, urbanization, had begun to make their impact; the agrarian base of social and political influence was shrinking. Throughout much of Europe, the formerly dispossessed classes were gaining political influence or, where influence was denied, were making ever greater demands upon the ruling strata of society. The felt necessity to repress, to forestall, or to accommodate such demands increasingly occupied the attention of the ruling classes of Europe.

War also occupied the attention of European rulers. Prussia and Austria had gone to war with France shortly after the French Revolution had begun. Thus began the first in a series of conflicts that continued intermittently until the peace settlement at Vienna, involving at one time or another every major power in Europe. It was war that provided the occasion for the rise of Napoleon and became the key instrument of his diplomacy.

Armed with the most formidable weapons of his day, Napoleon extended French rule, effecting constitutional revision in the states that fell to French control. He also radically altered the rules by which international politics in Europe had been played for roughly two hundred years. The grandiose territorial ambitions of Napoleon threatened to disrupt the European balance of power. Moreover, he violated the implicit agreement among the powers to pursue only limited territorial and other diplomatic objectives, even in war.

With Napoleon came the *levée en masse*, the concept of a nation in arms, mobilized in pursuit not only of universal ideals of liberty but also of the particular aspirations of French nationalism. As Crane Brinton has noted in his comparative analysis of the English, American, French, and Russian revolutions, the participants in such struggles "end up with a God meant indeed for all mankind, but brought to mankind, usually a not altogether willing mankind, by a Chosen People."[7] In the aftermath of the French Revolution, it was the expansionist nationalism of Napoleonic France that carried the universal message of revolution to other parts of Europe. As this message spread, so also did nationalism—French nationalism among some people where French culture was already strong (for instance, Savoy), but more often nationalism of indigenous people banding together in opposition to French rule.

Those who assembled at the Congress of Vienna in 1814–1815 made efforts to restore those rules of the game that had governed international politics before the French Revolution and the Napoleonic era.[8] These efforts were partially successful, that is, until Europe exploded into war a century later, diplomacy remained largely the art of compromise and accommodation, and large-scale conflict was avoided. However, the trend toward expansion of the popular voice in government could not be reversed at Vienna; nor could the rising tide of nationalism.

EUROPEAN TURMOIL AND
AMERICAN FOREIGN POLICY

The pertinence of the changes in Europe during the period 1783–1820 to the concurrent emergence of a distinctive American orientation toward its world environment can be suggested briefly. First, the events and political circumstances that have been described generally distracted European rulers from affairs in the Western Hemisphere. Moreover, because their overseas commitments had lower priority than the heavy demands on the European continent, the European influence on events in the Western Hemisphere was reduced. The reduction of European interest and influence facilitated America's effort to secure its borders and promoted the expansion of American influence into areas where European control had diminished.

The Louisiana Territory, for example, was purchased from Napoleon at a time when such a transaction seemed expedient to him in the light of war commitments in Europe. Napoleon himself had acquired Louisiana only recently from the Spanish, who also subsequently yielded Florida to the United States, and whose colonies in Latin America in rapid succession asserted their independence from Spain.

Among European powers, Spain and Portugal in particular, both of which had had substantial holdings in the Western Hemisphere, were in a period of sharp decline as world powers. The vitality of each nation had diminished to the point that, as Ortega y Gasset said of Spain a century later, it was little more than "a cloud of dust that was left hovering in the air when a great people went galloping down the high road of history."[9]

Although there were rumors circulating in America after the Congress of Vienna that the series of conferences that were held (1817–1822) among the great powers of Europe (the so-called Concert of Europe) might take action to restore the Latin American colonies to Spanish control, the opposition of the British to such an idea effectively squelched it. Great Britain represented an exception to the generalization about the declining European interest and influence in the Western Hemisphere during the period. After suffering a major loss to her own imperial holdings with the successful revolt of her thirteen American colonies, Great Britain exploited the ever weakening hold of Spain and Portugal on their Latin American colonies to increase British trade and influence. These policies of Great Britain in the Western Hemisphere put her in major competition with the United States, which also was nurturing contacts in Latin America.[10] In time, however, British sea power became, in effect, a useful buffer between continental Europe and the United States, thereby working primarily to the benefit rather than to the detriment of American interests.

Finally, the turmoil, machinations, and bloodshed that characterized European politics during the period reinforced the preconceptions of American leaders that Europe was a decadent civilization—which provided all the more reason, therefore, for the United States to avoid becoming embroiled in the troubles of Europe. The great ocean that separated the United States from Europe helped to make such a policy of avoidance feasible.

THE EMERGING POLICY CONSENSUS

While significant changes in the world environment (especially in Europe) were occurring, American foreign policy was devoted primarily to making independence secure. By the time that this objective had been accomplished, a strong consensus had emerged among national leaders regarding American adaptive capabilities and the identity and destiny that set the new nation apart from Europe.

The observation that Alexis de Tocqueville made after visiting the United States early in the nineteenth century identifies figuratively if not literally the beliefs that had been prevalent among Americans for generations regarding their identity and place in history. The discovery of America, Tocqueville suggested, which provided an asylum for persecuted peoples from Europe, was as if America "had been kept in reserve by the Deity and had just risen from beneath the waters of the Deluge."[11] Early American colonists, especially the Puritans, had expressed similar beliefs. Puritan leaders expressed the conviction that they and their followers had been delivered from persecution by God in order to fulfill a unique mission on earth. Although the aspirations of Puritan leaders for the establishment of theocracy in America foundered, the sense of destiny did not. Rather, as initial hardship gave way to prosperity, the belief that initially had been drawn from passages in the Old Testament of a unique historical mission gave way to a less explicit sense of destiny that was supported by secular experience; this experience in its general characteristics was shared not only by New England Puritans, but by other American colonists as well.[12]

Leaders of the American revolution drew upon this sense of national destiny, in addition to the pragmatic as well as idealistic considerations of the benefits of independence from British colonial rule, in forming their images of the appropriate role that the nascent nation could and would play in world affairs. For example, Thomas Paine, the most famous pamphleteer of the cause of revolution, reiterated the early Puritan theme of Americans as a "chosen people" and anticipated the later observations of Tocqueville when he noted in his essay, "Common Sense," that the Protestant Reformation had been briefly preceded by the discovery of America, "as if the Almighty graciously meant to open a sanctuary to the persecuted in future years. . . ." His argument rested not only upon the idealistic claim that America was "the asylum for the persecuted lovers of civil and religious liberty from *every part* of Europe," but also upon the pragmatic assessment of the capabilities of the colonies to maintain their independence. Some leaders in the colonies argued that America could not survive without the protection afforded by the colonial connection to British mercantilism; Paine argued that independence would mean economic gain, not loss. "As Europe is our market for trade, we ought to form no partial connection with any part of it." To do so, he warned, "tends directly to involve this continent in European wars and quarrels, and set us at variance with nations who would otherwise seek our friendship, and against whom we have neither anger nor complaint."[13]

Avoidance of political entanglement with European nation-states was to become a central policy precept around which consensus among American national leaders would emerge. However, the consensus did not develop immediately. Washington, for example, was confronted during his two terms as President with squabbles that to a large extent had troubled the nation since the beginning of the movement for independence. Some leaders, such as Washington's first secretary of the treasury, Alexander Hamilton, argued that the future of the new nation was inexorably linked to the former mother country, upon which continued dependence could be a blessing, not a curse. Other leaders urged, at least until the rise of Napoleon, that the alliance with the French that had helped to achieve American independence ought to be maintained. Washington, however, subscribed instead to the belief that the United States had an identity and a set of interests that were distinct from those of Europe; he had therefore urged his fellow countrymen that the United States must remain aloof from European politics and retain her freedom of action. His most famous statement of such advice came in his farewell address as President.

WASHINGTON'S FAREWELL ADDRESS   "Europe has a set of primary interests which to us have none or a very remote relation," President Washington observed. "Hence she must be engaged in frequent controversies, the causes of which are essentially foreign to our concerns." He pointed to geographic considerations favorable to the course that he recommended: "Our detached and distant situation invites and enables us to pursue a different course." Combining a realistic assessment of national potential with an idealistic appeal to national pride, he urged, "If we remain one people, under an efficient government, the period is not far off when we may defy material injury from external annoyance; when we may take such an attitude as will cause the neutrality we may at any time resolve upon to be scrupulously respected; when belligerent nations, under the impossibility of making acquisitions upon us, will not lightly hazard the giving us provocation; when we may choose peace or war, as our interest, guided by justice, shall counsel."

As Lipset has observed, Washington's contribution to the development of the new nation was particularly great because he combined immense charisma with considerable restraint in using it. Not only did his personal appeal to Americans of various political leanings and from all sections of the country promote national unity, but the fact that he voluntarily retired from office at the end of a second term, rather than exploiting his popularity by remaining in office, paved the way for the institutionalization of a process of orderly succession in government and thereby furthered national harmony.[14] Thus, the image of the national self that Washington had promoted provided a rallying point around which, amidst external threats to destroy the nation and internal threats to abandon it, consensus could eventually develop.

When the Democratic-Republicans, with Thomas Jefferson as their leader, replaced the Federalists as the dominant power in the federal government, a major early test was presented of whether the orientation to world affairs defined by Presidents Washington and Adams would be maintained. In his first inaugural address, President Jefferson suggested the continuity that would follow, when he argued for "peace, commerce, and honest friendship with all nations, entangling alliances with none. . . ."

It was under Jefferson, too, that great impetus was given to the expansionist thrust in American foreign policy with the purchase of Louisiana in 1803. The size and the cost of the territorial acquisition far exceeded Jefferson's expectations. When he sent James Monroe to assist Robert Livingston, the minister to France, to negotiate with Napoleon, their instructions were only to try to obtain New Orleans, or at least the land in the Mississippi delta that would guarantee Americans complete freedom of navigation from the Mississippi River to the Gulf of Mexico. Moreover, Jefferson had been committed to a strict interpretation of the Constitution, which precluded the purchase of additional territory for the Union. But as early as 1801, Jefferson had expressed a view that justified abandoning constitutional scruples in order to take advantage of the unexpected opportunity to acquire all of Louisiana. "However our present interests may restrain us within our own limits," he had written to Monroe, "it is impossible not to look forward to distant time, when our rapid multiplication will expand itself beyond those limits, and cover the whole northern if not the southern continent."[15]

How could a hemispheric conception of national interests such as the one Jefferson had articulated in his letter to Monroe be reconciled with avoidance of involvement in European politics, when several nation-states of Europe (notably Spain, France, England, Russia, and Portugal) continued to have political interests in the Western Hemisphere that could conflict with the expansion of the influence of the United States? An occasion for answering this question occurred during the presidency of James Monroe, two decades later.

THE MONROE DOCTRINE   This situation was the one mentioned previously, in which restoration of the former Spanish colonies in Latin America seemed threatened by the Concert of Europe. As indicated, however, the British revealed strong opposition to any such action by the Concert. In fact, in order to strengthen their own position, the British sought the collaboration of the American government in issuing a statement warning the continental powers to leave the Latin American nations alone.

It was in this context that the American Secretary of State John Quincy Adams suggested, in lieu of collaboration with the British, a unilateral declaration by the United States. Such a course would be "more candid, as well as more dignified . . . than to come in as a cockboat in the wake of the British man-of-war," Adams urged.[16] The Monroe Doctrine, which was drafted largely by Adams in implementation of his suggestion, provided the occasion for at once defining American interests in hemispheric terms while maintaining and attempting to bolster a course of action independent of European entanglements or interference.

The continuity between the self-confident assertion of an American sphere of interest, which the Monroe Doctrine represented, and the earlier territorial acquisitions, such as the Louisiana Purchase, which made self-confidence in an expanded notion of national interests possible, is apparent. In fact, as Frederick Jackson Turner noted on the centennial of the Louisiana Purchase, "The Monroe Doctrine would not have been possible except for the Louisiana Purchase. It was the logical outcome of the acquisition."[17]

In summary, by the time of Monroe, a consensus among national leaders had emerged regarding American capabilities and the precepts that should guide foreign policy. Threats to the borders, and perhaps to the continued independence, of the United States had been all but eliminated. Moreover, the size of America had doubled. American adaptive capabilities were perceived as substantial if utilized to promote the future development of the nation in the Western Hemisphere, rather than pitted against the still superior forces of the major European powers. Paine, Washington, Jefferson, and other early leaders had all spoken of the pragmatic advantages of freedom of action that the avoidance of political entanglements in Europe would provide. They had also foreseen a period of future national greatness if their advice were followed. By the time of

Monroe, the sense of national destiny had become articulated more explicitly in terms of American supremacy in the Western Hemisphere. Warning European nations against further encroachments in the hemisphere satisfied the sense of national identity, which was defined especially in contrast to the perceived tyranny of Europe; the warning was also congruent with pragmatic beliefs about the benefits to be derived from maintaining maximum freedom from the interference of European powers in the extension of American influence in the hemisphere.

THE 1890s AND THE TURN OF THE CENTURY

THE PATTERN OF CONTINUITY

At the risk of some oversimplification, the period from the 1820s to the 1890s may be described as one of remarkable continuity in the broad orientation that the United States maintained toward the world environment. A key policy precept that sustained this orientation was that of avoiding political entanglement with European states. Nonentanglement did not imply isolation from the world. Indeed, during this period the United States was in the forefront of diplomatically opening China to the West. Commodore Perry and his "black ships" steamed into Yokohama harbor, and subsequent conversations with the Mikado led to the first treaty between Japan and a Western nation. Diplomatic contacts were established with Korea. Hawaii became an American colony. The islands of Midway, a thousand miles west of Hawaii, were acquired. Filibustering expeditions in the Caribbean extended American interests southward. Commerce was maintained and expanded in Europe. American commercial outposts in Africa were established. In other words, the United States was by no means cut off from the rest of the world; on the contrary, points of contact were numerous. Adherence to the nonentanglement doctrine meant, however, that the United States should incur no binding political obligations to other nation-states—especially European states—in pursuing its foreign policy interests.

A second key element in the foreign policy posture of the United States was that of territorial expansion; the period under consideration was the heyday of expansion. The vast territory of Texas was annexed in 1845, by joint resolution of the United States Congress. The Oregon territorial issue with Great Britain was settled by treaty in 1846. War with Mexico was declared the same year, by a nearly unanimous vote of the Congress; as a result of the Treaty of Guadalupe Hidalgo in 1848, which ended the war, the United States acquired an enormous stretch of territory from the western border of Texas to and including California, plus all or part of the present states of Nevada, Utah, Arizona, Wyoming, Colorado, and New Mexico. In 1853, an additional strip of territory along the southern edge of what are now the states of Arizona and New Mexico was acquired by purchase. In 1867, the territory that was to be the largest in the union, Alaska, was purchased from Russia.

Although Alaska was the last significant territorial acquisition during the period, the occupation and consolidation of the lands acquired and the development of systems of communication and transportation across the continent greatly consumed the energy of the nation from the end of the Civil War to the 1890s. From the viewpoint of the American government at the time, this was domestic policy. American Indians, however, not Americans of European stock, occupied much of the land that was acquired during the period, and they had not been consulted in the negotiations by which the land had been ceded to the United States government. From a different perspective, therefore, the consolidation by the American government of the territory during the post-Civil War era, which involved fighting nearly a thousand separate engagements with Indian tribes, may be regarded as foreign policy activity designed to secure by force the fruits of expansion.[18]

OBSOLESCENCE OF IMAGES
OF NATIONAL IDENTITY
AND NATIONAL INTEREST

The basic prerequisite for a change of the traditional foreign policy posture was a dissolution of the consensus among national leaders in their images of the national identity, the nation's vital interests, and the prevailing assumptions regarding American capabilities to promote and protect those interests in a world environment that was undergoing rapid transformation.

CHANGING ENVIRONMENT   The period after the American Civil War was one of important industrialization and social and political change, both in the United States and in Europe, with effects that were felt throughout the world. The political structures and boundaries in Europe were changed dramatically with the consolidation of Italy and Germany as nation-states. Industrialization of the nation-states of Europe was accompanied by a rapid population growth (the population of Europe increased two and a half times from 1800 to 1900); by urbanization; and by increasing insecurity among the masses of people, foreshadowing the problems that would come to a head in the twentieth century. The nineteenth-century German philosopher Friedrich Nietzsche saw a trend in Europe toward "numerous, talkative, weak-willed, and very handy workmen who *require* a master, a commander, as they require their daily bread. . . ."[19]

As the European nations became industrialized, they turned their attention to the Middle East, to Asia (to which access had been facilitated by the steamship and by the opening in 1869 of the Suez Canal), and to Africa for raw materials, markets, and colonies. A rough indication of the frenzied pace of competition that ensued is provided by the fact that before 1875 less than one tenth of the territory in Africa was under European colonial rule; by 1895, all but one tenth of Africa was under European colonial rule. In the 1880s and the 1890s, European international politics were aggravated not only by imperialistic competition, but also by a growing rigidity of relationships into opposing military alliances and pacts. Alliances included war plans that were to go into effect almost automatically in the case of a triggering incident or provocation, since the growing belief was that future wars would be short (like the Franco-Prussian War of 1871) and that the first strike or maneuver probably would be decisive (reflected, for instance, in the development of elaborate plans for surprise attacks, such as the celebrated Schlieffen Plan, developed in 1903 and imperfectly implemented by Germany in 1914 against France).

INCREASING AMERICAN CAPABILITIES   For the United States, the post-Civil War decades produced many impressive accomplishments and rapidly developing capabilities.[20] In the 1870s, the

United States attained a favorable balance of trade for the first time in its history. Between 1870 and 1880, American export trade increased more than 200%. The same period was also one of rapid industrialization, railroad building, and general growth. The total population of the country increased by roughly 100% from 1860 to 1890; the number of those engaged in manufacturing and in mechanical or mining industries increased by over 170%. During the nineteenth century as a whole, the population of the United States had increased from 5.3 million to 76.0 million (compared with an increase in population in Europe by a factor of 2.5).[21]

As historian Thomas A. Bailey has observed, by almost any set of indexes, the capability of the United States compared favorably with that of other major powers as the end of the nineteenth century drew near.

> By 1890 we were the number two white nation in population, still trying to catch up to the Russians. We had bounded into first place in total manufacturing, including top rank in iron and steel—the standard indices of military potential. In addition, we held either first or second place in railroads, telegraphs, telephones, merchant marine, and in the production of cattle, coal, gold, copper, lead, petroleum, cotton, corn, wheat, and rye. The armies and navies were not there, but we had the means of creating them when we needed them—and did.[22]

It is not surprising, then, that most American national leaders in the 1890s drew the conclusion that to Bailey and the rest of us is apparent in retrospect: the United States had attained capabilities sufficient for the exercise of a role as a great world power.

NEW EXPANSIONISM AND ADVOCATES   With the impetus of such changes as those described above, American foreign policy, for a period beginning in the late 1890s, became more aggressively competitive with the great powers of Europe than previously. To be sure, some of the actions of the United States around the turn of the century might be described as relatively natural extensions of the traditional definitions of the national interest. The intense concern with events in Cuba, for instance, culminating in a war with Spain (1898), was rooted in a long interest in the Caribbean. Likewise, the assertion by the Theodore Roosevelt administration of a right to intervene in Santo Domingo to force the government there to pay debts was explicitly rationalized as a corollary to the Monroe Doctrine. Similarly, the American show of force in support of Panama's independence from Columbia (1903), with the subsequent development of a United States-controlled Panama Canal, reflected long-standing interests in the Western Hemisphere, although the canal also provided convenient new access to trade routes to Asia.

A number of other American actions, however, represented a sharp departure from tradition, especially from the tradition of nonentanglement in world politics. For instance, the United States became a colonial power, with the acquisition of Puerto Rico, Guam, and the Philippines, as a result of war with Spain. The Hawaiian islands, 2,400 miles from the California shore, were annexed in 1898.

In 1899 and 1900, "Open Door" notes were sent to the major powers with colonial interest in Asia, indicating American interests in preventing the control of China or of Chinese trade by any other power. The United States participated for the first time in an international diplomatic conference with European powers.[23] The American government made available its good offices to mediate in a war between Russia and Japan and to provide facilities for a peace conference (at Portsmouth, New Hampshire, in 1905). Likewise, the United States took the initiative in organizing a conference among European powers to resolve a dispute over colonial interests in North Africa (the Algeciras Conference of 1906).

Advocates of the vigorous expansionism of this period were led by a relatively close-knit group of prominent persons, including Theodore Roosevelt, Brooks Adams, Whitelaw Reid, John Hay, Henry Cabot Lodge, and Albert Beveridge.[24] This core group had in common a patrician contempt for the crass materialism of the nouveau riche in American society (which partly explains the later identification of Roosevelt and Beveridge, for instance, with the Progressive movement). Members of the group had also in common a belief, articulated in terms that were quite distinct from traditional images of the national identity and the national interest, that the United States stood at a historical watershed. This belief, rooted in a variety of ideas ranging from Social Darwinism to analysis of British success as an imperial power, provided the basic rationale for advocating an aggressive new role for the United States in world affairs.

71

Theoretical abstractions were synthesized with practical considerations in their arguments. The United States could compete successfully with the great powers of Europe in virtually any region of the
world. Furthermore, the acquisition of new possessions in the Pacific
(such as Hawaii, the Philippines, and Guam) could provide coaling
stations to support a first-rank navy and convenient access to new
markets and sources of raw materials in Asia. Moreover, to fail to
engage in imperialistic competition, they warned, would mean that
European powers would gain an advantage that in the future would
again relegate the United States to second-class status. A few of
the intellectual origins of ideas to which the advocates of vigorous
expansionism were committed and some of the central themes that
they expressed, will be identified briefly.

SOCIAL DARWINISM   The first American edition of Charles
Darwin's On the Origin of Species appeared in 1860. Although the
immediate impact of Darwin's work was not as great in the United
States as it was in England, by the 1870s Darwin's theory of natural
selection was creating a radical transformation not only of theories
in the natural sciences, but also in religion and in popular theorizing
about the evolution of human beings and of nations. The appeal
of such ideas in late nineteenth-century America, especially to
those who were amassing fortunes in the industrial boom, is understandable. As Richard Hofstadter has noted, "With its rapid expansion, its exploitative methods, its desperate competition, and its
peremptory rejection of failure, postbellum America was like a vast
human caricature of the Darwinian struggle for existence and survival of the fittest."[25]
Although the direct appeal of social Darwinism had waned somewhat by the 1890s, indirectly social Darwinism had an even greater
impact at that time because it had become assimilated into the
thought and writings of a whole generation of American scholars
and public officials. Advocates of a stronger governmental role in
the economy and in social welfare, as well as critics of such a role,
typically expressed their views in Darwinian or neo-Darwinian
form.[26] Social Darwinism could also be, and was, synthesized with
earlier notions that the United States had a manifest destiny to
fulfill. Likewise, in discussions of the fate of nations and civilizations, adaptations of social Darwinism were common. Theodore
Roosevelt, for example, saw in the events at the turn of the century

a test of the collective manhood of America. Seen in this light, imperial competition with European powers was to be sought rather than avoided.

INTERPRETATIONS OF HISTORICAL EXPERIENCE   Interpretations of historical experience were another important source of the ideas expressed by the advocates of vigorous expansion. The writings of Frederick Jackson Turner, Alfred Thayer Mahan, and Brooks Adams were particularly influential.

Frederick Jackson Turner, professor of history at the University of Wisconsin, set forth what came to be known as "the frontier thesis" in 1893. Turner observed that the U.S. Census Bureau report of 1890 had indicated that westward migration in the United States had ceased; the frontier, which had been moving steadily west, had reached the coast. Turner agreed that the frontier had been of vital importance in American history, stimulating the development of democratic institutions, through the promotion of egalitarian norms as well as economic development. Such an interpretation of the American past raised the obvious question of what the consequences would be now that the frontier was apparently closed (although in retrospect, we know that westward migration continued for decades).

The frontier thesis expounded by Turner had a profound impact. Theodore Roosevelt described Turner's ideas as important because they "put into definite shape a good deal of thought which has been floating around rather loosely."[27] The concept of a new frontier for the United States crystallized an idea that many people had been seeking as a solution to the mounting social and economic problems from a severe economic depression in 1893.[28] The new frontier envisioned by its proponents in the 1890s lay primarily in the vast reaches of Asia, where the lure of new markets and sources of raw materials seemed not only appealing but urgent, in the light of the precarious condition of China, whose seemingly imminent collapse might lead to the carving up of that land and its resources among European imperial powers.

The concern for greater American involvement in the political struggle in Asia was also underlined by the theories of Captain Alfred Thayer Mahan, whose lectures at the Naval War College shaped the thought of a generation of American naval officers and whose writings had an enduring impact on a far broader audience.

73

His seminal work, *The Influence of Sea Power on History, 1660–1783,* was published in 1890. Drawing primarily upon analysis of the growth of the British empire, Mahan argued that control of land masses could be attained through control of the seas. As imperial competition heightened in the 1890s, Mahan saw the United States at a critical juncture. The Eurasian land mass, he maintained, was the area of which control was crucial for achieving world power.[29] Only a strong navy coupled with an alliance with Great Britain, the world's strongest naval power, could stave off the expansion of the Russian empire and its eventual domination of the Eurasian land mass. Construction of a canal across the Panama isthmus would provide convenient access from the Atlantic to the Pacific; acquisition of areas such as Hawaii and the Philippines would be useful additional steps to enable the American Navy to operate most effectively.[30]

Theodore Roosevelt was among those who followed Mahan's works closely and who regarded his theories as having profound significance. After his appointment as assistant secretary of the Navy by President McKinley, Roosevelt kept in close touch with Mahan. Less than a year after lecturing officers at the Naval War College that "no triumph of peace is quite so great as the supreme triumphs of war," Roosevelt sent the famous dispatch that triggered Admiral Dewey's attack at Manila Bay, the first battle fought following congressional declaration of war on Spain.[31] The acquisition of the Philippines followed.

The theories of Brooks Adams reinforced the policy implications of Mahan's theories. Brother of Henry Adams and a direct descendant of two presidents of the United States and of the ambassador to Great Britain during the Civil War, Brooks Adams was a serious student of world history, from which he derived a cyclical pattern of the rise and decline of great civilizations.[32] The center of civilization, he thought, had been moving westward. Thus, by the 1890s he believed nature had "cast the United States into the vortex of the fiercest struggle which the world has ever known. She has become the heart of the economic system of the age, and she must maintain her supremacy by wit and by force, or share the fate of the discarded."[33]

Adams was critical of those of his contemporaries who, in his view, lacked the vision to move from outworn traditions, rooted in a world that Washington and Jefferson had known, to new policies dictated by new realities. The key to future power lay in Asia, Adams contended, especially in China. He saw Germany and Russia as presenting a growing challenge in the competition for dominance in that region. Like Mahan, Adams favored entering the competition through an Anglo-American alliance (with the United States as senior partner); failure to compete for an empire, he warned, would place the future of American civilization in jeopardy.

Policies of an expanded American role in Asia to support the acquisition of new markets and resources appealed to various groups. Although, as Julius W. Pratt has suggested, many leading American businessmen were initially unsympathetic to the possibility of war with Spain, once the Philippines had fallen into American hands and Hawaiian annexation had been secured, business support for expansionist policies increased markedly.[34] Groups such as the American-China Development Company, founded by leading American industrialists and financiers in 1895, and the American Asiatic Association, organized in 1898 by leading cotton growers and other businessmen, worked actively to persuade the government to support American interests in Asia and especially to prevent Russia from attaining a dominant sphere of interest in China.

The activities of these and other interested groups were rewarded by the notes issued by Secretary of State John Hay to the major imperial powers in 1899 and 1900, calling for the maintenance of Chinese territorial integrity and for the preservation of an "open door" for all interested powers in their relations with China.[35] Hay's own contribution to drafting the first of the "Open Door" notes appears to have been slight; nevertheless, the policies propounded in the notes, which followed a long-standing British approach to relations with China and in effect aligned the United States and Great Britain, were consistent with Hay's own views. When his close friend Roosevelt assumed the presidency at the death of McKinley, even stronger working ties with the British were forged.[36]

LINGERING TRADITION

As suggested by the preceding discussion, Theodore Roosevelt was the pivotal figure in a core group of expansionists. The initial successes of the group in influencing the direction of American foreign policy made it appear for a time that a new foreign policy consensus had emerged, or would emerge, around the ideas propounded by Roosevelt, Mahan, Brooks Adams, and other leading spokesmen of the group. The outbreak of the Spanish-American war, for example, appears to have served as a national catharsis, temporarily unifying disparate elements of the society.

With Dewey's victory at Manila, however, and the imminent prospect of an American empire, several prominent persons began to question the departure from American foreign policy tradition. The Anti-Imperialist League, organized in Boston in November 1898, claimed 30,000 members within a year. Leading spokespersons for the anti-imperialist cause formed a heterogeneous group which included intellectuals and writers, such as Mark Twain, Finley Peter Dunne, and William James; college presidents, such as David Starr Jordan of Stanford and Henry Wade Rogers of Northwestern; social reformers, such as Jane Addams; political reformers, such as Carl Schurz; and a few business tycoons, such as Andrew Carnegie. In 1900 William Jennings Bryan made anti-imperialism a major campaign slogan in his unsuccessful bid for the presidency.

While lack of unified leadership and internal frictions among disparate elements diluted the effectiveness of the anti-imperialist movement, it would be erroneous to conclude, on the other hand, that the advocates of imperialism were completely successful. Rather, as Richard W. Leopold has noted, the imperialist movement at the turn of the century withered in a domestic environment that failed to provide it with enduring nourishment.[37] A symbol of the limits of the policy commitment to imperialism was the failure to create a colonial office in the American government. Moreover, growing pacifist sentiments in the nation exerted pressure upon policy makers to tone down the rhetoric of aggressive expansionism and to talk instead of peace. Even Theodore Roosevelt was responsive. As Osgood observed, "It was a sign of the times that the man who had been distinguished for his bellicosity in 1898 was awarded the Nobel Peace Prize in 1906."[38] Roosevelt's successor, Taft, was even more ambivalent in his foreign policy posture. Both he and his secretary of state, Philander Knox, seem to have been committed at least in principle to the nineteenth-century tradition of avoiding political entanglement with the great powers of the world.

NATIONAL LEADERSHIP
IN TRANSITION

That there was no enduring consensus among American national leaders favoring imperialism may be attributed not only to the continuing hold of the traditional values and conceptions of the national identity among important national leaders at the turn of the century but also to the changing composition of national leadership. It is not possible here to identify precisely the impact on the composition of national leadership produced by such phenomena as immigration (nine million immigrants entered the United States between 1901 and 1910 alone); the growth of labor unions; the proliferation of socialist, anarchist, and other movements committed to radical change; and the widespread discrediting of politicians and government officials by the "muckrakers" and by the popular cry of the Progressives to "give government back to the people." It is possible to suggest with confidence, however, that the impact of such phenomena was cumulatively felt on the composition as well as on the attitudes of national leadership.

Frederick A. Ogg has suggested that the election of 1908 "was the harbinger of a great shift in party power."[39] This shift was occurring not only in the growing strength of grass-roots elements in the Democratic party and in the inroads that Democrats were making in previously secure Republican areas but also in the national political structure as a whole. The changes that were taking place within the two-party system were of particular significance, however, since the two major parties in the United States have tended to assimilate or to co-opt the demands, if not the leadership, of third parties and of dissident groups in the society when such groups become strong enough to pose a political threat to them. Samuel Lubell has shown how the assimilation into the Democratic party of immigrants and other socially dispossessed groups in urban areas produced a shift in national voting patterns that, beginning in the 1930s, culminated in a long period of Democratic dominance in American politics.[40] The elections of 1908 may be described as an early symptom of the process that Lubell has described as continuing into the 1940s and the 1950s. The political effects of the process are still being felt.

77

The restructuring of the composition of national leadership, although begun only slightly in the years between the end of the nineteenth century and World War I, further contributed to the cleavages among national leaders regarding their images of national identity and national interest. No enduring foreign policy consensus among national leaders emerged until a process of domestic policy struggle had allowed previously dissident elements to be more fully assimilated into the political system.

In short, dissension among national leaders with regard to the national identity and the national interest contributed to nearly half a century of vacillation in the orientation of the United States toward the world environment. The pattern fluctuated between the active embroilment in world politics in the Spanish-American War and in World War I to the more traditional posture in the period before World War I and the even greater efforts to avoid entangling international commitments during the 1930s as symbolized by the Neutrality Acts. With World War II, however, the global system was radically transformed, and a new foreign policy consensus was forged.

NOTES

1. A third important period of change, which began with World War II and accelerated in the postwar years, is discussed in Chapter 4. The current transitional period, which began essentially with the war in Vietnam, is examined in Chapter 5.
2. See Gerald W. Hopple, ed., *Biopolitics, Political Psychology and International Politics: Towards a New Discipline* (New York: St. Martin's Press, 1982); James N. Rosenau, *The Study of Political Adaptation* (New York: Nichols, 1981); Kenneth E. Boulding, *Ecodynamics: A New Theory of Societal Evolution*, paperback ed. (Beverly Hills, Calif: Sage, 1981).
3. Rosenau, *The Study of Political Adaptation*, p. 38.
4. Harold and Margaret Sprout, *The Ecological Perspective on Human Affairs* (Princeton, NJ: Princeton University Press, 1965).
5. Georges Lefebvre, *The Coming of the French Revolution*, trans. R. R. Palmer (New York: Vintage Books, 1959), p. 19.
6. Georg Wilhelm Friedrich Hegel, "Concerning the Most Recent Internal Affairs in Wurttemberg, and More Especially the Shortcomings of the Constitution of City Magistrates," in *The Philosophy of Hegel*, Carl J. Friedrich ed. and trans. (New York: Modern Library, 1953), p. 523.
7. Crane Brinton, *The Anatomy of Revolution*, revised ed. (New York: Vintage Books, 1952), p. 206.
8. An interesting case study of the Congress of Vienna that depicts classical diplomacy as it was performed by the masters of the art assembled at Vienna has been written by Henry A. Kissinger, "The Congress of Vienna," in *Power and Order* eds. John G. Stoessinger and Alan F. Westin (New York: Harcourt Brace, 1964), pp. 1–32.

9. Jose Ortega y Gasset, "Particularism and Disintegration," in *Readings in Twentieth-Century European History* eds. Alexander Baltzly and A. William Salomone (New York: Appleton, 1950), p. 227. The selection is extracted from the author's work, *Invertebrate Spain* (New York: Norton, 1937).

10. A penetrating analysis of British diplomacy in the period is provided by William W. Kaufman, *British Policy and the Independence of Latin America, 1804–1828* (New Haven: Yale University Press, 1951). American policies are discussed by Arthur P. Whitaker, *The United States and the Independence of Latin America* (Baltimore: Johns Hopkins Press, 1941).

11. Alexis de Tocqueville, *Democracy in America,* ed. Phillips Bradley, 2 vols., paperback ed. (New York: Vintage Books, 1957), 1:302. First English translation, 1835.

12. As expressed by Daniel J. Boorstin, Americans tended to draw key tenets of their political faith from a sense of their "givenness" in the American historical experience, rather than from theological or ideological sources. Boorstin, *The Genius of American Politics* (Chicago: University of Chicago Press, 1953).

13. Thomas Paine, *Thomas Paine: Representative Selections,* ed. H. H. Clark (New York: American Books, 1944), p. 18–34; excerpted in Avery Craven, Walter Johnson, and F. Roger Dunn, eds., *A Documentary History of the American People* (Boston: Ginn, 1951), pp. 154–158. Emphasis in the source cited. "Common Sense" was first published, anonymously, in January 1776.

14. Seymour M. Lipset, *The First New Nation* (New York: Basic Books. 1963), pp. 16–23.

15. Jefferson to Monroe, quoted in Charles A. Beard, *The Idea of National Interests: An Analytical Study in American Foreign Policy* (New York: Crowell-Collier-Macmillan, 1934), pp. 53–54.

16. Adams diary, quoted in William A. Williams, ed., *The Shaping of American Diplomacy,* 2 vols., paperback ed. (Chicago: Rand McNally), I:160.

17. Frederick Jackson Turner, "The Significance of the Louisiana Purchase," *Review of Reviews* 27 (May 1903): 578–584, reprinted in Williams, *The Shaping of American Diplomacy,* I:71–81.

18. A noted military historian has cited 943 engagements with the Indians by the U.S. Army from 1865–1898: Russell F. Weigley, *History of the United States Army* (New York: Crowell-Collier-Macmillan, 1967), p. 267.

19. Friedrich Nietzsche, "Beyond Good and Evil," in *The Works of Friedrich Nietzsche,* ed. Orson Falk (New York: Tudor, 1931), 2:64–66; also excerpted in Alexander Baltzly and A. William Salomone, eds., *Readings in Twentieth-Century European History* (New York: Appleton, 1950), p. 10).

20. Merle E. Curti, Richard H. Shryock, Thomas C. Cochran, and Fred Harvey Harrington, *An American History,* 2 vols. (New York: Harper & Row, 1950), 2: 306–314.

21. U.S. Bureau of the Census, *Historical Statistics of the United States: Colonial Times to 1957* (Washington, D.C.: Bureau of the Census, 1960), p. 8.

22. Thomas A. Bailey, "America's Emergence as a World Power: The Myth and the Verity," *Pacific Historical Review* 30 (1961): 1–16, reprinted in Harry Howe Ransom, ed., *An American Foreign Policy Reader* (New York: Crowell-Collier-Macmillan, 1965), pp. 87–102; quoted at p. 101.

23. The Hague Conference of 1899 to discuss the peaceful settlement of disputes and the laws of war. American delegates also attended the second Hague Conference in 1907.

24. See *The Education of Henry Adams* (New York: Random House, Modern Library edition, 1931); Robert Seager, II, "Ten Years Before Mahan: The Unofficial Case for the New Navy, 1880–1890," *Mississippi Valley Historical Review* 40 (Dec. 1953): 491–512, reprinted in Williams, ed., *The Shaping of American Diplomacy* I:338–343; William E. Leuchtenburg, "Progressivism and Imperialism: The Progressive Movement and American Foreign Policy, 1898–1916," *Mississippi Valley Historical Review* 39 (Dec. 1952): 484–504;

Julius W. Pratt, *Expansionists of 1898* (Baltimore: Johns Hopkins Press, 1936).

25. Richard Hofstadter, *Social Darwinism in American Thought*, rev. paperback ed., (Boston: Beacon Press, 1955), p. 44. The present discussion draws heavily from Hofstadter's discerning analysis.

26. Goldman contrasts "Reform Darwinism" with "Conservative Darwinism" in the thought of this era. Eric F. Goldman, *Rendezvous with Destiny*, rev. abridged paperback ed. (New York: Vintage Books, 1958).

27. Arthur A. Ekirch, Jr., *Ideas, Ideals, and American Diplomacy* (New York: Appleton, 1966), p. 86, quoting from *The Letters of Theodore Roosevelt*, ed. E. E. Morison (Cambridge, MA: Harvard University Press, 1951–54), I:363.

28. The idea of a new frontier found appeal again during the Kennedy administration in the early 1960s but for different reasons and with different content.

29. Mahan's views influenced those of British strategist H. J. Mackinder, and in turn those of German contemporaries responsive to Mackinder's notion that "who rules the World Island commands the World." See Harold and Margaret Sprout, *Foundations of International Politics* (Princeton, NJ: Van Nostrand, 1962), chap. 10.

30. Useful treatments of Mahan and his foreign policy views and influence include W. D. Puleston, *Mahan* (New Haven: Yale University Press, 1939); Robert E. Osgood, "Mahan and Premonitions of World Power," in *Ideals and Self-Interest in America's Foreign Relations*, ed. R.E. Osgood. (Chicago: University of Chicago Press, 1953), chap. 1; Peter Karsten, *The Naval Aristocracy* (New York: Free Press, 1972).

31. Roosevelt is quoted by Richard Hofstadter, *The American Political Tradition* paperback ed. (New York: Vintage Books 1959), p. 213.

32. Brooks Adams, *The Law of Civilization and Decay* (New York: Crowell-Collier-Macmillan, 1896).

33. Brooks Adams, *The New Empire* (New York: Crowell-Collier-Macmillan, 1902), p. xxxiv.

34. Pratt, *Expansionists of 1898*, chap. 7.

35. Charles S. Campbell, Jr., "American Business Interests and the Open Door in China," *Far Eastern Quarterly* 1 (1941):43–58, reprinted in *Major Problems in American Diplomatic History: Documents and Readings*, ed. Daniel M. Smith (Boston: D. C. Heath, 1964), pp. 335–346.

36. George F. Kennan, *American Diplomacy 1900–1950* (New York: New American Library, Mentor, 1951), pt I, chap. 2; Foster Rhea Dulles, "John Hay (1898–1905)," in *An Uncertain Tradition: American Secretaries of State in the Twentieth Century*, ed. Norman A. Graebner (New York: McGraw-Hill, 1961), pp. 28–33.

37. Richard W. Leopold, "The Emergence of America as a World Power: Some Second Thoughts," in *Change and Continuity in Twentieth-Century America*, ed. John Braeman, Robert W. Bremner, and Everett Walters (Columbus: Ohio State University Press, 1964), pp. 3–34.

38. Osgood, *Ideals and Self-Interest*, p. 77.

39. Frederick A. Ogg, *National Progress 1907–1917*, The American Nation: A History, vol. 27 (New York: Harper & Row, 1918), pp. 16–17.

40. Samuel Lubell, *The Future of American Politics* (New York: Harper & Row, 1952).

SUGGESTED ADDITIONAL READING

COMBS, GERALD A. *American Diplomatic History: Two Centuries of Changing Interpretations.* Berkeley, CA: University of California Press, 1983.

EKIRCH, ARTHUR A., JR. *Ideas, Ideals, and American Diplomacy.* New York: Appleton, 1966.

FERRELL, ROBERT H. *American Diplomacy.* 3d ed. New York: Norton, 1975.

HOFSTADTER, RICHARD. *Social Darwinism in American Thought.* Revised paperback edition. Boston: Beacon, 1955.

KARSTEN, PETER. *The Naval Aristocracy.* New York: Free Press, 1972.

KENNAN, GEORGE F. *American Diplomacy 1900–1950.* New York: New American Library, 1951.

KRASNER, STEPHEN D. *Defending the National Interest.* Princeton, NJ: Princeton University Press, 1978.

PATERSON, THOMAS G.; CLIFFORD, J. GARRY; and HAGAN, KENNETH J. *American Foreign Policy: A History.* 2 vols. paper. Lexington, MA: Heath, 1983.

ROSENBERG, EMILY S. *Spreading the American Dream: American Economic and Cultural Expansion 1890–1945.* New York: Hill and Wang, 1982.

SCHLESINGER, ARTHUR, JR. "Foreign Policy and the American Character." *Foreign Affairs* 62 (Fall 1983): 1–16.

SONDERMANN, FRED A. "National Interest." *Orbis: A Journal of World Affairs.* 21 (Spring 1977): 121—138.

THOMSON, JAMES C., JR.: STANLEY, PETER W.; and PERRY, JOHN CURTIS. *Sentimental Imperialists.* New York: Harper & Row, 1981.

TOMPKINS, E. BERKELEY. *Anti-Imperialism in the United States: The Great Debate, 1890–1920.* Philadelphia, PA: University of Pennsylvania Press, 1970.

WILLIAMS, WILLIAM APPLEMAN. *America Confronts a Revolutionary World: 1776–1976.* New York: William Morrow, 1976.

81

CHAPTER 4

〜

Adapting to Post-World War II Challenges

"We have torn up 150 years of traditional American foreign policy. We have tossed Washington's Farewell Address into the discard. We have thrown ourselves squarely into the power politics and the power wars of Europe, Asia and Africa. We have taken the first step upon a course from which we can never hereafter retreat."

—Diary entry of Senator Arthur H. Vanderberg March 1941, following the congressional enactment of Lend-Lease

". . . My convictions regarding international cooperation and collective security for peace took firm form on the afternoon of the Pearl Harbor attack. That day ended isolationism for any realist."

—Vandenberg recalling his sentiments December 1941

"In a sense we are a tragic generation, despite our blessings and our place in the sun. We have been drawn into two World Wars. We finally won them both, and yet we still confront a restless and precarious peace. Something has been wrong. It is our supreme task to face these present realities, no matter how we hate them, and to mend the broken pattern if such be within human power. . . ."

—Vandenberg diary entry, April 1947

FROM ISOLATIONISM
TO INTERNATIONALISM

For two decades after the heated post-World War I debates over American participation in a League of Nations, antagonists tended to be identified as "internationalists" or "isolationists," with the preferences of the latter most often reflected in American foreign policy. The internationalists (so-called because they favored involvement in world affairs commensurate with the expansion that had been occurring in American resources, technology, and global prestige) suffered from two significant political liabilities. First, policy proposals such as that of American participation in the League were readily described by critics as a compromise of American sovereignty and thus of "the national interest." Second, the degree of involvement in international affairs recommended by internationalists was contrary to a tradition that, if already frayed, was still accorded deference.

The vulnerability of the internationalist position was noted by critics such as William Borah, Republican Senator from Idaho, who had been one of the leading opponents of U. S. membership in the League of Nations. Still regarded as a champion of isolationism into the Franklin Roosevelt administration, Borah warned in 1934 that if internationalism

> means anything more than the friendly cooperation between separate, distinct and wholly independent nations, [it] rests upon a false foundation. And when undertaken, it will fail as in the name of progress and humanity it should fail.[1]

Invoking the spirit of George Washington in a later speech, Borah added that the best foreign policy would be one that "offers peace to all nations, trade and commerce with all nations, honest friendship to all nations [but] political commitments, expressed or implied, with none."[2]

American isolationist tendencies in the 1930s were reinforced by the widespread preoccupation with the domestic consequences of the Great Depression and by the anxieties associated with the war clouds hovering over Europe and Asia. The United States must isolate itself from foreign quarrels, so advocates of policies such as the Neutrality Acts reasoned, and thereby permit American energies and resources to be utilized fully for domestic recovery.

The German attack on Poland in September 1939 provoked a revival of internationalist concern, however; this led to growing support in the Congress for preparedness measures and a dilution of neutrality legislation. With the Japanese attack on Pearl Harbor in December 1941 even those Americans who had been among the most vociferous isolationists now tended to champion the fight against tyranny. The wartime commitment became not only a means of gaining collective exoneration for the profound departure from the tradition of nonentanglement but also a vehicle for achieving an element of social cohesion in a nation badly fractured by the domestic battles of the depression. Wartime magazine essays and articles as well as movies, whether governmentally commissioned or commercially inspired, fostered the image of a nation totally united in pursuit of heroic goals. As one historian recalls the dominant themes:

> Democracy and decency were at last on the verge of total triumph over dictatorship and degradation. Participation in the war was a cathartic act that would sweep away the sense of shame and guilt and futility that had so gripped the United States throughout the depression decade. Global war, it was promised, would give the lost individual of the thirties a renewed sense of place and purpose.[3]

Concerned observers of American politics, however, wondered whether the domestic foreign policy consensus could survive the transition to a peacetime environment, with its inevitable host of problems more divisive in nature than that of fighting a common enemy.

There were some hopeful signs. Leaders of both major political parties were operating during the war on the premise that partisanship "stops at the water's edge." When policy discussions began to focus on postwar planning, Republican leaders expressed views close to those being articulated by the Democratic Roosevelt administration about the need for a new era of global responsibilities for the United States. Wendell Willkie, for instance, who had been the Republican standard-bearer in the 1940 presidential election, contended in 1944 that the arguments that in the past had been used to keep the United States from becoming involved in international institutions had become invalidated by current and emerging needs. Participation in a new international organization designed to keep the peace ought not to be regarded as an infringement upon American sovereignty but rather as an opportunity to exercise leadership creatively in order to solve the complex problems of the postwar era. "To use [world] leadership for our own enrichment and that of mankind will not be to weaken the sovereign power of the American people," Willkie wrote, "it will be to widen it and make it more real."[4]

If Willkie's reputation as a "one-worlder" somewhat undercut his ability to mobilize the support of others in his party for these views, an especially significant role in forging a bipartisan approach to postwar foreign policy problems rested with Republicans who had been prominent spokesmen for isolationist views in the prewar years. The most notable example is Arthur Vandenberg of Michigan, leading Republican spokesman for foreign affairs in the Senate, whose "conversion" from prewar isolationist to postwar proponent of American support for international commitments such as the United Nations and the NATO alliance was widely discussed. As his influential journalist contemporary, Walter Lippmann, noted:

> When a sudden and tremendous change of outlook has become imperative in a crisis, it makes all the difference in the world to most of us to see a man whom we have known and trusted, and who has thought and has felt as we did, going through the experience of changing his mind, doing it with style and dash, and in a mood to shame the devils of his own weakness.[5]

On the other hand, the bipartisan policy consensus regarding American acceptance of major world responsibilities always threatened to come apart over the question of the continuing relationship between the United States and its wartime allies. Distrust of the British was expressed by many American politicians; even more so was distrust of the Soviet Union.

Careful students of world history recognized that the prospects of continued close cooperation among wartime allies into the postwar era were slim. Once wartime victory was assured, the mutual self-interest that formed the basis of the alliance, which lay primarily in neutralizing the threat of Germany, was eliminated. Especially for the two nation-states that emerged from the war as superpowers, the threat that each could pose to the self-interest of the other now exceeded the probable gain to be derived from continuing to work as partners unless each could be certain that the other was perfectly trustworthy. But it is precisely the absence of such trust that characterizes the system of sovereign nation-states.[6]

Although the failure of cooperative efforts between the United States and the Soviet Union may seem to have been predictable, at the time such failure was of major concern, particularly as it undermined the Rooseveltian vision of the structure of postwar peace. It seems doubtful that a consensus in support of continued cooperation with the Soviets could have been sustained in the postwar era, even if Roosevelt had lived to provide leadership for this approach. Many politicians otherwise sympathetic to the needs for bipartisan unity in foreign policy identified with the views of "the average American," which Vandenberg expressed in his diary in March 1943:

> I think [the] average American wants to be very sure that American spokesmanship at the peace table is at least as loyal to America's own primary interests as Mr. Stalin is certain to be in respect to Russia and Mr. Churchill . . . to the British Empire. This average American is scared by the Vice President's [Henry Wallace's] "international milk route" and by kindred Pollyanna crystal gazing . . . He is neither an isolationist nor an internationalist. He is a middle-of-the-roader who wants to win this war as swiftly and as cheaply as possible; who then wants a realistic peace which puts an end to military aggression; who wants justice rather than force to rule the postwar world; who is willing to take his full share of responsibility in all of these directions; but who is perfectly sure that no one is going to look out for us . . . unless we look out for ourselves and who wants "enlightened selfishness" mixed with "generous idealism" when our course is charted.[7]

After Roosevelt's death in April 1945, it became increasingly evident that a foreign policy consensus would be forged in the postwar years only if a central assumption incorporated into policy was that the Soviets had expansionistic ambitions that must be contained. The consensus that did emerge in the postwar years supported a radical departure from prewar policies in terms of American global commitments, but support was sustained in terms of a refurbished image of American uniqueness and mission. America must now accept global responsibilities but do so on the basis of "tough-minded" realism rather than "wooly-headed" idealism.

CHALLENGES OF
THE POSTWAR WORLD

In an important sense, the foreign policy experience of the United States in the postwar years is a study in adaptation to a radically changed environment. A careful examination of the pattern of policy response to the varied and complex challenges posed by the postwar world reveals, however, that as adaptive energies increasingly were consumed by Cold War concerns, several important issues were not resolved. Rather they were deferred, to plague American foreign policy in the 1960s, the 1970s, and the 1980s.

In later chapters, the pattern of American response to the vexing challenges of recent decades will be considered. Here the post-World War II experience will be reviewed for the insight that it provides into the emergence of themes that would come to dominate American foreign policy discussions for a generation.

Among the major challenges that the United States faced after World War II were these: (1) reconciling American global responsibilities and commitments with American capabilities as a world power; (2) developing a workable system for maintaining the peace in a world that had experienced untold devastation from major war twice within the span of a generation; (3) the challenge of containing and bringing under control the awesome development of weapons of mass destruction, as represented by the atomic bomb; (4) designing and managing postwar economic recovery on a global basis; (5) identifying and coping with the rising expectations of peoples of the Third World, especially in areas under colonial rule; and (6) the challenge of continuing collaboration with the wartime allies sufficient to ensure that the other challenges could be met.

The last of these challenges merits discussion first, because the American response to it conditioned the response to the other challenges.

POSTWAR RELATIONS
WITH WARTIME ALLIES

President Franklin Roosevelt and his top advisors were sensitive in varying degrees to each of the challenges that the postwar world would pose. Although a design for postwar policy was worked out only sketchily in Roosevelt's thinking, a principal working assumption was that continued collaboration among the wartime allies was essential if other postwar challenges also were to be met.

As frictions among the allies grew in the waning months of the war, few of Roosevelt's advisors or political associates expressed confidence that a postwar foreign policy could be sustained based upon the collaboration assumption. Roosevelt himself had forebodings. In his final State of the Union address to the Congress in January 1945, Roosevelt warned that "the nearer we come to vanquishing our enemies the more we inevitably become conscious of differences among the victors." Therefore, he emphasized:

> We must not let those differences divide us and blind us to our more important common and continuing interests in winning the war and building the peace.
>
> International cooperation on which enduring peace must be based is not a one-way street.
>
> Nations, like individuals, do not always see alike or think alike, and international cooperation and progress are not helped by any nation assuming that it has a monopoly of wisdom or of virtue. . . .
> In our disillusionment after the last war we preferred international anarchy to international cooperation with nations which did not see and think exactly as we did. We gave up the hope of gradually achieving a better peace because we had not the courage to fulfill our responsibilities in an admittedly imperfect world.
>
> We must not let that happen again or we shall follow the same tragic road again—the road to a third world war.[8]

At the Yalta Conference early in 1945, cooperation with the Soviets in the postwar period still seemed to most American policy makers not only essential to the preservation of peace in the postwar world but feasible. As President Roosevelt's close adviser Harry Hopkins described the prevailing sentiment, "The Russians had proved that they could be reasonable and farseeing and there wasn't any doubt in the minds of the President or any of us that we could live with them and get along with them peacefully for as far into the future as any of us could imagine."[9]

During the few climactic months of the war after Yalta, however, American-Soviet relations had deteriorated so far that Acting Secretary of State Joseph Grew could predict in May 1945 that "a future war with Soviet Russia is as certain as anything in the world can be certain."[10] An aura of cautious optimism and international goodwill had permeated the Opera Hall in San Francisco a month earlier when delegates had gathered for the founding of the United Nations only days after the death of Roosevelt. But as conference deliberations progressed, according to a reporter on the scene, "Day and night . . . there was only one topic [among conferees]: Soviet Russia."[11]

In calling the reporter's observation to the attention of a radio audience, Republican Congresswoman Clare Booth Luce said that her reporter friend had wondered whether the Soviets really deserved all that attention. "Of course he knew the answer," Luce added, "they do." According to Luce, delegates from all parts of the world were legitimately concerned about the Soviets because of the moral bankruptcy of their ideology and ambitions. "No American wants to go to war over this," she noted. "But surely we have learned in the last decade that appeasement is the road to war. And if we want to keep out of war with communism we must not appease communism."[12]

Even if unwilling to accept the proposition that a showdown with the Soviet Union was inevitable, most top American policy makers agreed that an emerging pattern of Soviet actions seemed evident. It was a pattern of increasing belligerency, of willingness to ignore wartime agreements, and of intent to expand Communist control by any means, including the use of force. The tactics of the Soviets in installing a government in Poland that would staunchly support Moscow and in subverting, through the arrest of key leaders as well as other means, the efforts of the Polish government-in-exile to regain control became a symbol to Western leaders of Soviet intentions to dominate Eastern and Central Europe. A series of bitter Communist-led strikes in France and Italy suggested a possible plan of extending Soviet control to Western Europe as well. Efforts to work out an amicable agreement with the Soviets for areas to be administered jointly seemed increasingly futile in Germany, in Korea, and at the time in Austria. The Soviets were subjecting Turkey to intense pressure to sign a new treaty with them defining their access to the straits of the Bosphorus and the Dardanelles, ceding them territory along the Black Sea, and leasing them military bases. Soviet armed forces that had occupied the northern provinces of Iran during the war remained there after the war had ended to allow indigenous Communists to attempt to establish an autonomous province of Azerbaijan that would be sympathetic to Moscow.

Soviet intentions seemed evident in their speech as well as in their actions. In February 1946, in an address reported publicly in the party newspaper *Pravda*, Stalin spoke of the inevitability of conflict with the capitalist powers. He urged the Soviet people not to be deluded that the end of the war meant that the nation could relax. Rather, intensified efforts were needed to strengthen and defend the homeland.[13]

Roughly a week after the Stalin speech, George F. Kennan, the second-ranking civilian diplomat in the American embassy in Moscow, sent to the State Department an 8,000-word cable assessing the motivations of Soviet leadership. The cable was widely circulated among policy makers in Washington and became important in crystallizing their beliefs. After exploring the roots of Soviet motivation and the implications of their positions, Kennan noted, "In summary, we have here a political force committed fanatically to the belief that with [the] U.S. there can be no permanent modus vivendi, that it is desirable and necessary that the internal harmony of our society be disrupted, our traditional way of life be destroyed, the international authority of our state be broken, if Soviet power is to be secure."[14]

A few weeks later, Winston Churchill spoke at Westminster College in Fulton, Missouri, with President Truman beside him on the platform. "From Stettin in the Baltic to Trieste in the Adriatic," Churchill observed, "an iron curtain has descended across the continent."[15] While warning of the threat of Communist expansion and subversion, Churchill nevertheless assured his audience that he did not believe that the Soviet Union desired war. Still, he contended that the pattern of Soviet expansion and subversion could only be met by strength and determined resistance on the part of the United States and Britain.[16]

Such "determined resistance" was given tangible form in an American military and financial commitment to Greece and Turkey (most notably in response to an urgent message from the British indicating that their own support of the Greek government in combating Communist-led insurgents could not be sustained). The key principle that President Truman enunciated in a March 1947 speech requesting congressional funding for aid to Greece and Turkey was that "it must be the policy of the United States to support free peoples who are resisting attempted subjugation by armed minorities or by outside pressures."[17] The Truman Doctrine, as it came to be known, thus enunciated principles seemingly global in applicability. The far-reaching implications of a commitment to oppose Communist expansion gave the speech immense significance as a statement of American policy. However, it was precisely these implications and the crusading language in which they were cast that led some persons, including the author of the "containment" concept, George Kennan, to criticize the Truman Doctrine.[18]

Critics were in a distinct minority, however. A consensus had been growing among policy makers in the Congress as well as in the executive branch in support of the position that Churchill had advocated and that Truman now gave policy form. This consensus, however, was obtainable mainly because strong emphasis was being placed on meeting the challenge of containing Soviet expansion with the result that institutional and emotional energies were becoming so consumed by meeting the perceived threat of Communism that other challenges tended to become defined as mere variations on the theme of the primary struggle.

RECONCILING RESPONSIBILITIES AND COMMITMENTS WITH CAPABILITIES

The images that American policy makers had had of the nation and its vital interests inevitably were altered by the experience of American leadership with the wartime alliance. A vast increase in global responsibilities and commitments was to be anticipated with peace, commensurate with the growth in American capabilities. Amidst the devastation of the final months of World War II, it was the United States, to a far greater extent than the other victor that also came to be known as a "superpower," that was now dominant in terms of economic, technological, and human resources.

The Soviet claim to superpower status rested on its military strength and dominance of Eastern Europe. In the final drive westward in the winter and spring of 1945, the Soviets had been able to mass nearly 250 divisions against the Germans.[19] At the end of the war, these units were deployed along a line from the Elbe River in Germany south to the Czech-German border and along a line west of Vienna, which defined the Soviet zone of occupation in

Austria. On the other hand, the Soviets had a relatively small navy and a small air force.

In the final months of the war, the United States Army also had impressive strength, but of the approximately sixty American divisions that had fought in the final European campaign, great numbers were transferred to the Pacific theater as soon as the war with Germany ended. Moreover, as soon as the surrender of Japan was announced, the American armed forces began a rapid demobilization. In a letter to the President in May 1945, Churchill questioned Truman on the consequences of this, asking, "What will be the position in a year or two, when the British and American Armies have melted and the French has not yet been formed on any major scale, when we may have a handful of divisions, mostly French, and when Russia may choose to keep two or three hundred on active service?"[20]

Nevertheless, at the war's end, President Truman responded to what he felt was massive public pressure for rapid demobilization. Within a month after the Japanese surrender, the United States Army was discharging over 15,000 soldiers per day; the President pledged that the number would be increased to 25,000 discharges per day by January 1946.[21] Thus, from a wartime peak strength of roughly 6 million men and women, the Army had been reduced to fewer than 1.5 million by mid-1946 and to fewer than 700,000 by mid-1947. An air force of 2 million persons and a navy of 3 million persons had been reduced by mid-1947 to approximately 300,000 and 500,000, respectively. Moreover, because the massive exodus from the services had included trained personnel in key positions, many of the Army, Navy, and Air Force units that remained were in a poor state of combat readiness.[22]

In spite of massive demobilization, the United States possessed at least one fearsome military advantage over all other powers— atomic weapons. A single bomb had virtually destroyed the city of Hiroshima in August 1945; a second had obliterated Nagasaki a few days later. At the war's end, the United States had a monopoly on both atomic weaponry and the scientific knowledge that had produced such unprecedented destruction. Even before the explosive potential of the atom bomb had been proved, some officials sensed that it could effect a radical change in the game of international politics. Secretary of War Stimson, for instance, urged that vital negotiations with the Soviets be postponed until the United States held "the master card."[23] The United States, he believed, would then be bargaining with "a royal straight flush and we mustn't be a fool about the way we play it. . . ."[24]

The United States emerged from the war with a number of other important advantages over the Soviet Union, too. These first included the fact that the United States had suffered no damage to its homeland in contrast to the vast devastation to the Soviet Union and the enormous task of reconstruction. Moreover, approximately one tenth of the prewar Soviet population had been killed in the war. The magnitude of the loss can perhaps be appreciated by the fact that the ratio of Soviet to American war deaths was about seventy to one. While nearly 300,000 Americans had been killed in the war, the number of Soviets killed has been estimated at 20 million.

Closely related to the differences between the two powers in the amount of physical punishment from the war were the differences in economic productivity. In spite of the problems caused by conversion from a peacetime to a wartime economy, manpower relocation, shortages of certain commodities, and a number of highly publicized strikes, the war had been tremendous boon to the economy of the United States. In constant dollars (1953 base), the gross national product of the United States had risen from $239.2 billion in 1941 to $329.3 billion in 1944. Agriculture production had increased nearly 25 percent during the war; between 1939 and 1944, civilian consumption of goods and services, as one index of trends in the standard of living, had risen by 20 percent.[25]

In contrast, the economy of the Soviet Union had been seriously impaired by the war. Vast industrial areas had been laid to waste, transportation and communication networks had been destroyed or damaged, and industrial production had been cut almost in half. Millions of persons from the Soviet Union returned at the end of the war as refugees, having spent months or years in concentration camps or work camps in Germany, where their health had deteriorated. The system of Soviet agriculture, which had been maintained during the war almost entirely by women, had suffered severely and food was scarce.[26]

Although by the end of the war the Soviets had gained control of substantial territory and resources in Central and Eastern Europe that they exploited to bolster their own economy, maintaining control in those areas required an enormous investment of personnel and equipment that to a large extent offset the economic gain. Moreover, the Soviets had been unsuccessful in persuading the United States and Great Britain that the wealthy industrial area of the Ruhr should be under international control with Soviet participation. Instead, the Ruhr remained in the British zone of occupation, and its resources were utilized for the postwar recon-struction of West Germany.

The United States also led its allies in capital investment and research innovation, which enhanced further productivity. During the war the American government had made substantial investment in basic and applied scientific research which, although undertaken for military purposes, had led to major breakthroughs with potential applicability to civilian needs in areas such as atomic energy, elec-tronics, jet propulsion, aircraft design, and the development of synthetic fabrics. Beyond the $2 billion that the government had spent in the development and production of atomic weapons, another half billion had been invested in scientific research.[27]

In short, at the end of World War II the United States had vast economic advantages over the Soviet Union. Moreover, the Soviets expected and needed American help in their reconstruction effort. As the American ambassador to the Soviet Union, Averell Harri-man, explained in a conference with President Truman only a week after the death of Franklin Roosevelt, the desire of the Soviets to retain American economic assistance would enable the United States to take a firm line on important issues "without running serious risks"; Truman assured Harriman that he intended to stand firm and agreed, as he has recorded in his memoirs, that "the Russians needed us more than we needed them."[28]

DEVELOPING A STRUCTURE FOR PEACE

Continuing cooperation with the Soviets was needed, however, to carry out the vital task of creating a set of institutions capable of maintaining peace in the world. The American approach to the task was characterized by a sense of urgency but ambivalence. Policy makers were convinced the American prestige and resources must be committed to the creation of a new international organization to succeed the League of Nations, but they were equally convinced that realism must prevail over naive Wilsonian idealism in entrust-ing authority to an international body and that American sovereignty must not be compromised.

Although Wilson had been the most zealous champion of the nascent League of Nations after World War I, the United States had not become a League member because of opposition in the Senate. Widespread feelings of guilt that the United States had failed to accept its responsibilities as a world power no doubt contributed to the desire of leading Republicans as well as Democrats to commit the United States to a successor to the League after World War II. At the same time, many remained convinced that a commitment to "collective security," which became the core of the United Nations peacekeeping approach as it had been in the League, could not and should not be translated into requiring an automatic commitment of American forces in situations that might seem remote from or contrary to American vital interests.[29]

Drafters of the Charter of the United Nations made the Security Council the centerpiece of the collective security mechanism, to be assisted by a military staff drawn from the chiefs of staff of the major powers. Each of five members given a permanent seat on the Security Council was given a veto over substantive action by the Council. The veto provision reflected the acknowledgement by the founders of the United Nations that it was unrealistic to expect any of the major powers of the world to join an international organization that might have the authority to commit force against a key member of the body.

In discussions before the San Francisco founding conference of how United Nations peacekeeping might work in practice, Franklin Roosevelt invoked the image of "four policemen"—the United States, the Soviet Union, Great Britain, and China—patrolling the world community to maintain order. Because in fact China was an economically underdeveloped country torn by war and internal strife, and Great Britain was too enfeebled even to hold its empire together, the "policemen" were essentially two. Thus, Roosevelt's "Yalta axioms," as they have been termed by Daniel Yergin, especially included an emphasis on continued collaboration with the Soviet Union as the key to world peace.[30]

As Yergin notes, however, the "Yalta axioms" did not outlive Roosevelt. They were replaced by what Yergin terms the "Riga axioms," so-called because they were a postwar version of assumptions that had been expressed during and after the period of the Stalinist purges of the 1930s by American diplomats stationed in Riga on the Baltic Sea. The key assumption was that given the "messianic drive for world mastery" on the part of Stalin and his fellow Communists, fruitful cooperation with the Soviet Union was impossible.[31]

Nevertheless, the illusions (1) that the United States accorded primacy to maintenance of world peace through the instrumentality of the newly created United Nations and (2) that the United Nations would be able to function effectively as an instrument of collective security were fostered not only by Truman administration rhetoric but also by United Nations action at the outbreak of the Korean War in June 1950. A United States-sponsored resolution that denounced the invasion of South Korea by the Communist North Korean forces and called on United Nations members to help the South Koreans repel the attack was approved by the Security Council.

The incident was more an example of American ability at the time to dominate the United Nations than it was of collective security operating according to the logic of its precepts, however. A Soviet veto, which would certainly have been cast to protect the Soviet Union's North Korean allies from the effects of the American-sponsored resolution, was prevented by unusual circumstances. Previously American influence had been demonstrated in persuading the United Nations to permit the government of Chiang Kai-shek to continue to represent China in the United Nations, despite the fact that with the culmination of the civil war in 1949, all of mainland China was now ruled by the Communist government of Mao Zedong, with Chiang and his forces having fled to Taiwan. In order to demonstrate his government's indignation at this denial to their Communist allies of their rightful seat, the Soviet delegate had boycotted the Security Council and was still absent at the time of the vote on the resolution condemning the North Korean invasion.

Although Truman and his top advisors may have continued to harbor the belief that collective security through the United Nations was workable, the fact is that as a policy collective security had become subordinated to collective defense against Soviet or Soviet-sponsored aggression. Whereas collective security presupposes a situation in which all members are pledged to respond to the aid of a victim if any one of them violates the pact by committing aggression against another member, collective defense commits the members of a military alliance to mutual assistance in the event of an attack by an external enemy.

Beginning in 1947 with the Rio Pact (formally the Inter-American Treaty of Reciprocal Assistance), the Truman administration embraced the concept of collective defense. As Europeans became increasingly alarmed (as did American officials) about Soviet pressures on Norway in the north, Turkey in the south, the continuing Communist-led insurgency in Greece, and (in 1948) a Communist coup in Czechoslovakia, American and West European governments entered into discussions designed to organize a collective defense arrangement similar to the Rio Pact.[32]

The resulting North Atlantic Treaty Organization (NATO), founded in 1949, took on added importance with the outbreak of war in Korea in June 1950. The alliance commitment seemed to be working to deter aggression in Europe, whereas in the absence of such a commitment in Korea, an attack occurred. A few months before the attack, Secretary of State Dean Acheson had announced that Korea was outside of the "defense perimeter" of the United States. When the attack came, the American government assumed that it must have been okayed if not planned in Moscow. The conclusion followed that future Soviet-sponsored aggression could be deterred only by the tangible American demonstration of a willingness to respond through alliance commitments.

When General Dwight D. Eisenhower, former commander of the allied powers in Western Europe, became president in 1953 succeeding Truman, the American policy commitment to collective defense on the NATO model increased still further. Eisenhower's secretary of state, John Foster Dulles, was a staunch believer in the collective-defense concept. The containment of Communism, to which Dulles was fervently committed, could be given real substance, Dulles believed, if the Soviet Union and Communist China could be entirely encircled with American-sponsored collective-defense pacts. Within two years of assuming office as secretary of state, Dulles had expanded the network of collective defense treaties with which the United States was affiliated to include over forty nations.

CHOOSING BETWEEN THE QUICK AND THE DEAD: HARNESSING NUCLEAR TECHNOLOGY

The key elements in the Eisenhower/Dulles strategic arsenal were nuclear weapons, which when carried by long-range bombers enabled the United States to pose a threat of "massive retaliation" in response to any Soviet aggression. Yet only a few years earlier, it had appeared that the United States was seeking to rid the world of such awesome instruments of war and that a carefully conceived plan for doing so actually had been developed.

Presiding over the first meeting of the United Nations Atomic Energy Commission in June 1946, Bernard Baruch, the American representative to the commission, had described the urgency of the task before the group:

> We are here to make a choice between the quick and the dead. . . .
> We must provide the mechanism to assure that atomic energy is
> used for peaceful purposes and preclude its use in war. . . . We must
> answer the world's longing for peace and security. . . . The search
> of science for the absolute weapon has reached fruition in this
> country. But she stands ready to proscribe and destroy this
> instrument, to lift its use from death to life, if the world will join
> in a pact to that end.[33]

With these words, Baruch had unveiled an American plan for international control of atomic energy. Prepared in draft form under the supervision of Under Secretary of State Dean Acheson and scientific consultant David Lilienthal, the plan called for the creation of an International Atomic Development Authority (IADA). The composition of the IADA was unspecified except that its members were to be highly knowledgeable in atomic energy and recruited on an international basis. Key aspects of the authority to be entrusted to the IADA were "managerial control or ownership of all atomic energy activities potentially dangerous to world security"; "power to control, inspect, and license all other atomic activities"; and primacy in engaging in research and development in atomic energy.[34] The body was to have power to impose penalties upon any violator; IADA investigations or the imposition of sanctions by the IADA were not to be prevented by the veto of any nation-state (in contrast to procedures in the UN Security Council).

The Baruch Plan provided assurances of the willingness of the American government to stop the manufacture of atomic bombs, to dispose of its existing stockpiles, and to provide the IADA with full information essential to the development of atomic weapons, "when an adequate system of control of atomic energy, including the renunciation of the bomb as a weapon, has been agreed upon and put into effective operation and condign punishments set up for the violations of the rules of control which are to be stigmatized as international crimes . . . "[35]

At the second meeting of the United Nations Atomic Energy Commission, Soviet representative Gromyko proposed an alternative to the Baruch Plan. Agreeing with Baruch that the issue was urgent, he added his view that inherent in the existing atomic weapons situation were "reasons that can only increase the suspicion of some countries in regard to others and give rise to political instability. . . ."[36] He therefore recommended that an international convention take place as soon as possible to devise a treaty prohibiting the production and employment of atomic weapons, with all existing stockpiles of atomic weapons, completed or uncompleted, to be destroyed within three months from the day the treaty became active. He further recommended that an international committee for the free exchange of scientific information be established immediately, with the task of working out details of the treaty, including provisions for control of atomic energy, policing, and sanctions.

Details of subsequent debate of the American and Soviet proposals need not concern us here. It is sufficient to note that the two positions proved to be irreconcilable; thus the United States continued its production and testing of atomic weapons, and the Soviets their research and development, which led to the successful test of an atomic device in 1949. The surprisingly rapid acquisition by the Soviets of an atomic capability in turn stimulated the American government, by a process that one observer has described as "how to decide without actually choosing," to push ahead to an even more "super" weapon (in the terminology of officials)—the hydrogen bomb.[37]

Available evidence suggests that President Truman and his key advisors wanted to believe that the Baruch Plan would be acceptable to the Soviets.[38] Quite apart from its inspection provision, however, the Baruch Plan was almost certain to be repudiated by the Soviet Union because of its tolerance of a continued American monopoly of atomic weapons, pending IADA assumption of control. Acceptance could be based only on Soviet faith in the American government until such time as the IADA had supervised destruction of the American atomic stockpile. The mutual distrust between American and Soviet leaders in 1946 made the probability that the Baruch Plan (or the Soviet alternative) would be accepted infinitesimal. One may suppose that, had the shoe been on the other foot, with the Soviets in sole possession of atomic weapons and offering the United States a control plan along the lines of the Baruch Plan, American government leaders would have found it impossible to agree to such a proposal.

Nevertheless, however improbable the realization of the Baruch Plan may have been, it was widely regarded at the time as an imaginative and magnanimous act on the part of the United States government. Many persons in the United States and abroad who had been at the forefront of public discussion about the dangers of atomic war enthusiastically supported the plan. Scientists who had worked on the Manhattan Project, for instance, and who had experienced agonizing cleavages in their ranks over the issue of dropping the bomb on Japan, were temporarily unified by the Baruch Plan. It seemed to offer a rational design for transforming the awesome scientific developments from a threat to mankind into a positive contribution to its betterment.[39]

Having proposed a seemingly reasonable and generous plan for the international control of atomic energy, the American government was able to depict Soviet intransigence on the issue as the only obstacle to a world freed from the threat of atomic war. Favorable world and domestic reaction served to provide an aura of legitimacy to an American nuclear arsenal, which would grow to proportions never imagined in the 1940s.[40]

REBUILDING WARTORN ECONOMIES

Another important dimension of the adaptive challenge that the transition to the post-World War II era represented for the United States was that of rebuilding wartorn economies and dealing with problems stemming from the profound impact that the war had had on national economies worldwide.

The war had taken a frightful toll, not only in human life, but also in economic infrastructures. Industries had to be rebuilt from rubble in many wartorn countries, agriculture revived, returning soldiers absorbed into economies, and systems of transportation and communication erected. Millions of refugees on the world scene had to be fed, housed, and relocated. Inflation was rampant, and economies with severe shortages of basic commodities such as food were experiencing the additional problem of black markets and hoarding.

Emergency relief assistance made severe demands upon American resources. However, because such assistance was less likely to provoke political controversy than were longer-range programs of economic reconstruction and restructuring, planning for the former was separable from planning for the latter and led to tangible results even in the middle of war. Following months of discussions between the American government and its wartime allies, the parties to the negotiations were able to announce in 1943 the creation of a United Nations Relief and Rehabilitation Administration (UNRRA). The UNRRA would become the principal instrument in 1945 and 1946 for coping with such urgent problems as the repatriation of dispossessed persons and of providing emergency food, clothing, shelter, and medical supplies to refugees and other needy persons.

Devising an international monetary system was a more politically sensitive problem (with consequences noted below). However, under the leadership of the secretary of the treasury, Henry Morgenthau, the United States was able to persuade forty-three other governments to meet in Bretton Woods, New Hampshire, in 1944, for the purposes of endorsing a new system. Its principal components were an International Monetary Fund and an International Bank for Reconstruction and Development (known as the World Bank).

Planning for the occupation, upon their defeat, of Italy, Germany, Austria, and Japan was even more susceptible to heated differences among the wartime allies. Nevertheless, plans were laid, reflecting the outcome of countless staff studies, exchanges of cables, and above all, discussions among Roosevelt, Churchill, and Stalin.

It is impossible in a few paragraphs or pages to describe fully the complex elements of economic and related problems that policy makers confronted in the postwar era, nor to trace in detail the tortuous evolution of programs, institutions, and plans such as those cited in previous paragraphs. It is possible only to convey a sense of the fragmentary nature of economic planning and the controversy that important issues engendered. The longer-range economic issues were not so much resolved as they were redefined in Cold War terms.

Planning for the various postwar tasks—emergency relief, revision of the world monetary system, occupation policies, rebuilding war-torn economies—was elaborate but lacking in real coherence. Plans could be based only on "guesstimates" of the magnitude and nature of problems to be faced, and each of the departments and agencies involved in the planning process had its own agenda, its own domain of responsibility and concern, and its own priorities.[41]

Efforts to consolidate planning across departments were far more successful on paper than in practice.[42] To an even greater extent, the same is true of efforts to coordinate planning among wartime allies. Planning problems at all levels were compounded before Roosevelt's death by the proclivity of the President for keeping subordinates in doubt about his real preferences, seeming one week to support the postwar policy recommendation of one advisor and the following week to praise a contradictory proposal of another advisor.[43]

When Harry Truman assumed the presidency, additional problems in the implementation of policy plans were generated by abrupt reversals of policy. The most serious of these in terms of American relations with its wartime allies was the sudden termination of lend-lease, a week after the Japanese surrender in August 1945. Through lend-lease appropriations, which had passed Congress by narrow margins at the outset of American involvement in the war, the United States had shipped $46 billion in supplies to the allies (especially Great Britain, the prime recipient of aid, the Soviet Union, and China).[44]

In an effort to rectify the diplomatic harm done by what Truman would later confide was the worst mistake of his presidency,[45] the administration managed to extend aid to the Chinese government of Chiang Kai-shek, which was then engaged in a civil war with the Communist forces of Mao Zedong, and to negotiate a $3.75 billion loan to the British.[46] Soviet protestations and requests for a loan to aid in rebuilding a devasted economy, however, fell upon deaf ears.

Moreover, termination of American support brought the activities of UNRRA to an end in 1946, despite the pleadings of the American commander in Europe, General Dwight D. Eisenhower, and of UNRRA Director-General Fiorello LaGuardia (former mayor of New York City), that the needs for UNRRA assistance were urgent.[47] Furthermore, the estimate (which proved to be sadly accurate) was that the winter of 1946–1947 would be unusually severe, aggravating the distress of those in need of food, shelter, clothing, and medical supplies.

Dean Acheson, an active participant in wartime planning for

the postwar era as an assistant secretary and then the under secretary of state, has acknowledged in retrospect that he and his governmental associates failed to anticipate

> not only . . . the extent of physical destruction, damage, and loss caused by the war, but even more of social, economic, and political dislocations undermining the very continuance of great states and empires. Only slowly did it dawn upon us that the whole world structure and order that we had inherited from the nineteenth century was gone and that the struggle to replace it would be directed from two bitterly opposed and ideologically irreconcilable power centers.[48]

The growing conviction among American policy makers that the real struggle was between "two bitterly opposed and ideologically irreconcilable power centers" was increasingly shaping the approach of the United States to postwar economic problems. The real objection to UNRRA had been that the international agency provided assistance not only to needy peoples in countries friendly to the United States but also to peoples in countries hostile to the United States. Similarly, the lines were being drawn in developing a postwar monetary system. The Soviets ratified neither the International Monetary Fund proposal nor that for the World Bank, the twin components of the Bretton Woods system.[49]

The British had felt compelled to become affiliated with the Bretton Woods system, although dissatisfied with American-imposed provisions designed to end preferential economic treatment within the British Commonwealth. However, the desperate economic plight of the British that drove them to accept American terms for a postwar monetary system also led them in early 1947 to plead with the American government to take up the burden that the British had assumed for supporting the Greek monarchy against a Communist-led insurgency. It was this plea, invoking the danger of the spread of Communism in the strategically vital eastern Mediterranean, that led to the Truman Doctrine.

Moreover, it was the spectre of expanded Communist influence in the context of desperate economic conditions throughout Western Europe that led to a major new American initiative for economic recovery. George Kennan, who early in May 1946 assumed his duties as head of a new policy planning staff in the State Department, told an audience at the National War College in Washington, D.C., that the Russians

> feel . . . that Europe is in reality theirs, although Europe may not know it; that they have already woven an invisible network of economic dependence around those proud nations of the continent which still fancy themselves to be free; and that they have only to await patiently the day when American failure to relieve the intolerable economic conditions of those areas will allow them to . . . draw tighter the cords . . . and bring the west of Europe into the shadows which have already enveloped the east.[50]

Later in the month, Kennan submitted to Secretary of State George Marshall a series of policy recommendations for dealing with the economic crisis in Europe.[51] In June, in a commencement speech at Harvard University, the secretary set forth the broad outline of a European recovery program that would be known as the Marshall Plan. Described subsequently by Winston Churchill as "the most unsordid act in history," the program committed unprecedented amounts of peacetime assistance from the United States to Europe. However, the program received requisite levels of funding by Congress not because it was an act of pure generosity but rather because members of Congress became convinced, as the administration emphasized, that in the context of economic crisis and a growing threat of Communist influence, a major American effort to promote European recovery was in the national interest.[52]

A major effort to rebuild the European economy necessarily meant rethinking the goals of occupation policy for Germany. A similar reappraisal of policy goals in the light of mounting concern with Communism was occurring in regard to Japan. The intense wartime concern with defeating the Axis powers (Germany, Italy, Japan) had led quite naturally to a consideration of postwar policies that would ensure that the aggressors from World War II never again would be able to instigate war. The goals were to demobilize and demilitarize the aggressors, and possibly even to dismember Germany to render it impotent. However, as some analysts pointed out in the early stages of postwar planning, the revitalization of German industry was vital not only to Germany but to European recovery generally; Japanese industry likewise had importance for regional economic health and not only for the Japanese economy.

The policy shift came gradually. Efforts to demilitarize Germany and Japan initially continued side by side with a new commitment to rebuild their economies. However, a decision to rearm West Germany came in the wake of crises such as the Berlin blockade and the Communist coup in Czechoslovakia, and following the creation of NATO. (The commitment of the Truman administration as of the early 1950s was to rearm the Germans within the context of an integrated European Defense Community; when it proved impossible to secure French approval for the latter, the United States supported the rebuilding of West German armed forces as a component of NATO.)[53] The key stimuli to rearming Japan were the Communist victory in 1949 in the civil war in China (followed almost immediately by a Sino-Soviet defense pact), and the invasion of South Korea by the armed forces of Communist North Korea in June 1950.

A new Constitution, drafted by General MacArthur's headquarters and accepted by the Japanese Diet of 1946, had proclaimed that "land, sea, and air forces, as well as other war potential, will never be maintained. The right of belligerency of the state will not be recognized."[54] Within weeks following the outbreak of the Korean War, however, the United States promoted the organization of a "National Police Reserve" in Japan. The following year, a change of policy made it possible for officers who had served in the Japanese armed forces before and during World War II to join the organization. In September 1951, representatives of the United States and the Japanese government concluded a peace treaty, formally terminating the state of war between the two nation-states, in which Japan's "inherent right of individual or collective self-defense" was specifically recognized.[55]

The same day on which the peace treaty was signed, the United States concluded a security treaty with Japan, providing for the retention of U.S. troops in and around Japan, "in the expectation, however, that Japan will itself increasingly assume responsibility for its own defense. . . ."[56]

The theme that had come to dominate American economic as well as military and diplomatic planning was that of the threat of Soviet-sponsored aggression. As explained by George Kennan in an article on "The Sources of Soviet Conduct" published anonymously in the influential journal *Foreign Affairs* the same month that the Marshall Plan was announced, "the main element of any United States policy toward the Soviet Union must be that of a long-term, patient but firm and vigilant containment of Russian expansive tendencies."[57] By mid-1947, there were few prominent Americans who disagreed.

THE REVOLUTION OF RISING EXPECTATIONS

A final challenge was one the full nature and significance of which were only dimly foreseen by American policy makers in the 1940s. Outside of the industrialized countries, much of the world's population was experiencing a "revolution of rising expectations."

One important dimension of the revolution was represented by the demand of peoples under colonial rule for self-determination. Given voice in the aftermath of World War I, the demand was reaching a crescendo in the aftermath of World War II. Independence was near or at hand not only for peoples formerly subjugated by the now-defeated powers—Italy, Germany, and Japan—but also for those who had experienced colonialism at the hands of nations that ostensibly were victorious in World War II. The latter included the United States, which granted independence to the Philippines on July 4, 1946, but also the imperial powers of Europe such as the British, the French, and the Dutch. The ability of the European powers to maintain overseas colonies was taxed to the breaking point by the requirements of rebuilding their domestic economies, although in some instances, such as French Indochina and Algeria, the effort to maintain control would be made, with bloody results.

Nations that would be granted self-rule or that would obtain it by armed struggle typically faced monumental difficulties of governance, with only a fragmentary political infrastructure ready to cope with underdeveloped economies and skyrocketing aspirations from their people. Even in countries that had known formal independence from foreign rule for many decades, a growing mass awakening to social, political, and economic inequities provided the stimulus to political unrest in the post-World War II years. The unrest assumed distinctive forms in particular cultural settings, varying, for example, from the Arab world to Latin America to Asia. Regardless of the setting, however, the problem of comprehension for American policy makers was severe, involving not only coming to terms with foreign cultures, but also trying to grasp the meaning and probable consequences of changes occurring at a dizzying pace.

Compassion on the part of policy makers was not lacking. A program of technical assistance for the developing nations of Latin

America, Africa, and Asia was announced by President Truman in January 1949 and enacted into law in mid-1950. Known as Point Four (the fourth of four courses of action to which the President committed the nation in his 1949 inaugural address), the program authorized the dispatch overseas of American technicians to aid local peoples in improving food production, preventing disease, improving transportation, and providing vocational education. The motivation reflected a combination of humanitarian, ideological, and pragmatic impulses. In his memoirs, Truman explains

> Point Four was aimed at enabling millions of people in underdeveloped areas to raise themselves from the level of colonialism to self-support and ultimate prosperity. . . . [The program] was a practical expression of our attitude toward the countries threatened by Communist domination. It was consistent with our policies of preventing the expansion of Communism in the free world. . . . Thus the plan was realistic as well as idealistic. Common sense told me that the development of these countries would keep our own industrial plant in business for untold generations.[58]

However beneficial the Point Four assistance in humanitarian terms, neither this program nor other American programs initiated at the time brought American policies in tune with the chorus of social and political discontent that was shaping the destiny of the Third World. American policies toward developing nations and toward the people under colonial rule tended to be ad hoc rather than carefully planned and triggered by Cold War concerns rather than by a response to indigenous needs and demands.

The policies that were pursued by the United States in Korea following the surrender of Japan (which had exercised colonial rule in Korea) are illustrative. A wartime agreement had been hastily devised whereby Soviet troops were to move into Korea from the north and American troops from the south to receive the Japanese surrender, with the 38th parallel designated as a dividing line until a permanent settlement of the postwar status of Korea could be reached. Of the first contingent of Americans to arrive in Korea in August 1945, none spoke a word of Korean. Little was known of Korean customs and traditions. Some Koreans who had gained status in exile as champions of Korean independence from Japanese colonial rule were known to some Americans (for example, Syngman Rhee, who became the first president of the Republic of

Korea in 1948, had been a student of Woodrow Wilson). But the Truman administration had little in-depth knowledge of the Korean struggle for independence, nor of the factional allegiances and rivalries that would dominate Korean politics in the months and years that followed.[59]

Policies pursued by the United States for several months after the arrival of American forces consisted primarily of pursuing negotiations with the Soviets, which would prove to be futile, for the establishment of a trusteeship for all of Korea. Under such an agreement, one nation would agree to act as trustee on behalf of the United Nations, governing Korea until a UN determination was made that the Koreans were ready for self-rule. In the absence of a successful trusteeship agreement, the United States supported the creation of an anticommunist regime in the south as a counter to a Soviet-supported Communist regime in the north. Korea remained (and remains) divided into two countries—its northern half controlled by a communist regime, its southern half by an anticommunist regime, with neither acknowledging the legitimacy of the other. These circumstances led to war in 1950.

The trusteeship idea (too vaguely formulated to be described as a plan) had its origin in President Roosevelt's belief that the American tutelage of the Philippines over a period of decades, but with the promise of self-rule in 1946, provided a model that other colonial powers should emulate. The continuing expression by American officials in the months following the surrender of Germany and Japan of support for self-rule by peoples that had been under colonial domination for a long period antagonized European colonial powers such as France, Britain, and the Netherlands, which wished to proceed according to their own time schedule and in the light of their own imperial interests.

However, vaguely articulated expressions of the virtues of self-determination and of American sympathies for independence from colonialism proved to be a frail guide for foreign policy. The fact was that it was Europe, not Asia—nor other regions—that assumed top priority in American foreign policy formulations in the months after the end of World War II. Thus, African affairs were ignored almost totally. In the Middle East, the United States granted recognition to Israel almost immediately upon the announcement of its statehood in 1948, but paid little attention to other than commercial developments (oil) in the Arab states. Iran was a source of policy concern during the 1946 crisis when the Soviets failed to withdraw their forces from the Azerbaijan region, as they had pledged to do during the war. But once pressure had been applied sufficient to bring about the desired result, Soviet withdrawal, the American focus on the Persian Gulf region subsided—until revived again in the early 1950s, when American covert support for the Shah enabled him to survive a left-wing populist movement designed to free the country from British and other neocolonial pressures.

Even the countries of Latin America, in the "back yard" of the United States, were not so much ignored as they were taken for granted. The Rio Pact reaffirmed the semblance of solidarity under "Yankee" leadership that had prevailed during World War II (with the notable exception of the Argentine defection). Only when the growing tide of social discontent took on the coloration of Marxism, as in Guatemala in 1954, did the American government pay close heed. However, the resultant success in promoting, at a relatively low investment of American resources (through CIA activity), the ouster of a Marxist-oriented government in favor of a government sympathetic to United States interests meant that the low priority of Latin America in U.S. policy calculations was not really altered. The alteration would come only after the stoning of Vice President Nixon by left-wing protesters during a tour of Latin America in 1958, followed shortly thereafter by the revolution in Cuba that brought Fidel Castro to power.

SUMMARY AND CONCLUSIONS

The attention devoted on previous pages to problems neglected, misunderstood, or treated solely in Cold War terms should not obscure the remarkable transformation that occurred in American foreign policy in roughly a ten-year period, from the late 1930s to the late 1940s. To a degree unprecedented since the founding of the Republic, formidable foreign policy challenges were posed by the transition from war to peace from the mid-1940s into the 1950s. These included (1) redefining the relationship with wartime allies; (2) reconciling America's responsibilities and commitments in the postwar world with the dramatic increase in American global capabilities; (3) developing an effective structure for the maintenance of world peace; (4) bringing under control the awesome developments that had occurred in weapons of mass destruction; (5) rebuilding war-torn economies and restructuring the world's monetary and economic systems; (6) coping with the revolution of rising expectations among peoples of developing nations, many of whom were struggling to be free of colonial rule.

If the monumental difficulties associated with the various challenges inevitably brought frustration and setbacks, it was nevertheless an unusually exciting time to be a part of the policy process. A new era was dawning, and as a Secretary of State (Dean Acheson) from this period would put it, one had the feeling of being "present at the creation."[60] Or as expressed by an official who participated in deliberations that resulted in such important new policy departures as the Truman Doctrine and the Marshall Plan, the period was "one of those rare times in history when shackles fall away from the mind, the spirit, and the will, allowing them to soar free and high for a while and to discover new standards of what is responsible, of what is promising, and of what is possible."[61]

Although the participant's description provides a romanticized picture of policy making in the early postwar years, there can be little dispute (1) that the vast expansion of the scope of American involvement in global issues and the profound alteration of foreign policy orientation were extraordinary, and (2) that a broad consensus emerged in support of the unprecedented new role of American leadership in world affairs. By these measures, at least, American foreign policy in the postwar years was remarkably adaptive to the exigencies of the time.

However, as the more complete assessment of the postwar transition in American foreign policy as provided here reveals, although some unprecedented obstacles were overcome, other problems were merely deferred, ignored, or misinterpreted. Moreover, if the nation was united in a feeling of pride at the American contribution to the allied victory in war and generally convinced of the righteousness of the American mission in the postwar world, there remained an element of malaise.

For example, despite his support for the Truman policies, Republican foreign policy leader Arthur Vandenberg had been uneasy. He expressed his concern to his Senate colleagues in a speech in support of Truman's request for aid to Greece and Turkey (excerpts of which constitute the final quote at the outset of the present chapter). "In a sense we are a tragic generation," Vandenberg observed, "despite our blessings and our place in the sun."[62]

The sense of anguish which had become pervasive was given further expression by American poet Archibald MacLeish, who had been assistant secretary of state for public and cultural relations during the war. In an article in *The Atlantic Monthly* in August 1949, MacLeish expressed his fear that the United States had lost its way, "precisely at the moment when the United States, having engineered a tremendous triumph and fought its way to a brilliant victory in the greatest of all wars, had reached the highest point of world power ever achieved by a single state." What was tragically absent in these times, MacLeish contended, was a national assertion of moral purpose.

> We have not yet denied that purpose—the cock has not crowed for the second time—but we have failed to assert it. We have not yet changed the direction of our national life but we have lost our momentum, we have lost our initiative. We have not yet rejected our role as a revolutionary people moving with the great revolutionary current of history but we have ceased to move, we have begun to resist, to oppose. It does not require a prophet to see that we have come to a moment of critical decision—a decision which is none the less critical because it may be taken unaware.[63]

The founders of the American Republic, MacLeish observed, would be distressed at the abandonment of their commitment to moral purposes. "Only by moral action at the highest level," he asserted, "only by affirmative recommitment to the revolution of the individual which was the vital and creative impulse of our national life at the beginning of our history—only by these means can we regain ourselves."[64]

America had become the dominant world power, but with some deep uncertainties about how and for what ends power should be exercised.

NOTES

1. Senator William E. Borah, speech before the Council on Foreign Relations, New York, Jan. 8, 1934, quoted by Wendell L. Willkie, "Our Sovereignty: Shall We Use It?", *Foreign Affairs* 22 (April 1944): 348.
2. Borah quoted by Willkie, *Foreign Affairs* 22 (April 1944): 348.
3. Lisle A. Rose, *Dubious Victory: The United States and the End of World War II* (Kent, Ohio: Kent State University Press, 1973), pp. 43–44.
4. Willkie, *Foreign Affairs* 22 (April 1944): 361.
5. Walter Lippmann as quoted by Arthur H. Vandenberg, Jr., ed. with Joe Alex Morris, *The Private Papers of Senator Vandenberg*, (Boston: Houghton Mifflin, 1952) p. xxi.

6. Quite apart from ideological and cultural sources of mistrust, an important element in an explanation of the failure of the United States and the Soviet Union to remain partners after World War II is simply that the alliance now violated what Riker has described as the "size principle." This principle states that parties to a contest will "create coalitions just as large as they believe will ensure winning and no larger." William H. Riker, *The Theory of Political Coalitions*, paperback ed. (New Haven: Yale University Press, 1962) p. 47.

7. Vandenberg, *The Private Papers*, p. 35.

8. Franklin D. Roosevelt, State of the Union address to the Congress, Jan. 6, 1945, in *Vital Speeches of the Day* 11 (Jan. 15, 1945): 198–199.

9. Quoted in Robert E. Sherwood, *Roosevelt and Hopkins* (New York: Harper & Row, 1948), p. 870.

10. Joseph C. Grew, *Turbulent Era: A Diplomatic Record of Forty Years*, ed. Walter Johnson, 2 vols. (Boston: Houghton Mifflin, 1952), 2: 1446.

11. Clare Booth Luce, "America and World Communism," radio broadcast over Blue Network, May 29, 1945, in *Vital Speeches of the Day* 11 (Aug. 15, 1945): 647–649.

12. Luce, *Vital Speeches* 11 (Aug. 15, 1945): 647–649.

13. *Pravda*, Feb. 9 and 10, 1946, as cited in Marshall D. Shulman, *Stalin's Foreign Policy Reappraised*, paperback ed. (New York: Atheneum, 1965), pp. 14–26.

14. Long excerpts from the cable, including the passage quoted, are contained in George F. Kennan, *Memoirs 1925–1950* (Boston: Little, Brown, 1967), app. C, pp. 547–559.

15. Excerpts from the speech of March 5, 1946, are contained in William A. Williams, ed., *The Shaping of American Diplomacy* (Chicago: Rand McNally, 1956), pp. 992–994.

16. Churchill speech of March 5, 1946, as excerpted in Williams, *The Shaping of American Diplomacy*, pp. 992–994.

17. Background of events leading to the Truman Doctrine and the Marshall Plan and a detailed description of the process by which each decision was made are provided in highly readable form by Joseph Marion Jones, *The Fifteen Weeks*, paperback ed. (New York: Harcourt Brace, 1964). The full text of the President's speech to Congress of March 12, 1947, is contained as an appendix to Jones, pp. 269–274.

18. See Kennan, *Memoirs 1925–1950*. Walter Lippmann also criticized Truman's speech on similar grounds, in a newspaper column entitled, "Policy or Crusade". On roughly the twentieth anniversary of Truman's speech, President Johnson singled out Lippmann as opposing aid to Greece and Turkey in 1946. In reply, Lippmann had reprinted his 1947 criticism of the Truman Doctrine. In fact, Lippmann had supported aid to Greece and Turkey but had argued that "since the reasons are sufficient why Congress should vote the authority to intervene in the Middle East, it does not necessarily follow that it should endorse the idea that our intentions are henceforth to become general and global." *World Journal Tribune* (New York), April 6, 1967, p. 26.

19. T. D. Stamps, Vincent J. Esposito, and associates, *A Military History of World War II*, 2 vols. (West Point: U.S. Military Academy, 1953), 1: 276.

20. Winston S. Churchill, *The Second World War*, vol. 6, *Triumph and Tragedy*, (Boston: Houghton Mifflin, 1954), p. 573. In the same letter, using phraseology that became famous in a speech the following year in Fulton, Missouri, Churchill observed of the Soviets, "An iron curtain is drawn down upon their front."

21. Harry S. Truman, *Memoirs*, vol 2, *1945: Year of Decision* (New York: New American Library by arrangement with Doubleday, 1965), p. 558.

22. W. W. Rostow, *The United States in the World Arena* (New York: Harper & Row, 1960), p. 172 and notes, p. 265.

23. H. L. Stimson, *Diary*, May 15, 1945, cited in Gar Alperovitz, *Atomic Diplomacy: Hiroshima and Potsdam* (New York: Simon & Schuster, 1965), p. 57.

24. Stimson, *Diary*, May 14, 1945, cited in Alperovitz, *Atomic Diplomacy*, p. 61.

25. Figures are from Walter Johnson, *1600 Pennsylvania Avenue*, paperback ed. (Boston: Little, Brown, 1960), pp. 156–164, and notes, p. 342.
26. Data are from Alexander Werth, *Russia at War, 1941–1945* (New York: Avon, 1964), pp. 904–907.
27. I. Stewart, *Organizing Scientific Research for the War: The Administrative History of the Office of Scientific Research and Development* (Boston: Little, Brown, 1948), p. 332.
28. Both the Harriman and the Truman quotations are from Truman, *Memoirs*, 1:86.
29. Inis L. Claude, Jr., *Power and International Relations* (New York: Random House, 1962); also Claude, *Swords into Plowshares*, 4th ed. (New York: Random House, 1971).
30. Daniel Yergin, *Shattered Peace: The Origins of the Cold War and the National Security State* (Boston: Houghton Mifflin, 1977).
31. Yergin, *Shattered Peace*, p. 11.
32. For a thorough account of events and discussions leading to the creation of NATO, see Alan K. Henrikson, "The Creation of the North Atlantic Alliance, 1948–1952," *Naval War College Review* 32 (May–June 1980): 4–39, reprinted in *American Defense Policy*, 5th ed., eds. John F. Reichart and Steven R. Sturm (Baltimore, Md: Johns Hopkins University Press, 1982), pp. 296–320.
33. United Nations, Atomic Energy Commission, *Official Records* (New York: Hunter College, June 14, 1946), no. 1, pp. 4–5. Cited hereafter as UN, AEC *Records*.
34. UN, AEC *Records*, no. 1, p. 7.
35. UN, AEC *Records*, no. 1, p. 8.
36. UN, AEC *Records*, (June 19, 1946), no. 2, pp. 23–30.
37. Warner R. Schilling, "The H-Bomb Decision: How to Decide without Actually Choosing," *Political Science Quarterly*, 76 (March 1961): 24–46; reprinted in Davis B. Bobrow, ed., *Components of Defense Policy* (Chicago: Rand McNally, 1965), pp. 390–409.
38. A recent study of nuclear-arms diplomacy concurs that provisions of the Baruch Plan made it "difficult to imagine" that the Soviets would give their consent, "but there is no evidence that Truman expected the Plan to fail." Michael Mandelbaum, *The Nuclear Revolution: International Politics Before and After Hiroshima* (Cambridge: Cambridge University Press, 1981), p. 191. See also Mandelbaum, *The Nuclear Question: The United States and Nuclear Weapons 1946—1976* (Cambridge: Cambridge University Press, 1979).
39. Attitudes of the American scientific community toward the Baruch Plan are described by Robert Gilpin, *American Scientists and Nuclear Weapons Policy*, paperback ed. (Princeton: Princeton University Press, 1965), pp. 39–63.
40. Not only the Baruch Plan, but also subsequent United States–Soviet negotiations regarding arms control and disarmament illustrate Cold War tactics. Such an interpretation is provided by John W. Spanier and Joseph L. Nogee, *The Politics of Disarmament: A Study in Soviet-American Gamesmanship* (New York: Praeger, 1962).
41. Even within a single department it proved to be next to impossible to achieve full coherence in planning. Within the State Department, Secretary Cordell Hull established two committees that were to assume primary responsibility for economic planning for the postwar world. However, among the important issues that fell outside of the purview of these committees were international monetary arrangements, relief and rehabilitation, and the occupation of Germany. Dean Acheson, *Present at the Creation: My Years at the State Department* (New York: W. W. Norton, 1969), p. 64.
42. For example, the 1941 directive creating a cabinet-level Economic Defense Board (later, Board of Economic Warfare), with responsibilities for postwar as well as wartime planning, provided that there must be a "complete exchange of information, mutual consultation and mutual confidence" among all concerned departments and agencies. As noted wryly by Dean Acheson, then serving as Assistant Secretary of State for Economic Affairs, implementation of the directive suffered from the fact that "none [of these ingredients] existed or was likely to exist." Acheson, *Present at the Creation*, p. 42.

43. Problems of coordinating postwar policy plans for the critical issue-area of the occupation of Germany are treated in detail by Paul Y. Hammond, "Directives for the Occupation of Germany: The Washington Controversy," in *American Civil-Military Decisions*, ed. Harold Stein (Birmingham: University of Alabama Press for the Twentieth-Century Fund and Inter-University Case Program, 1963), pp. 311—460.

44. Truman, *Memoirs*, 1:525–526.

45. Acheson, *Present at the Creation*, p. 122.

46. See Michael Schaller, *The U.S. Crusade in China, 1938–1945* (New York: Columbia University Press, 1979), pp. 270–272.

47. Charles Robertson, *International Politics Since World War II*, 2d ed. (New York: John Wiley & Sons, 1975), pp. 39–40.

48. Acheson, *Present at the Creation*, p. 726.

49. See Joan Edelman Spero, *The Politics of International Economic Relations*, 2d ed. (New York: St. Martin's Press, 1981); see also David P. Calleo and Benjamin M. Rowland, *America and the World Political Economy* (Bloomington: Indiana University Press, 1973).

50. Kennan, *Memoirs 1925–1950* p. 330.

51. Kennan's recommendations drew upon staff studies prepared by the policy planning staff, others prepared for the State-War-Navy Coordinating Committee, and upon comments and speeches by Under Secretaries Will Clayton and Dean Acheson. See Kennan, *Memoirs 1925–1950*, chap. 14; see also Jones, *The Fifteen Weeks*.

52. See Jones, *The Fifteen Weeks*; see also Hadley Arkes, *Bureaucracy, the Marshall Plan, and the National Interest* (Princeton, NJ: Princeton University Press, 1972).

53. Laurence W. Martin, "The American Decision to Rearm Germany," in *American Civil-Military Decisions*, ed. Harold Stein (Birmingham: University of Alabama Press, 1963), pp. 645–660.

54. Constitution of Japan, Art. 9. Official English translation in U.S. Dept. of State Pub. 2836, Far Eastern Series, 22 (Washington: U.S. Government Printing Office, 1947).

55. U.S., Department of State, *Conference for the Conclusion of the Treaty of Peace with Japan: Record of Proceedings* (Washington: 1951, Dept. of State Pub. 4392, International and Conference Series, 2; Far Eastern Series, 3: 102–119.

56. U.S., Department of State, *U.S. Treaties and Other International Agreements* (Washington: 1952), TIAS 2491, TIAS 2492, vol. 3, Pt. 3, 3330–3419.

57. The background of the "X" article, as Kennan relates it, plus a fascinating critique by Kennan of his own piece in retrospect, is contained in his *Memoirs: 1925–1950*, pp. 354–367. The article has been reproduced in full in Kennan's *American Diplomacy: 1900–1950*, paperback ed. (New York: New American Library, Mentor 1952), pp. 89–106.

58. Truman, *Memoirs*, 1: 269.

59. See Bruce Cumings, *The Origins of the Korean War: Liberation and the Emergence of Separate Regimes 1945–1947* (Princeton, NJ: Princeton University Press, 1981); see also Gregory Henderson, *Korea: The Politics of the Vortex* (Cambridge, MA: Harvard University Press, 1968); Carl Berger, *The Korea Knot: A Military-Political History* (Philadelphia: University of Pennsylvania Press, 1967); E. Grant Meade, *American Military Government in Korea* (New York: Columbia University Press, 1951).

60. Acheson, *Present at the Creation*.

61. Jones, *The Fifteen Weeks*, p. 264.

62. Vandenberg, *Private Papers*, p. 348.

63. Archibald MacLeish, "The Conquest of America," *The Atlantic Monthly* 184 (August 1949): 17–22.

64. MacLeish, *The Atlantic Monthly* 184 (Aug. 1949): 22.

SUGGESTED ADDITIONAL READING

ACHESON, DEAN. *Present at the Creation: My Years at the State Department.* New York: Norton, 1969.

ARKES, HADLEY. *Bureaucracy, the Marshall Plan, and the National Interest.* Princeton, NJ: Princeton University Press, 1972.

BLOCK, FRED. *Origins of International Economic Disorder.* Berkeley, CA: University of California Press, 1977.

BLOOMFIELD, LINCOLN P. *The United Nations and U.S. Foreign Policy: A New Look at the National Interest.* Boston, MA: Little, Brown, 1960.

CAUTE, DAVID. *The Great Fear: The Anti-Communist Purge Under Truman and Eisenhower.* New York: Simon and Schuster, 1978.

DONOVAN, ROBERT J. *Conflict and Crisis: The Presidency of Harry S. Truman, 1945–1948.* New York: Norton, 1977.

EICHELBERGER, CLARK M. *Organizing for Peace: A Personal History of the Founding of the United Nations.* New York: Harper & Row, 1977.

JONES, JOSEPH MARION. *The Fifteen Weeks: An Inside Account of the Genesis of the Marshall Plan.* New York: Harcourt, Brace, and World, 1955, paperback ed. 1964.

LATHAM, EARL. *The Communist Controversy in Washington.* Cambridge, MA: Harvard University Press, 1966.

MANDELBAUM, MICHAEL. *The Nuclear Question: The United States and Nuclear Weapons 1946–1976.* New York: Cambridge University Press, 1979.

PATERSON, THOMAS G. *On Every Front: The Making of the Cold War.* New York: Norton, 1979.

PATTI, ARCHIMEDES L. A. *Why Viet Nam: Prelude to America's Albatross.* Berkeley, CA: University of California Press, 1980.

SPANIER, JOHN W. and NOGEE, JOSEPH L. *The Politics of Disarmament: A Study in Soviet-American Gamesmanship.* New York: Praeger, 1962.

SPERO, JOAN EDELMAN. *The Politics of International Economic Relations.* 2d ed. New York: St. Martin's, 1981.

YERGIN, DANIEL. *Shattered Peace: The Origins of the Cold War and the National Security State.* Boston: Houghton Mifflin, 1978.

PART THREE

The Foreign Policy Process in a New Era

CHAPTER 5

∽

The Modern Quest for Unifying Goals: The Politics of Consensus Building

"Our next frontier is to find peace within ourselves. Let us begin by restoring our self-confidence. In the past dozen years, we have lost one President through murder, another through Viet-Nam, and another through scandal. We have agonized through our longest and most inconclusive war. Our once-predominant strength has been challenged and our once-predominant dollar battered. We have endured riots, assassinations, racial and generational confrontations, a cultural revolution, and Watergate.

"Yet we have surmounted these traumas, showing a resiliency that inspires the envy of others."

> —Winston Lord, State Department official
> in the Ford Administration, November
> 1974

In Chapter 2, the imaginary world of the IIMMP was contrasted with the real world of foreign policy making. In the real world, the challenge of foreign policy leadership is less that of "discovering" what "the national interest" requires than it is of mobilizing a national consensus on behalf of goals and priorities that accommodate competing interests. The additional component of leadership that has been emphasized in Chapters 3 and 4 is that of keeping foreign policy goals and the basic underlying assumptions on which foreign policy rests in tune with changing world realities, with changing American capabilities, and with the changing needs of the nation. Only if this is done can the central imperative of foreign policy, namely, purposeful adaptation to the world environment, be accomplished. The process of foreign policy adaptation, with its imperfections as well as its successes, was illustrated by the formative experience of the late eighteenth and early nineteenth centuries, by the turbulent experience of the turn of the century, and by the major reappraisal of foreign policy during and after World War II.

The present chapter provides still another example of the adaptive challenge of altering policy goals and assumptions to fit changing world and domestic realities and needs, and the difficulties of mobilizing and sustaining a policy consensus in a time of flux. The fragility of the Cold War consensus of the late 1940s and 1950s is discussed briefly. A discussion of the dissolution of this consensus in the 1960s, under the strain of Vietnam, Watergate, and energy and monetary crises, is followed by an examination of the quest for a unifying sense of national purpose—a quest that became the preoccupation of administrations from Nixon to Reagan.

The chapter has the additional objective of clarifying the linkage between goal-setting and consensus building. In contrast to the neat and logical procedures depicted in the IIMMP, goal-setting in the real world emerges from the hurly-burly of politics. Foreign policy goals represent not only guideposts that orient the nation-state toward its world environment but also the outcomes of political competition. Examination of goal-setting as a political process reveals the interplay of political elites with one another and with the mass and attentive publics. It reveals also the influence of the mass media in defining the idiom of policy debate and in evaluating policy options.

The idiom of debate can be an important determinant of the kinds of policy alternatives that receive serious and sustained attention, and it can provide the basis for interpreting and evaluating particular alternatives. The struggle to control policy outcomes, therefore, becomes in part a struggle to control the idiom of debate. Moreover, for policy makers, the effort to mobilize consensus becomes in part a problem of articulating goals in terms that will elicit broad support.

The risk, to which democracies are especially vulnerable because those in power must always be conscious of the probability that their programs will be subjected to criticism and challenge, is that the rallying symbols selected by an administration will magnify threats to the point of public hysteria and will arouse undue expectations of quick solutions to the problems at hand. Such "oversell" of threat and remedy is illustrated by the promotion of the foreign policy of containment in the Truman and Eisenhower years.

THE SENSE OF MISSION: "AN AMERICAN CENTURY"

"The world of the 20th century," influential *Time/Life* publisher Henry Luce had observed on the eve of American entry into World War II, "must be to a significant degree an American Century."[1] The vast increase in American power and involvement in world affairs that came with World War II and its aftermath provided grounds for supposing that Luce's wishful proposition had been accurate. So also did the increase in opportunities for Americans at every social level. As Goldman has noted in describing this as the "crucial decade," by the end of the war,

> Jews seeking admission to professional schools had a ten-to-fifteen percent better chance than the applicant of 1929. First-generation Catholics of eastern or southern European backgrounds reported far less difficulty in purchasing homes in upper-middle-class neighborhoods. . . . Negro representatives on labor grievance committees were becoming accustomed to speaking up as freely as their white colleagues. . . . Hundreds of thousands [of veterans] who had thought of the university as a preserve of the rich found themselves headed for an A.B.—in many cases, toward the highest of professional degrees.[2]

However, Goldman also notes that the national mood quickly shifted from exhilaration at victory and at the new opportunities to frustration at the mounting problems at home (e.g., inflation, unemployment, strikes) and at the seeming intractibility of problems abroad. In their growing anxiety and irascibility, policy makers reflected the changing public mood.

President Truman was plagued with disaffection both from Henry

Wallace supporters and from the Dixiecrat wing of his own party and by sharp criticism from the Robert Taft wing of the Republican party. Beginning with special intensity after the so-called "fall" of China to the Communists late in 1949, blistering attacks against the Truman administration were made by Senator Joseph McCarthy and his allies, accusing the administration of being "soft" on Communism.[3] After an initial upsurge in popularity at the outset of the commitment of American troops to Korea in 1950, Truman's personal standing among the public plummeted, especially in 1951 with his dismissal from command of the legendary General Douglas MacArthur. Nevertheless, as Truman himself modified Asian policies to accommodate hardline critics, a consensus in support of the Truman containment policies was sustained.[4]

Because of Republican control of the Congress after the 1946 elections, Truman had to work vigorously to forge a bipartisan coalition in support of his foreign policies. In this effort, Republican Senator Arthur Vandenberg was a key figure. It was Vandenberg who, when in 1947 Truman sought the support of congressional leaders for a program of aid to combat Communist pressures on Greece and Turkey, had urged the President to "make a personal appearance before Congress and scare hell out of the country."[5]

The Truman Doctrine and related declaratory policies were consistent with Vandenberg's advice and generally produced the support which Truman sought. As Samuel Huntington has demonstrated in an analysis of polling data from 1945–1960, "where the Administration did not take a strong stand, public opinion was, at the least, passive and permissive, and at the most, very favorably disposed toward stronger defenses." When the President spoke out strongly of the vital interests at stake requiring support of programs such as the Truman Doctrine or the commitment to NATO (but as noted above, not in regard to a prolonged war in Korea), the public displayed a readiness to follow the President's lead.[6]

A consensus was obtained, but the process of forging it was costly, involving the technique that Theodore Lowi has aptly described as "oversell"—an overselling of problems to be resolved, of threats to national interests, and of remedies to deal with problems and threats. Thus, the struggle with international Communism became a crusade, arousing popular expectations of a decisive triumph of good over evil. As Lowi notes, inflated rhetoric tends to produce a vicious cycle. Foreign policies that, given the complexities of international politics, must be regarded as experiments, "may be partially successful, but after oversell partial success must be accepted as failure. Failure leads to distrust and frustration, which lead to more oversell and to further verbal excesses, as superlatives become ordinary through use."[7]

Americans in the 1950s rallied to the Cold War leadership of World War II military commander, President Dwight D. Eisenhower. However, the practice of eliciting consensus through oversell continued, especially in the moralistic rhetoric of Secretary of State John Foster Dulles.[8] By the end of Eisenhower's second term of office, an increasing number of critics were complaining that the policies of the administration meant stagnation and that the reliance on the threat of "massive retaliation" to a Soviet provocation or attack merely increased the risks of war without credibly ensuring that Soviet expansion, through surrogates fomenting insurgencies in developing nations, would be halted.

Thus, the election of the youthful John F. Kennedy (the first American president born in the twentieth century) revived the traditional American sense of mission, but with a renewed fervor. "The torch has been passed to a new generation of Americans," Kennedy announced in his inaugural speech, "Let every nation know, whether it wishes us well or ill, that we shall pay any price, bear any burden, meet any hardship, support any friend, oppose any foe to assure the survival and the success of liberty." To his fellow citizens, Kennedy appealed for the commitment of loyalty, energy, and talents: "Ask not what your country can do for you—ask what you can do for your country."[9]

Thousands of Americans responded to the challenge—as Peace Corps volunteers, as recruits to the military Special Forces whose role in counterinsurgency attained new importance under Kennedy, as volunteers to rebuild urban areas and work for civil rights. However, the American "Camelot era" was brief and ended tragically. President John F. Kennedy was killed by an assassin's bullet in Dallas in November 1963. Less than five years later, assassinations had felled still other prominent Americans, including civil rights leader Martin Luther King, Jr., and John Kennedy's brother, Robert, the latter killed as he campaigned for the nomination to the Presidency.

These were years "When Dreams and Heroes Died," in the words of the author of a portrait of the American college student of the

1970s.[10] Yet as Garry Wills has noted, youthful rejection of the crusading sense of American mission that had symbolized the Kennedy era is explicable not merely in terms of despair at the death of charismatic leaders. Rather such rejection was fed by disillusionment that a system in which young Americans had wanted to believe had failed them. As Wills observed:

> Kennedy, leading a rebellion against the quiet years, liberalized young people, sent them out on beneficent missions—Peace Corps kids in Africa, "advisers" in Vietnam, Green Beret counterinsurgents in training camps, and Cubans democratically reclaiming their own land. But he also radicalized the kids who saw this new activism as imperialist, however kind its intent. Under Eisenhower, one could still claim that a person (Dulles, say) or an aberrant policy (massive retaliation) was at fault. These were lapses within the System, a System which could be tinkered with. But under Kennedy, if things went wrong, it was not because the wrong party or the wrong man was in charge of the System; the fault must be in the System itself.[11]

In particular, Kennedy had been responsible for thrusting the United States into a role of support for the authoritarian but anticommunist regime of South Vietnam. Critics could plausibly charge that this was little more than a continuation of the colonial role which the French had vacated after the Geneva accords of 1954. President Eisenhower had initiated the direct assistance to the Saigon regime; but the number of American military advisors in Vietnam was increased from several hundred to nearly 20,000 during the Kennedy years.

After Kennedy's death his successor, Lyndon Johnson, had escalated the commitment still further to full American combat units, with corresponding increases in the military conscription of young American men—and before long, dramatic increases in American casualties. By 1968, the United States had half a million military personnel in Vietnam, and had suffered nearly 30,000 battle deaths. The public support that Kennedy and Johnson initially had enjoyed for the Vietnam venture had been largely dissipated by 1968. Instead, the society was becoming bitterly divided over the war.

Although it was especially the young who took to the streets to protest, older Americans too, even if not radicalized, came increasingly to wonder if the institutions and policies that they associated with American democracy continued to merit their support. Political leaders had been assassinated. The government seemed as inclined to the use of violence to maintain order (as in Chicago during the Democratic national convention of 1968) as were extremists among antiwar protesters. And the world that had seemed so malleable at the hands of American policy makers only a few years before seemed to have become chaotic.

For example, the international monetary system that had been created at Bretton Woods was in a shambles by the late 1960s, and in 1971 President Nixon felt compelled to bring an end to the fixed relationship of the dollar to gold ($35 an ounce) and devaluate the dollar. A quadrupling of the price of oil in 1973–1974 was triggered by demands from the Organization of Petroleum Exporting Countries (OPEC). (Within ten years, the price would rise to ten times the pre-1973 price.) Once self-sufficient in oil, the United States found itself increasingly dependent upon foreign sources, especially those in the Middle East.

Bitterly accentuating the sense of dependency was the boycott that the Arab members of OPEC placed on shipments of oil to the United States in retaliation for American support of Israel in war with neighboring Arab states in 1973. Further contributing to the seige mentality of the administration during the 1973 Middle East crisis was the resignation from office of Nixon's vice president, Spiro Agnew, in disgrace because of financial irregularities and income tax evasion. And in 1974, Nixon himself resigned rather than face almost certain impeachment during congressional investigation of White House involvement in planning a burglary at Democratic Party headquarters in the Watergate apartment complex in Washington.

Public disenchantment was pervasive, as Yale University President, Kingman Brewster, Jr., wrote in the influential journal, *Foreign Affairs*, in 1972:

> It would be wrong to say that Americans do not believe in their country. Fundamentally they do. But for the very reasons that their expectations are so high, their distress is very deep. They want terribly to believe in the rightness of America. Yet, even those who are not overcome with a sense of wrongness yearn for the energetic, optimistic self-confidence which made all things seem possible until a few years ago.[12]

THE END OF PAX AMERICANA: RESTORING LOST CONFIDENCE

No longer was there talk of Pax Americana and "The American Century." Instead, pundits spoke of "the end of American exceptionalism" and "the decline of the West." Not merely the sense of mission but also the sense of common purpose were gone. In the late 1960s and early 1970s, it appeared to more pessimistic observers that the American society, torn apart by protest and bitter differences, might have lost not only its global dominance but also its internal cohesion. Presidents Nixon, Ford, Carter, and Reagan, in turn, would be confronted in varying degrees with the lost sense of national purpose, and with the task of reviving American confidence, and in so doing rebuilding a foreign policy consensus.

From the early months of his administration, President Nixon and other top officials warned that adverse reaction to the involvement in Vietnam was generating a new mood of isolationism in the country. However, although the public were calling for withdrawal of American forces from Vietnam, and then insisted that there must be "no more Vietnams," little evidence of isolationist sentiment along the lines of American views of the 1920s and 1930s was evident. Rather, what increasing numbers of Americans were calling for simply was a redefinition of American goals and interests in the light of current global realities and American capabilities. As the editors of one prominent opinion journal put it:

> The chances of an American "withdrawal from the world and international responsibilities" [as President Nixon warned] are infinitesimal. The question is just what are our "responsibilities" and what are our "irresponsibilities." And how, in fact, is the U.S. to be *responsible* in modestly defining our national interest and recognizing the limits of prerogatives and capacities?[13]

Moreover, the recognizable consensus in support of the proposition that there must be "no more Vietnams" obscured important disagreements regarding the nature of the "failure" that was not to be repeated and regarding the desired steps to be taken in order to avoid "another Vietnam." Had Vietnam been a failure of American strategy and technique? A failure of perseverance? A failure to weigh the probable costs and benefits of intervention? A failure to understand the nature of revolutionary change? There were prominent advocates on behalf of each of the various interpretations, as there were on behalf of each of a variety of mutually incompatible alternative courses of action that "must" be taken if future "Vietnams" were to be avoided.[14]

Beyond the diversity of views regarding the Vietnam experience itself, important differences emerged regarding America's interests and purposes in a world that had changed profoundly in the years since World War II. The challenge was to define new goals and articulate them in ways that could command broad popular support. As Secretary of State Henry Kissinger put it in a speech in Washington in 1973:

> We find that our most difficult task is how to apply limited means
> to the accomplishment of carefully defined goals. We can no longer
> overwhelm our problems; we must master them with imagination,
> understanding, and patience.
> —For a generation our preoccupation was to prevent the cold
> war from degenerating into a hot war. Today, when the danger of
> global conflict has diminished, we face the more profound problem
> of defining what we mean by peace and determining the ultimate
> purpose of improved international relations. . . .
> Questions once obscured by more insistent needs now demand
> our attention: What is true national interest? To what end stability?
> What is the relationship of peace to justice?[15]

Ironically, even as it perpetuated the war in Vietnam, the Nixon administration in fact was charting a new foreign policy course designed to prevent "another Vietnam" (as in the Nixon Doctrine, which shifted the burden of counterinsurgency from American soldiers to those in the societies experiencing insurgency). More broadly, new policies such as the diplomatic overtures to the People's Republic of China and the policy of detente with the Soviet Union were efforts to cope with a changing world reality.

In the aftermath of Vietnam and then Watergate and in the midst of a monetary crisis and an energy crisis, however, a policy consensus was unattainable. Rather, critics on the left of the political spectrum pushed for cuts in military spending, a sharp curtailment if not total end to CIA covert activity, and a redirection of federal attention to domestic needs. Critics on the right, on the other hand, charged that the policy of detente was a new form of appeasement of Communist dictatorships and that the Nixon—and then Ford—administrations were displaying a failure of nerve.[16]

The verbal attacks led Kissinger to complain

> Our greatest foreign policy problem is our divisions at home. Our greatest foreign policy need is national cohesion and a return to the awareness that in foreign policy we are all engaged in a common national endeavor. . . . [Yet] one group of critics undermines arms control negotiations and cuts off the prospect of more constructive ties with the Soviet Union while another group cuts away at our defense budgets and intelligence services and thwarts American resistance to Soviet adventurism. Both combined will—whether they have intended it or not—end by wrecking the nation's ability to conduct a strong, creative, moderate, and prudent foreign policy. The result will be paralysis, no matter who wins in November.[17]

Such divisive criticisms continued into the Carter administration. The allegation that the nation had "lost its will" was given further credence in a commencement speech at Harvard in June 1978 by Soviet exile Alexsandr Solzhenitzyn. The Nobel-prize winning author contended that "The Western world has lost its courage."[18] Jimmy Carter had inherited the problem, as Ronald Reagan would after him, of establishing a policy consensus in a society still reeling from the effects of the policy setback of the late 60s and early 70s.

The success of Carter and Reagan in turn as political campaigners was attributable in no small part to the ability of Carter in 1976 and of Reagan in 1980 to tap the yearning of the American public for a leader who could inspire confidence in a climate of anxiety. As Carter explained in 1976, "At one level . . . there is the traditional debate over such issues as defense, health care, tax policy, and the economy. But . . . the other level of this year's campaign, the less tangible issue, is simply the desire of the American people to have faith again in government, to want a fresh start."[19]

The magnetism of Jimmy Carter as a presidential candidate, as noted by one of his most perceptive biographers,

> was based on the appeals he made at this other level. Where he differed from most other candidates was in his recognition of these

deeper longings of the voters, and his ability and willingness to make bold, breathtaking, and original claims that he was the one who could satisfy those longings.[20]

The oratory, style, and political organization that generate success in a presidential election, however, are no guarantee of success in developing and maintaining support for the policies and programs of governance. Ironically, it was Carter's failure in inspiring confidence as president that provided the basis for Ronald Reagan's success as a presidential aspirant. As Elizabeth Drew recorded in her journal on the eve of the 1980 election, Carter had been "trying to ride the crocodile" at least since the seizure of American hostages in Iran a year earlier. To many Americans, the hostage crisis had become "a symbol of what they saw as a decline in our power," Drew observed.

> And it has added to an impression of Carter as hapless. This had to do very much with his style: the term that came to be used about him in private conversations was that he was a "wimp," and he began to be portrayed in cartoons as peanut-sized and looking bewildered. When he tried to explain the point of being patient, the futility of force, he could not do it forcefully. When he used force, he botched it, and was never able to explain to critics on any side why the plan made sense. Carter is an articulate man, yet he has not been successful at explaining himself.[21]

Ronald Reagan, in contrast, "presented himself as the candidate bringing hope, faith, freedom, and prosperity to an electorate sorely in need of good news. As opposed to President Jimmy Carter, who spoke so mournfully [in a widely publicized address in 1979] about the passing of the American dream, Mr. Reagan held out the promise of a bright future."[22]

It was especially through television appearances that Reagan proved himself master of the medium and capitalized on popular yearnings for leadership in a time of tribulation. A half-hour advertisement run on TV on the eve of the election exemplified the appeal. Reagan, seated in an easy chair, asked his audience, "What kind of country, what kind of legacy, will we leave to [the] young men and women who will live out America's third century?" Noting that many Americans were "wondering, searching—feeling frustrated and perhaps even a little afraid," Reagan offered reassurance,

"I believe we can embark on a new age of reform in this country and an era of national renewal." He reported that his friend John Wayne had commented shortly before his death, "Just give the American people a good cause, and there's nothing they can't lick." "Duke Wayne did not believe that our country was ready for the dustbin of history," Reagan remarked, then added, "We do not shirk history's call."[23]

Although differing considerably from one another in style and also in skill in using the mass media, Carter and Reagan each made the presidental office a "bully pulpit," as Teddy Roosevelt had described it. Efforts were made to restore American pride and sense of purpose and thereby to rally support for the administration's policies. The human rights theme, which became a centerpiece for the Carter foreign policy, is an example. Early in his presidency, the President appointed Patricia Derian to the newly created post of Assistant Secretary of State for Human Rights and Humanitarian Affairs. Ambassadors throughout the world were required to submit regular reports on human rights conditions in the countries in which they served, and the State Department itself began preparing extensive annual reports on human rights conditions worldwide. The Congress could consult these reports before making decisions on foreign assistance and other programs. President Carter lost few opportunities to call to the attention of the American people the priority that he was placing upon human rights. As he said in a major foreign policy address at the University of Notre Dame in May of his first year in office, "It is a new world that calls for a new American foreign policy—a policy based on constant decency in its values and on optimism in our historical vision."[24]

This is not the place for a detailed evaluation of the results abroad of the Carter human rights policies; even sympathetic observers have tended to conclude that the record was mixed. Carter's emphasis on human rights must be understood not simply in terms of the aspirations for reform abroad, but also in terms of the President's desire to rekindle idealism and a sense of purpose in the American people.

Similarly, the strident Cold War rhetoric that characterized the Reagan administration, especially during the President's first months in office, must be assessed not simply in terms of the impact that a "get tough" approach had on U.S.-Soviet relations. Rather, more broadly the rhetoric must be assessed in terms of what Reagan's first secretary of state, Alexander Haig, called "the crucial psychological element in any foreign policy . . . [displaying] confidence in ourselves . . . . [and thus restoring] confidence in American leadership abroad."[25]

President Reagan, like his predecessor, found that themes that had elicited broad support on the campaign trail were no guarantee of broad support for presidential programs. However, the point at hand is that every president has found it essential to attempt to rally support through appeals to popular symbols.

THE IDIOM OF POLICY DEBATE

LEVELS OF ABSTRACTION

The preceding discussion is designed to help clarify the function that is served by the articulation of goals in broad, relatively abstract terms. The popular appeal of a commitment to "fighting Communism," "championing human rights," "promoting individual liberty," or "defending the Free World" may provide the rallying cry for building a national consensus. Conversely, the breakdown of consensus is likely to promote the search for new or alternative symbols.

It is important to note, however, that the debate of policy issues typically occurs at various levels of abstraction in various policy arenas (Table 5-1). An abstract formulation of goals might serve to mobilize a popular consensus; but as participants in the policy process debate the solutions to particular problems, the discussion typically moves to a lower level of abstraction.

A goal is described as "a lasting peace settlement among Israel and its Arab neighbors in the Middle East," for instance, or "improved relations with Latin America." The general priorities that are established among policy goals, i.e., identifying some interests as "vital" and others as "secondary" or "minor," also tend to be made at a mid-level of abstraction. For example, policy makers might assert that "continued American access to oil in the Persian Gulf is a vital policy goal." Broad assumptions tend to be made regarding issue salience, threats to interests, and patterns of opportunity; the assumptions help one to identify policy priorities. Thus, the assumption may be that "the Soviets are launched on a campaign

TABLE 5-1 Levels of Abstraction in the Foreign Policy Idiom

LEVEL OF ABSTRACTION	NATURE OF CHARACTERISTIC IDIOM	EXAMPLES
High	Images of the national identity	America as a beacon to the Free World
	Images of the national purpose	Manifest Destiny
Medium	National interests, goals, and priorities	Peace in the Middle East Improved relations with Latin America Access to Gulf oil is vital
	Broad policy assumptions	Soviets seek strategic superiority Falklands/Malvinas issue damaged US-Latin American relations
Low	Operational assumptions	Risk of hostilities in Lebanon is low Diplomatic benefits outweigh costs in support of Latin American position in UN
	Instrumental goals and strategies	Marines as peacekeeping force while pressing for broad Middle East peace Support UN vote reopening negotiations on Falklands/Malvinas

to achieve strategic superiority," or that "U.S. support of the British in the Falklands/Malvinas dispute was injurious to U.S.-Latin American relations."

Examination of alternative courses of action, however, requires that assessments be made of the detailed nature of particular problems and situations, of the implications of these problems for specific American interests, and of the capabilities of the United States to deal with the problems, given situational exigencies. Thus, for example, the dispatch of U.S. Marines to Lebanon may be predicated on the operational assumption that the risk that the Marines will become involved in hostilities is low (so the President assured the Congress in 1982 in an effort to defuse concern about the applicability of the War Powers Resolution, although in 1983 he tacitly acknowledged the applicability of the resolution in seeking an eighteen-month guarantee of congressional support for a Marine role in Lebanon.) Or the administration might decide (as it did in early November 1982) that the costs in injury to relations with the British by supporting a UN resolution to reopen negotiations on the status of the Falklands/Malvinas will be outweighed by benefits derived from demonstrating to Latin American governments the U.S. effort to be sympathetic to their views.

This is not to say that broad, generalized statements of foreign policy goals and purposes are irrelevant to policy outcomes. On the contrary, the paradox is that although the appraisal of complex foreign policy issues demands the application of highly specific facts and analysis, to the extent that the issues become the object of widespread debate, the policy options are likely to be defined at a relatively high level of abstraction and choices made accordingly. The remainder of the chapter is devoted primarily to explaining this paradox and tracing its implications, with examples drawn from recent foreign policy experience. The explanation requires an examination of the role of public opinion in foreign policy, key characteristics of the public debate of policy issues, and the influence of policy elites.

The paradox is one that many observers of foreign policy prefer to deny or, if acknowledged, to regard as a source of intolerable frustration. For example, in an editorial urging readers to vote "no" on nuclear freeze referenda in 1982, the New York Times complained that the freeze proposal "remains a simplistic, sloganeering response to a complex issue."[26] Leaving aside the merits or demerits of the case for a nuclear freeze, there can be no doubt that the Times was right; the freeze referenda focused on a simple idea, cast primarily in the form of a slogan. What the Times editorial failed to note, however, is that opponents as well as advocates of a nuclear freeze are engaged in sloganeering, recognizing that the symbolic terms in which the issue comes to be defined may well determine the policy outcome.

A political action committee seeking to enlist support for the freeze, thus calls itself the "U.S. Committee Against Nuclear War," implicitly conveying the message that any responsible person who opposes nuclear war ought to support a nuclear freeze. Reply in kind has come from groups such as the American Security Council. In letters to prospective supporters, the ASC has warned that "nuclear freezniks" favor policies that would lead only to a "phased surrender" of the Free World to Communism; the only realistic alternative is said to be American "Peace Through Strength."

Contending arguments on the nuclear freeze issue are not devoid of factual considerations—the numbers of warheads possessed by the two superpowers, for instance, or the quantitative and qualitative improvements that have been made in nuclear technology by both sides in the past fifteen years. However, the policy battle will not be fought or won primarily as an exercise in mobilizing statistics or of meticulously detailed analyses of policy alternatives. To paraphrase Holmes, the life of policy making is not logic, it is politics. To expect issues to be resolved on the basis of the logic and evidence associated with respective policy positions is to neglect vital considerations of power. Moreover, the student of the policy process who focuses too closely on the concrete facts and particular inferences that are associated with various policy alternatives may fail to recognize the political functions that are being served by ambiguity and abstraction in political debate.[27] It also is to assume a capacity for clarity of communication among parties to political debates and an agreement on what really is at issue that often has been notable by its absence.

Public participation in the foreign policy process is examined in the following section of the chapter, with emphasis on the nature of public debate and the clustering of opinion that is characteristic. In the subsequent section, the focus is on the role of political elites in influencing policy outcomes, with a critical review of theories of elite dominance.

THE PUBLIC, FOREIGN POLICY, AND SYMBOLIC SECURITY

American policy makers invariably express a concern for formulating policies that are responsive to public wishes and needs. Whether the shaping of American foreign policy actually is influenced by public opinion, and the extent to which policy should be influenced by public opinion, however, are other questions. Some observers, such as the celebrated journalist Walter Lippmann, who had the ear of Presidents from the time of Woodrow Wilson all the way into the Vietnam years, argued emphatically that the public exerted too much influence on foreign policy. The public tend to be uninformed, Lippmann correctly noted, and also fickle; thus, according to Lippmann, their influence on policy tends to be pernicious.[28]

Others, however, have argued that the real failing of the American system has been that the public has been ignored. If policy makers had been more sensitive to popular needs and desires, so some critics maintain, policy failures such as the major escalation of the war in Vietnam might have been averted.

An answer to the question of the desirability of shaping foreign policy in response to public opinion must hinge not only upon one's normative preferences but also upon available evidence of the actual influence of public opinion on the policy process.

PUBLIC AND ELITE INFLUENCE   A useful distinction, introduced years ago by Gabriel Almond, is one between the public as a whole—the "mass public"—and that relatively small percentage, probably less than 10% of the total, who follow foreign policy matters with some regularity. The "mass public" will exert influence upon foreign policy only to the extent that policy makers carry with them images (accurate or inaccurate) of what "the public wants"—images that Douglass Cater has usefully described as the "synthetic public." The "attentive public", in contrast, because they follow foreign policy issues and debates at least part of the time, are the ones who are in a position to express their views directly to policy makers through letters, phone calls, and directly or indirectly through participation in interest groups and public policy organizations.[29]

Almond also identified the existence of opinion elites whose role in the system is important because they help to mold the opinions of others. An obvious example is the members of the mass media—TV commentators, editorial writers, and others—who have a regular audience for their views. Less obvious but also important are men and women in other positions of leadership in local communities and in organizations who command both regular audiences and respect and thus are able to influence opinion.

The mass media have come to play an enormously important role in modern politics. Television, in particular, has radically altered the life-style of the average American family (for better or worse). Within a decade, from 1950 to 1960, the percentage of

135

American families owning television sets increased from 11 to 88. By the 1980s, it was an exceptional family that owned less than one set. Moreover, since the early 1960s, television has been the principal medium that Americans depend on for information about and interpretation of political events (supplanting the newspaper).[30]

The access to every home that television represents has revolutionized the techniques which politicians utilized to market their wares, and has put a premium on the skills of professional image-makers. Nevertheless, it would be an exaggeration of public gullibility to suppose that television now enables politicians to effect unlimited manipulation of public attitudes and opinions on policy issues. The process by which opinions are formed often is complex. Even a national leader with the experience and skill in utilization of the mass media as President Ronald Reagan has found that televised messages to the public are no guarantee of public approval of the President's stated proposals and ideas. TV commentators and spokespersons for opposing policy positions also reach the public through this medium. Moreover, before the public have formed firm opinions on issues that the President has raised, they are likely to have heard many other persons in their community or workplace express their views.

One ought to be cautious about assuming that the process of foreign policy opinion formation reflects a hierarchy of wisdom and influence, with the intelligent and well-informed people at the top, and information and opinions filtering down to the "rednecks" and the "know-nothings" among the mass public. For example, consider the phenomenon of permissiveness toward presidential leadership that some opinion analysts have termed the "father knows best" or "president knows best" syndrome.

THE "PRESIDENT KNOWS BEST" SYNDROME   "Father knows best" refers to a tendency to grant the President the benefit of the doubt when he takes new policy initiatives and to assume that he is doing the right thing for the country. At the outset of almost every foreign policy crisis the President is virtually assured of a large majority of popular support providing only that he does something and preferably something that appears decisive in response to the crisis.[31]

Thus, President Harry Truman's commitment of American troops to Korea when war broke out in June 1950 was supported by a majority of the American public. So also was Lyndon Johnson's commitment of combat units (as distinguished from mere military advisors) to Vietnam as the political situation there deteriorated in 1965. The American commitments to Korea and to Vietnam ultimately became unpopular. However, perhaps more surprising than the decline in support over time was the distribution of support among various sectors of the public, as John Mueller's careful study reveals. The "follower mentality," that is, the readiness to fall in line behind the President's policies in Korea and in Vietnam, tended to be more characteristic of relatively well-educated Americans than it was of the less well-educated. Moreover, contrary to the romantic mythology that suggests that the young are invariably rebels, young Americans were more likely to support the involvement in war than were the old, even when the data were controlled for education. Incidentally, consistent with other opinion polls over a number of years, Mueller found that men tended to be somewhat more ready to support the use of force in foreign policy than were women.[32]

The Mueller data are interesting because they also help to explain a plausible but perplexing interpretation of the pattern of American involvement in Vietnam, known as the "stalemate machine" thesis. Explaining the pattern of American involvement as a "stalemate machine" is but one of many interpretations. Nine alternative theories are described by Leslie Gelb, for example, only to be rejected in favor of a variation on the "stalemate" theme. Gelb argues paradoxically that the American political system "worked" in the sense that "while each President was [an architect of the policy consensus], he also was a part and a prisoner of the larger political system that fed on itself, trapping all its participants in a war they could not afford to lose and were unable to win quickly."[33]

Contrary to those who have asserted that presidents stumbled blindly into a "quagmire," Gelb and other analysts, such as Daniel Ellsberg and Paul Kattenburg, have argued that presidents escalated the American involvement in Vietnam despite their realization that the prospects for success were bleak. At least until 1968, the President was subjected to political cross-pressures: on the one hand not to lose Vietnam to Communism and on the other hand not to become drawn into an unlimited commitment of force that could lead to World War III. The result was a policy that perpetuated stalemate. As Kattenburg has summarized the thesis, "The objectives of the United States in Indochina were neither to win at a cost which presidents knew would be exorbitant, nor to lose in the sense of a negotiated settlement incorporating the Communists in the government of South Vietnam."[34]

The "stalemate machine," as Mueller's data reveal, was fueled by a symbiotic relationship between the President and those who until 1968 followed his lead. The pre-1968 followers were drawn disproportionately from the ranks of the well educated, also were more likely to be politically active, and thus in turn to be the ones whose views the President respected. The better educated were prepared to become involved, if the President said it was desirable; but they were generally opposed to the extremely hawkish positions of all-out war. By 1968, a larger percentage of better-educated than of less-educated Americans had become disillusioned by the war experience to the point of opposing continuing American involvement. Until then, however, they provided support for the halfway escalatory measures that had been followed.

"PRESIDENT KNOWS BEST" AND GRENADA   The more recent experience of Grenada reveals that the "president knows best" tendency can lead the public to ignore or minimize evidence that might call policy commitments into serious question. The American invasion of Grenada in October 1983 shocked and angered various governments, including many of America's closest allies as well as America's adversaries and neutrals. Prime Minister Margaret Thatcher of Great Britain was openly critical of the invasion of the former British colony, for instance, and opposition to the installation in Great Britain of American intermediate-range nuclear missiles increased because many of the British populace interpreted the Grenadan invasion as evidence that the American government could not be trusted to exercise restraint in the use of nuclear weapons in the event of a confrontation with the Soviet Union. The Grenadan invasion left the Reagan administration susceptible also to the charge that the United States contemptuously was resorting to military force in blatant disregard of provisions both of the United Nations Charter and of the Charter of the Organization of American States, both of which prohibit intervention in the internal affairs of sovereign states. The claim that the intervention was justified in order to rescue American medical students in Grenada, critics complained, was unfounded.

Evidently more persuasive to the majority of the American public, however, was the rationale for action provided by President Reagan in a televised address to the nation. Grenada, the President explained, had been in a state of virtual anarchy in the two weeks following a bloody coup d'etat on October 12. The lives of some 1,000 Americans on Grenada, 800 of them students at St. George's University Medical School, were endangered. Moreover, the President contended, Grenada was "a Soviet-Cuban colony being readied as a major military bastion to export terror and undermine democracy." Thus, when six members of the Organization of Eastern Caribbean States requested American military action, the President agreed to "a military operation to restore order and democracy to Grenada."[35]

The President disarmed potential critics of his action with assertions such as "we're all Americans before we are anything else, and when our country is threatened, we stand shoulder to shoulder in support of men and women in the armed forces." The events in Grenada and the emotional presidential appeal came at a time when the American public was still shocked and grieving at the death of more than 200 American Marines in a terrorist attack in Beirut. In an atmosphere of crisis, the President conveyed an image of a leader who was ready to act decisively; his ratings in the polls rose accordingly.

One may argue that the "father knows best" syndrome may be essential to the well-being of the nation in providing the cohesion it needs to survive crises. However, obviously the syndrome has its hazards. "Father" may be wrong, or he may be pursuing policies that are in his interests but not those of large numbers of his people. The best interests of the country might then be served by a popular receptivity to early criticism of his policies, generating pressures that might bring about a policy change, if that is in order.

To the extent that the public looks to multiple sources of leadership rather than to the President alone, a climate is provided for the debate of policy alternatives as an essential prerequisite to action. However, even when such debate occurs, it tends to occur with crucial effect upon opinion at the level of abstract symbols and rallying slogans, despite the facts and figures that may be used to buttress particular points of view. The operational assessments and instrumental goals and strategies upon which foreign policy has been predicated are seldom unchallengeable. Critics of administration policies may mobilize evidence to dispute the assumptions on which such policies are built. Policy analysts may hassle over competing interpretations of the situation and estimates of what is required for policy success. Abundant data on public opinion and foreign policy, however, suggest that attitudes tend to cluster according to affective predispositions rather than to vary according to specific details of policy issues.[36]

As one opinion specialist put it, "mass opinion is short on detail, sometimes rather unspecific, and often sluggishly unresponsive on exact issues of policy choice, except as these have direct and obvious bearing upon the individual's continuing, conscious concern for his immediate welfare."[37]

For example, focusing on "national security" as a central issue area of concern to Americans, one may reasonably assume that for the vast majority of the public, the concept is best understood in its simple literal rendering. That is, the nation is secure to the extent that we as a people feel secure. The policies of an administration expressed in terms of promoting national security are likely to receive popular endorsement to the extent that they are associated in the public eye with a feeling of security, and to be denied support to the extent that they are associated with feelings of insecurity, even though the causal link between feelings of insecurity and particular policies may be remote or nonexistent.

Of course, the public expects the government, as the repository of expertise and access to privileged intelligence sources, to be in a better position than is the average citizen to apprise the people of previously unforeseen threats to the nation's security. However, it is a reasonable hypothesis that the credibility of such warnings will be a function of the general feelings of security or insecurity that the society has experienced, as well as the basis of trust or mistrust that has been established between governing officials and the populace.

Thus, no amount of posturing from Washington could convince large numbers of Americans in 1979 that a Soviet brigade in Cuba posed a substantial threat to the American national security. On the other hand, the extent of grass-roots support in the early 1980s for a nuclear freeze suggests a degree of popular insecurity regarding the dangers of nuclear war in circumstances in which both superpowers are armed "to the teeth" that policy makers in Washington obviously had not fully anticipated.

The point is that it is especially at the level of abstract affective images and at the level of broad policy goals and assumptions rather than at the level of operational assumptions and particular details of strategic doctrine or plans that the public is able to interpret and evaluate foreign policy. It is at the former levels also that public opinion may have an impact on the foreign policy process. Mass opinion tends to be expressed not in the form of endorsements of or challenges to the operational designs of particular policy actions, but rather in the form of support for or opposition to the general orientation of policy in a given area. Particular crises may give public concern a policy focus (Berlin, Korea, Cuba, Vietnam, Iran, Poland, Lebanon, Grenada), but it is what particular actions symbolize about an administration's ability and determination to act in the nation's best interests, rather than specific details of the actions themselves that are likely to be the focus of popular concern.

It is in this sense that Almond's notion of shifting "moods" has continuing analytical relevance. Almond tended to agree with Walter Lippmann that the mass public was fickle in its views. The American culture as a whole provided continuity in foreign policy through a set of stable deep-rooted values and beliefs. But public opinion itself tended to manifest itself in "moods" that were fluid and unstable. The mood of the public, Almond argued, would tend to fluctuate in rather erratic cycles between a sense of superiority and a sense of inferiority relative to other nations, between optimism and pessimism regarding world affairs, between enthusiasm for intervention in the affairs of others and isolationist sentiment.[38]

Caspary's critical review and updating of the Almond data tell us only what we already knew based on Huntington's 1961 analysis: namely, that in the first decades after World War II, the Cold War mood of the American public was relatively stable and highly permissive toward military spending.[39] However, as Russett has demonstrated based upon data extending to the late Vietnam years, such permissiveness is not irrevocable. Whereas those who favored reducing defense expenditures had been limited to a minority of 20% to 25% of American adults throughout the 1950s and 1960s, opposition rose to roughly half of those surveyed beginning in 1968 (the year of the Tet offensive by Viet Cong and North Vietnamese forces in Vietnam, arousing widespread disillusionment with the war in the United States).[40]

Polling data used for such analyses appropriately focus on questions at a broad level of abstraction—not "should we build more aircraft carriers," or "are American jet aircraft superior to Soviet jet aircraft?" but rather "How do you feel about the money the government is spending for defense? Is it too much? Too little? About right?" It is at this level of generality that the average citizen can be expected to formulate opinions with some confidence. To the extent that politicians in the 1970s sensed the nature and intensity of those opinions, the basis was provided for reductions in the size the armed forces, the end of military conscription, and foreign policies that were in accordance with the deemphasis on the military instrument.

On the other hand, whereas the public mood of the late 1970s was one that called for reductions in U.S. military involvement abroad, distrust of the Soviet Union remained high and continues to remain high in the 1980s.[41] Polls showing high levels of public support for SALT II tended to be misleading, therefore, in tapping a popular desire for an end to the nuclear arms race whicle ignoring other popular concerns, such as apprehension about Soviet motives.[42]

One might expect that in a climate of public uncertainty regarding the merits and demerits of competing policy positions on a complex issue such as the Strategic Arms Limitation Talks (SALT), policy makers are likely to resolve their own doubts in favor of the views of those who can provide solid and detailed answers to complex questions—namely, the experts. Detailed analysis did play an important role, especially during the months of forging the American negotiating position.[43] Even when Congress became deeply involved in the process, in the final months before the Vienna summit and subsequently in the treaty ratification stage, discussions focused on various complex and sometimes highly technical questions of throw-weight, fractionation, equivalence, and verification. Expert witnesses were called to testify before the armed services committees of both houses of Congress. The Intelligence Committee conducted closed-door sessions of several-weeks duration to consider verification provisions of the treaty.[44] The Senate Foreign Relations Committee conducted extensive hearings, leading to a 550-page report weighing the pros and cons of the treaty.

However, as I. M. Destler has noted, the hearings and report had little effect on support or opposition in the Senate. SALT II was "a pawn in a larger game," and ultimately was rejected because of a substantial body of opposition in the Senate to any agreement with the Soviets that would seem to endorse the strategic status quo.[45] Only when President Carter agreed to a 5% increase in real terms in the defense budget were some opponents of SALT II prepared to commit themselves to ratification, and even that commitment was withdrawn with the Soviet invasion of Afghanistan in December 1979.

One might argue that the extensive participation by scientists in the debate of 1969–1970 regarding construction of a defense network of anti-ballistic missiles (ABM) provides a contrary example of the resolution of important policy issues on the basis of careful assessment of technical detail. Such an argument does not stand up to critical scrutiny, however. It is true that dozens of scientists were called as expert witnesses to testify before the Senate Armed Services Committee on the probable effectiveness of the Spartan and Sprint missiles and radar capabilities on which the ABM system was dependent. However, those adamantly opposed as well as those supportive of an ABM system were able to summon on their behalf the testimony of scientists buttressing mutually contradictory arguments with impressive arrays of data. The activities of "expert" witnesses were thereby transformed into a political donnybrook, leading one informed observer to compare the debate to "the great bomb shelter controversy that plagued President Kennedy in his first year in the White House. . . . It is arousing much the same fears felt in 1961, namely that whatever is decided may be decided in the worst possible way for the worst possible reasons."[46]

The ABM controversy also had parallels with the debate in the early 1950s on the appropriate American response to the Soviet development of an atomic-bomb capability.[47] In none of these policy debates were conclusions at the lowest level of abstraction about operational assumptions and instrumental goals and strategies determinant of the policy outcome. Rather, as Slater has noted of the ABM dispute, the debate in each case tended to become one of competing catchwords. In the case of the ABM, it

> had become a symbolic issue. Growing frustrations about the Vietnam war and a generally antimilitary shift in public and congressional opinion had made it even more difficult to consider the ABM on whatever merits it might have had. In the Senate, the ABM became a surrogate for congressional futility over rising military expenditures and the Indochina war.[48]

A similar pattern is observable in the recent MX missile dispute.

Over the years since the first deployment of intercontinental ballistic missiles (ICBMs) in the late 1950s, more than thirty distinct concepts of alternative basing of the missiles had been subjected to detailed review and appraisal by the government before President Jimmy Carter announced in 1979 that the newest "generation" of ICBMs, the MX (missile experimental), would be produced and deployed in a "racetrack" mode. The technical feasibility and desirability of the plan became the subject of extensive critical examination in various specialized as well as popular journals.[49] The view that perhaps received the widest currency was one expressed in 1980 by presidential candidate Ronald Reagan, echoing earlier critics, who described the Carter plan as a "Rube Goldberg" scheme.

Upon assuming the presidency himself, because he had objected only to the basing scheme but not to the development of the MX, President Reagan launched a new series of detailed studies of basing alternatives. In December 1982, the administration announced the results of the studies: missiles would be grouped together in a "dense pack" mode. In a major policy address in December 1982 designed to enlist support for the needed appropriations for MX production, the President referred to the new generation of ICBMs as "Peacekeepers."[50] Substantial numbers of the members of Congress, however, had doubts about the wisdom of proceeding with the development of an MX to be committed to a "dense pack" deployment. As noted by Senator Henry Jackson, generally supportive of the MX but dubious about the basing plan, "the public has gotten the idea that it's a boondoggle, a Rube Goldberg . . . You can't explain it."[51]

Thus, appropriations for the production of the MX were held in abeyance pending still another study, by a presidential commission headed by former national security advisor Brent Scowcroft. The Scowcroft Commission report, which was published in April 1983, provided a wide range of recommendations, from advocacy of further research and development of a "Midgetman" missile, much smaller than the MX, to support for alternatives such as airborne missiles. From the perspective of many members of Congress, the policy issue remained unresolved. It is fair to say that the mood of intense hostility toward the Soviets that was produced by the downing of the South Korean airliner in September 1983, more so than any set of facts and figures related to a particular MX basing plan, tipped the scales in favor of congressional funding for MX.[52]

FOREIGN POLICY SUBCULTURES

Common to the ABM, SALT II, and MX controversies has been a tendency for debate at the level of detailed comparisons of operational assumptions regarding technical feasibility as well as desirability to become transformed into a debate at the level of broad generalities about the nation's goals, purposes, and priorities. Common also to these controversies has been a tendency of key participants to attempt to define the issues in terms of an idiom compatible with their own ideological biases and organizational or partisan perspectives. The use of the English language by all parties to the debates belies important idiomatic differences among participants. Such differences are revealing, not only as barriers to communication and policy consensus, but also as clues to political alignments and prevailing patterns of influence.

Drawing upon his experience in the British government during World War II, working with scientists as well as with career civil servants, C. P. Snow has explored the communication problems that are associated with contacts between these "two cultures."[53] In the American foreign policy context, the communication problems may be even greater, as foreign policy debates illustrate. The most popular categories used by the mass media in labelling participants to policy debates are "conservative" and "liberal." However, on foreign policy issues such items often are not helpful—partly because persons who espouse "liberal" causes in domestic politics may identify with their "conservative" colleagues on foreign policy issues, and vice versa, and partly because often it is not clear what the terms mean when applied to foreign policy issues. For example, self-proclaimed "liberals" as well as self-proclaimed "conservatives" have supported increases in defense spending throughout much of the period since World War II. Some "liberals" who became opposed to continued American military involvement in Vietnam in the late 1960s and early 1970s favored American military involvement elsewhere, for example, military assistance to Israel. Some "conservatives" have opposed particular defense programs; some have argued against defense spending increases in the interests of reducing federal deficits. In short, the clustering of attitudes and interest groups on foreign policy issues tends to defy classification according

145

to a simple "liberal-conservative" dichotomy, or even according to political party affiliation.[54]

Nevertheless, political alliances do tend to be forged, with some variation from one issue to another, according to shared interests, values, and beliefs. In other words, the clustering of groups in the political arena tends to reflect distinctive political subcultures. Using for purposes of illustration the dimension of foreign policy alluded to with the MX, ABM, SALT, and other cases discussed above, we may speak of distinctive "foreign policy subcultures"— clusters of individuals who share priorities among policy-relevant values and beliefs and who tend to attach common connotations to familiar terms in the policy lexicon (e.g., deterrence, nuclear freeze, strategic parity).

Five of the most prominent foreign policy subcultures may be described as "technocrats," "strategic supremacists," "pragmatists," "reformers," and "Consciousness III radicals". No argument is made here that in number or character these categories are definitive. However, the categorization suffices to illustrate important differences that do exist among those who participate, with regularity, in foreign policy debate. Such differences tend to be manifested in differing uses of the foreign policy idiom, as Table 5-2 and the following discussion suggest. Examples are drawn from national security debates that have served to bring to light contrasting policy assumptions and perspectives in recent years. However, the reader will recognize that similar distinctions might be made focusing upon foreign economic policies, issues relating to American participation in international organizations, and other realms of foreign policy.

TECHNOCRATS

The term *technocrats* is used here to refer to participants in the foreign policy process whose expressed interests lie primarily with technical details of policy application. The technocrat is not entirely apolitical; but to the extent that he or she discusses politics, it is likely to be in terms of Cold War slogans which are accepted as "givens" rather than as objects of useful debate and inquiry. Little attention is likely to be paid to debates about policy goals or about the probable consequences of policy commitments—such as the possible effects on arms control discussions if the United States were to make a "no-first-use" pledge to the Soviet Union regarding

TABLE 5-2 The Foreign Policy Subcultures

ISSUES AND IDEAS	TECHNOCRATS	STRATEGIC SUPREMATISTS	PRAGMATISTS	REFORMERS	CONSCIOUSNESS III RADICALS
Lessons of Vietnam	Faulty technique	Failure of will	Mixed lessons	Failure of U.S. comprehension	Immoral
Soviet intentions	Hostile	Global conquest; Finlandization	Hostile but. . .	Hostile, with reason	Willing to be reasonable
Soviet capabilities	Gaining edge	Strategic superiority	Strategic parity	Strategic parity, with problems	Strategic inferiority
Third World	Market for U.S. arms	Source and object of terrorism	Turbulent	Turbulent, needs high priority	Liberation struggles continue
Nuclear deterrence	Peace through strength	Peace through strength	Needs Refinement	Outmoded	Evidence of U.S. militarism
Arms control, disarmament nuclear freeze	Arms control, U.S. terms	Arms control, U.S. terms	Freeze plus new SALT	Freeze plus new SALT mutual disarmament	Freeze plus disarm Now
Economic dimensions of security	Improve capitalism	Improve and defend capitalism	Important; requires multilateral approach	Important; North-South dialogue needed	Capitalism source of insecurity

nuclear weapons. The technocrat is likely to find an interest in questions such as these: Can a workable anti-ballistic missile (ABM) system be developed? How can command and control systems be perfected to permit communication with submerged nuclear sub-marines? Which is preferable, investing in fewer state-of-the-art jet aircraft and aircraft carriers, or in more, but cheaper, systems that exhibit less "gold plating"? To the extent that political issues are of concern to the technocrats, they are likely to be intimately associated with issues of technology, such as with the relevance of the capability of the AWACS rather than to the question of whether its sale to Saudi Arabia was in the national interest.

Doubtless technocrats are found in large numbers in all advanced industrial societies, socialist as well as capitalist. They are in clear evidence among career military personnel, among civilians in the defense bureaucracy, and in defense-related industries. Many of the specialized journals that have a defense-industrial base provide a forum for the technocratic perspective: *Aerospace*, published by Aerospace Industries Incorporated, for instance, or the journal, *National Defense*, published by the American Defense Preparedness Association.

STRATEGIC SUPREMACISTS

In his pioneering study of American military professionals, Morris Janowitz distinguished between those who were *absolutists* and those who were *pragmatists* in their strategic outlook, linking the former viewpoints to professionals whose World War II identification was with General Douglas MacArthur ("no substitute for victory"), and the latter to those whose identification was with General George Marshall.[55] The views that Janowitz associated with the absolutist approach can continue to be observed in foreign policy discussions. Such views include a "worst case" approach in assessing Soviet intentions, a corresponding skepticism regarding the desirability or even the feasibility of reaching meaningful arms control agreements with the Soviets, and a determination to continue to invest heavily in defense spending with the goal of maintaining American strategic supremacy. However, even among the most rigidly doctrinaire military and civilian participants in foreign policy discussions, the deep cultural strain of American pragmatism is likely to be evident to a degree that makes absolutism seem an inaccurate label. Thus, in lieu of absolutists it seems appropriate to speak of *strategic supremacists* as a distinctive subculture, with values and beliefs shared by some civilians as well as some career military personnel.

The new dimension of this outlook in the years since the mid-1970s has been the sense of urgency that is expressed regarding the maintenance of American strength in comparison to the Soviet buildup of strategic arms. The sense of urgency has been fed also by a conviction that in the aftermath of Vietnam, many Americans—including a number in key policy positions—have lost the "will" and "sense of national purpose" that are essential to the preservation of the American power position in world affairs. The neoconservative journal *Commentary* has become one of the key outlets for this subcultural perspective, for reasons explained in agonizing detail by Norman Podhoretz.[56] The American Security Council and the Heritage Foundation have sponsored a number of publications designed to mobilize support for the perspective of strategic supremacy. The rallying cry, "peace through strength," also is the theme of resolutions that have been introduced in a number of state legislatures and other forums.

PRAGMATISTS

The subculture that is here termed *pragmatism* is less cohesive in its outlook than is the strategic supremacist subculture. Pragmatists by their very nature are apt to find it possible to live with diverse views, even when some of the views are somewhat inconsistent with one another. Nearly all foreign policy pragmatists will have been identified with support for the American military involvement in Vietnam during its early stages, but their retrospective critiques of that involvement are likely to differ considerably one from another. Similarly, it is possible to label as foreign policy pragmatists both some individuals who have endorsed the notion of a nuclear freeze and others who have not, some who have come out in favor of "no first use" as a principle that the American government should adopt publicly, and some who have expressed opposition to this idea.

At least among those who are in the forty-or-over age group, pragmatists are likely to be individuals who have made strong commitments to the strategy of deterrence since the peak Cold War years but who also have identified with the efforts over many years to forge strategic arms control agreements with the Soviets. The foreign policy pragmatist is likely to regard himself or herself as a "tough-minded realist" regarding Soviet intentions, but at the same time to regard continuing negotiation as imperative and potentially holding great hope for the future. The journals *Foreign Policy* and *International Security* provide important forums for the expression of the views of pragmatists, as has *Foreign Affairs* in airing the nuclear freeze proposal of McGeorge Bundy, George Kennan, Robert McNamara, and Gerard Smith.[57]

REFORMERS

Those who are described here as "reformers" share with the pragmatists long association with debates over the continuing efficacy of American deterrence strategy and long involvement in arms control discussions. Some of those who, according to the present classification, would be categorized as "reformers" have been labelled by some strategic supremacists as dangerous radicals, presumably because the former tend to be consistently critical of the policy positions of the latter. Reformers also differ from some pragmatists and all strategic supremacists in assigning major blame for the failure to reverse the arms race to the United States.

Prominent foreign-policy "reformers" include: Richard Barnet and his associates of the Institute for Policy Studies; Roger Molander and other leaders of the "Ground Zero" movement; and Rear Admiral Gene LaRocque and associates of the Center for Defense Information, which publishes the *Defense Monitor*.[58] Like the strategic supremacists, reformers have a deep sense of urgency about the current climate of superpower relations. However, for the reformers, the grave danger lies in actions that perpetuate the nuclear arms race and thereby increase the dangers of war by miscalculation or by accident. Although dubious about proposals for drastically altering the American political and economic systems, reformers tend to be convinced that the paradigms that are applied in viewing global issues can be (and must be) altered and that the "decision rules" that govern the identification and selection of policy options can (and ought to be) be changed. The lesson of Vietnam, in the minds of reformers, is not simply that of tactical mistakes, nor of well-meaning but ultimately disastrous incremental steps into a "quagmire". Rather, the foreign-policy reformer sees the lesson as one of a trained incapacity to comprehend the fundamental nature of the problem; only when structural and procedural changes are made can such failures be avoided in the future.

CONSCIOUSNESS III RADICALS

The final category consists of those who, adapting a voguish concept of the early 1970s to present needs, may be described as "Consciousness III Radicals" (the modifier borrowed from Charles Reich).[59] Nearly all participants in current foreign policy debates regard defense and arms control problems as priority issues. Most participants would favor some types of disarmament under some circumstances. What distinguishes Consciousness III radicals from persons whose views have been discussed previously is the conviction of the former that the issue of arms control and disarmament is linked inextricably to the need for raising the consciousness of the masses and effecting radical social and political change.

As Reich noted in describing Consciousness III, a key to understanding this view of policy issues is the underlying sense of betrayal that is associated with attitudes toward American governmental officials. The conclusion is that the political system itself requires total restructuring. The writings of Noam Chomsky, among others, reveal the pattern of continuity, from allegations that American policies in Vietnam were immoral to arguments that the system of capitalism continues to foster exploitation of the Third World.

THE STRUGGLE TO CONTROL
THE IDIOM OF DEBATE

Each of the five categories above includes participants in foreign policy debates who are attentive and informed. Even among informed and attentive participants, policy debate moves inexorably from differences over specific details to mid-level assumptions, value priorities, and legitimizing symbols. The differences that sometimes become intense among competing foreign policy subcultures are explicable in part in terms of communications failures, which are to be expected when parties to policy discussions bring to these discussions fundamentally differing assumptions regarding the issues and differing connotations attached to key concepts that are central to the resolution of the issues. However, intense differences sometimes are rooted not in misunderstanding but in a clear recognition by parties to political debate of the threat to their own interests and policy preferences that are posed by a competing set of assumptions and symbols of policy legitimacy. The struggle to define the idiom of debate becomes a mechanism for controlling the selection of policy alternatives. The outcome of this struggle is dependent not merely on skillful rhetoric but also on other political resources.

POLITICAL ELITES AND
THE FOREIGN POLICY CONSENSUS

It is because political resources are distributed unequally that the concept of "political elites" has relevance. "Political resources" are the means available for exercising political influence. Depending upon the context, the issues, and the parties that have stakes in the outcomes, the means may include such political resources as money, social status, control of key information, highly valued skills (such as media skills), organization (including numbers of members and effectiveness of control), and access to key positions in government. A "political elite" is the portion of the political system that is especially influential, that is, a group that is able to bring political resources to bear in ways that have major influence on policy.

Even if relatively open, democratic political systems are compared with closed, highly authoritarian systems, the contrast is not between the absence and presence of political elites. Rather, the contrast is between a system in which multiple elites compete with one another and one that is largely or totally dominated by a single, relatively cohesive elite. It is between a system in which persons not currently influential have realistic opportunities to become members of the elite in the future and a system in which such opportunities are effectively precluded.

Most serious observers agree that the extent to which American political practice has conformed to the open, democratic model has varied from one historical epoch to another, and perhaps from one issue to another. The question for the student of American foreign policy is not, have political elites influenced United States foreign policy, but rather, to what extent and over what kinds of issues have political elites determined the course of American foreign policy?

Space limitations preclude full consideration of the wide variety of answers to the question that has been posited by serious observers.[60] For purposes here of simply highlighting important differences of interpretation, two especially important contrasting interpretations are discussed: "power elite" theories and "pluralist elite" theories. Both schools of thought accept the proposition that some groups (elites) wield considerably more political influence than do others. However, the "power elite" school attributes cohesion and continuing influence to a single elite. Proponents of the "pluralist" argument, in contrast, tend to see policy as resulting from competition among contending elites. If a particular elite exercises a dominant influence over policy in a given issue area, according to the pluralist school such dominance is likely to be temporary. Moreover, "pluralists" maintain that it is feasible for persons not presently influential to become part of the political elite in the future.

"POWER ELITE" OR "PLURALISM"?

At various points in American history, the picture of a handful of powerful men making deals in the citadels of power while the masses of the population remain politically impotent has been one that many persons have taken as an accurate representation of reality. For instance, groups that can be loosely described as populist in political orientation have characteristically rallied to the cry that the voice of the people was being ignored while a band of powerful men ruled the nation. The verbal attacks of William Jennings Bryan on the "organized wealth" of the industrialists of the East Coast, of Huey Long on the "moguls" of business, of Joseph McCarthy on "commies and fellow-travelers" and of George Wallace on the Supreme Court and on "pseudo-intellectuals and agitators" all have in common the attribution of a small minority of persons as a dominant and perverse influence over the political fortunes of the nation.

Among the theories of elite dominance that have focused specifically on the American foreign policy process, those advanced during the period of the Senate munitions investigation of the early 1930s are a prominent and instructive illustration. The investigation was a direct outgrowth of disillusionment with American involvement in World War I, which at the time had been justified in such idealistic terms as helping "to make the world safe for democracy" and as participating in a "war to end wars." In the postwar atmosphere of disillusionment, critics of the decision to involve the United States in the war unearthed evidence that to many persons seemed to explain the decision in crassly materialistic rather than idealistic terms.

Revisionist theories of why the Wilson administration committed the nation to enter the war on behalf of England and France attributed a dominant influence to the manufacturers of arms, munitions, and ships. Such manufacturers had promoted American participation in the war, according to the theory, in order to advance their own profits. In the spring of 1934, an article presenting such a thesis was published in *Fortune* magazine. The article was inserted into the *Congressional Record* at the request of Gerald Nye, a forty-two-year-old Republican senator from North Dakota. A condensed version was published in the *Reader's Digest*. A book by other authors, entitled *Merchants of Death: A Study of the International Armament Industry*, became a best seller and a Book-of-the-Month Club selection in the spring. A number of groups, notably the Women's International League for Peace and Freedom, sought to arouse public opinion and to enlist government support to investigate the alleged responsibility of arms manufacturers for American involvement in World War I. It was in this atmosphere of mounting popular concern that the Senate instructed a special committee, headed by Senator Nye, to investigate the manufacture and sale of munitions.[61]

The investigation was able to unearth evidence to show that various manufacturers of arms and ships had reaped enormous profits during World War I and that bribery of foreign governments and blatant violations of American arms embargoes had been among the devices used to expand the markets for their goods. However, after two years of committee hearings, the broader thesis that American involvement in World War I had been caused by profit-hungry manufacturers remained unsubstantiated by the facts. The author of the most thorough study of the Nye committee investigation suggests that, of the committee's achievements, "perhaps the most notable one was debunking—inadvertently to be sure—the merchants-of-death thesis."[62]

It is instructive that the next major rash of popular concern for alleged elite domination of foreign policy came in the 1960s, a period of "Camelot" hubris followed by disillusionment, as described earlier in this chapter. A work that had been published in the mid-1950s received renewed attention, as receptivity increased to the argument that major policies in the United States were dictated by *The Power Elite*.[63] The thesis that its author, C. Wright Mills, developed was given special credence in the aftermath of a surprising warning from President Dwight D. Eisenhower in his farewell address in January 1961. Eisenhower, a former army general and certainly no subscriber to the full dimensions of Mills's thesis, nonetheless warned in a famous passage that "in the councils of government, we must guard against the acquisition of unwarranted influence, whether sought or unsought, by the military-industrial complex." According to a close associate, it was Eisenhower's prior military experience, coupled with the resistance that he had encountered as president to his efforts to cut the defense budget, that had convinced him that he had an understanding of pressures for excessive military spending that successors to the presidency might lack unless he gave the issue emphasis.[64]

Lucrative defense contracts in the 1960s, a time of increased military spending by the United States, helped to provide a receptive audience for dozens of books and articles in that era attesting to the alleged dominance of the "military-industrial complex" over American policies. However, the allegation eventually received critical scrutiny by scholars, who carefully examined the solid links that were said to exist among various elements of the military establishment and defense industry and found them to be weak and who scrutinized the alleged control over policy and found it to be largely missing.[65]

If the pattern of American foreign policy in recent decades defies simple explanation in terms of control by a cohesive "power elite," one must add that the enthusiasm of most social scientists for "pluralist" descriptions of the pattern may be oversimplified as well. Especially influential in forstering such enthusiasm was an award-winning study by Bauer, Pool, and Dexter, which seemed to demonstrate that elite dominance was a myth.

> The stereotype notion of omnipotent pressure groups becomes completely untenable once there are groups aligned on both sides. The result of opposing equipotent forces is stalemate. But, even

taken by themselves, the groups [studied] did not appear to have the raw material of great power. We noted shortages of money, men, information, and time. It was a particular surprise to us to find how dilute vast sums could become when divided among dozens of pressure groups.[66]

Contrary to persons who viewed public policy as being at the mercy of a dominant business elite, the authors found business leaders to be frequently paralyzed by inaction at crucial policy junctures, oblivious to contending sources of influence, and ignorant of political realities. Such findings have led many students of politics to identify Bauer, Pool and Dexter as proponents of a "pluralist" interpretation of the policy process. However, a recent treatise by Eric Nordlinger cites the study along with other evidence to bolster the claim that even pluralist images of the policy process exaggerate the influence of elites. Policy in democratic states, Nordlinger argues, frequently reflects the exercise of autonomy from elite influence by the state (that is, by governmental policy makers).[67]

Although the provocative Nordlinger thesis helps to keep alive the debate over the degree and pattern of elite influence over policy, in the foreign policy realm it is useful to recall the findings from Lowi's earlier study of the American experience since World War II. Lowi found that *"the only instances in which the makers of foreign policy were truly separated and insulated from broad publics and worked truly in unison, even if not always in harmony, were crisis."*[68]

Lowi's argument, as developed more fully, is that elite involvement in and influence upon the policy process varies with the issues at stake.[69] It follows that the degree of flexibility that the President and other key policy makers enjoy in the formulation and execution of foreign policy varies somewhat from issue to issue. Although an element of autonomy may be provided sometimes, typically the price of authority for the conduct of foreign policy is the forging of coalitions and compromises among political elites, and the moulding of a popular consensus in support of policy.

The "president knows best" syndrome alluded to earlier in the chapter can be helpful in the development of support for presidential policy initiatives. So also can the commonality of values and beliefs that tends to provide a basis for compromise in the American political system, even when competing groups have divergent policy perspectives.[70] Ultimately, however, the challenge is one of leadership—a requisite of foreign policy adaptation that is examined in Chapters 6 and 7 in discussing the President and the bureaucracy, and in Chapter 8 in exploring the relationship of the President with Congress.

NOTES

1. Henry R. Luce, "The American Century," *Life* 10 (Feb. 17, 1941): 61–65.
2. Eric F. Goldman, *The Crucial Decade: America, 1945–1955* (New York: Alfred A. Knopf, 1959), pp. 12–13.
3. See David Caute, *The Great Fear: The Anti-Communist Purge Under Truman and Eisenhower* (New York: Simon & Schuster, 1978).
4. See John E. Mueller, *War, Presidents and Pubic Opinion* (New York: John Wiley & Sons, 1973). See also William R. Caspary, "The 'Mood Theory': A Study of Public Opinion and Foreign Policy," *American Political Science Review* 64 (June 1970): 536–546. Caspary challenges the thesis expounded by Gabriel Almond, in his landmark study, *The American People and Foreign Policy* (New York: Harcourt, Brace, 1950) that American public opinion tends to vacillate between sharply contrasting "moods." However, Caspary acknowledges that a "weaker formulation" of the Almond thesis would be consistent with public opinion data into the 1950s, with a prediction of a sharp reduction of popular support for international commitments if the sense of threat from the Soviet Union were to decline.
5. Vandenberg, quoted by Walter Johnson, *1600 Pennsylvania Avenue: Presidents and the People Since 1929*, paperback ed. (Boston: Little, Brown, 1963), pp. 205–206.
6. Samuel P. Huntington, *The Common Defense: Strategic Programs in National Politics* (New York: Columbia University Press, 1961), p. 235.
7. Theodore J. Lowi, "Making Democracy Safe for the World," in *Domestic Sources of Foreign Policy*, ed. James N. Rosenau (New York: Free Press, 1967), pp. 295–331. In updated form, the article is incorporated into Lowi's *The End of Liberalism*, 2d ed. (New York: W. W. Norton, 1979), chap. 6.
8. See Townsend Hoopes, *The Devil and John Foster Dulles* (Boston: Little, Brown, 1973).
9. Inaugural speech, January 20, 1961, in *Public Papers of the Presidents of the United States: John F. Kennedy, 1961* (Washington, D.C.: Government Printing Office 1961).
10. Arthur Levine, *When Dreams and Heroes Died: A Portrait of Today's College Student*, prepared for the Carnegie Council on Policy Studies in Higher Education (San Francisco: Jossey-Bass, 1980).
11. Garry Wills, *Nixon Agonistes: The Crisis of the Self-Made Man* (Boston: Houghton Mifflin, 1970), p. 369.
12. Kingman Brewster, Jr., "Reflections on Our National Purpose," *Foreign Affairs* 50 (April 1972): 399–415.
13. "The Myth of Neo-Isolationism," *Commonweal* 94 (Mar. 26, 1971): 51–52. Emphasis in original text. See also John L. Steele, "How Real is Neo-Isolationism?" Time Essay, *Time* 97 (May 31, 1971): 24–25; James A. Johnson, "The New Generation of Isolationists," *Foreign Affairs* 47 (Oct. 1970): 136–146.
14. Earl Ravenal, *Never Again: Learning From America's Foreign Policy Failures* (Philadelphia: Temple University Press, 1978).
15. Henry Kissinger, Secretary of State, address before the Third Pacem in Terris Conference sponsored by the Center for the Study of Democratic Institutions, Washington, D.C., Oct. 8, 1973, published in the *Department of State Bulletin* 69 (Oct. 29, 1973): 525–531.

16. For example, see "America Now: A Failure of Nerve? A Symposium," *Commentary* 60 (July 1975): 16–96.

17. Henry Kissinger, Secretary of State, address to the Boston World Affairs Council, March 11, 1976, published in the *Department of State Bulletin* 74 (April 5, 1976): 425–432.

18. See Ronald Berman, ed., *Solzhenitsyn at Harvard: The Address, Twelve Early Responses, and Six Later Reflections* (Washington, D.C.: Ethics and Public Policy Center, 1980).

19. Jimmy Carter, quoted by Betty Glad, *Jimmy Carter: In Search of the Great White House* (New York: W. W. Norton, 1980), p. 321.

20. Glad, *Jimmy Carter*, pp. 321–322.

21. Elizabeth Drew, "A Reporter at Large," *The New Yorker* 56 (Dec. 1, 1980): 180–181.

22. Lewis H. Lapham, "Reagan's Academy Award," *Harper's* 262 (Jan. 1981): 8.

23. Ronald Reagan, quoted by Drew, *The New Yorker* 56 (Dec. 1, 1980): 184–185.

24. The quote is included in a portion of his memoirs in which he describes the rationale for the human rights emphasis: Jimmy Carter, *Keeping Faith: Memoirs of a President* (New York: Bantam Books, 1982), pp. 141–151. Patricia Derian provides an early discussion of the Carter administration human rights objectives in U.S. Department of State, Bureau of Public Affairs, *Human Rights: A World Perspective*, Current Policy series no. 42, Nov. 1978, p. 4. An account of the administration's program from a three-and-a-half year vantage point is provided by Deputy Secretary of State Warren Christopher, in U.S. Department of State, Bureau of Public Affairs, *Human Rights and the National Interest*, Current Policy series no. 206, Aug. 4, 1980, p. 4. A critique of the Carter approach by the woman who became Ronald Reagan's choice to become United States Ambassador to the United Nations is provided by Jeane Kirkpatrick, "Dictatorships and Double Standards: A Critique of U.S. Policy," *Commentary* (Nov. 1979). A useful comparison is provided by Roger Hamburg, "American and Soviet Views of Human Rights," *Conflict* 2 (1980): 163–175. The Carter policies are set in perspective by A. Glenn Mower, Jr., *The United States, the United Nations, and Human Rights: The Eleanor Roosevelt and Jimmy Carter Eras* (Westport, CT: Greenwood, 1979).

25. Secretary of State Alexander Haig, "A New Direction in U.S. Foreign Policy," address to the American Society of Newspaper Editors, Washington, D.C., April 24, 1981, Current Policy Document No. 275, U.S. Department of State, Bureau of Public Affairs, Washington, D.C., 1981.

26. *New York Times*, October 24, 1982, p. 22.

27. See Harold Lasswell, *Politics: Who Gets What, When, How* (New York: Meridian Books, 1958); first published 1936 by McGraw-Hill); T. D. Weldon, *The Vocabulary of Politics* (Baltimore: Penguin Books, 1953); Murray Edelman, *The Symbolic Uses of Politics* (Urbana: University of Illinois Press, 1964).

28. Walter Lippmann, *Public Opinion* (New York: Macmillan, 1960); originally published by Harcourt, Brace, 1922).

29. Gabriel A. Almond, *The American People and Foreign Policy* (New York: Praeger, 1960; originally published by Harcourt, Brace, 1950). Douglass Cater, *The Fourth Branch of Government* (Boston: Houghton Mifflin, 1959). See also James N. Rosenau, *Public Opinion and Foreign Policy* (New York: Random House, 1961); and Bernard C. Cohen, *The Press and Foreign Policy* (Princeton, NJ: Princeton University Press, 1963).

30. A vivid description of the impact of television on presidential elections, in particular, is provided by Theodore H. White, *America in Search of Itself: The Making of the President 1956–1980* (New York: Harper & Row, 1982), Chap. 6. For counterpoint, see Thomas E. Patterson and Robert D. McClure, *The Unseeing Eye: The Myth of Television Power in National Elections* (New York: Putnam's Sons, 1976). Vivid essays on some of the subtle effects of television in interpreting foreign policy events to the public were provided in pieces by Michael J. Arlen originally published in various issues of *The*

New Yorker and collected in *Living Room War* (New York: Viking, 1969; Penguin Books, 1982).

31. See Daniel Yankelovich, "Farewell to 'Presidents Know Best'," *America and the World 1978*, ed. William P. Bundy (New York: Pergamon and *Foreign Affairs*, 1979), pp. 696–713). Yankelovich notes that the effect of experiences such as Vietnam and Watergate has been to make the public less willing to grant the President uncritical support for his policies.

32. Mueller, *War, Presidents and Public Opinion*.

33. Leslie H. Gelb, with Richard K. Betts, *The Irony of Vietnam: The System Worked* (Washington, D.C.: Brookings Institute, 1979), p. 25.

34. Paul M. Kattenburg, *The Vietnam Trauma in American Foreign Policy, 1945–1975* (New Brunswick, NJ: Transaction Books, 1980), p. 250. See also Daniel Ellsberg, *Papers on the War* (New York: Simon and Schuster, 1972).

35. President Ronald Reagan, transcript of address to the nation, Oct. 27, 1983, in *New York Times* Oct. 28, 1983, p. 5. One of the few members of Congress who publicly criticized the Reagan administration for the Grenadan venture was Democrat Les Aspin of Wisconsin. See U.S., Congress, House, *Congressional Record*, 98th Cong., 2d sess., 130, pt. E49–52 See also Eldon Kenworthy, "Grenada as Theater," *World Policy Journal* 1 (Spring 1984): 635–651.

36. Irving L. Janis and M. Brewster Smith, "Effects of Education and Persuasion on National and International Images," in *International Behavior*, ed. Herbert C. Kelman (New York: Holt, Rinehart & Winston, 1965), pp. 188–235; also Michael A. Maggiotto and Eugene R. Wittkopf, "American Public Attitudes Toward Foreign Policy," *International Studies Quarterly* 25 (Dec. 1981): 601–631.

37. Milton J. Rosenberg, "Images in Relation to the Policy Process: American Public Opinion on Cold War Issues," in *International Behavior*, edited by Herbert C. Kelman (New York: Holt, Rinehart & Winston, 1965), p. 284.

38. Almond, *The American People*.

39. Caspary, "The 'Mood Theory'," 544–546. Samuel P. Huntington, *The Common Defense: Strategic Programs in National Politics* (New York: Columbia University Press, 1961).

40. Bruce M. Russett, "The Revolt of the Masses: Public Opinion on Military Expenditures," in *New Civil-Military Relations*, ed. John P. Lovell and Philip S. Kronenberg (New Brunswick, NJ: Transaction Books, 1974), pp. 57–88.

41. Eighty percent of those surveyed in an ABC News/*Washington Post* poll in late April 1982 agreed with the statement, "The Soviet Union would try to cheat on any nuclear freeze agreement and get an advantage over the United States". *Public Opinion* (August–September 1982), pp. 34–35.

42. David W. Moore, "SALT and Beyond: The Public is Uncertain," *Foreign Policy* 35 (Summer 1979): 68–73.

43. Strobe Talbott, *Endgame: The Inside Story of SALT II* (New York: Harper & Row, 1979).

44. Stephen J. Flanagan, "The Domestic Politics of SALT II: Implications for the Foreign Policy Process," in *Congress, The Presidency and American Foreign Policy*, ed. John Spanier and Joseph Nogee (New York: Pergamon Press, 1981), pp. 44–76.

45. I. M. Destler, "Trade Consensus, SALT Stalemate: Congress and Foreign Policy in the 1970s," in *The New Congress*, ed. Thomas E. Mann and Norman J. Ornstein (Washington, DC: American Enterprise Institute for Public Policy Research, 1981), pp. 329–359.

46. Max Frankel, "Great Sentinel Debate," *New York Times*, Feb. 13, 1969, p. 16.

47. George H. Quester, "Population Defenses: Have We Been All Through It Before?" *Public Policy* 18 (Fall 1970): 703–731.

48. Jerome Slater, "Population Defense Reconsidered: Is the ABM Really Inconsistent with

Stability?" in *American Security Policy and Policy-Making*, ed. Robert Harkavy and Edward A. Kolodziej (Lexington, Ma: Lexington Books, 1980), p. 104.

49. For example, see Bernard T. Feld and Kosta Tsipis, "Land-based Intercontinental Ballistic Missiles," *Scientific American* 241 (Nov. 1979): 50–61; Eliot Marshall, "MX Missile to Roam 200 Racetracks," *Science* 206 (Oct. 12, 1979): 198–200; Russell E. Dougherty and Mark O. Hatfield, "Should the United States Build the MX Missile?" *AEI Foreign Policy and Defense Review* 2 (1980): 2–23.

50. "Peacekeeper" was the name selected after "Peacemaker" (favored by National Security Advisor William Clark), "Guardian Missile" (favored by Secretary of Defense Caspar Weinberger), and "Themis" (proposed by the National Security Council, as a symbolic link to the Greek goddess) had been rejected. *Time* (Dec. 6, 1982), p. 14.

51. Senator Henry Jackson, quoted in the *Washington Post*, Dec. 9, 1982, p. A10.

52. See Michael R. Gordon, "The Midgetman Missile—A Counterpoint to the Giant MX, But Will It Work?" *National Journal* 15 (Oct. 1, 1983): 2000–2003.

53. C. P. Snow, *The Two Cultures: And a Second Look*, 2d. ed. (Cambridge, England: Cambridge University Press, 1963).

54. Careful students of the political process have provided some more refined typologies. Arthur Herzog described the "war-peace establishment" in terms of three distinct schools of thought (deterrers, experimentalists, peace movement), each of which in turn was divisible into subsets, for a total of eight subcultures. Herzog, *The War-Peace Establishment* (New York: Harper & Row, 1963). Ole Holsti and James Rosenau provide empirical support for the assertion that since Vietnam, American foreign policy attitudes tend to fall into three clusters: Cold-War internationalists, post-Cold-War internationalists, and isolationists. Ole R. Holsti, "Three-headed Eagle: The United States and System Change," *International Studies Quarterly* 23 (1979): 339–359. See also Ole R. Holsti and James N. Rosenau, "A Leadership Divided: The Foreign Policy Beliefs of American Leaders, 1976–1980," in *Perspectives on American Foreign Policy*, ed. Charles W. Kegley, Jr. and Eugene R. Wittkopf (New York: St. Martin's Press, 1983), pp. 196–212. In an analysis of 1974 survey data, Michael Maggiotto and Eugene Wittkopf provide empirical support for a four-fold typology (essentially the Holsti-Rosenau typology, with internationally minded "accommodationists" added). M. Maggiotto and E. Wittkopf, *International Studies Quarterly* 25 (Dec. 1981): 601–631.

55. Morris Janowitz, *The Professional Soldier* (Glencoe, Il: Free Press, 1960).

56. Norman Podhoretz, *Breaking Ranks: A Political Memoir* (New York: Harper & Row, 1979).

57. McGeorge Bundy, George F. Kennan, Robert S. McNamara, Gerard Smith, "Nuclear Weapons and the Atlantic Alliance," *Foreign Affairs* 60 (Spring 1982): 753—768.

58. See Richard J. Barnet, *Real Security: Restoring American Power in a Dangerous Decade* (New York: Simon & Schuster, 1981).

59. Charles A. Reich, *The Greening of America* (New York: Random House, 1970).

60. See for example the range of views presented in G. William Domhoff and Hoyt B. Ballard, eds. *C. Wright Mills and the Power Elite* (Boston: Beacon Press, 1968). See also John C. Donovan, *The Cold Warriors: A Policy-Making Elite* (Lexington, Ma: D. C. Heath, 1973); Martin Weil, *A Pretty Good Club: The Founding Fathers of the U.S. Foreign Service* (New York: W.W. Norton, 1978); Richard Barnet, *Roots of War* (New York: Atheneum, 1972); Kenneth M. Dolbeare and Murray J. Edelman, *American Politics: Policies, Power and Change*, 3d ed. (Lexington, Ma: D. C. Heath, 1977); Michael Parenti, *Democracy for the Few*, 3d ed. (New York: St. Martin's Press, 1980).

61. A detailed account and analysis of the activities of the Nye committee is provided by John Edward Wiltz, *In Search of Peace* (Baton Rouge: Louisiana State University Press, 1963).

62. Wiltz, p. 231.
63. C. Wright Mills, *The Power Elite*, (New York: Oxford University Press, 1956).
64. Dwight D. Eisenhower, farewell radio-television address to the American people from Washington, D.C., Jan. 17, 1961; reprinted in U.S. Office of the Federal Register, National Archives and Record Service, *Public Papers of the Presidents of the United States: Dwight D. Eisenhower 1960–61* (Washington, 1961), pp. 1035–1040. The speech is interpreted in "Pressures from 'Military-Industrial Complex' Focus on New Secretary of Defense," *Congressional Quarterly Weekly Report* 81 (May 24, 1968), pt. 1: 1155–1156.
65. For example, see the studies in Steven Rosen, ed., *The Theory of the Military-Industrial Complex* (Lexington, Ma: D. C. Heath, 1973).
66. Raymond A. Bauer, Ithiel de Sola Pool, and Lewis Anthony Dexter, *American Business and Public Policy: The Politics of Foreign Trade* (New York: Atherton, 1963), p. 398.
67. Eric A. Nordlinger, *On the Automomy of the Democratic State* (Cambridge, Ma: Harvard University Press, 1981).
68. Lowi, in *Domestic Sources*, ed. Rosenau, p. 324. Emphasis in the original.
69. Building upon the Lowi thesis, Hayes has demonstrated that pressure group influence on Congress varies according to (1) the degree of consensus or conflict regarding the issue at hand, and (2) the type of legislative action that is being considered ("cosmetic" delegation of authority, granting of discretionary authority, substantive rule of law). Michael T. Hayes, "The Semi-Sovereign Pressure Groups: A Critique of Current Theory and an Alternative Typology," *Journal of Politics* 40 (February 1978): 134–161.
70. A recent study of the American political system from a comparative perspective finds a good deal of integration among American political elites in terms of underlying values, sustained by regular communications within a common social network. John Higley and Gwen Moore, "Elite Integration in the United States and Australia," *American Political Science Review* 75 (Sept. 1981): 581–597.

SUGGESTED ADDITIONAL READING

"America Now: A Failure of Nerve? A Symposium." *Commentary* 60 (July 1975): 16–96.

BARNET, RICHARD. *Roots of War*. New York: Atheneum, 1972.

BARON, DONA, ed. *The National Purpose Reconsidered*. New York: Columbia University Press, 1978.

BELL, CORAL. *The Diplomacy of Detente: The Kissinger Era*. New York: St. Martin's, 1977.

CHOMSKY, NOAM. *Towards a New Cold War: Essays on the Current Crisis and How We Got There*. New York: Pantheon, 1982.

COHEN, BERNARD C. *The Public's Impact on Foreign Policy*. Boston: Little, Brown, 1973.

FORSBERG, RANDALL. "The Freeze and Beyond: Confining the Military to Defense as a Route to Disarmament." *World Policy Journal* 1(Winter 1984): 285–318.

FOSTER, H. SCHUYLER. *Activism Replaces Isolationism: U.S. Public Attitudes 1940–1975*. Washington, D.C.: Foxhall, 1984.

GADDIS, JOHN LEWIS. "The Rise, Fall and Future of Detente." *Foreign Affairs* 62(Winter 1983–84): 354–377.

GRABER, DORIS A. *Mass Media and American Politics*. Washington, D.C.: Congressional Quarterly Press, 1980.

HOLSTI, OLE R. and ROSENAU, JAMES N. *American Leadership in World Affairs: Vietnam and the Breakdown of Consensus*. Boston: Allen and Unwin, 1984.

KISSINGER, HENRY. *Years of Upheaval*. Boston: Little, Brown, 1982.

QUESTER, GEORGE. "Consensus Lost." *Foreign Policy* no. 40 (Fall 1980): 18–32.

SANDERS, JERRY W. *Peddlers of Crisis; The Committee on the Present Danger and the Politics of the Containment.* South End, 1983.

THOMPSON, W. SCOTT, ed. *National Security in the 1980s: From Weakness to Strength.* San Francisco, CA: Institute of Contemporary Studies, 1980.

TUCKER, ROBERT W. *The Purposes of American Power: An Essay on National Security.* New York: Praeger, 1981.

WHITE, THEODORE H. *America in Search of Itself: The Making of the President, 1956–1980.* New York: Harper & Row, 1982.

CHAPTER 6

〜

The Presidency
and the Bureaucracy

"Everybody now expects the man inside the White House to do something about everything. Laws and customs now reflect acceptance of him as the Great Initiator, an acceptance quite as widespread at the Capitol as at his end of Pennsylvania Avenue. But such acceptance does not signify that all the rest of government is at his feet. It merely signifies that other men have found it practically impossible to do *their* jobs without assurance of initiatives from him. Service for themselves, not power for the President, has brought them to accept his leadership in form."

> —Richard Neustadt, author of *Presidential Power*

". . . The White House is an ideal cloak for intrigue, pomposity, and ambition. No nation of free men [and women] should ever permit itself to be governed from a hallowed shrine where the meanest lust for power can be sanctified and the dullest wit greeted with reverential awe. Government should be vulgar, sweaty, plebeian, operating in an environment where a fool can be called a fool and the motivations of ideological pimpery duly observed and noted."

> —George E. Reedy, former Special Assistant to President Lyndon B. Johnson

The inability of a succession of administrations since the late 1960s to rebuild a firm foreign policy consensus is not necessarily symptomatic of a failure to adapt to changing requirements, but it may represent an inexorable byproduct of the adaptive process. That is, in times of turbulence and rapid change, it is to be expected that contending interpretations of the patterns of change will be offered by various participants in the policy process, and conflicting policy options will be vigorously debated. The democratic practice of debate is no guarantee that policy alternatives which ultimately receive official sanction will embody wisdom, but to the extent that democratic practices are maintained, the opportunity is provided for at least subjecting policies to critical scrutiny, thereby making it possible for errors of fact and judgment to be recognized and corrected. As John Stuart Mill observed,

> Complete liberty of contradicting and disproving our opinion is the very condition which justifies us in assuming its truth for purposes of action. . . . If any opinion is compelled to silence, that opinion may, for aught we can certainly know, be true. To deny this is to assume our own infallibility.
>
> Secondly, though the silenced opinion be an error, it may, and very commonly does, contain a portion of truth; and since the general or prevailing opinion on any subject is rarely or never the whole truth, it is only by the collision of adverse opinions that the remainder of the truth has any chance of being supplied.
>
> Thirdly, even if the received opinion be not only true, but the whole truth; unless it is suffered to be, and actually is, vigorously and earnestly contested, it will, by most of those who receive it, be held in the manner of a prejudice, with little comprehension or feeling of its rational grounds.[1]

Presidential leadership is essential for mobilizing foreign policy consensus. Even more fundamentally, it is an essential ingredient of the process by which the political system adapts to changing global and domestic demands and opportunities. Leadership, like love, however, is a widely valued but poorly understood facet of human relationships. An effort to identify the requisites of presidential leadership, in particular, requires a consideration not only of the qualities and skills of those who assume the office of the presidency, but also of the nature of the office, of the institutional context within which policies are developed and executed, and of the policy challenges to be confronted.

164

THE NATURE OF PRESIDENTIAL LEADERSHIP

Being elected to the office of President serves as evidence that the incumbent has satisfied a plurality of voters that he or (before long) she has demonstrated the potential for presidential leadership, but assumption of the office is no guarantee that leadership will be exercised. As Richard Neustadt notes in the recent edition of his landmark study of the subject which is quoted at the outset of the chapter,

> A President, these days, is an invaluable clerk. His services are in demand all over Washington. His influence, however, is a very different matter. Laws and customs tell us little about leadership in fact.[2]

In other words, leadership is not something to which Presidents are entitled simply upon occupying the White House. Rather, as a popular TV commercial has John Houseman saying of money-making by an investment house, when presidents exercise leadership, they do it "the old fashioned way—they *earn* it." "Earning it" is rarely simple. As James MacGregor Burns defines "leadership" in a book exploring the subject in depth, it is "a reciprocal process of mobilizing . . . various economic, political, and other resources, in a context of competition and conflict, in order to realize goals independently or mutually held by both leaders and followers."[3]

The Burns definition is helpful in conceptualizing leadership in terms of several interrelated components: (1) leadership as a process; (2) reciprocity between leader and followers; (3) competition and conflict as the inevitable context; (4) the realization of both leader and follower goals as the objective of leadership; and (5) the mobilization of resources as the means to the end.

1. Leadership is, first of all a process of human interaction. Leadership is not usefully equated with whatever actions someone in authority (such as the President) takes; nor is it useful analytically to conceptualize leadership merely in terms of particular

human traits, such as "decisiveness" or "forceful personality." Such traits may be observable in particular instances of the exercise of leadership; but awareness of leadership as a process calls attention to the need to recognize that alternative traits may be crucial to the exercise of leadership under varying circumstances.

2. Leadership is not a one-way relationship; it is reciprocal, between a leader and his or her followers. Key determinants of the extent to which the President "leads" the nation are not only what the President says and does, but also how presidential statements and actions are perceived and interpreted. In short, what the public thinks and does are elements of the leadership equation. Presidential leadership of his advisors, of his party, of the bureaucracy, and of the Congress, in turn, and the leadership that the President brings to alliances of which the United States is a part, will be a function not merely of the style, approach, and techniques of the President but also of the initiatives and responses of these various constituencies.

3. The nature of politics is conflictual. The attainment of the policy preferences of some groups and individuals precludes the adoption of policy preferences of competing groups and individuals. Leadership is most vividly demonstrated not when a sizeable policy consensus prevails within the society, but rather when conflict over goals and values is intense. The exercise of presidential leadership is not simply the choosing of sides among competing interests, nor is it necessarily the adoption of policies that represent a perfect middle-ground between contending points of view. Rather, it is acting in ways that reflect a sensitivity to the diverse needs of various sectors of the society while mobilizing the nation's energies and resources on behalf of goals that the President has determined are essential.

4. Thus, the fourth component of leadership as identified by Burns is that of pursuing goals that will fulfill the needs of followers as well as those of leaders. Conceptualizing leadership in this way is to make a normative statement, one that distinguishes "leadership" from mere "manipulation," for instance, of followers for ends selected by the manipulator with little or no regard for the needs of followers. As applied to the American foreign policy process, the emphasis on follower as well as leader goals is to underscore the complexity of the challenge of presidential

leadership, which must seek to identify accurately the wishes of the members of an extremely heterogeneous society even as those members are called upon to support goals that may differ from their preferences.

5. Fifth, in order to realize leader and follower goals, a President must be able to mobilize the nation's resources and its skills and talents. No President, however knowledgeable and however vast the authority entrusted in him, can achieve this mobilization on his own. Essentially the task is one of organization in its broadest sense—assembling, structuring, coordinating, and energizing the human and physical components of the political and economic system in ways that will facilitate goal-attainment, and, of more fundamental importance, that will facilitate adaptation to the ever-changing demands of the world and domestic environments.

THE BUREAUCRATIC CHALLENGE

Optimally, the organizational apparatus of government facilitates foreign policy efficiency as well as effectiveness. "Effectiveness" refers to goal attainment, including adaptation to changing demands whereas "efficiency" is used here to refer to task accomplishment with the minimum waste of human and material resources.

For the past 200 years, the organizational task that American presidents have confronted has never been one of weaving from whole cloth. Rather, each president has inherited from his predecessors a set of institutions, procedures and, to a considerable extent, a group of civilian and military personnel trained in governmental operations. The challenge has been variously to streamline, to augment, to restructure, to revitalize the inherited machinery.

There are several interrelated elements of the organizational challenge: (1) managing organizational growth; (2) cultivating organizational norms, values, and traditions; (3) selection, promotion, and retention of foreign policy personnel; (4) structuring authority and communication within and among foreign policy organizations in ways that will promote effectiveness and efficiency; (5) gathering and utilizing foreign policy intelligence; and (6) development of procedures for making and implementing foreign policy decisions.

The first three of these tasks are discussed in the remainder of this chapter; the final three are discussed in Chapter 7. The discussion highlights the paradox of bureaucratic development: measures that have been taken in order to meet the organizational challenge, in response to a changing pattern of demands in the post-World War II environment, have in some important respects created new impediments to foreign policy effectiveness and efficiency.

To an important degree, the difficulties of meeting the organizational challenge were anticipated by the discussion in Chapter 2 of the gap between the real world of policy practice and the imaginary ideal of the IIMMP. Here those insights are applied more explicitly to the departments and agencies that constitute the foreign policy bureaucracy.

In the contemporary context, the focus is especially on the presidency, including the Office of Management and Budget, in relation to the departments of State and Defense, and the Central Intelligence Agency. Some historical perspective is useful, however, in viewing the current problems that these elements of foreign policy organization confront. In particular, it is helpful to understand the pattern of organizational growth and bureaucratization.

Bureaucratization has become a pejorative term used to describe a feature of modern life that many persons find annoying. However, as applied to a consideration of the historical evolution of the organizational structure of American foreign policy, bureaucratization may be seen as both inescapable and in important respects a positive rather than negative response to changing demands. On the other hand, the susceptibility of bureaucracy to various pathologies (several of which are identified below) also needs to be recognized by the student of foreign policy.

As noted by Max Weber, a scholarly pioneer who described the process of bureaucratization in ancient civilizations such as Egypt and in modern ones such as Great Britain, the process was an element of societal adaptation to increasingly complex demands. Bureaucracy represented the quest for rationality in problem solving, a quest that was often elusive and sometimes illusory.[4]

As applied explicitly to the evolution of the organizational apparatus involved in the formulation and execution of American foreign policy, bureaucratization represented an organizational adjustment to vastly changing demands (Table 6-1). The bureaucratic transformation and various problems and pathologies associated with it are evident along several organizational dimensions: growth and

TABLE 6-1 Idealized Goals and Actual Problems of Bureaucratization of Foreign Policy Institutions

	ORGANIZATIONAL SIZE AND COMPLEXITY	RECRUITMENT AND PROMOTION CRITERIA	ORGANIZATIONAL SUBCULTURE	INTELLIGENCE PRACTICES	STRUCTURE OF AUTHORITY AND COMMUNICATION	DECISION-MAKING PROCEDURES; POLICY EVALUATION AND LEARNING
Eighteenth–Nineteenth Century U.S. Foreign Policy Apparatus	Small, simple	Personalized, patronage	Generalist	Reliance on diplomats and citizens abroad	Decentralized and fluid	Ad hoc, tradition
Potential or Actual Weaknesses	Inadequate to demands on world power	Favoritism, incompetence	Amateurism, lack of expertise	Innocent of actions and intentions of devious adversary	Inconsistent, fragmented	Erratic, mistakes repeated
Idealized Gains from Twentieth Century Bureaucratization	Increased capability to cope with new demands	Impersonal, merit criteria	Specialization professionalization	Thorough, competitive edge	Clear, centralized control	SOPs, systematized, expeditious
Current Problems and Pathologies	Cumbersome, uncoordinated	Careerism	Parochialism, tunnel vision	Selective search, lack of accountability	Competitive, informal organization	Rigidities, dogmatic "lessons", groupthink

169

complexity, changing organizational subculture, systematized re-cruitment and promotion criteria, hierarchical authority and com-munications structure, standardized intelligence practices and deci-sion-making procedures.

ORGANIZATIONAL GROWTH AND COMPLEXITY

By comparison with the enormous bureaucracy that today is in-volved in the formulation and execution of United States foreign policy, the organizational structure that existed in the early days of the republic was tiny and simple. It is useful briefly to elaborate on the comparison.

THE HISTORICAL PATTERN OF GROWTH

During the early stages of the American war for independence, the major responsibility for making contact with other nation-states was delegated by the Continental Congress to a committee of five men. Termed initially the Committee of Secret Correspondence, the name was changed in 1777 to the Committee for Foreign Affairs. When by 1781 it was evident that the burden of interna-tional relations was too great for a small committee, the Continental Congress created a Department of Foreign Affairs, later (1789) redesignated the Department of State.

The first Secretary of Foreign Affairs (the title from 1781 to 1789), Robert R. Livingston, received an annual salary of $4,000 and was assisted by two under secretaries, a clerk, and an interpreter-translator. Even 120 years later, at the start of the twentieth cen-tury, there were fewer than 100 personnel assigned to the State Department in Washington, although the number of U.S. diploma-tic and consular personnel abroad had increased to more than 1,100. The number remained virtually unchanged, however, in the follow-ing four decades until the outbreak of World War II.

The war with Spain had given added foreign policy importance to the departments of War and Navy. However, the Army entered the war in 1898 with only 28,000 soldiers on active duty. Its ranks were expanded by volunteers and National Guard units during the war but cut back again when fighting ceased. Until war broke out in Europe fifteen years later, the army remained under 100,000. The Congress as well as a series of Presidents had become convinced of the need for naval expansion toward the end of the nineteenth century. However, although new battleships and heavy cruisers were under construction at the turn of the century, naval personnel numbered only 2,000 officers and 24,000 seamen.[5]

Moreover, personnel from the War and Navy Departments occupying positions in Washington from which they could exercise an influence on foreign policy were relatively few in number, and their structure more closely resembled that of separate fiefdoms than a tightly organized hierarchy. The War Department at the turn of the century, for instance, closely resembled the structure that had been created when John C. Calhoun was secretary of war after the War of 1812. Ten bureaus, with responsibilities for domains such as engineering, quartermaster, and medicine, operated with virtual autonomy (budgeted separately by the Congress) within the War Department.[6]

The War department was reorganized under Secretary of War Elihu Root in the first decade of the twentieth century, and the armed forces were expanded during World War I. At the end of the war, however, the armed forces were sharply reduced, and the foreign policy role of top-ranking military personnel and the civilian secretaries of the War and Navy Departments remained minimal.

Although a sizeable bureaucracy was created during the New Deal of the 1930s to carry out domestic programs, it was not until World War II that dramatic expansion of the foreign policy apparatus occurred. Nearly all of the increase occurred in war-related agencies. The State Department not only grew little during the war itself, but in relative terms it became relegated to a secondary position in many crucial policy decisions.

After the war, the State Department did experience growth. The armed forces, in contrast, were rapidly demobilized in the months immediately after the cessation of combat. Even before the outbreak of war in Korea in 1950, however, a growing emphasis on national security concerns, combined with the far-reaching demands upon the United States for the exercise of responsibilities in world affairs, were leading to an expansion and restructuring of the national security-related bureaucracy.

It is unnecessary to retrace the evolution of American foreign policy in the years since World War II. This was done in Chapters

4 and 5 with an emphasis on describing policy goals and the effort to define the national purpose in terms that could elicit and sustain a foreign policy consensus. Here the focus is simply on the organizational consequences in the 1980s of post-World War II increases in the size and complexity of the foreign policy bureaucracy.

THE CURRENT ORGANIZATIONAL STRUCTURE

In sharp contrast to the handful of persons that assisted Secretary Robert Livingston, today there are more than 8,000 State Department personnel stationed in the United States and nearly 6,000 other departmental personnel stationed abroad. The Department of Defense (DOD), which has assumed extraordinary importance in foreign policy since its establishment by a 1949 amendment to the National Security Act of 1947, is considerably larger. Approximately 2.1 million men and women serve in the Army, Navy, Marine Corps, and Air Force, the constituent units of the DOD. Although the number of personnel in the Central Intelligence Agency (also created by the National Security Act of 1947) is a government secret, it is estimated to be slightly larger than the total number employed by the State Department.

Even the President's immediate entourage has grown dramatically relative to the pre-World War II practice. In addition to advisors who are frequently in the public eye, such as the President's Counselor (later Attorney General-designate), Edwin Meese III, and the presidential Chief of Staff, James A. Baker III, the White House office under Ronald Reagan was operating with nearly one hundred assistants, deputy assistants, and special assistants with various specialized responsibilities. In contrast, when the White House office was formally created in the Franklin Roosevelt administration under the Reorganization Act of 1939, it consisted of three secretaries to the President, three administrative assistants, a personal secretary, and an executive clerk.

The complexity of the foreign policy structure is a function not simply of numbers of personnel and their various and sometimes overlapping responsibilities but also of the numbers of departments and agencies that participate in the foreign policy process. For instance, in addition to State and Defense, several of the other eleven cabinet-level departments have some important responsibilities in foreign policy, including Treasury, Commerce, Agriculture, and Energy. Even the Department of Interior has an Office of Territorial and International Affairs. The Department of Transportation, although committing much of its organizational resources to its responsibilities for federal highways, railways, and aviation administration, has important foreign-affairs responsibilities through the St. Lawrence Seaway Development Commission, the Maritime Administration, and the U.S. Coast Guard.

The executive office of the President also is deeply involved in the foreign policy process and now includes not only the White House office but also the Office of Management and Budget, the Council of Economic Advisors, the National Security Council and its staff, the Office of Policy Development, the Office of the United States Trade Representative, the Council on Environmental Quality, the Office of Science and Technology policy, and the Office of Administration. In addition, there are numerous bureaus or agencies with a status independent of departments and the executive office that play important foreign policy roles, notably including the Arms Control and Disarmament Agency, the Peace Corps, and the U.S. Information Agency (all in existence less than three decades).

The increased complexity of the bureaucracy has complicated the foreign policy process in various ways. Problems of policy coordination, communication, control, and information gathering are examined in Chapter 7. Here it is sufficient to note that every President at least since Franklin Roosevelt has had occasion to express his frustration with the sluggishness of the bureaucracy and its apparent unresponsiveness to his commands. At the height of the crisis of October 1962, for example, when John F. Kennedy and his advisors were seeking to design a course of action that would persuade the Soviet Union to withdraw missiles from Cuba, the President learned to his dismay that American Jupiter missiles targeted on the Soviet Union had remained in Turkey. The President had wanted American missiles removed because the liquid-fueled weapons had become technologically obsolete; he was furious at being caught in a position where their removal might become a demand which the Soviets would make as a condition for the removal of Soviet missiles from Cuba. Moreover, if American military action against missile installations in Cuba was required, the missiles in Turkey were highly vulnerable to a Soviet retaliatory attack. Kennedy was angry because five months earlier the State Department had been directed to contact the Turkish government and get the missiles removed. Moreover, when in August the President had learned that the ordered removal had not been effected, he again had personally directed that the missiles be removed. The State Department had failed to carry out the orders not because its personnel wished to have the missiles remain in Turkey, and certainly not out of an effort to sabotage presidential policies—but simply because the wheels of bureaucracy ground slowly, and resistance by the Turkish government to the removal of the missiles had led to delays that resulted in a major obstacle at the time of the Cuban crisis.[7]

POLICY MILIEU AND ORGANIZATIONAL SUBCULTURE

Increases in the number, size and complexity of the organizations that are involved in the foreign policy process define an important component of the change that has occurred in the structural context within which American foreign policy is formulated. In addition, one must note the change that has occurred in organizational milieux, with shifting priorities and policy perspectives. Of special interest is the emergence after World War II of national security as a "commanding idea" in the minds of policy makers.

PRE-WORLD WAR II POLICY ORIENTATION

Even into the 1930s, a sharp distinction tended to be made between the responsibilities of the War and Navy Departments for military affairs and the responsibility of the State Department for foreign policy. The Republican administrations of the 1920s that followed the wartime administration of the Democratic President, Woodrow Wilson, prided themselves on trimming the military establishment to the bone.[8] Isolationist fervor became intense. Domestic issues assumed still higher priority when Franklin Roosevelt assumed office at the onset of an economic depression, despite an awareness of strategic realities on Roosevelt's part that exceeded those of both his Republic predecessors and his Democratic Secretary of State.

Until late in his second term, Roosevelt's overriding preoccupation was with his New Deal program for economic recovery, and he was content to rely heavily on Secretary of State Cordell Hull in defining the orientation of American foreign policy.

Hull's outlook was archetypical of the "legalistic-moralistic approach to international problems" that George Kennan has described as a characteristic American weakness.[9] He believed, as had Wilson, that "power politics" in world affairs had become outmoded and that an enlightened spirit of peaceful negotiation could and must prevail.[10] Under his leadership, the State Department was expected to promote peace, such as through reciprocal trade agreements, not to prepare for distasteful contingencies that would require the commitment of American armed forces.

It was contrary to Hull's principles that the military should be included in the design of foreign policy. In the months following Germany's invasion of Poland in September 1939, however, President Roosevelt increasingly turned to military advisers to help him reshape American programs for possible involvement in war. Hull's resentment at the loss of exclusive prerogative for shaping foreign policy was increasingly expressed in the form of withdrawal from the arena of policy discussion. For example, he declined comment on proposals submitted by the military chiefs to the President in late 1940 calling for rearmament in the Pacific on the grounds that "the recommendations were of a technical military nature outside the proper field of his Department." And when the military delegation that had attended an Anglo-American conference to discuss joint strategic planning circulated its reports early in 1941, Hull refused to look at them.[11] After Pearl Harbor, he was virtually a nonparticipant in the strategic policy process.

For their part, American military officials in the interwar years had lamented the isolationist mood and feared the consequences of a policy of unpreparedness. Yet most of them adhered strongly to the traditional view that the military professional must have no concern for political matters nor should he have any voice in shaping policy beyond giving advice regarding issues of a narrowly technical military nature.[12]

The military viewpoint that was characteristic at the time was stated in authoritative terms by the Army Command and General Staff College:

> Politics and strategy are radically and fundamentally things apart. Strategy begins where politics ends. All that soldiers ask is that once the policy is settled, strategy and command shall be regarded as being in a sphere apart from politics.[13]

175

THE EMERGENCE OF NATIONAL SECURITY
AS A COMMANDING IDEA

World War II and especially American involvement after Pearl Harbor moved military professionals from the periphery to the center of the policy process and resulted in a radical alteration of views. Although the State Department under Cordell Hull tended to be shunted aside by the shift in emphasis to wartime concerns, other components of the civilian sector became far more involved than ever before in the policy process as a result of wartime mobilization.

Industrialists, many of whom had been held at arm's length during the peak New Deal years, became active in wartime production. Organized labor became involved in manpower planning and farmers in lend-lease programs. Thousands of academics moved into administrative and research assignments in government or into positions to assist in the design of military recruitment, testing, and training programs. Scientists, who traditionally had remained aloof from and wary of government, became heavily involved in wartime roles of crucial importance.[14]

It is not surprising that a key lesson almost universally drawn from the wartime experience by civilian and military officials alike was that the American response to the exigencies of the postwar era would require intelligence and policy coordination on a scale lacking early in the war (for example, at Pearl Harbor) but largely achieved by the war's end. A related lesson, for which Munich and Pearl Harbor were appropriate shorthands, was that democracies could never again afford to indulge in wishful military unpreparedness.[15]

However, the success achieved in World War II was not attributable to the armed forces alone—far from it. Only the integrated efforts of all sectors of government and the population as a whole had made success possible, and only comparable integration of effort could ensure security in the future. As Daniel Yergin has aptly observed, the concept of "national security" became a "commanding idea" in American postwar policy discussions, providing a framework for linking together otherwise disparate foreign policy concerns and giving a sense of urgency to policy discussions.[16]

The most important institutional manifestation of the "commanding idea" was the National Security Act of 1947. Under provisions of the act, the armed forces were unified (albeit loosely) under a secretary of defense (as of 1949 the Department of Defense). The collective wisdom of the various service chiefs was to continue to be available to the President, as it had been during the war, through formalization of the Joint Chiefs of Staff (JCS). Intelligence gathering was to be coordinated by a Central Intelligence Agency (CIA). A National Security Resources Board, a Munitions Board, and a Research and Development Board, respectively, were to institutionalize the means whereby the skills of scientists, engineers, economists, industrialists, and others from the civilian sector could be brought to bear on issues affecting the nation's security. (None of these three bodies survived subsequent reorganization.) Finally, to provide the President with a top-level advisory body that represented leadership of the key departments involved in national security matters and that drew on the intelligence provided by the CIA, the National Security Council (NSC) was created.

The organizational structure created by the act, although certainly not an inevitable outcome of postwar planning in its specific content, was a highly predictable outcome in terms of general scope and purposes. As explained by James Forrestal, the key architect of the act, in testimony supporting it, "The complexity of the modern world, the telescoping of the factors of time and space, require the closest relationship possible between our military and our national policy-making organizations—that is, between the War and Navy Departments and the Department of State."[17]

An effective military establishment was the keystone of a successful national security policy, and some civilians—notably those in the State Department who had experienced the muffling of their voices relative to those of the military during the war—feared military dominance of the national security apparatus. What is notable about the National Security Act, however, is not the prominence given to the military role in policymaking but rather the prominence given to civilians as key advisers to the President in national security matters. All of the statutory members of the NSC were (and are) civilians, with the Joint Chiefs of Staff in turn serving as advisers to the NSC. Civilians headed the National Security Resources Board, the Munitions Board, and the Research and Development Board. The CIA was an important exception to the pattern, with a military man selected as its head, although large numbers of persons in key positions in the agency were civilians. The armed forces were subordinate not only to the President as commander-in-chief but also to a civilian secretary of defense and civilian secretaries of the three principal arms of service. The secretary of defense, in turn, was prohibited by provisions of the Act of 1947 from having his own military staff.

Moreover, there were related developments with the creation of largely civilian-staffed organizations conducting analyses pertinent to national security affairs. These included the Air Force sponsored Rand Corporation, the Operations Research Office of the Army, the Navy's Operations Evaluation Group, and the General Advisory Committee of the Atomic Energy Commission. Civilians thereby began to shape strategic doctrine and military planning to a degree that had been unthinkable in the prewar era.

ORGANIZATIONAL SUBCULTURE
AND THE RISK OF GROUPTHINK

In short, contrary to the fears of some persons in the early postwar years, the policy structure that was created was not one dominated by the military establishment. However, the structure, which in its basic elements remains intact, did represent an institutional commitment to national security as a "commanding idea." Moreover, as noted in Chapter 4, American policy makers in the early post-World War II years became preoccupied with the struggle with Soviet-led communism. The commitment to national security became an intensely ideological commitment to anticommunism, with domestic overtones that had not only a chilling effect upon public discourse but also some devastating repercussions upon foreign policy institutions. Intimidated by allegations by Senator Joseph McCarthy and others that the "fall of China" to Communism in 1949 was attributable to the infestation of the Foreign Service with Communist sympathizers, top officials in the Truman administration and later the Eisenhower administration effectively purged the State Department of its China experts.[18] Foreign policy personnel who remained in the government learned from the McCarthy-era experience the risks of expressing controversial views, and conversely, the career benefits of caution and adherence to prevailing norms and attitudes that are associated with the organizational "operational code".

Richard Barnet's description of the "operational code" that

evolved among "national security managers," civilian as well as military, in the early post-World War II years usefully calls attention to elements of commonality among participants in the foreign policy process.[19] However, it is also important to recognize differences in perspective among policy participants that are explicable in terms of variations in "organizational subcultures". The term, "subculture," is used here to refer to the values, traditions, beliefs, and sometimes even sense of élan that, for its members, define an organization's character and purpose.

In order for an organization to function effectively, it needs to cultivate the identification of its members with organizational goals and practices. Optimally, the result is a sense of organizational loyalty and esprit that inspires individuals within the organization to a heightened sense of commitment to the tasks at hand.

For example, Theodore Sorensen observed of "the Kennedy team," the men selected to work closely together in key advisory roles to President John F. Kennedy,

> They were, like him, dedicated but unemotional. . . . There were no crusaders, fanatics or extremists from any camp; all were nearer the center than either left or right. All spoke with the same low-keyed restraint that marked their chief, yet all shared his deep conviction that they could change America's drift. They liked government, they liked politics, they liked Kennedy and they believed implicitly in him. Their own feelings of pride— *our* feelings, for I was proud to be one of them—could be summed up in a favorite Kennedy passage from Shakespeare's *King Henry V* in his speech on the St. Crispin's Day battle: " . . . we . . . shall be remembered—We few, we happy few, we band of brothers . . . And gentlemen . . . now abed Shall think themselves accurs'd they were not here."[20]

The risk of "team spirit" in a policy body, however, is the fostering of conformity and a resultant reduction of the willingness or capacity of individuals to bring critical judgment to bear on prevailing assumptions and policy preferences. In short, as Irving Janis puts it, the risk is one of "groupthink."[21]

Winning and retaining the esteem of one's organizational colleagues makes one sensitive to cues regarding the range of behavior and viewpoints that are acceptable in various situations. Nearly 80 percent of the 580 members of the U.S. Foreign Service Corps who were surveyed some years ago indicated that "winning respect of colleagues in the Corps" was a factor that they considered crucial to their success. None of another fifteen factors rated in terms of importance to success in the Foreign Service received a high rating by such a substantial portion of the FSO sample.[22] Doubtless similar findings would emerge from a survey of career personnel in the armed forces, in the CIA, and in other sectors of the foreign policy structure.

Just as "groupthink" can result from the desire of members of a group or organization to be considered good "team members," so parochialism in policy discussions with representatives of other organizations can be fostered. Biases stemming from organizational affiliation and loyalty have been evident in the American foreign policy process not only on the part of representatives of the major organizational participants, such as State, DOD, and CIA, but even within such organizations among representatives of various subordinate units (for example, Army, Navy, Air Force, and Marine Corps within DOD).

A useful shorthand for explaining the policy parochialism and bias that are attributable to organizational affiliation and role is Miles's Law: "Where you stand depends upon where you sit." That is, a familiar tendency of bureaucratic behavior, highlighted in Graham Allison's important study of the action of various key actors in the Cuban Missile Crisis, is for individuals to advocate policy positions or to carry out their policy responsibilities in ways that reflect the narrow concerns or standard operating procedures of the organizations that they represent. For example, representatives of the CIA argued with those of the Air Force over which organization should assume responsibility for flights of U-2 intelligence aircraft over Cuba during the crisis. The Air Force view prevailed (in U-2s that the CIA controlled), but only after a delay of several days while the interdepartmental squabble was being resolved.[23]

Of course, the student of foreign policy must be wary of drawing inferences about probable policy behavior on the basis of facile observations about organizational interests and role stereotypes. In a careful study of foreign policy crises dating from before the Korean War through the period of the deepest American involvement in Vietnam, Richard Betts found, contrary to stereotypical views, that top U.S. military advisors to the President were no more likely than were top civilian advisors to advocate the use of force to resolve the crises.

Betts's study demonstrates that Miles's Law must be applied with care, not that it must be discarded. Consistent with Miles's Law, Betts found that once a policy decision to commit force had been made, the preference of military advisor tended to be for "quickly, massively, and decisively" extending the military commitment.[24]

ORGANIZATIONAL PAROCHIALISM AND TUNNEL VISION

The influence which one's organizational ties has on one's behavior can lead to "tunnel vision." In his assessment of national policy needs, and thus in the policy advice that he renders, the organizational chauvinist is apt to attach undue importance to the organization's mission, doctrine, and technology. A vivid example of such behavior was provided during the several decades leading up to World War II by spokesmen of the horse cavalry. The horse cavalry was maintained as an elite combat element of the U.S. Army throughout this period, despite technological developments such as the rapid-fire machine gun and long-range artillery, which dramatically increased the vulnerability of the cavalry, and despite innovations such as the tank and fighter and reconnaissance aircraft, which persuaded critics that the horse cavalry was obsolete. In the United States, as in Europe where the longevity of such units also was remarkable, the horse cavalry was essentially "a club, an exclusive one, made up at the officer level of those who could afford to ride when young, hunt, dress, and play polo when older."[25]

Similarly, airborne units of Army paratroopers, having attained prominence and prestige during World War II, became elite elements of the U.S. Army during the Cold War years. Despite mounting evidence that parachute drops of sizeable units would sustain unacceptably high levels of casualties in modern warfare, given the availability of mobile defenses to an adversary, airborne proponents continued to press with some success for the training and equipping of large numbers of jump-qualified airborne personnel.[26]

The 1970 ceremony in which General William Westmoreland, Army chief of staff, received his "wings" as a helicopter pilot, symbolized a shift in organizational status away from airborne qualification to helicopter credentials. Westmoreland had emerged in the early post-World War II years as one of the most promising of a crop of prestigious airborne-qualified officers, at a time when helicopter pilots tended to be "marginal men" in the Army, their role seen as peripheral to the Army combat mission. Especially after the Korean War, however, the Army attached growing importance to the helicopter, not only as an instrument of combat mobility, but also as a symbol of their desire to retain an aviation capability independent of that provided by the Air Force. By the early 1970s, the Army's struggle for its own aviation capability had succeeded to the point that there were more pilots on active duty in the Army than there were in the Air Force. The Army maintained 12,000 aircraft, including 3,500 helicopters in Vietnam alone, giving it control of the world's third largest fleet of aircraft—only the U.S. and Soviet air forces had more planes. Whether this growth, which was centered on the helicopter-assault concept, was fully justified in terms of military requirements or whether the now command-supported Army aviation subculture had been engaging in empire-building was a question that troubled some members of Congress and some critics within the military establishment.[27]

If specialists in particular technologies gain dominance in the key leadership positions within an organization, the policy orientation of the entire organization is likely to take on the hue of the subordinate element, as the enthusiasm of Army leaders by 1970 for the helicopter assault concept illustrated. Similarly, whereas the policy advice provided by top naval personnel before World War II reflected the paramount position of admirals whose careers had been built through service on battleships, so the shift in policy orientation in the postwar years reflected the ascendancy of submariners and, to an even greater degree, naval aviators.[28]

When the Air Force became an independent arm in 1947, the dominant elite group within the force consisted of bomber pilots. As a detailed study by Perry Smith has shown, the strategic mission of bomber units had provided a more powerful argument for independence of the Air Force from the Army than had other missions, such as tactical support of ground forces or aerial reconnaissance.[29] Thus, bomber pilots, assigned to the Strategic Air Command (SAC), became key advocates of a strategic bombing capability as the core element of an American deterrence strategy. However, as policy emphasis at the presidential level shifted (beginning in the second Eisenhower administration and continuing more dramatically in the Kennedy administration) away from a "massive retaliation" strategy to "flexible response" to a variety of conflict contingencies, the organizational status of SAC within the Air Force and within DOD declined somewhat.[30]

Similar fluctuations in the fortunes of rival subcultures within the CIA are discernible. Former CIA agent Victor Marchetti and his coauthor, John Marks, distinguish between CIA personnel who are engaged in conventional roles of intelligence collection and analysis, and those who are engaged in "covert action" abroad. Writing in the mid-1970s, the authors argued that the agency had become dominated by the latter subculture to the point that clandestine activity was a virtual cult. The policy significance of the trend, according to the authors, was that the:

". . . clandestine mentality" is a mindset that thrives on secrecy and deception. It encourages professional amorality—the belief that righteous goals can be achieved through the use of unprincipled and normally unacceptable means.[31]

William Colby, who became Director of the CIA during the Ford administration, has described a similar trend, but with greater differentiation. From its inception, Colby contends, "the CIA constituted a loose confederation of three compartmented and competing 'cultures'."[32]

Of the staff of eighty persons who came to the CIA when it was created in 1947 to take the place of a Central Intelligence Group, which had operated under Presidential authority for the previous year, most were well-educated specialists in research and analysis.

Second, there was a "CA" (covert action) subculture, composed of specialists in psychological warfare and propaganda and in bringing American influence to bear on political activities in other countries. It was this section of the CIA, for instance, that was especially active in support of anticommunist candidates in the 1948 elections in Italy and throughout the Cold War in supporting anti-Soviet propaganda in Eastern Europe. In the 1980s, the CA portion of the CIA would become instrumental in supporting guerrilla forces in Soviet-dominated Afghanistan.

Third, an "FI" (foreign intelligence) subculture within the organization consisted of those persons assigned to the Office of Special Operations, which was charged with espionage and counterespionage abroad. Colby asserts that by the Nixon years, it was the FI subculture that was dominant within the CIA. Whereas more than 50% of the CIA's highly classified budget had been allocated to covert action in the 1950s and 1960s, CA funding had dropped below 5% of the total by the 1970s (although the Pentagon had assumed responsibility for much covert activity that previously had been the responsibility of the CIA).[33]

Another trend, which resulted in the emergence of a "technician subculture," was the increased reliance on electronic listening devices and other features of advanced technology for intelligence gathering. Beginning as early as the late 1950s, U-2 planes capable of high-altitude photography were gathering information over the Soviet Union and other territory. With further technological advances such as the successful launching of satellites into earth orbit, CIA officials such as Colby and his predecessors as director, John McCone and James Schlesinger, became convinced of the growing importance of technological expertise. Crucial to policy concerns such as the verification of arms control agreements, by the 1980s electronic intelligence-gathering had become a key element of CIA activity.[34]

In the State Department, organizational mores, values, and policy perspectives tend to reflect the outlook of members of the core elite, the Foreign Service. As noted by Andrew Scott,

> The starting point for understanding the Department lies in an appreciation of the nature and dominance of the Foreign Service corps. . . . To discuss the operation of the Department of State without considering the role of the subculture is like trying to explain tidal change without reference to the role of the moon.[35]

John E. Harr, himself the author of a detailed study of the State Department and Foreign Service, has observed that analysis of subculture of the type provided by Scott in the articles cited provides "a powerful explanatory tool for understanding the pathology of the State Department."

> One begins to understand that repeated attempts at reorganization are frustrated because the basic problem is cultural rather than organizational. One begins to understand why there is no vigorous policy debate within the Department, why the Department seems so sluggish and unimaginative, why the considerable power of the Secretary of State is so limited within the Department, why the Department "comes fairly close to being an institution without an organizational memory," why there is "about a twenty-year lag in adjusting to foreign policy realities," why the Department is unable to examine its own strengths and weaknesses, why it is so hostile to research.[36]

As if to disprove the Scott-Harr contention that the department was unable to reform itself, in 1969 Secretary of State William P. Rogers and other top departmental officials commissioned thirteen task forces, charged with studying various facets of departmental practices and procedures, and providing reports that highlighted strengths and weaknesses and recommended changes. The Rogers initiative had come not only in response to the call from President Nixon for "a decade of governmental reform" [sic], but also in response to pressures for change from "Young Turk" members of the department who had gained control of the American Foreign Service Association.

The report most germane to the present discussion of organizational subculture was that of Task Force VII, charged with examining creativity within the department. The assessment was highly critical:

> The Task Force was forced to the conclusion that conformity is prized in the Foreign Service above all other qualities. Its record in this regard may be no worse than that of other bureaucratic organizations but it is nonetheless unsatisfactory. The pressures to avoid rocking the boat, to avoid dress and behavior which depart from the norms of the group, to avoid the expression of controversial views are of the subtle, unspoken kind which are hard to document. But we have the testimony of a broad cross section of the officers whose views we sought that they are a powerful, all-pervasive influence. Such pressures, of course, are the death of the creative impulse. [37]

Although strongly recommending change, the report on behalf of the twenty-one members of Task Force VII expressed skepticism about the receptivity of top departmental leadership to meaningful change, despite having solicited the recommendations. [38] There was solid basis for such skepticism. Queried in 1974 about what had been done to put into effect the far-reaching proposals for change that had been made in the 1970 task force reports, a senior departmental official admitted candidly, "zilch". [39] While perhaps an unduly cynical appraisal of a process of change that has continued into the 1980s at a tortuously incremental pace, the remark nevertheless aptly summarized the sentiments of those within the department who had hoped that deep-rooted patterns and habits might be altered more significantly.

INTERORGANIZATIONAL RIVALRY

One area of activity where the department already had made changes was that of interdepartmental cooperation. Given the necessity for close working relationships with the Defense Department, in particular, in the post-World War II era, the State Department had taken various measures to help ensure that effective channels of communication were established. Each year, some State Department personnel were assigned to the Pentagon in liaison roles (with the Defense Department reciprocating). In addition, mid-career professionals from State were sent to the year-long program of instruction at each of the war colleges of the armed services. These practices continue in the 1980s.

However, not only in policy discussions including State and Defense but also in those among other departments and even within departments, the tendency is to view foreign policy requirements from the perspective of the organizational subculture. Especially if policy advisors represent organizations that are competing with one another for scarce resources, one can expect organizational parochialism to be displayed in virulent form. An instructive example was provided in response to President Truman's imposition of stringent ceilings on defense budgets in the years before the outbreak of the Korean War, pitting the armed services against one another in a struggle for funds. The ensuing dispute between the Navy and the Air Force was particulary bitter.

An important concern of naval aviators, who as noted above were becoming a dominant subculture in the Navy, was that the postwar elevation of the Air Force to the status of an independent arm of service would result in the amalgamation of naval aviation into the air force. Even if such merger could be prevented, could the Navy make an adequate case for support of its mission, with strategic airpower enthusiasts arguing that decisive to the outcome of the next war would be an American capability to strike at the heartland of the adversary with nuclear weapons? Given these concerns, naval leaders argued the importance of the modern flush-deck aircraft carrier from which, it was claimed, naval aircraft could carry the decisive blow to the enemy heartland.

Air Force spokesmen, in turn, led by the SAC elite, argued the necessity of a 70-group air force (each air-group consisting of several thousand planes and support personnel).

Although details of the Navy–Air Force rivalry in the late 1940s are now of but historical interest, the resulting poisoning of the policy atmosphere is worth noting. Barbed public addresses were made by admirals purporting to have evidence of the severe limitations of B-36 aircraft (then the centerpiece of SAC). Widely publicized articles sharply critical of naval aviation were written (by authors whom, many naval personnel believed, had been commissioned by the air force). Classified memoranda within the Pentagon that advocated particular policy positions for the purpose of strengthening the bargaining position of one service or the other were leaked to the press. By 1949, the Congress felt required to launch a full-scale investigation into the charges and countercharges. The results, while far from satisfying advocates of either service fully, at least tempered the interservice controversy. Some but not all of the funding for aircraft carriers was restored, while most but not all of the appropriations for the Air Force were provided that its proponents had requested.[40]

Internecine rivalry within the foreign policy bureaucracy is by no means peculiar to the military, nor is it a phenomenon that was peculiar to the 1940s and 1950s. For example, John M. Collins, who served for thirty years in the U.S. Army before joining the Library of Congress as a senior specialist in defense matters, has described a pattern of friction between the State Department and the Defense Department that continues into the 1980s. Although periods of relatively close interdepartmental cooperation are noted, such as the Korean War period and the period 1977–1980 during the Carter years, there have been numerous periods of bureaucratic infighting and intense competition. "Open warfare" is the term Collins uses to describe relations between State and Defense during the Reagan administration when State was headed by retired Army general Alexander Haig and DOD was headed by Caspar Weinberger. The same term is applied to interdepartmental relations during Henry Kissinger's stint as Secretary of State under President Nixon, when James Schlesinger (subsequently fired by President Ford) was Secretary of Defense.[41]

In short, interorganizational rivalry remains a recurring phenomenon in policy discussions, especially during annual budget negotiations between departments and the White House, as represented by the Office of Management and Budget (OMB). However, such rivalry must be understood not merely as the pursuit of vested organizational interests in the acquisition and accumulation of resources, but also as a common form of policy myopia. In testimony preparatory to being confirmed by the Senate as President Eisenhower's Secretary of Defense, Charles E. Wilson, who had served as president General Motors, explained away any potential conflict of interest with the assertion that he had long believed that "what was good for the country was good for General Motors, *and vice versa.*"[42] Wilson's assertion that the interests of GM were synonymous with those of America was ridiculed by critics as being extraordinarily arrogant or perhaps naive. But in fact, the tendency to confuse the national interest with the interests of the organization or groups with which one is affiliated is a familiar one.

THE PRESIDENT AND
INTERORGANIZATIONAL COMPETITION

The organizational imperative to seek to be indispensable to the President in the formulation of policy accentuates the tendency to translate organizational preferences into national priorities. The President's role both as the object of organizational attention and as a determinant of the outcome of interorganizational competition is illustrated by the struggle in recent years between advocates of arms control measures such as SALT II and advocates of increased defense spending.[43]

There are, of course, proprieties to be observed in bureaucratic infighting. No one in a position of responsibility in government can retain his or her claim to be humane and express total opposition to arms control agreements. Conversely, no one can retain the claim to being a patriotic American and oppose the maintenance of "sufficient" military strength. However, whereas all participants to policy discussions are likely to aver a concern both for adequate armed strength and for arms control, the differences among participants are notable. Such differences are evident in contrasting assumptions that are made about the nature and magnitude of threats to the American national security that exist, about the adequacy of the U.S. deterrent capability and the utility of particular additions to that capability, about the probable effectiveness of alternative diplomatic strategies in bargaining with the Soviet Union, and about the reliability and verifiability of agreements reached with the Soviets.

ACDA, THE PENTAGON, AND THE CIA   The contrasting assumptions tend to have their roots in competing organizational subcultures that vary from one policy organization to another. Of particular interest in recent arms control-defense policy debates have been differences among the Arms Control and Disarmament Agency (ACDA), the Defense Department (the Pentagon, for short), and the CIA.

The ACDA was created at the outset of the Kennedy administration as a symbol of American resolve to bring to a halt the nuclear arms race, beginning with the cessation of nuclear weapons tests (which had brought widespread opproprium worldwide). Throughout most of its history, ACDA has been characterized by an organizational ethos that stresses the importance of arms control as a national goal, an ethos sustained by the conviction that ways can and must be found to reach an agreement with the Soviet Union for the reduction of strategic arms and by the belief that the Soviets are unlikely to be brought to the bargaining table by crash programs of defense spending for the purpose of amassing "bargaining chips" to play in the negotiation process.

Conversely, the Pentagon has been a citadel for advocates of the imperative of American military preparedness. Such advocates have tended to be dubious about the desire of Soviet leadership to enter into or adhere to meaningful and verifiable arms control agreements and have pointed to American defense reductions in the 1970s, while the Soviets were increasing their military commitment, as evidence of the need in the 1980s to revive the traditional lesson that "the best way to maintain the peace is to be adequately prepared for war."

The prevalent policy outlook in the CIA regarding defense and arms control is more difficult to discern, largely because of the secrecy that is maintained but also because of fluctuations that have come to light with leadership changes. Of course, any generalizations about organizational doctrine and outlook must be tempered with the observation that within the CIA, ACDA, the Pentagon, and other governmental agencies a diversity of viewpoints can be found. The concept of organizational "subculture" refers to modal values and beliefs; it is not intended as an all-encompassing portrait. Moreover, as noted above, large organizations often contain rival subcultures within them.

CONTRASTING PRIORITIES OF CARTER AND REAGAN   Furthermore, through his actions, pronouncements, and appointments to office, the President may reinforce modal organizational values and beliefs or help to undermine them. That is, a President may take advantage of the policy orientation that prevails in a given organization in order to emphasize particular policy commitments of his own; or he may seek to effect change within an organization, countering whatever threat prevailing values and beliefs might present to his own policy preferences. The contrasting approaches of Presidents Carter and Reagan, in pursuit of opposing policy objectives, illustrate the point. Jimmy Carter sought to reinforce traditional ACDA subcultural values with his appointments in order to strengthen the institutional support for arms control. Ronald Reagan, convinced that false expectations regarding peaceful relations with the Soviets had been aroused by the arms control emphasis of his predecessors, sought to alter the ACDA subculture through replacing key personnel with appointees who shared his conviction that arms control must be subordinated to the policy goal of strengthening American defenses.

Carter entered the White House pledged to effect a major reduction in the nuclear arsenals of the superpowers and to bring to a successful conclusion the Strategic Arms Limitations Talks (SALT II) that had begun under his predecessor. The appointment of Paul Warnke as Director of ACDA and as chief SALT II negotiator symbolized the commitment and tended to reinforce the traditional ACDA ethos. Warnke was a controversial appointee, however, precisely because his well-known commitment to arms control was interpreted by a substantial number of critics, including influential Democrats such as Senator Henry "Scoop" Jackson, as evidence that he was "soft" at a time when "toughness" with the Soviets was needed.

Harold Brown, Carter's designate as Secretary of Defense, had credentials that were reassuring to the defense community in his previous experience as secretary of the Air Force and as director of defense research and engineering. However, he also had expressed his strong support for arms control as a delegate to the SALT negotiations and thus could exert leverage in mobilizing Pentagon support for Carter's arms control policies.

At the head of the CIA, Carter placed his Annapolis classmate,

Admiral Stansfield Turner, whose military credentials presumably could appease "hawkish" critics while Turner's well-known reputation as a defense intellectual could be helpful in making a reasoned case for arms control.

Ronald Reagan's views of defense requirements and arms control contrasted sharply with those of Jimmy Carter (although by his final year in office, Carter had retreated sharply from his early arms control posture and was calling for major increases in defense spending). During the 1980 presidential campaign, Reagan had termed SALT II a "fatally flawed" agreement that must be discarded. Moreover, for years he had been warning that the Soviets were making ominous strides in developing a strategic nuclear war capability and urging that the United States greatly expand its defense commitment.

An important outlet for Reagan's views in the mid-to-late 1970s had been the Committee on the Present Danger (CPD), a political interest group committed to increasing public awareness of the mounting Soviet threat and to increasing American capabilities to meet the threat. Eugene Rostow and Paul Nitze, co-founders of the CPD, were early appointees when Reagan became President, Rostow as Director of ACDA, Nitze as head of the American team to negotiate with the Soviets over control of intermediate-range nuclear forces (INF) in Europe. Vice President George Bush also was a CPD member. Other CPD-affiliated appointees to the Reagan team included Secretary of State Alexander Haig, Secretary of Defense Caspar Weinberger, Presidential Advisor for National Security Affairs Richard Allen, CIA Director William Casey, and numerous under secretaries, assistant secretaries, and other officials.

The Reagan appointments also represented the endorsement of the Team B assessment of Soviet strategic capabilities and intentions. During the Ford administration, CIA assessments of Soviet capabilities had been so consistently cautious that critics such as those affiliated with the CPD complained that the government was dangerously underestimating the danger. George Bush, Ford's CIA Director, was persuaded to appoint a team of consultants (Team B) to review the evidence that those within the CIA formally charged with analyzing the Soviet threat (Team A) had used, and to arrive at their own conclusions. The consultants, which included Richard Pipes, Lieutenant General Daniel Graham, Paul Nitze, and William Van Cleave, produced a report that depicted the situation as much more ominous than that portrayed by Team A. The Soviets not only had been making massive strides in developing their nuclear and missile-delivery capability but also were said to be basing their plans on the assumption that the Soviet Union could survive and win a nuclear war.

The gist of the Team B report was leaked to the press on the eve of Carter's 1976 election victory, providing leverage for critics who charged that Carter's policies were leaving the nation unprepared in the face of obvious peril. In time, President Carter did alter policy priorities sharply away from arms control in the direction of defense increases. From early to mid-1979, Carter attempted to satisfy both arms control proponents and those who favored "beefing up" America's military strength. He agreed to demands for increases in the defense budget as a means of trying to ensure Senate ratification of the SALT II treaty. After the Soviet invasion of Afghanistan at the end of 1979, however, Carter himself ordered the SALT II treaty withdrawn from consideration by the Senate and effectively abandoned his hopes for arms control in favor of increased emphasis on defense. However, it was the 1980 Reagan election victory that not only represented the full policy accommodation of Team B assumptions but also the incorporation of most Team B members into key roles in the new administration.

An interesting postscript to the Team A-Team B drama was provided late in 1983 when a new CIA report revised downward the estimate of Soviet military strength. Whereas the CIA had come to accept the Team B estimate that Moscow had been increasing its military expenditures by an alarming rate of 4 to 5 percent annually since the mid-1970s, the 1983 report indicated that the increase had been only 2 percent annually, with defense expenditures as a percentage of economic growth remaining stable over the period.[44]

RECRUITMENT AND PROMOTION OF FOREIGN POLICY PERSONNEL

Organizational subcultures are the product in part of the assigned "mission" that distinguishes one department or agency from another and defines its raison d'être. In part, subcultures also reflect the customs, procedures, and traditions that have evolved over time.

However, as the experience of the Carter and Reagan Administrations indicates, a President can reinforce or counter organizational subcultures with his key appointments. Moreover, even in the absence of presidential influence, the evolution of subcultures is partly the product of the types and outlooks of individuals who have been attracted to, or sought out for, and retained by the organization. That is, an organizational subculture is likely to be the product of prevailing patterns of recruitment, self-selection, promotion, and retention. It follows that as recruitment, promotion, and retention criteria change, organizational subcultures will change. The American foreign policy experience provides some vivid examples of this process.

RECRUITMENT, PROMOTION, AND RETENTION TRENDS

The historical trend in recruitment, in promotion, and retention patterns in the American foreign-policy bureaucracy resembles the bureaucratic ideal in important respects. There has been an increasing application of merit criteria to recruitment into and advancement within career positions in the military and civilian components of the foreign policy bureaucracy. For example, virtually all of the general officers who served in the American army at the time of the war with Mexico in 1845 were political appointees to these high-ranking positions; many had no previous military experience. However, the professionalization of the American armed forces already was underway, with the middle ranks of officers largely filled with career officers. Thus, by the time of the Civil War, both Union and Confederate Armies included general officers such as Ulysses S. Grant and Robert E. Lee who had begun their military careers at the Military Academy at West Point and who subsequently had served continuously as officers, promoted on the basis of a systematic review of their performance at each level.[45]

Continued evidence of professionalization in each of the armed services was provided by the expansion of a program of systematic education and training for career military personnel, with the founding of command and staff colleges and war colleges late in the nineteenth century, by the development of professional journals within which career military personnel published the results of strategic and historical studies and exchanged ideas, and by increasingly systematized methods for assignment and promotion.

193

Particularly in the period since World War II, the armed forces have created a specialized bureaucracy devoted exclusively to the management of careers of military personnel. Detailed personnel files are maintained on each individual, including annual performance ratings by supervisory personnel. Assignments are made taking into account the preferences of the individuals to be assigned, their previous experience and qualifications for particular tasks, and the needs for the service. When after a specified number of years in grade an individual becomes eligible for promotion, especially appointed boards of officers review the records of those eligible and make selections.

Similarly, the professionalization of diplomatic service in the State Department, which had begun early in the twentieth century, was given impetus and legal sanction with the passage of the Rogers Act in 1924. By this act, the Diplomatic Service and the Consular Service were combined into the Foreign Service of the United States, entry into which required successful passage of an examination and satisfactory performance during a probationary period.[46] By the post-World War II period, applicants had to pass a day-long written examination before becoming eligible for an oral interview, after which successful applicants were subjected to background checks and medical examinations. Those who cleared these hurdles entered the foreign service on probationary status.

In some respects, the most dramatic change has come in the recruitment of intelligence specialists. From the Revolutionary War period throughout the nineteenth century, intelligence gathering and analysis were done on an ad hoc basis, typically by diplomatic personnel. During World War I, the Army and Navy maintained small intelligence organizations. Important expansion came during World War II, not only of the intelligence components of the armed services but even more significantly with the creation of the Office of Strategic Services (OSS).[47]

Only with the initiation of a Central Intelligence Agency in 1947, however, can one really speak of career professionals in the American intelligence field. Subsequent to that act, recruitment into and promotion within the CIA have been systematized along the lines of foreign service recruitment and promotion.

Although the historical trend toward professionalization of recruitment and promotion practices in the civilian as well as military components of the foreign policy apparatus is significant, three important qualifications to the generalization must be noted: (1) Important discrepancies are evident even at junior levels in the application of objective, impersonal recruitment and promotion criteria; (2) at the level of selection to executive positions in the policy hierarchy, ascriptive criteria have continued to be employed; (3) the results in practice of applying achievement criteria (e.g., formal examinations) often are less distinguishable from the results in applying ascriptive criteria (e.g., patronage) than one might think.

DISCREPANCIES IN APPLYING ACHIEVEMENT CRITERIA

JUNIOR AND MID-LEVEL RECRUITMENT AND PROMOTION

The most obvious exception to the historical trend toward the recruitment of civilian and military personnel for positions in the foreign policy apparatus purely on the basis of their qualifications to perform assigned tasks is that until quite recently, most positions were available only to men, and among men, only to those of white extraction.

Blacks served in the American armed forces in every war beginning with the American Revolution, but throughout much of American history they were denied admission to officer ranks. Beginning with the Reconstruction Era, entrance to West Point was available to blacks who could obtain a congressional or presidential appointment. However, it was not until 1877 that the first black (Ossian Flipper) graduated from West Point, having successfully endured the harassment to which he was subjected.[48] Blacks such as Lieutenant Flipper who did become officers were only permitted to command all-black units.

By the time of World War I, a black officer had risen to the rank of full colonel. However, even though he rode a horse from his home in Ohio to Washington, D.C. to demonstrate the fallacy of the allegation that he was not physically equipped for combat command, he was retired from the service without being given the command or the promotion that came with it. Until late in World War II, black officers had similar experiences, and black units were kept from engaging in combat despite their appeals to do so in order to demonstrate their courage and patriotism (and thus their basis for enjoying the full rights of citizenship).[49]

The integration of the armed forces by presidential order began during the Truman administration. It was not until the 1960s, however, that the government began a concerted effort at affirmative action to rectify the inequities of opportunity in recruitment into and promotion within the officer ranks. The affirmative action programs were directed not only at the recruitment and promotion of blacks, but also as other minorities that had experienced discrimination, such as native Americans, Hispanic Americans and Asian-Americans.

The historical pattern of recruitment, promotion, and retention in the Foreign Service is similar to that in the officer corps of the armed forces, although there are some additional biases in Foreign Service recruitment. For example, since their founding, the armed service academies have tended to be quite representative of the distribution of the population geographically by virtue of the heavy statutory reliance of the academies on congressional appointments. The Foreign Service tended to recruit disproportionately from the Atlantic Seaboard, and especially from young men who had graduated from Ivy League schools (particularly Harvard, Princeton, and Yale).

Under similar presidential directives as were the armed forces during the Kennedy administration, the Foreign Service in the 1960s began a program to recruit minorities. Progress was slow. Of 3,453 Foreign Service Officers (FSOs) in 1967, there still were no native Americans, 9 Asian-Americans, 16 Hispanic-Americans, and 19 blacks.[50] However, by 1981, in a slightly smaller corps of FSOs, the minority representation had more than doubled, to about 5% of the total at junior and mid-levels, and about 4% at senior levels.[51] Likewise, in recent years the CIA has abandoned its lily-white recruitment practice in favor of one much more racially and socially representative.

Although women still not are not represented in foreign policy roles in numbers proportionate to their majority status in the total population, they are now being recruited, promoted, and retained in greater numbers than in the past in the Foreign Service, the CIA, and even in the armed forces (although barriers in combat assignments remain). For example, by the 1980s approximately 20% of entry-level Foreign Service Officers (FSOs) were women, up from 9% a decade earlier. Women constituted approximately 12% of the elite Foreign Service officer corps by 1980, compared with less than 5% in 1970.[52]

196

It is not quite accurate to assert that throughout most of American historical experience women were totally excluded from significant participation in the foreign policy process. A number of women have played significant foreign policy roles, as early as the 1920s, when Ruth Shipley began a thirty-three-year career as director of passport operations in the Department of State. Frances E. Willis, appointed in 1927, pursued a 37-year career in the Foreign Service, including appointments as the American Ambassador to Switzerland, Norway, and Ceylon, respectively. Eleanor Lansing Dulles was already a distinguished economist when she joined the government in the late 1930s. In the subsequent wartime and postwar periods, Dulles served in a number of important positions, including participation in the Bretton Woods conference of 1944. She assumed major responsibilities for postwar planning for Germany, France, Austria, and Belgium. Examples from recent years are far more numerous.[53] These include President Reagan's appointment of Jeane Kirkpatrick as United States Ambassador to the United Nations (the most recent in a long line of women, beginning with Eleanor Roosevelt, who have served in the United States delegation to the UN).

The informal roles that the wives of diplomats and career military personnel have assumed in the American foreign policy process over a period of two centuries also should be noted. The significant contributions made by wives, although without official titles or formal recognition, has been acknowledged at least implicitly. A departmental directive issued in 1972 declared that spouses no longer were to be treated as "associate unpaid employees" of the department; moreover, annual efficiency reports were no longer to include comments—favorable or unfavorable—about the wife and her contribution to the diplomatic community. As noted by several of the twenty-five women and men who participated in a symposium in 1981 assessing the effects of the directive, a dramatic change in the expectations associated with the role of spouse had occurred.[54] Still, pressures on spouses regarding their responsibilities to the diplomatic or military community remain, and methods for tempering the pressures and for recognizing the contributions remain imperfect.[55]

ASCRIPTIVE CRITERIA FOR TOP-LEVEL APPOINTMENTS   A second qualification must be made regarding the generalization that the historical trend in the recruitment and promotion of personnel in foreign policy positions has been toward reliance on achievement criteria. In top-level positions, ascriptive criteria are still applied. That is to say, whereas there are examination procedures stipulated by law for entry into lower-level positions in the civil service and in the Foreign Service, top-level positions (for example, departmental secretaries, under secretaries, assistant secretaries, and ambassadors) are filled by presidential appointment, subject to the advice and consent of the Senate.

Paradoxically, the application of ascriptive criteria at top levels of government does not necessarily conflict with affirmative action goals but may in fact enable the government to meet such goals more quickly. Women, blacks, Hispanics, or members of other minorities must work their way up through the ranks in career progression. Because affirmative action programs have been in existence only for a couple of decades, such individuals still are badly underrepresented at top levels of government. However, because he (or she) has the authority to make appointments to top-level positions, a President has the opportunity to effect changes in representation in executive positions more quickly than is feasible through the gradual process of career progression.

President Gerald Ford, for example, filled a record 14 percent of presidential appointments with women. His successor, Jimmy Carter, was able in four years to increase the number of women in executive positions to 22 percent of the total. Twenty-one percent of Carter's appointments to federal executive positions were minorities. It is also true that the percentages of minorities and women in presidentially appointed executive positions dropped during the first two years of the Reagan administration (to 8.2 percent and 8.0 percent, respectively, of 980 full-time positions). Discretionary authority in the hands of the President (with appointments subject to Senate ratification) can work either way—although as President Reagan learned, not without political outcry on the part of those who are underrepresented.[56]

Within the armed forces, those who are appointed to "executive positions," in the grades of brigadier general, rear admiral, or above, are selected from among eligible career officers rather than being drawn from civilian life as typically had been true in the early nineteenth century. Still, such top-level promotions are made into positions that by the nature of their characteristic interface with the civilian sector and the responsibility for being closely attuned to the policy orientation of civilian superiors (service secretaries, secretary of defense, president), have a political nature.

Sometimes the political hue of the promotion is highly visible, to the point of becoming the object of intraorganizational gossip and disputation. Such was the case when Alexander Haig moved from colonel to four-star general in less than four years during the Nixon years. Haig's rapid promotion reflected the prominent support of Henry Kissinger, on whose National Security Council staff Haig served, as well as that of the President, whom he subsequently served as White House advisor.

Even when selection is being made totally within the system of military promotion boards operating according to standardized procedures, promotion to the elite flag-rank positions is qualitatively different from promotion to lower grades. As Lieutenant General DeWitt Smith used to say when presiding over ceremonies to recognize the promotion of lieutenant colonels to full colonel, "This is the last time you will be promoted purely on merit."[57] Although the remark was made partly in jest, there is much truth to it. Richard Betts convincingly argues that for the civil servant, the Foreign Service Officer, or the military officer, the demarcation between being a "professional" and being a "political official" begins to blur at this level (brigadier general or rear admiral in the military, grade FSO-2 in the Foreign Service, grade GS-16 in the civil service). At higher grades, the requisites of one's responsibilities make the emphasis increasingly political.[58] The Reagan appointment of General John Vessey as Chairman of the Joint Chiefs of Staff is illustrative. General Vessey's well-known opposition both to the SALT II treaty and to President Carter's plan (later abandoned) to reduce American military forces in Korea had rendered Vessey out of contention for the top JCS post in the Carter administration. However, the views that had been political liabilities during the Carter administration became assets when Ronald Reagan was elected, leading to the Vessey appointment.[59]

Congress has left top-level policy positions to presidential appointment because of a recognition that a president needs to have full confidence in his principal subordinates. Moreover, the Congress recognizes that a certain amount of patronage is a requisite of the functioning of the political process. Presidents, like members of Congress, must be elected. Even the most incorruptible politician is likely to believe that the benefits of success at the polls ought to include recognition of the contributions to that success of staunch party members and loyal supporters among their constituents. If such constituents or party allies have expressed an interest in being appointed to an important policy position such as an ambassadorship or a secretarial position, they deserve at the very least to have their credentials reviewed.

Presidents typically ensure that their closest advisors will include close associates from the past, as Jimmy Carter did in drawing upon his Georgia entourage and as Ronald Reagan did in appointing those who had worked with him in California. However, the full process is much more complicated than turning to old friends and political colleagues. Successful candidates to the presidency compile long lists of prospects for each appointive position, with names supplied by key officials in their party, by members of Congress, by persons whom they already have selected as their White House staff or to head particular departments (a departmental secretary will expect to have a say in the appointment of his key subordinates), and by influential friends and political allies.[60]

Often the review of these candidates takes several weeks, or even months, and includes not only an FBI security check of the background of frontrunners but also informal checking with persons whose opposition to the candidacy might bring embarrassment to the administration or otherwise hamper the candidate if his or her appointment cleared Senate ratification.[61]

BLURRING OF THE DISTINCTION BETWEEN ASCRIPTIVE AND ACHIEVEMENT CRITERIA   Although it is reasonable to describe top-level appointments to government as being patronage appointments, it does not necessarily follow that the best-qualified individuals are thereby neglected in the process. Thus, the third caveat that must be offered regarding the generalization that the trend has been one toward increasing utilization of achievement criteria in recruitment and promotion is that in practice the distinction between applying ascriptive or achievement criteria often is blurred.

In the first place, "political appointees" often bring to their jobs highly relevant experience and expertise. For instance, a study of the backgrounds of 153 persons appointed to executive positions at the cabinet or subcabinet level in foreign affairs from 1946 to 1962 revealed that half of these had had more than ten years of prior experience in federal government; less than 10 percent of the executive appointees entered office with no prior experience in the federal government.[62]

Secondly, even if lacking the kind of formal experience that a career foreign policy official might have, a political appointee might have developed such an effective working relationship with the President or with the department head whom he or she will serve that the results in performance of executive tasks will be superior to those that would result from restricting selection to available career personnel.

Third, the converse of the second point is that the career bureaucrat may have developed a trained incapacity to provide fresh, innovative policy advice.

Henry Kissinger is among those who has argued that a bureaucratic career has precisely these results.[63] In lower and middle-level roles in the bureaucracy, specialization is fostered. The administrative routine requires the cultivation of skill in routing staff papers through multiple channels and facility in the expression of orthodox ideas and in the formulation of timely compromises that are essential to committee and staff work. However, at top leadership levels, these skills and work habits are dysfunctional. What is needed at the top is an ability to transcend the limited focus of the specialist, to see "the big picture," to have a capacity for innovation, for risking unpopularity with subordinates and associates by making difficult decisions and acting decisively.

There is no simple panacea for ensuring that those in leadership positions will bring to their roles the requisite qualities. Those appointed to key posts from outside the government, for example, may be equally orthodox if not more so in their thinking than are those who have made governmental service a career; the political appointee may be indecisive, lacking in creativity, mired in his or her own narrow perspectives.

However, the point at hand is that the application of merit criteria in recruitment and promotion is no guarantee of meritorious performance. Ironically, the formalized procedures that are instituted in order to ensure that merit criteria will be applied impersonally and equitably in recruitment and promotion decisions sometimes have contributed to the problem that Kissinger has described. On the basis of a detailed analysis of the State Department and the Foreign Service, John Ensor Harr has concluded that "the importance of the promotion system to the [Foreign] Service as a regulatory and governing process, and its impact on individual members, can scarcely be exaggerated."[64]

The Department's own management reform study concluded in a report by Task Force 9 examining "Openness in the Foreign Affairs Community" that

> For the Foreign Service officer, career advancement depends heavily upon the favorable judgment, periodically rendered, of a long list of supervisors. . . . These conditions inevitably move the Foreign Service officer to focus his attention upon his immediate superiors, to qualify present thinking and action with long-term career considerations, to think twice before taking possibly disquieting initiatives, to interpret his responsibilities narrowly and to develop a defensive reflex against obtrusive outsiders. The bias is against an attitude of openness.[65]

Chris Argyris, after extensively interviewing Foreign Service officers, found that a process had developed within the organizational subculture that tended to result in behavior in which individuals were

> minimizing risk-taking, being open and being forthright, as well as minimizing their feelings of responsibilty and their willingness to confront conflict openly. This, in turn, tends to reinforce those who have decided to withdraw, play it safe, not make waves, and to do so both in their behavior and in their writing. Under these conditions people soon learn the survival quotient of "checking with everyone," of developing policies that upset no one, of establishing policies in such a way that the superior takes the responsibility for them.[66]

Similarly, in a searching post-Vietnam examination of the institution that he served as a career military officer, Colonel William Hauser was critical of the system of annual ratings of the performance of Army officers. A consensus had developed, Hauser observed

> that ratings within this report system have become so inflated as to have lost much of their validity and that, as a consequence, officers fear that "one bad report" will be the ruination of an otherwise promising career. This sort of belief, valid or not, puts a premium on caution and prices moral courage very nearly out of the market.[67]

In response to concerns such as those expressed by Colonel Hauser, the Army has made changes in the officer evaluation report (OER) form and in the evaluation process. However, apart from the crucible of combat, there remain severe difficulties in making valid distinctions among officers in terms of their performance of the varied tasks in military organizations. The result is that, especially in promotions to field-grade and higher ranks, considerations other than performance, such as the "visibility" of the officer's previous career assignments, are likely to prevail in the selection process.[68]

PRESIDENTIAL LEADERSHIP AND FOREIGN POLICY ORGANIZATION

Whatever talent search may be utilized, even an optimal selection of "the best and the brightest" does not ensure the development of wise policies nor even that participants in the process will utilize their abilities to the fullest. The effective mobilization and utilization of human resources occurs only to the extent that structures and procedures are created and maintained that enable those entrusted with making key decisions and those charged with implementing them to fulfill these responsibilities. In short, we return to the topic of leadership, broadly defined, with which the discussion in the chapter began.

The impact of a president and his administration on the preexisting organization of foreign policy is felt in various ways, which in cumulative form represent the effects of presidential leadership in foreign policy: (1) through the imprint that the administration makes not only upon national foreign policy goals but also on the subsidiary goals of governmental organizations, partly through pronouncement but especially through resource allocation; (2) through the organizational mores and standards that are cultivated; (3) through the practices of recruitment, advancement, and retention that are instituted; (4) through the structuring of authority, communications and intelligence in the foreign policy process that is effected; (5) through decision-making procedures that are incorporated; and (6) through the techniques that are devised to evaluate policies that have been implemented and actions that have been taken, and to learn from experience.

The first three of these leadership tasks have been discussed in the present chapter in the context of an examination of the foreign policy bureacracy. The final three tasks are the subject of Chapter 7.

NOTES

1. John Stuart Mill, *On Liberty*, ed. annot. David Spitz (New York: W. W. Norton, 1975), pp. 20, 50. Mill adds (pp. 50–51), "Fourthly, the meaning of the doctrine itself will be in danger of being lost, or enfeebled, and deprived of its vital effect on the character and conduct; the dogma becoming a mere formal profession, inefficacious for good, but cumbering the ground, and preventing the growth of any real and heartfelt conviction, from reason or personal experience."

2. Richard E. Neustadt, *Presidential Power: The Politics of Leadership from FDR to Carter*, rev. ed. (New York: John Wiley & Sons, 1980), p. 7. Emphasis in the original.

3. James MacGregor Burns, *Leadership* (New York: Harper & Row, 1978), p. 425. Space limitations preclude pursuit here of the interesting distinction that Burns makes between "transactional" and "transformational" leadership.

4. Max Weber, *Theory of Social and Economic Organization*, trans. Talcott Parsons (New York: Free Press, 1947). Max Weber, *Theory of Social and Economic Organization* (New Brunswick, NJ: Transaction Books, 1981). Hans Gerth and C. Wright Mills, eds., *From Max Weber: Essays in Sociology* (New York: Oxford University Press, 1946).

5. Walter Millis, *Arms and Men: A Study in American Military History*, paperback ed. (New York: New American Library, 1956), pp. 140–182. See also Richard B. Morris, ed., *Encyclopedia of American History*, bicentennial ed. (New York: Harper & Row, 1976), pp. 343–345.

6. U.S. Army, Center of Military History, *From Root to McNamara: Army Organization and Administration, 1900–1963*, prepared by James E. Hewes, Jr., Special Studies Series, Washington: Government Printing Office, 1975, pp. 3–9. (Cited hereafter as Hewes, *From Root to McNamara.*)

7. Graham T. Allison, *Essence of Decision: Explaining the Cuban Missile Crisis* (Boston, MA: Little, Brown, 1971), esp. Chap. 4.

8. On the eve of the 1932 elections, the Republicans boasted proudly in campaign literature that the American Army "through successive reductions had reached the irreducible minimum consistent with self-reliance, self-respect and security." Republican Party National Committee, *Campaign Textbook 1932*, pp. 86–87.

9. George F. Kennan, *American Diplomacy 1900–1950*, paperback ed. (New York: New American Library, Mentor, 1959), pp. 86–87.

10. As Hull observed of the principles of international law and moral conduct he was promoting in the 1930s, "to me there was nothing vague about them. They were solid, living, all-essential rules. If the world followed them, the world could live at peace forever. If the world ignored them, war would be eternal . . . To me these doctrines were as vital in international relations as the Ten Commandments in personal relations." Cordell Hull, *The Memoirs of Cordell Hull*, 2 vols. (New York: Macmillan, 1948), I:536. See also the commentary by Donald F. Drummond, "Cordell Hull," in *An Uncertain Tradition: American Secretaries of State in the Twentieth Century*, ed. Norman A. Graebner (New York: McGraw-Hill, 1961), ch. 10.

11. Mark S. Watson, *Chief of Staff: Prewar Plans and Preparations*, United States Army in World War II (Washington: Chief of Military History Office, Department of the Army, 1950), p. 123, quoted with commentary by Harvey C. Mansfield, in Walter Millis, *Arms and the State: Civil-Military Elements in National Policy* (New York: Twentieth Century Fund, 1958), pp. 50–51.

12. The case can be overstated. Military men flew the mail when the postmaster general cancelled contracts with civilian carriers; they also participated in prominent New Deal programs such as the Civilian Conservation Corps (CCC). Moreover, the Army Industrial College, which had been created in 1924, was producing a small cadre of military officers (from all arms of services) familiar with problems of industrial mobilization in the event of war. However, as Bernard Baruch has observed, programs such as those of the Army Industrial College were "only small islands of concern in a sea of indifference": Bernard M. Baruch, *The Public Years*, (New York: Holt, Rinehart and Winston, 1957), pp. 264–265. See also Hewes, *From Root to McNamara*, pp. 50–56. Similarly, although by 1939 the War Plans Division was maintaining regular liaison with the Departments of State, Treasury, Interior, Agriculture, Commerce, and Justice, the breadth of perspective required of it made the Division an exception to the pattern within the Army General Staff, to say nothing of the military establishment as a whole. Ray S. Cline, *Washington Command Post: The Operations Division, United States Army in World War II, The War Department* (Washington: Office of the Chief of Military History, Department of the Army, 1951), chap. 2. The War Plans Division was redesignated the Operations Division in 1942.

13. U.S. Army, Command and General Staff School, *Principles of Strategy* (1936), pp. 19–20, quoted by Samuel P. Huntington, *The Soldier and the State* (Cambridge, Ma: Harvard University Press, Belknap Press, 1959), p. 308.

14. The dramatic change for scientists that occurred is described by Daniel S. Greenberg, *The Politics of Pure Science* (New York: New American Library, 1967), chap. 3–5. Greenberg notes that with the resulting altered relationship, in the early postwar years "it is evident that something between seduction and rape repeatedly occurred, but at various points it is by no means certain which party was the aggressor and which the victim," p. 124.

15. The shorthands were appropriate in the sense that they accurately refer to the historical events most salient to those that experienced them. This is not to deny that the lessons learned sometimes have been misapplied to more recent circumstances. See Ernest R. May, *The Lessons of the Past: The Use and Misuse of History in American Foreign Policy* (New York: Oxford University Press, 1973).

16. Daniel H. Yergin, *Shattered Peace: The Origins of the Cold War and the National Security State* (Boston: Houghton Mifflin, 1977).

17. U.S. Congress, House of Representatives, Committee on Expenditures in the Executive Department, *Hearings: National Security Act of 1947*, 80th Cong., 1st sess., 24 April 1947, p. 99.

18. Earl Latham, *The Communist Controversy in Washington* (Cambridge, MA: Harvard University Press, 1966). Also E. J. Kahn, Jr., *The China Hands: America's Foreign Service Officers and What Befell Them* (New York: Viking, 1975). During the first months of the Reagan administration, numerous Foreign Service Officers who were holding key positions of responsibility for Latin American affairs were dismissed or reassigned (three ambassadors to Central American countries, the assistant secretary and two deputy assistant secretaries). The abrupt "housecleaning" led some observers to express the fear that the pattern of early purges was being repeated. See George Gedda, "A Dangerous Region: Association with Carter's Central American Policies Proved Hazardous to the Careers of Several FSOs," *Foreign Service Journal* 60 (Feb. 1983): 18–21, 34.

19. Richard J. Barnet, *Roots of War: The Men and Institutions Behind U.S. Foreign Policy* (New York: Athenum, 1972).

20. Theodore C. Sorensen, *Kennedy*, (New York: Harper & Row, 1965), p. 256.

21. Irving L. Janis, *Groupthink: Psychological Studies of Policy Decisions and Fiascoes*, 2d ed. (Boston: Houghton Mifflin, 1982).

22. John Ensor Harr, *The Professional Diplomat* (Princeton, NJ: Princeton University Press,

1969), pp. 210–214. Sample selection and survey instrument are discussed in appendices to the book.

23. Graham Allison, *Essence of Decision: Explaining the Cuban Missile Crisis* (Boston: Little, Brown, 1971), pp. 121–123. Miles's Law is attributed to Rufus Miles, formerly a career administrator at the Department of Health, Education and Welfare. Along with dozens of other homey aphorisms and maxims, it has been collected by Paul Dickson, *The Official Rules* (New York: Dell, 1978).

24. Richard K. Betts, *Soldiers, Statesmen, and Cold War Crises* (Cambridge, Ma: Harvard University Press, 1977), esp. pp. 4–5.

25. Edward L. Katzenbach, "The Horse Cavalry in the Twentieth Century: A Study in Policy Response," *Public Policy* 8 (1958): 120–149, excerpted in *Readings in American Foreign Policy: A Bureaucratic Perspective*, ed. Morton H. Halperin and Arnold Kanter (Boston: Little, Brown, 1973), p. 177.

26. As William Cockerham notes, airborne training is a rite of passage, successful completion of which provides acceptance into "an elite subgroup." The subgroup "exists not only as a formal organization but also as a social perspective based upon an elaborate construction of symbolic meanings representing a social experience unique to those involved." Cockerham, "Selective Socialization: Airborne Training as Status Passage," *Journal of Political and Military Sociology* 1 (1973): 215–229.

27. See Frederic A. Bergerson, *The Army Gets an Air Force: Tactics of Insurgent Bureaucratic Politics* (Baltimore: Johns Hopkins University Press, 1978).

28. Vincent Davis, *Postwar Defense Policy and the U.S. Navy, 1943–1946* (Chapel Hill: University of North Carolina Press, 1966).

29. Perry McCoy Smith, *The Air Force Plans for Peace, 1943–1945* (Baltimore: Johns Hopkins University Press, 1970).

30. A subtle empirical analysis by Arnold Kanter of Air Force officer promotion data over an 18-year period is instructive. Kanter has shown that in the 1950s, mid-career officers in SAC were more likely than their peers in other Air Force commands to be promoted, but by the 1960s SAC officers were slightly disadvantaged in promotion relative to those serving in "limited war commands." Kanter, *Defense Politics: A Budgetary Perspective* (Chicago: University of Chicago Press, 1979), pp. 104–110.

31. Victor Marchetti and John D. Marks, *The CIA and the Cult of Intelligence* (New York: Knopf, 1974), pp. 5–6.

32. William Colby, *Honorable Men: My Life in the CIA* (New York: Simon & Schuster, 1978). The discussion of subcultures within the CIA draws primarily from Colby's account. See also a review essay by David H. Hunter with accompanying bibliography, "The Evolution of Literature on United States Intelligence," *Armed Forces and Society* 5 (Fall 1978): 31–52.

33. Colby, *Honorable Men*, pp. 293–301.

34. Colby, *Honorable Men*, pp. 186, 292–298, 461–465.

35. The quote is from two sources: Andrew M. Scott, "Environmental Change and Organizational Adaptation: The Problem of the State Department," *International Studies Quarterly* 14 (March 1970): 86, and Scott, "The Department of State: Formal Organization and Informal Culture," *International Studies Quarterly* 13 (March 1969): 1. See also Chris Argyris, *Some Causes of Organizational Effectiveness within the Department of State*, Occasional Paper no. 2, Center for International Systems Research (Washington: Department of State, 1967).

36. Harr, *The Professional Diplomat*, p. 96.

37. U.S., Department of State, *Diplomacy for the 70s: A Program of Management Reform for the Department of State*, Dept. of State Publ. 8551, Dept. and Foreign Service Series 143, Washington: Government Printing Office, 1970, p. 310.

38. The report asserted that departmental top officials "must now ask themselves whether

they are really prepared to live in an organization where creativity flourishes—where the habitual mode is innovative, skeptical, nonconformist, where the received wisdom is habitually questioned, where established policy is habitually challenged as a matter of sound professional practice, where the Ambassador's leadership reposes less on traditional status than on sound management principles, where youth is allowed to participate in the decisionmaking process." U.S., Dept. of State, Diplomacy for the 70s, p. 336.

39. Author's conversation with bureau chief, Department of State, Washington, D.C., 1974.

40. Paul Y. Hammond, "Super Carriers and B-36 Bombers: Appropriations, Strategy and Politics," in American Civil-Military Decisions, ed. Harold Stein (Birmingham: University of Alabama Press, with the Inter-University Case Program, 1963), pp. 465–564.

41. John M. Collins, U.S. Defense Planning: A Critique (Boulder, Co: Westview Press, 1982), Fig. 12, pp. 98–99 and accompanying discussion.

42. Charles E. Wilson, testimony before U.S. Senate, Committee on Armed Services, Hearings: On Nominee Designates, 83d Cong., 1st sess., 15–16 Jan. 1953, p. 26. Emphasis added.

43. The literature on arms control and defense needs is massive. For some helpful background on the debate as it occu. ᵣᵈ within the government during the Carter and Reagan years, see the following. Thomas Powers, "Choosing a Strategy for World War III," The Atlantic 250 (Nov. 1982): 82–110; Robert Scheer, With Enough Shovels: Reagan, Bush and Nuclear War (New York: Random House, 1982); Richard Pipes, "Why the Soviet Union Thinks It Could Fight and Win a Nuclear War," Commentary (July 1977).

44. Stephen S. Rosenfeld, "Knockdown of a Soviet 'Buildup'," Washington Post, Nov. 18, 1983, p. A19. See also accounts of earlier fluctuations in intelligence estimates. William P. Lee, Understanding the Soviet Military Threat: How CIA Estimates Went Astray, Agenda Paper no. 6 (New York: National Strategy Information Center, 1977). John Prados, The Soviet Estimate: U.S. Intelligence Analysis and Russian Military Strength (New York: Dial, 1982).

45. Huntington, The Soldier and the State. This is not to say that favoritism had been eliminated completely, but only to make a point about the historical trend in the direction of applying merit criteria to recruitment and promotion.

46. Harr, The Professional Diplomat, pt. I.

47. Thomas F. Troy, Donovan and the CIA: A History of the Establishment of the Central Intelligence Agency (Frederick, Md: University Publications of America, 1981).

48. Henry Ossian Flipper, The Colored Cadet at West Point (New York: Arno Press, 1969). Flipper, Negro Frontiersman: The Western Memoirs of Henry O. Flipper, First Negro Graduate of West Point (El Paso: Texas Western College Press, 1963).

49. See Richard M. Dalfiume, Desegration of the U.S. Armed Forces: Fighting on Two Fronts, 1939–1953 (Columbus: University of Missouri Press, 1969); Jack D. Foner, Blacks and the Military in American History: A New Perspective (New York: Praeger, 1974); Morris J. MacGregor, Integration of the Armed Forces, 1940–1965) (Washington, D.C.: U.S. Army Center for Military History, 1981).

50. U.S., Department of State, Diplomacy for the 70's, p. 278.

51. U.S., Commission on Civil Rights, Equal Opportunity in the Foreign Service: A Report, Washington, D.C.: Government Printing Office, June 1981, Appendix A. See also Elmer Plischke, "Profile of United States Diplomats: Bicentennial Review and Future Projection," in Modern Diplomacy: The Art and the Artisans, ed. Elmer Plischke (Washington, D.C.: American Enterprise Institute for Public Policy Research, 1979), pp. 237–253.

52. Barbara J. Good, "Women in the Foreign Service: A Quiet Revolution," Foreign Service Journal 58 (Jan. 1981): 47–50, 67.

53. See U.S., Department of State, Deputy Under Secretary for Management, Women in the Department of State: Their Role in American Foreign Affairs, Department of State publ.

8951, Foreign Service series 166 (Washington, DC: Government Printing Office, September 1978). Also Eleanor Lansing Dulles, *Chances of a Lifetime: A Memoir* (Englewood Cliffs, NJ: Prentice-Hall, 1980).

54. A similar change has occurred regarding the role of spouses of military officers.

55. Martin F. Herz, ed., *Diplomacy: The Role of the Wife, A Symposium* (Washington, D.C. Georgetown University Institute for the Study of Diplomacy, Edmund A. Walsh School of Foreign Service, 1981).

56. U.S., Commission on Civil Rights, *Equal Opportunity in Presidential Appointments*, Washington, D.C.: Government Printing Office, June 1983, 22 pp. Most of the increase in the representation of women and minorities in executive positions in the federal government has come in departments and agencies that have primarily a domestic focus. Of fifty-one Carter appointments to the Defense and State departments, six were minorities, and four were women. Of seventy-five Reagan appointments to these two departments (as of 1983), none were minorities, one was a woman. President Reagan, however, had selected Jeane Kirkpatrick as U.S. Ambassador to the United Nations and Loret Ruppe to be Director of the Peace Corps.

57. Author's personal observation. Lieutenant General DeWitt Smith presided over these promotion ceremonies as Commandant, U.S. Army War College. The author was a visiting professor at the college at the time.

58. Betts, *Soldiers, Statesman*, fig. 1, p. 39, and accompanying discussion. See also John G. Kester, "Politics and Promotions," *Parameters, Journal of the U.S. Army War College*, 12 (Dec. 1982): 2–13.

59. See Brad Knickerbocker, "Power of Joint Chiefs Chairman could grow under General Vessey," *Christian Science Monitor*, March 8, 1982.

60. A useful description of the process is provided by Dean E. Mann, with Jameson W. Doig, *The Assistant Secretaries: Problems and Processes of Appointment* (Washington, D.C.: Brookings Institution, 1965). On the process used by President-elect Carter, see Betty Glad, *Jimmy Carter: In Search of the Great White House* (New York: W. W. Norton, 1980), pp. 412–416. On the process used by President-elect Reagan, see the following articles in vol. 12 (1980) of the *National Journal*: Dom Bonafede, "Keep an Eye on the Cabinet" (Nov. 22), p. 1990; Dick Kirschten, "First Among Equals" (Nov. 29), p. 2042; Dick Kirschten, "Wanted: 275 Reagan Team Players; Empire Builders Need Not Apply" (Dec. 6), pp. 2077–2079.

61. The views of Senator Jesse Helms were frequently sought in the initial Reagan appointments, although some appointments were made even though they failed to meet the Helms "litmus test" for right-wing political views.

62. Derived from figures reported by James L. McCamy, *Conduct of the New Diplomacy* (New York: Harper & Row, 1964), table 14, p. 237.

63. Henry A. Kissinger, "The Policymaker and the Intellectual," *The Reporter* 20 (March 5, 1959): 30–35.

64. Harr, *The Professional Diplomat*, p. 227.

65. U.S., Department of State, *Diplomacy for the 70s*, p. 381.

66. Argyris, *Some Causes of Ineffectiveness*, p. 33.

67. William L. Hauser, *America's Army in Crisis: A Study in Civil-Military Relations* (Baltimore: Johns Hopkins University Press, 1973), p. 223.

68. See David W. Moore and B. Thomas Trout, "Military Advancement: The Visibility Theory of Promotion," *American Political Science Review* 72 (June 1978): 452–468.

SUGGESTED ADDITIONAL READING

ALLISON, GRAHAM T. *Essence of Decision: Explaining the Cuban Missile Crisis.* Boston: Little, Brown, 1971.

ART, ROBERT. "Bureaucratic Politics and American Foreign Policy: A Critique." *Policy Sciences* 4 (1973): 467–490.

BACCHUS, WILLIAM. *Foreign Policy and the Bureaucratic Process.* Princeton, NJ: Princeton University Press, 1974.

BARBER, JAMES D. *The Presidential Character.* 2d ed. Englewood Cliffs, NJ: Prentice-Hall, 1977.

BURNS, JAMES MACGREGOR. *Leadership.* New York: Harper & Row, 1978.

DAVIS, VINCENT, editor. *The Post-Imperial Presidency.* New Brunswick, NJ: Transaction Books, 1980.

DESTLER, I. M. *Presidents, Bureaucrats and Foreign Policy.* Princeton, NJ: Princeton University Press, 1972.

HALPERIN, MORTON, and KANTER, ARNOLD, eds. *Readings in American Foreign Policy: A Bureaucratic Perspective.* Boston: Little, Brown, 1973.

JANIS, IRVING L. *Groupthink: Psychological Studies of Policy Decisions and Fiascoes.* 2d ed. Boston, MA: Houghton Mifflin, 1982.

NELSON, WILLIAM E. *The Roots of American Bureaucracy: 1830–1900.* Cambridge, MA: Harvard University Press, 1982.

NEUSTADT, RICHARD E. *Presidential Power: The Politics of Leadership with Reflections from FDR to Carter.* 3rd ed. New York: John Wiley & Sons, 1980.

SIMPSON, SMITH. *The Crisis in American Diplomacy: Shots Across the Bow of the State Department.* North Quincy, MA: The Christopher Publishing House, 1980.

U.S., DEPARTMENT OF STATE, Deputy Under Secretary for Management. *Women in the Department of State: Their Role in American Foreign Affairs.* Department of State Publ. 8951, Foreign Service Series 166. Washington, DC: GPO, Sept. 1978.

WARWICK, DONALD P. *A Theory of Public Bureaucracy: Politics, Personality, and Organization in the State Department.* Cambridge, MA: Harvard University Press, 1975.

CHAPTER 7

ॐ

The Structure and Process of Foreign Policy Decision Making

". . . It is time I recognized that my Planning Staff, started nearly three years ago, has simply been a failure, like all previous attempts to bring order and foresight into the designing of foreign policy by special institutional arrangements within the department. Aside from personal shortcomings, the reason for this seems to lie largely in the impossibility of having the planning function performed outside the line of command."

> —Diary entry of George Kennan, November 1949

"The advice of every member of the Executive Branch brought in to advise [the President] was unanimous—and the advice was wrong."

> —President John F. Kennedy reflecting on the failure of the 1961 Bay of Pigs invasion

". . . It never suited the purposes of the American government . . . to level with the American people on the nature of [the war in Vietnam], to level with the Congress, or even to level with itself. Indeed, at the root of many of the large and small deceptions that characterized America's Vietnam policy over the years, there was that most fatal flaw of all—namely, collective self-deception."

> —James Thomson, Asian specialist formerly with the State Department, conference on Vietnam, 1983

A major irony of the American involvement in Vietnam is that decisions that produced abysmal failure were made by "the best and the brightest" of individuals (to use David Halberstam's apt description).[1] Not only was the assignment of policy responsibility to talented persons no guarantee of virtuous and wise policy decisions but, on the contrary, such a clustering of talent seems to have contributed to a sense of hubris that fostered and perpetuated disastrous policies.

Some of the particular failings of the State Department in recent decades are susceptible to a similarly ironic explanation. As noted by Stewart Alsop during the period of the 1960s when State had come under attack by presidents as well as by pundits, the problem was *not* that of a dearth of committed, talented individuals in the department.

> The trouble is not only that there are too many people in the State Department; there are too many *able* people. A bureaucracy hums along happily enough if it consists very largely of drones, content to shuffle their papers and collect their pay checks. But the presence of large numbers of intelligent and able people produces near-chaos. An able man wants to earn his salary, and when something important is afoot, he wants to get into the act. Getting into the act means attending the meetings of the committees and "task forces" (another, more activist-sounding name for committees) dealing with the major crises of the moment.
>
> These committees thus keep getting bigger and bigger [and ultimately become unmanageable].[2]

In short, foolish policies may emerge even from a system with individuals of extraordinary experience and intelligence at the helm. Conversely, sensible and successful policies may be developed by persons of only modest abilities. For an explanation of this paradox, one must look beyond recruitment practices to the organizational context of policy making.

In part, this context is defined by organizational subcultures, as noted in the discussion in Chapter 6. It is also defined, as we emphasize in the present chapter, by organizational structure and process.

Put in other terms, the choices that are made day-in and day-out at all levels of the foreign policy apparatus—at lower levels by junior FSOs or Army lieutenants, for example; at top levels by the

President and his key advisors—are constrained by, and therefore shaped by, the existing structure and process.

By structure, is meant the patterning of roles within the government—who is assigned which tasks, who is able to talk with whom about which matters, and who decides? By process, is meant especially the rules and procedures that govern behavior—how is information obtained about present and future needs, requirements, capabilities, and threats? How, when, and by whom are problems and issues identified, analyzed, and resolved?

The prevailing structures and processes thus not only will help to determine which choices among various policy or action alternatives are most probable but also will tend to dictate which among possible options even will be considered.

In theory, to echo the theme introduced early in the previous chapter, bureaucracy is created in order to bring rationality and predictability to the policy process. To focus particularly on tasks that are the subject of the present chapter, bureaucratization theoretically provides a means for systematizing policy planning, for ensuring the rigorous gathering and analysis of pertinent intelligence and the orderly flow of information to those who need it in order to make decisions, for formulating options in a manner that will enable policy makers to make choices that are optimal in terms of national interests and priorities, and for monitoring the implementation of policy in order to correct errors and adjust to changing circumstances.

In practice, the operation of the foreign policy process departs in significant ways from a rational model. One need not dwell on the pathologies of bureaucratic behavior to recognize the dilemmas that typically confront policy makers in the real-world of policy making. Here the structuring of four important facets of foreign-policy making and implementation will be examined: policy planning, intelligence and communications (especially in relationship to crisis management), decision making, and policy evaluation and learning. Key dilemmas associated with each of these tasks include the today-or-tomorrow dilemma of planning, the conceal/control and expedite/get-it-right dilemmas of intelligence, the take charge/delegate dilemma of decision making, and the sunk costs/sunk hopes dilemma of policy evaluation and learning.

POLICY PLANNING

The American foreign policy planning process includes efforts to identify trends and thereby to forecast events. It includes assessing the implications of trends and future contingencies for American interests and for existing policies and identifying policy options in the event that contingencies materialize. Finally, planning includes the design of strategies and programs of resource allocation that will enable the United States to meet future contingencies.

If foreign policy is to serve as the instrument of *purposeful adaptation* of the political system to an ever-changing world environment, then policy makers must have a capacity to transcend day-to-day concerns. That is to say, there must be a capacity for planning.

Successful adaptation requires the effective and economical utilization of human energies and skills as well as natural and material resources. To the extent that foreign policy problems can be anticipated, major failures can be averted and costly surprises avoided. On the other hand, in a complex and rapidly changing world, existing plans are bound to be at least partially inadequate much of the time, and perhaps fatally inadequate if adhered to rigidly. Given an incessant flow of problems, large and small, to be solved daily, policy makers must exercise flexibility and judgment rather than becoming the prisoners of SOPs (standard operating procedures) and "cook-book" solutions.

The result of these cross-pressures may be termed the *today-or-tomorrow* dilemma of policy planning, using the terms in a figurative rather than literal sense. *Today* refers to the demands of the moment—short-run concerns that are on the agenda of current policy operations. *Tomorrow* is used here to refer to the future—considerations several months or years ahead. Foreign policy makers cannot totally ignore *tomorrow* anymore than they can totally neglect the demands of the present. However, they are repeatedly confronted with having to decide how to allocate resources and energies to deal with immediate operational demands as compared with commitments to planning, and with having to decide how the planning component of government shall be organized in relationship to the operational element.

There are at least two features of organizational behavior that

213

compound the dilemma in practice. The first of these relates to the variation in organizational subcultures discussed in Chapter 6 and is rooted in differences in outlook that tend to develop between those with planning roles and those with operational roles in the foreign policy apparatus. The second is that even when those who have authority for making policy decisions or for carrying them out make a commitment to planning, short-range or immediate policy demands tend to dominate attention to the neglect of long-range planning.

PLANNERS AND THE "IVORY TOWER" STIGMA

There is an important sense in which it is accurate to regard planning as the responsibility of all foreign policy officials at executive levels. That is, from the President and the members of the National Security Council down at least to the level of the country desk officer in the State Department, or the division chief in the Arms Control and Disarmament Agency, or the battalion commander in the Army, there is a need to look beyond the pressing demands of today to prepare for future contingencies.

All executive-level officials do spend part of their time with planning. Moreover, every unit of government commits part of its organizational resources and energies to this task. In practice, however, the planning function has become sufficiently specialized that it is possible to identify components of organizations that have a major responsibility for devising plans for their organization and to identify individuals whose training and assignments label them as "planners."

The today-or-tomorrow dilemma is compounded in practice by the tendency of individuals who occupy operational roles in the system to become impatient with the efforts of planners and to regard formal plans as largely irrelevant to their needs; in turn, planners are inclined to be irritated at the neglect in decision making of planning efforts to which they have made major commitments of time and creative energy.

THE PRESSURES OF THE MOMENT

To the extent that planners are able to satisfy the demands of those in operational roles that the plans they devise be "relevant," the tendency is to make commitments to the immediate, and neglect long-range concerns. Thus, an oft-cited example of the allegedly "golden age" of planning in the State Department is the period shortly after the creation of a policy planning staff headed by George Kennan. Whereas others in the department were so deluged by the flood of day-to-day problems and issues that it was almost impossible for them to think creatively about future requirements, the latter responsibility would be assigned to the new group of six planners. As Secretary of State George Marshall told Kennan when he summoned him to set up the planning staff, "he had only one bit of advice . . . 'Avoid trivia'."[3]

It is instructive, however, to note the specific task that Marshall then assigned to Kennan. The problems of postwar reconstruction in Europe were to be analyzed and recommendations for American policy in regard to these problems devised—with results back to the Secretary in ten days or two weeks![4]

Although Kennan and his staff were preoccupied with devising solutions to immediate policy problems, at least the planning staff was having a direct impact on policy decisions. Under Marshall's successor, Dean Acheson, however, the planning staff was kept at a distance. Kennan's frustrations mounted, as indicated in his expression of failure quoted at the outset of the chapter. When Paul Nitze relieved Kennan as director late in 1949, a central policy role again was assigned to the planning staff. Once again, however, the crisis-at-hand tended to take priority over long-range projections and analyses. Acheson turned to Nitze, for example, for advice and even service as a governmental emissary abroad during a crisis in which the Iranian government headed by a fiery nationalist named Mossadegh had nationalized the oil facilities in Iran.[5] (With substantial help from the CIA, a successful plot was devised two years later to oust Mossadegh as premier, thereby returning Iranian oil to private hands, and restoring the young Shah to power. The Shah would remain close to the United States until his own downfall in 1979, to be succeeded by an Islamic regime headed by the Ayatollah Khomeini.)

In the 1980s, the policy planning staff continues to perform a major planning role within the State Department, often operating under similar demands for "relevance" to immediate needs. Other units of government with specialized planning responsibilities are too numerous to list completely. For example, they range from the Office of Defense Research and Engineering, which conducts research in defense-related areas such as weapons systems, telecommunications, and command and control systems, to the Council of Economic Advisors, which provides advice to the President on present and future economic needs, to the Office of Defense Programs in the Department of Energy, which directs research and planning in areas such as laser, particle beam, and nuclear energy.

For purposes of illustrating the today-or-tomorrow dilemma in policy planning, it especially is useful to examine (1) the budgetary process as a central means by which the President endeavors to impose discipline on the planning efforts of the various departments and agencies of government,[6] and (2) the role of the National Security Council in coordinating policy plans in the national security realm.

THE BUDGETARY PROCESS AND POLICY PLANNING

The rationale for the creation of a Bureau of the Budget in 1921 was to provide the President with an organizational means for imposing order on the process of developing the annual federal budget. A change of terminology in 1970 to the Office of Management and Budget reflected a growing emphasis on managerial control of federal programs.

Such emphasis was evident as early as the 1950s. In that period, increasing interest was being expressed in the writings of budgetary experts who advocated supplementing line-item budgeting with program budgeting. Line-item budgeting provides a tally of the cost of discrete items to be purchases in a given year (5-ton trucks, jet aircraft, gallons of gasoline, and so forth). Because such line-items are likely to refer indiscriminantly to the resources of a variety of departments and agencies, it is not possible from a review of a line-item budget to make a carefully reasoned assessment of the policy wisdom of resource allocations. It is not feasible, for instance, to see if planned increases or decreases in particular line-items correspond to desired changes in policy priorities.

If planned expenditures could be aggregated according to the commitment of resources to particular programs—strategic defense of the United States, for instance, or developmental assistance to Third World countries—then within the executive branch and within the Congress it would be possible to make budgetary decisions according to policy preferences. This was the rationale for program budgeting, which first became adopted most systematically within the Defense Department.

The defense portion of the federal budget provides a particularly useful illustration of the effort to apply the budget as a planning and management tool for at least three additional reasons. First, the vast majority of federal expenditures that relate to foreign policy fall under the heading of defense. Even if the cost of domestic programs is included, the defense portion of the federal budget has accounted for approximately one fourth of total outlays for the past ten years, or even more if one were to include military-related programs not normally reported in the defense budget, such as military aspects of the space program and veterans benefits.

Second, to a much greater degree than is true of the domestic portion of the budget, the defense portion is controllable from one year to the next. That is, governmental officials can effect substantial increases or decreases in defense spending according to their estimate of policy requirements, rather than being largely "locked into" budgetary commitments by law, as they are in regard to commitments to federal programs such as Medicare or Social Security. To eliminate a major weapons system from the budget, for instance, or even to delay production for a year or two, can result in budgetary reductions of billions of dollars.[7] Conversely, a decision to build a new major weapons system carries a price tag that is likely to be far more visible in the total budget than are new commitments in various domestic programs.[8]

Third, the successes and failures in the effort to utilize the defense budget as a management tool are particularly instructive in revealing how, in practice, the best-laid policy plans often become compromised in response to immediate political realities—a phenomenon that can be described as a variation of the today-or-tomorrow dilemma.

The formative period in the effort to systematize defense planning by means of the budgetary process was that of the Kennedy administration, when Robert S. McNamara was secretary of defense. Especially as developed by McNamara's Comptroller, Charles Hitch, an economist formerly with the Rand Corporation, a series of major reforms in defense budgeting was instituted. Two innovations were particularly important, the Planning-Programming-Budgetary System (PPBS), with an emphasis on systems analysis, and the Five-Year Defense Plan (FYDP).

The basic idea of PPBS was to delineate long-range policy objectives clearly, to bring systems analysis techniques to bear in the evaluation of programs that could be justified in terms of their probable effectiveness in reaching the objectives, and to allocate resources in ways that would be cost effective, given policy priorities and available alternatives in "packaging" programs to meet policy objectives. Whereas PPBS would provide a key management tool for the development of the annual defense budget, the FYDP would provide a means for projecting policy and program plans into the near-term future, thereby encouraging planners at every level to adjust their design of current programs to longer-range needs and plans.

Although administrations subsequent to the Kennedy/McNamara era have made numerous modifications in the utilization of PPBS and the FYDP, the basic concept of their use as management tools remains intact, as is evident annually in fiscal year projections. Since 1974, the fiscal year has been designated as a twelve-month period beginning on 1 October.[9]

The budget cycle begins approximately two-and-a-half years before the start of the fiscal year, with presidential guidance to the various departments and agencies provided, in the case of component units of the Department of Defense, by the director of the Office of Management and Budget (OMB) and the Office of the Secretary of Defense (OSD). Thus, such guidance for the fiscal 1987 budget, which begins 1 October 1986, was provided in the spring of 1984; guidance for the fiscal 1988 budget was provided a year later, and so forth.

The initial guidance represents, in effect, an updating of the FYDP. The various departments and agencies utilize the guidelines that are provided to them as the basis for formulating their projections of defense requirements that relate to their organizational missions. These requirements are submitted in early summer (summer 1985 for FY88) through the Joint Chiefs of Staff (JCS) to the OSD for comment. Through a process of negotiation involving the JCS, OSD, and representatives of the various departments and agencies, preliminary decisions about national defense requirements and objectives are made.

Utilizing guidance provided by the OMB, the Secretary of Defense then is able to provide memoranda (in early 1986 for FY88) to the various departments and agencies establishing budgetary constraints (floors and ceilings) that are to be employed in translating plans and requirements into specific defense program proposals (for example, a strategic defense program, an anti-terrorist program, a military assistance program, and so forth). Through a process of negotiation involving the OSD, JCS, the various service secretaries, and representatives of subordinate units, decisions regarding defense programs are made.

Beginning in late summer (of 1986 for FY88), the task of making cost estimates of various programs begins. As specific budgets for each of the various departments and agencies are formulated, negotiations involving the OMB (on behalf of the President, who indicates his own priorities and demands), the OSD, and various subordinate units continue. Final decisions are made by the end of the year in order to enable the President to present his budget request to the Congress in January (of 1987 for FY88).

IMPERFECTIONS OF BUDGETARY PLANNING

Leaving aside here the effects of congressional bargaining and log-rolling, which of course can drastically alter the substance of the budget as it emerged from the executive branch, at least three imperfections must be noted in the effort to utilize the budget as an instrument of systematic foreign policy and defense policy planning: (1) the reality of practice during and since the McNamara reforms has departed substantially from the promised ideals; (2) although some gains have been realized in imposing order on a cumbersome process, there have been some unanticipated costs; (3) the present system carries a heavy risk that the illusion of precision in calculation will be confused with the reality of resource allocations made in response to political necessity.

The central observation is not the one that has become a cliché in writings about bureaucratic politics: namely, that the policy process departs significantly from a rational model. As Jordan and Taylor aptly note, the dichotomy between "rationality" and "politics" can be misleading, perhaps especially as applied to a description of the budgetary process. Rather, the process is both—as when (the example that they cite) the conclusion was drawn through systems analysis that the optimum number of launching tubes to be installed on Polaris submarines would be thirty-two; ultimately half that number were installed because of the aversion of submarine officers to the large submarines that would be required if the number were larger.[10]

The program budgeting, PPBS, and FYDP reforms have endured, with modifications, because they have helped to rationalize the budgetary process. On the other hand, the promise of these reforms as suggested in the writings of their early proponents has not been fully realized. For example, in a careful study of defense budgeting, Arnold Kanter found that to the extent that long-range plans were developed and embodied in the FYDP, these bore little relationship to the actual commitments that were made in the annual budget. The annual budgets were not derivable from the FYDP nor did program decisions necessarily dictate budget decisions, contrary to the rationale for PPBS. In fact, as Kanter's study reveals, top policy officials such as the secretary of defense and the President continue to respond to the exigencies of the time in making short-run judgments about budgetary needs in a manner that does not differ significantly from the seemingly arbitrary practice of imposing budget ceilings that prevailed in the years before the PPBS approach was adopted.[11]

A second point to be made is that there have been some unanticipated consequences of the budgetary reforms, some of them making planning more difficult rather than facilitating it. For example, budgetary practice before the implementation of PPBS and systems analysis was criticized for permitting only a fragmentary, incremental review of policy requirements. As Aaron Wildavsky warned in a landmark early critique, however, by exposing full programs to scrutiny, reforms such as program budgeting and PPBS increased the probability that partisan lines would be drawn for or against entire programs rather than for or against a little more or a little less money for defense, as was the case with the earlier format.[12]

Furthermore, by calling upon the major participants in the process to formulate or review budget requests from the vantage point of overall policy needs, one may be making unreasonable demands upon a capacity to transcend parochial perspectives. As Wildavsky puts it, "Requiring an individual to commit suicide for the public good may at times have an acceptable rationale; suggesting that it become a common practice can hardly claim as much."[13] Moreover, when the "suicide" required is of one or more of the armed services in the form of abandoning or reducing cherished programs in response to the claim by civilian analysts that broad considerations of systems analysis and cost effectiveness require the cuts, organizational morale may suffer in unanticipated ways—as the military response to the highly centralized civilian control that was imposed in the McNamara Pentagon reveals.[14]

Third, one must note the illusion of precision that is fostered by translating policy and program decisions into alternatives that allegedly can be compared systematically in cost-benefit terms. The candid admissions of David Stockman, the Director of OMB in the Reagan administration, are revealing in this regard. Programming all relevant variables into the computer during his first months in office early in 1981, Stockman was able to make judgments about the probable effects of various budgetary commitments, including increased allocations to defense, allowing for promised reductions in taxes, and estimates of probable levels of inflation.

He was stunned to find that the Reagan program would lead to federal deficits that would increase to $116 billion by 1984.[15] Distressed by the prospect of large deficits, Stockman worked feverishly to restructure the budget in order to meet the estimated defense needs while also fulfilling the Reagan promise to achieve a balanced budget by 1984. Negotiations were undertaken between OMB and the various cabinet departments, including especially the Pentagon and then subsequently between Stockman representing the White House and key members of Congress. In the final phases of this process during Reagan's first year, however, whatever formulae had seemed appropriate in the initial programming of the computer were abandoned. As Stockman put it,

> The defense numbers got out of control and we were doing that whole budget-cutting exercise . . . frenetically. . . . The pieces were moving on independent tracks—the tax program, where we were going on spending, and the defense program, which was just a bunch of numbers written on a piece of paper.[16]

THE NATIONAL SECURITY COUNCIL
AND POLICY PLANNING

The today-or-tomorrow dilemma of policy planning also can be illustrated by the activities of the National Security Council (NSC). In his appearance before the Senate Subcommittee on National Policy Machinery in 1960, President Eisenhower's Special Assistant for National Security Affairs, Robert Cutler, emphasized that the

NSC "does not serve as a planning or operational mechanism."[17] It was a curious argument, given Cutler's role as chairman of the NSC Planning Board and service as a member of the NSC Operations Coordinating Board. Presumably what Cutler intended to stress, however, was that the NSC itself was created by the National Security Act of 1947 to provide advice to the President on national security matters. The actual tasks of planning and the coordination of operations would be performed by staff members reporting to the NSC.

The distinction that Cutler sought to make obscures rather than highlights the responsibilities of the NSC, since the utilization of planning and oversight of the coordination of operations are crucial to the advice that the NSC provides to the President. In recent years, the planning role of NSC has been acknowledged more clearly, as with the designation by the Reagan administration of the Vice President, the secretary of defense, the secretary of state, the director of the CIA, the national security advisor, and three other presidential assistants as members of a National Security Planning Group.

John Endicott has usefully distinguished among the types of planning in which the NSC becomes involved.[18] The first of these is the formulation of assumptions about trends and the future state of affairs, which may be crucial to the selection among policy options. For example, how many nation-states will have a nuclear weapons capability by the end of the century, and what are the implications of nuclear proliferation for American foreign policy? What are the prospects for further revolutionary activity in Central America in coming years, and what are the pros and cons of alternative American military, economic, and diplomatic responses to such activity?

A second type of planning involves developing recommendations of actions that must be taken in order to achieve an effective integration of policies and programs with a common regional or country focus. For example, personnel within such departments as State, Defense, Treasury, Commerce, and the CIA have responsibilities that relate to U.S. policy toward Israel; others have responsibilities for U.S. policy toward Egypt; others deal with Saudi Arabia; others with Syria; others with Iran, and so forth. An effective set of policies for the United States in the Middle East requires coordination of these various efforts, taking into account a variety of factors, such as anticipated actions by the Israelis, probable policies of Arab states in the Middle East, estimates of trends in oil production and oil prices, projected developments in the Islamic revolution, and so forth.

Third, the NSC engages in contingency planning. If a coup d'etat should occur in unstable country X, what policy options would be available to the United States, and what circumstances ought to be considered in deciding which of the options should be pursued?

Planning in each of these forms contributes to NSC discussions. As Endicott notes, however, to the extent that the first occurs, it is more likely to be reflected in the efforts of an individual preparing a position paper than in the collective activities of the NSC. The second, integrative planning, presupposes a breadth of perspective in planning activity that, given a small staff, "usually is not possible and can only occasionally be accomplished."[19]

Contingency planning is perhaps the most common of the three within the NSC and its staff; but the contingencies that are most likely to be considered are those that emanate from a crisis that already is at hand or is believed to be imminent. As John Collins has noted in his detailed study of defense planning, even when the President and his top advisors have made explicit commitments to an emphasis on planning—as did Richard Nixon, for instance, or as did Jimmy Carter—a preoccupation with immediate operational concerns tends to overcome the concern with planning.[20] This is not to say that policy makers respond only to the exigencies of the moment with no consideration of what may occur in the future; but the priority concern is with information and analyses that will enable them to act effectively now. It is this priority that illustrates the intimate relationship of planning to intelligence.

INTELLIGENCE

The growing emphasis on crisis management in the American government in the years since the Cuban missile crisis of 1962 is testimony to top-level sensitivity to the close line between intelligence and planning. The concept of *crisis management* is that a systematic effort should be made to anticipate contingencies in world events that could generate significant threats to important

American interests. Such planning should forestall most foreign policy crises by preventing surprise, and thereby avoiding the necessity to respond in haste to unforeseen threats. Should crises develop, however, the idea is to have the organizational apparatus and repertoire of responses available that will enable policy makers to control or "manage" the crisis, minimizing the untoward effects on American interests.

The crisis management concept reveals the crucial relationship between the intelligence specialist and the decision maker—the consumer of intelligence. As with policy planning, it is correct to say of intelligence that it is a function that must be performed by every department and agency in the foreign policy apparatus, and it is necessarily a concern of all policy officials at executive levels. Like planning, however, the intelligence function has come to require specialized skills. Thus, particular units of government (identified below) have been assigned the major responsibility for foreign policy intelligence, and specially trained individuals (most of them devoting their careers to this specialty) have been assigned to the intelligence organizations.

In theory, the intelligence process is set in motion in response to the expressed needs of those in decision-making positions. In practice, however, there is a recurring tension between intelligence specialists, whose chronic complaint is that policy makers fail to make their needs clear, and decision makers, who complain that pertinent intelligence is not available when needed and that much of the information that is provided is irrelevant.[21]

As a study by a Senate subcommittee noted some years ago, policy makers often had found themselves inadequately informed not simply in spite of the receipt of daily intelligence from various sources including embassies all over the world, but partly because of the enormous volume of this information. As the report indicated, routines had not been adequately established that would provide clear guidelines for the kinds of information to collect and the kinds to report. "No one knows how to issue general instructions on who should be told what and when. As a result the rule seems to be, Report Everything."[22]

Properly performed, the intelligence function includes not only gathering information (by open means and by espionage, by individual intelligence agents, and by electronic means and photo-

224

graphy), but also analyzing the information, evaluating it to sort out rumor and falsehood from fact, synthesizing information received from various sources, and making it available in a form that decision makers can use.

The vital importance of being able effectively to utilize as well as collect intelligence data was indelibly impressed upon American officials following the Japanese attack on Pearl Harbor in December 1941. In a thorough study of American intelligence activity during the months before the Japanese attack, Roberta Wohlstetter found that American unpreparedness for the attack was not attributable to lack of evidence about Japanese intentions. Such evidence was relatively abundant, thanks largely to the success of American cryptologists in breaking the Japanese code. By decoding Japanese top-secret cables and radio messages, United States intelligence analysts had alerted American policy makers to the imminence of a major Japanese attack on western bases in the Pacific.

However, American policy makers in Washington and military forces in Hawaii still were caught by surprise on 7 December when Japanese planes launched a devastating assault on American warships anchored at Pearl Harbor. The surprise is attributable neither to a dearth of advance warning nor to the conspiracy thesis that some domestic critics found plausible in the aftermath of the attack (contending that because the Roosevelt administration surely knew an attack was coming, they must have left American ships vulnerable to a sneak attack in order to have a provocation sufficient to get the American people to support United States entry into war against the Axis powers).

Rather, as Wohlstetter demonstrates, policy makers were lulled into inattentiveness for security measures at Pearl Harbor by their conviction that the Japanese would attack targets much closer to Japanese traditional interests in the Pacific (Singapore or Hong Kong, for example), rather than undertaking a risky attack thousands of miles from their home bases. "In short," Wohlstetter concludes, "we failed to anticipate Pearl Harbor not for want of the relevant materials, but because of a plethora of irrelevant ones. Much of the appearance of wanton neglect that emerged in various investigations of the disaster resulted from the unconscious suppression of vast congeries of signs pointing in every direction except Pearl Harbor."[23]

THE MODERN INTELLIGENCE COMMUNITY

The Pearl Harbor attack more than any other single experience provided the motivation for creating an organization in the postwar years that would have the responsibility and the authority for coordinating intelligence activity for the government and for ensuring that the President would be receiving solid advice based upon available intelligence.[24] Thus, a Central Intelligence Agency (CIA) was founded with the National Security Act of 1947.

Intelligence functions are performed by a variety of governmental organizations in addition to the CIA. Such organizations notably include the Bureau of Intelligence and Research (INR) in the State Department; the Defense Intelligence Agency (DIA); and the National Security Agency/Central Security Service (NSA), which has the dual mission of providing cryptological support and communications security for the government and collecting, processing, and disseminating signals intelligence, such as that gathered by satellites.

It is the CIA, however, that stands at the apex of the American intelligence community, with the director of the agency (DCI) serving as the President's principal advisor on intelligence matters. The DCI fulfills this responsibility especially as statutory advisor to the National Security Council (NSC), which the President heads.

As indicated in Chapter 6, since its founding, the CIA has been assigned a variety of activities in addition to those which, strictly speaking, are part of the intelligence function. For example, covert action, propaganda, and counterintelligence are activities that fall within the CIA domain and that have embroiled the agency in controversy. Especially notable in this regard were activities that became the object of widespread publicity and extensive investigation in the 1970s.

INTELLIGENCE AGENCIES IN THE 1970s AND 1980s: FLUCTUATING FORTUNES

Just as the Pearl Harbor attack and the experience of World War II provided the stimulus to expanding American intelligence capabilities, so the revelations in the mid-1970s of abuses or failings on the part of intelligence agencies provided the stimulus to curbing their activities. The hostility that was directed at the CIA and other intelligence agencies in the 1970s must be understood as an element of a more profound popular disillusionment with government.

For instance, suspicions that the CIA had been involved in a coup d'etat in Chile in 1973, which brought about the overthrow of the constitutionally established Marxist government of Salvador Allende, was one of the factors that led the Congress to increase its oversight of CIA activity. By provision of the Hughes-Ryan amendment to the foreign aid act of 1974, the executive branch was required to report to the appropriate committees of Congress any covert actions undertaken "by or on behalf" of the CIA.

A Senate Select Committee on Intelligence was created the following year, headed by Democrat Frank Church of Idaho, (who previously had presided over an investigation of allegations that the International Telephone and Telegraph Company had made available financing to prevent Allende's election in 1970).[25] Just a few months before the establishment of the Church committee on intelligence, Richard Nixon had resigned from the presidency rather than face impeachment for his role in the Watergate coverup. Public disenchantment also had been fostered by the prolonged and costly United States involvement in Vietnam, the denouement of which was written in 1975 with the collapse of the American-supported Thieu regime and the hasty evacuation of the last American personnel from Saigon.

A House of Representatives Select Committee on Intelligence, headed by Otis Pike of New York, critically reviewed the adequacy of intelligence of various foreign policy crises, including the 1968 Tet offensive in Vietnam, the 1973 war in the Middle East, and the crisis in Cyprus with the Turkish invasion in 1974.

Considerable media attention was directed to the various investigations and reports, the result of which was to reinforce widespread suspicions (1) that the intelligence community had been proved inadequate in important respects in carrying out is primary responsibility for providing policy makers with adequate intelligence; (2) that intelligence agencies had overstepped the bounds of legality and perhaps of morality with their actions (the reference here emphatically included the FBI, not previously mentioned because its focus is domestic rather than foreign); and (3) that neither the President nor the Congress had exercised adequate control of the intelligence agencies.

With the executive branch bearing the brunt of criticism of intelligence abuses and failings, President Gerald Ford appointed a blue-ribbon committee headed by Vice President Nelson Rockefeller to make recommendations of changes in the ways in which the intelligence agencies were organized and controlled. However, several members of the Rockefeller commission, including former California governor Ronald Reagan, were convinced of the importance of an effective clandestine capability for the United States and were opposed to many of the more far-reaching proposals for reform that CIA-critics had made. The result was that the Rockefeller report was relatively bland, providing the basis for only modest changes during the Ford administration.

President Jimmy Carter was determined to effect more sweeping reforms of the intelligence agencies, however. As a presidential candidate in 1976, Carter had been highly critical of various publicized intelligence failings and alleged violations of the constitutional and legislative mandate for the CIA. In 1978, he issued an executive order considerably curtailing the covert action role of the agency. Carter had appointed his Naval Academy classmate, Admiral Stansfield Turner, to be the director of Central Intelligence, in which capacity he was to implement a major reduction in CIA personnel and activities and impose tighter control over the agency. The Congress, in turn, passed a Foreign Intelligence Surveillance Act in 1978, restricting domestic surveillance activities of intelligence agencies and providing for expanded congressional oversight of intelligence activities.

Even before his election to the White House in 1980, Ronald Reagan was among those who had denounced what he saw as an overreaction to alleged failures in the intelligence community, with severe resultant damage, Reagan claimed, to the ability of the United States to keep track of the activities of deadly adversaries. Upon assuming office, President Reagan acted on his conviction by loosening several of the restrictions on covert action and other programs of the intelligence agencies.

The contrast between the Carter and Reagan approaches to the utilization and control of the CIA and other intelligence agencies illustrates fluctuations that have occurred in the effort to resolve a central dilemma for a democratic society. Especially when the object of intelligence or covert activity is an adversary that may be intent on doing harm to the United States or its citizens or interests, secrecy in the conduct of intelligence or clandestine activity can be crucial to success. On the other hand, democratic practice demands, as a minimum, that those who act in the name of the state are held accountable for their actions. Accountability, in turn, presupposes access by those who have oversight responsibility (for example, the Congress on behalf of the citizenry) to full information regarding CIA activity. However, the wider the circle of those to whom access to such information is provided, the greater the probability that secrecy will be compromised. The democratic society thus faces what may be termed the conceal/control dilemma in regulating the intelligence function (here expanding the concept of "intelligence" to include covert action). How much concealment or secrecy is required for success, and how much is permissible without compromising accountability? Conversely, how much control over such activity by monitoring bodies such as the Congress can be exercised without hampering the effectiveness of intelligence agencies?[26]

THE EXPEDITE/GET-IT-RIGHT DILEMMA

Another important dilemma that confronts policy makers in regard to intelligence may be termed the expedite/get-it-right dilemma. The problem is especially severe in time of a foreign policy crisis— that is, during a situation in which a significant threat is posed to important American interests and the time for formulating a response to the threat is limited. In such a situation, policy makers experience competing impulses. On the one hand, there is a felt need to expedite action in response to a threat because delay might prove to be exceedingly costly. On the other hand, because information about the situation is likely to be incomplete in important respects, policy makers are inclined to want to take the time to "get it right"—that is, to improve the quantity and quality of information on which to base their decisions.

In a climate of uncertainty and ambiguity in intelligence, considerations beyond the need for better information may contribute to delay. Such considerations apparently help to explain the failure of military commanders to take actions that might have prevented the loss of the lives of 241 U.S. Marines in October 1983, when a truck carrying the equivalent of over 12,000 tons of TNT crashed into the headquarters building where the Marines were billeted, and exploded.

United States Marines had been dispatched to Lebanon in September 1982 as a component of a four-nation peacekeeping force. However, the political situation in Lebanon had deteriorated rapidly. The U.S. embassy in Beirut was destroyed by a terrorist bomb in the spring of 1983, and several Marines were killed or wounded in encounters with guerrillas or terrorists in subsequent months. Despite the mounting evidence of risk to Marine installations, the Marine Corps unit was expected to maintain a visible presence to demonstrate that its mission was peacekeeping, not combat. Thus, orders were given neither to withdraw the troops from the area nor to take more vigorous measures to protect them. The result was disaster. Investigating the costly failure subsequently, a Defense Department commission concluded

> that the combination of a large volume of unfulfilled threat warnings and perceived and real pressure to accomplish a unique and difficult mission contributed significantly to the decisions of . . . commanders regarding the security of their force. Nevertheless, the commission found that the security measures in effect in the . . . compound were neither commensurate with the increasing level of threat confronting the [peacekeeping force] nor sufficient to preclude the catastrophic losses such as those that were suffered on the morning of 23 October 1983.[27]

The expedite/get-it-right dilemma is made acute by the fact that intelligence preceding or during a crisis is rarely if ever 100% complete or accurate—and policy makers must assume that it never can be. Ambiguities and uncertainties, such as those regarding the intentions of hostile parties in Lebanon in 1983, must be confronted. If it appears that the quantity and quality of intelligence could be improved with further effort, the gains to be derived thereby often must be weighed against the costs of delay in taking action. The best that can be hoped for is that when action is taken, the problem has been diagnosed correctly, that an accurate assessment has been made of American capabilities to deal with the problem, and that remaining gaps or inaccuracies in intelligence will not be fatal.

Sometimes decisions must be made even when crucial bits of information are missing. As noted in chapter 2, in May 1975, President Gerald Ford, acting with the advice of his National Security Council, gave orders setting in motion a military operation to rescue the U.S. container ship *Mayaguez* and its crew from the

Cambodians, who had forcibly seized the ship sixty miles off the Cambodian mainland. Distress signals from the *Mayaguez* as it was being seized revealed that the ship was to be towed to an unknown port. President Ford and his advisors felt compelled to act, even though the most crucial bits of information—the precise location of the ship and the crew several hours after the distress message had been sent—were missing.

The precedent of the 1968 seizure of the American intelligence ship *Pueblo* loomed large in the minds of American policy makers in 1975. The *Pueblo* had been boarded off the coast and forced to North Korean shores, where the crew members were held prisoners for eleven months. A rescue mission had been deemed unfeasible, without endangering the lives of the crew. Only after months of futile diplomatic efforts had the Johnson administration agreed to make a humiliating apology to the North Koreans, which resulted in the release of the American prisoners.

Determined to avoid a repeat of such humiliation, the more so in the wake of Communist victories in Cambodia and Vietnam, the Ford administration decided that an effort must be made—despite important gaps in intelligence—to rescue the *Mayaguez* crew before the captors had succeeded in getting them to the Cambodian mainland.[28] Thus orders were given for an assault on the island where the crew was believed to be held. The result of twenty-four hours of intense combat was that 18 U.S. Marines were dead or missing and another 50 wounded. The fact that the crew had been released by the Cambodians, unknown to President Ford and his advisors, before the launching of the attack on the island only underscores the agonizing nature of the expedite/get-it-right dilemma.

COMMUNICATION, CONTROL, AND DECISION MAKING

In recent years, considerable improvements have been made in American capabilities for transmitting and processing information and intelligence expeditiously.[29] However, advances in communications technology do not solve the information problem in foreign policy decision making. As Paul Hammond has observed in testimony before Congress on information problems that face the Joint

Chiefs of Staff, one way to conceptualize "organization" is "in terms of the secrets people keep from one another".[30] In other words, the way an organization actually is structured (the "informal organization," which may differ considerably from the formal organization) largely determines who talks to whom about what and which kinds of information are shared within and across organizations.

"Organization" conceptualized in this way places emphasis on interrelationships among planning, intelligence, and communication and the ways in which authority and responsibility are allocated. In recent years, such interrelationships have been especially acknowledged in Defense Department writings through frequent references to the importance of C^3I: command, control, communications, and intelligence.[31]

Individuals as well as governments in advanced industrial societies have become dependent upon access to information through modern modes of communication such as the telephone, radio, and television. The extent of this dependence can be appreciated through imagining the consequences of a disaster such as a nuclear war (as depicted, perhaps in tame form, in the 1983 television drama, "The Day After"). American strategic planners have been especially concerned that such an eventuality might actually result in "nuclear decapitation"—that is, damage of such severity that major command would be destroyed or rendered incapable of communicating with subordinate commands (and thereby controlling the response that might be made to the attack). A limited number of nuclear explosions, if they are targeted selectively by an enemy, might suffice to achieve "nuclear decapitation".[32] Thus, considerable emphasis in defense planning has been devoted to such facets of preparedness as surveillance and warning sytems, electronic countermeasures to defend against missile attack, communications jamming, and redundancy of communication equipment and channels through which commanders and subordinates can communicate with one another.

The C^3I concept may be usefully applied well beyond the conventional usage that associates the acronym especially with nuclear war scenarios and military planning. More broadly, the concept has relevance for the foreign policy as a whole, assuming that one understands C^3I capabilities to refer to much more than electronic gadgetry and technological sophistication. Ultimately, such capabilities lie at the heart of the challenge of organizing in ways that will facilitate the making of wise decisions and carrying them out effectively.

THE TAKE CHARGE/DELEGATE DILEMMA

Each president has had his own approach to organizing the government in ways that, in his judgment, would enable him to exercise leadership most effectively.

"The buck stops here," the sign on Harry Truman's desk in the White House said, indicating the acceptance by the President of the responsibility for making the difficult decisions that may have intimidated his subordinates. On the other hand, neither Truman nor any other President has managed to cope with the responsibilities of office without delegating a sizeable portion of decision-making responsibility to subordinates. Invariably there must be a mixture of responses to problems, some of them laid on the desk of the President, where "the buck stops," and some of them delegated to subordinates for resolution. But what kind of mixture is appropriate to the maintenance of policy effectiveness and democratic principles? How can authority and responsibility be allocated so as to optimize the capacity of the system for dealing with an enormous flow of problems while maintaining coherence in policy and clear accountability for actions taken?

It is easy to get agreement in the abstract to the proper resolution of what may be termed the take charge/delegate dilemma. The decisions of greatest importance should be made at the top of the government or the organization. Problems that originate or are detected at lower levels should be fed upward through channels to the top if major decisions of policy are required. On the other hand, because it is desirable that those in key executive positions have time for reflection and for creative consideration of the total context within which policies must be formulated, minor problems should be dealt with at lower levels.

If the dilemma is easy to resolve in the abstract, in practice it defies simple solution. Which problems, especially when detected in the early stages, can be safely labelled as "minor," to be dealt with exclusively by lower-ranking policy officials? And if countless problems on the policy agenda are "major" at least in terms of their potential implications for the United States, how can the President be apprised of them all without being so overwhelmed that rash judgments are made and needed time for reflection is denied? If (as happens in practice) problems are to be studied in depth by those elements of government with responsibilities most germane to the problem at hand before bringing the issues to the President for final consideration, by what process of selectivity are issues to be assigned to various departments and agencies?

Complex problems tend to have implications for the organizational missions of several departments and agencies. How can responsibility for the analysis and resolution of such issues be allocated or shared without making the decision-making process unduly cumbersome? How much information and intelligence among participants in the process must be shared at each stage in order to assure sound option development and appraisal? And how much of this information must be passed up the hierarchy to enable key policy officials to make informed judgments without overwhelming these officials with detail?

No pat formulae are available for answering these questions. Presidents and their advisors have structured the decision-making apparatus to fit their perceptions of requirements at the time, in accord with their stylistic preferences, and the personal relationship which they have developed with key advisors.[33] Marked contrasts are evident, for example, between the elaborate structure that was developed in the Nixon administration and the simpler, more ad hoc systems that characterized the Kennedy and Johnson administrations and, more recently, the Carter and Reagan presidencies.

Richard Nixon had been Vice President during the Eisenhower presidency and thus had experienced the former general's preference for an orderly structuring the advice to the President. Eisenhower had made use of weekly meetings of the National Security Council as a forum for consideration of major policy issues and had insisted that staff members present analyses of the issues to the Council in highly digested form, with policy alternatives clearly distinguished.

As President, Nixon took the formal structuring of the flow of information and advice within the executive branch several steps further. At his direction, a network of interdepartmental groups and committees reporting to the National Security Council was created. Each committee was assigned responsibility for a particular issue area, such as strategic arms limitation talks (SALT), crisis management, intelligence, covert operations, defense programs, international energy, Vietnam.

With the exception of an under secretaries committee, which was chaired by the Deputy Secretary of State, each of the committees was chaired by the presidential assistant for national security affairs. Henry Kissinger held the position beginning in 1969 and this position as well as that of secretary of state from September 1973 until early 1976, when he relinquished the former position to General Brent Scowcroft. The system was a highly centralized one, with Kissinger acting as the dominant advisor to the President to a degree that made him virtually Nixon's surrogate for foreign policy matters.

John F. Kennedy, in contrast, had adopted a more collegial style, with a somewhat fluid structuring of the flow of information and advice on foreign policy issues. During the Cuban missile crisis of 1962, Kennedy relied upon an ad hoc group of advisors that became known as the ExCom (Executive Committee of the National Security Council), although the group was considerably larger than the formal composition of the NSC. In order to encourage a free and candid exchange of views, Kennedy absented himself from the early deliberations of the ExCom. On other occasions, however, Kennedy often involved himself directly in the details of foreign policy issues even when problems were still being studied at lower levels of the government.

Whereas Eisenhower, for example, had eschewed detail, Kennedy immersed himself in it, often bypassing channels to communicate directly with those at lower echelons who could provide him with the information he sought about a particular matter. As one associate put it, "President Kennedy is a desk officer at the highest level."[34] An advantage of such an approach is that if bureaucratic channels have become bogged down, top leaders can sometimes energize the bureaucracy by probing directly into affairs at lower levels, thereby also getting an idea of the key points at which communications within the bureaucracy are being clogged. As critics have observed of the Kennedy presidency, however, the effect of such an approach is likely to be that of funneling proportionately more problems to the top for decision. As one observer has put it, "The great risk of the Kennedy method is that no single mind, even a presidential mind, can absorb the information or muster the wisdom necessary for sound judgment of many intricate issues pouring upon the President."[35]

If the criticism is applicable to the Kennedy style, however, it is applicable to an even greater degree to a highly centralized system such as the one that placed Henry Kissinger at the hub of virtually all significant foreign policy information-processing and decision-making activity.

Conscious of this limitation of relying so heavily on an elaborate committee structure that funnelled information and issues for resolution to a single source, the Carter administration simplified the design. The NSC staff, which had been doubled in size under Kissinger, was reduced. Two interdepartmental committees, one given the task of relatively long-term projects and plans, the other assigned responsibility for crisis management, SALT, and covert operations, replaced the previous system.

In practice, however, the National Security Advisor to the President continued to exert major influence on the decision-making process. The incumbent to this position, Zbigniew Brzezinski, went to considerable lengths to distinguish his role in the process from the dominant one that Kissinger had played. However, frictions that surfaced between Brzezinski and other top officials, such as Secretary of State Cyrus Vance and Secretary of Defense Harold Brown, revealed that the National Security Advisor remained a kingpin in the structure.

When Ronald Reagan became President in 1981, a simplified interdepartmental committee structure, similar to that which President Carter had used, was adopted. A conscious effort was made to redefine the role of National Security Advisor from that of a primary source of foreign policy advice to that of coordinator and facilitator of advice from the departments of State, Defense, CIA, and other departments and agencies. Other White House advisors, however, such as Counsellor to the President Edwin Meese III and Presidential Chief of Staff James A. Baker III, came to assume considerable influence in the decision-making process, with the result that the pattern of friction among key participants in the process such as the secretaries of State and Defense with those in the White House who were close to the President continued as it had in varying degrees in earlier administrations.

In all administrations, the tendency is to process policy problems that are routine in nature or, like those dealing with the law of the sea or trade negotiations, ones that remain current for an extended period of time through channels in the bureaucracy. In time of crisis, administrations tend to impose a much more centralized structure on the flow of information and decision making and to limit the number of participants in the process.

There is a tendency also during crises for the President and his top advisors to become directly involved in the management of actions that are taken at the site of operations. An Army colonel who served in Washington as legal advisor and legislative assistant to the Chairman of the Joint Chiefs of Staff during the *Mayaguez* crisis of 1975 and in Korea as theater judge advocate and special advisor to the Commander-in-chief of United Nations Forces during a crisis in the Demilitarized Zone (DMZ) between the two Koreas in 1976, has identified the frustrations that are experienced in a crisis, depending upon one's location. "In Washington you feel an absence of information and an abundance of power," the colonel observed, "On the ground [at the crisis site] you feel an abundance of information and an absence of power."[36] To the extent that it is possible to do so, policy makers in Washington are inclined to cope with the frustrations associated with such uncertainties by increasing their control over actions that are taken.

Developments in communications technology in recent decades have made such exercise of control increasingly feasible. Officials in Washington can virtually command the precise movements of ships at sea, for example, as Pentagon officials did at times during the imposition of a "quarantine" (the euphemism used for blockade) during the Cuban missile crisis. They can telephone instructions directly to embassy personnel abroad during crises, as State Department officials did to Ambassador William Sullivan in Tehran (to the latter's annoyance) on the eve of the fall from power of the Shah of Iran. They can monitor with some precision the movements of secret military missions thousands of miles from Washington, as President Carter did in cancelling Desert One, the April 1980 mission to rescue the American hostages in Iran, when the President learned that mechanical breakdowns and a crash had reduced the helicopter capability to an unsatisfactory level.

The tendency of policy makers to want to exercise full control of distant actions in time of crisis is understandable; but such top-level tinkering with operational detail can prove to be an impediment rather than a sure road to success. Despite the means that have become available for providing policy makers in Washington with rapid access to information about distant actions and events as they occur, persons with operational responsibilities who are on the scene are likely to have a more detailed picture of the unfolding situation. If given adequate freedom to exercise their own judgment, personnel on the scene can tailor their actions to the nuances of change they detect in the situation.

POLICY EVALUATION AND LEARNING

Painful experience may reinforce the tendency of a president or other top policy makers to want to exercise maximum control over action rather than trust in the judgment of subordinates. The change in President Kennedy's approach to key military and CIA advisors during the Cuban missile crisis in 1962 after having experienced failure in the Bay of Pigs operation of 1961 is illustrative.

A deterioration in relations between the United States and Cuba after Castro came to power on New Year's Day in 1959 had led President Eisenhower to order the CIA to begin training Cuban exiles for an invasion of the island in order to overthrow the Castro regime. When Kennedy assumed the presidency in January 1961 he could have cancelled the invasion plans, of course. However, he had used the spectre of a Marxist regime "ninety miles off our shores" during the campaign in criticism of the alleged ineffectiveness of Republicans in dealing with the threat of Communism. To cancel invasion plans now would seem to be a rejection of the active opposition to Castro that Kennedy had demanded.

Moreover, time for deliberation was limited. For a variety of reasons (an impending rainy season, improving Cuban defense capabilities, growing frictions among exile groups being trained for the invasion, pressures from the Guatemalans to vacate sites in that country that were being used for training), action was required soon or not at all.

The subordinates who had been assigned operational responsibility for planning and executing the invasion provided Kennedy with reassurances. Military and intelligence experts argued that the prospects for success were high, at least for the limited objective of establishing a sizeable guerrilla force in Cuba, which in turn could serve as a rallying point for dissident elements, thereby eventually bringing the downfall of Castro. Some took an even more optimistic view, that spontaneous uprisings throughout the island in response to the invasion would lead Castro to capitulate almost immediately.

Thus, Kennedy gave the go-ahead. When put to the test for three agonizing days beginning April 17, 1961, the plan for the invasion of Cuba at the Bay of Pigs proved to have been constructed on a series of tragic miscalculations. When the failure was complete, the invasion force decimated, and the prestige of the United States badly marred, President Kennedy lamented to an advisor, "How could I have been so far off base? . . . All my life I've known better than to depend on the experts. How could I have been so stupid, to let them go ahead?"[37]

Accounts of the Bay of Pigs fiasco have been provided by several persons who participated in the foreign policy process at the time. Roger Hilsman, Arthur Schlesinger, and Theodore Sorensen, for instance, attribute Kennedy's hesitancy to challenge the views of the established experts who had designed and organized the Bay of Pigs invasion to the newness of the President to his office and his unfamiliarity with the strengths and weaknesses of various advisers.[38] In contrast, as Elie Abel has observed in one of the most detailed accounts of the decision-making process during the 1962 missile crisis, from the outset "Kennedy meant to control events, not to be swept along by them. The political initiative was to be his alone."[39]

APPLYING LESSONS OF THE PAST
TO VIETMAM

If one may agree with Schlesinger that "failure in Cuba in 1961 contributed to success in Cuba in 1962,"[40] it is far from clear that Kennedy and his advisors were uniformly wiser in their approach to foreign policy in the final months of his administration than they were during the first months. The Vietnam experience, for instance, reveals a pattern in which "lessons" of the past provided the Kennedy administration with a rationale for increasing the American involvement.

The first of the "lessons" was one that conditioned the outlook toward Communism not only of the Kennedy administration but of an entire generation of American policy makers. The struggle of the West with Communism was seen as "the Munich test" all over again. At a conference in Munich in 1938, leaders of the European democracies had attempted to appease Adolph Hitler by granting him territorial concessions in Czechoslovakia. Rather than reducing the risks of war, appeasement had whetted Hitler's appetite for further expansion. When German tanks rolled into Poland in 1939, leaders of the European democracies realized that their only recourse was to declare war on Germany; five-and-a-half years of bloodshed followed. For a generation of postwar policy makers, Munich became the symbol of what happens when democracies fail to stand firm against aggression. Because Communism was seen as inherently aggressive, it followed that a firm reaction to it was required.

As Ernest May has demonstrated, historical "lessons" often have been misapplied by American policy makers.[41] The parallel between the struggle that the revolutionary, Ho Chi Minh, was leading in Vietnam in the post-World War II years and the actions of Nazi Germany in the 1930s was tenuous, at best. However, for the Kennedy administration the struggle for control of Vietnam was seen in the context of the worldwide conflict with Communism. Especially when the response to provocations elsewhere had been ineffective, as with the Bay of Pigs invasion and with the futile protests that the administration lodged following the construction of the Berlin Wall in 1961, Vietnam assumed special importance as a test of the administration's ability to fight Communism. It was a test from which, given the "hairy-chested realism" that characterized the prevailing policy outlook, the Kennedy administration could not shrink.[42]

Partly at issue was the "Munich test" of resolve against aggression (so the actions of the Viet Cong and North Vietnamese were defined). In particular, however, the test was seen as that of an ability and determination to counter the guerrilla threat with which the Kennedy administration had become deeply concerned, not only in Southeast Asia but also in Latin America and in other parts of the Third World. In the minds of Kennedy and his advisors, the Soviet leader, Nikita Khrushchev, had thrown down the gauntlet in January 1961 in a speech expressing support for "wars of national liberation" worldwide. The Kennedy counter to "wars of national liberation" was a major program of "counterinsurgency," with Vietnam destined to become a key testing ground. As Kennedy told the Association of Newspaper Editors a few days after the Bay of Pigs invasion:

> it is clearer than ever that we face a relentless struggle in every corner of the globe that goes far beyond the clash of armies, or even nuclear armaments. The armies are there. But they serve

primarily as the shield behind which subversion, infiltration, and a host of other tactics steadly advance. . . . We dare not fail to see the insidious nature of this new and deeper struggle. We dare not fail to grasp the new concepts, the new tools, the new sense of urgency we will need to combat it—whether in Cuba or South Vietnam.[43]

When Kennedy assumed office, there were approximately 800 American military advisors in South Vietnam. By the time of Kennedy's death in November 1963, authorization had been given for increasing the number of American military personnel in Vietnam to nearly 22,000.[44] It may be, as several of Kennedy's close advisors have argued, that if Kennedy had lived, he would have withdrawn American troops rather than escalate the war by committing full combat units, as Lyndon Johnson did in 1965. What is clear, however, is that by substantially increasing the American commitment to South Vietnam, Kennedy had made it difficult for Lyndon Johnson to change course—the more so, given Johnson's anxieties about being as "macho" as his martyred predecessor had been.[45]

Just as Johnson had "inherited" the commitment to South Vietnam from Kennedy, so Kennedy had inherited it from Eisenhower; Eisenhower, in turn, had inherited the commitment from Truman, albeit in the form of aid to the French beginning in 1950 to fight a colonial war in Indochina. At virtually every critical juncture throughout these four administrations, Presidents elected to increase the commitment that had been made of American resources and prestige to the containment of Communism in Vietnam.

The concept of "critical junctures" is important to an understanding of the limits that are imposed on administrations that under some circumstances might effect a change of direction in foreign policy. On the one hand, successful foreign policy adaptation to a changing environment requires a capability for learning from experience. It requires the monitoring and evaluation of programs that have been instituted and of actions that have been taken, with policy adjustments made in response to evaluative conclusions.

On the other hand, the President and key advisors realistically do not have the luxury of reviewing major global policy commitments with an eye to needed changes on a daily or even on a weekly basis. Rather, only as circumstances change in ways that might call into question the assumptions that undergird major commitments, as policy priorities change, or as key personnel change (as with a change of administration) is there likely to be an occasion for a top-level review and reconsideration of previous decisions.

THE SUNK COSTS/SUNK HOPES DILEMMA

During the American involvement in Vietnam from the Truman era through the Johnson years into the Nixon administration, one can identify at least a dozen such occasions at which significant opportunity was provided to review the commitment that had been made.[46] The pattern of the decisions that were made during this period highlights what may be termed the "sunk costs/sunk hopes" dilemma of policy evaluation and learning. On the one hand, the more resources and prestige that are invested in a given policy commitment (sunk costs), the more incentive there is, even in the face of adversity, for continuing the commitment in order to salvage the investment. On the other hand, prudent policy evaluation requires an ability to recognize when the probability of success for a given venture is so overshadowed by the probability of failure (sunk hopes) that losses should be cut and the commitment abandoned.

If each of these occasions is treated in isolation, with an effort to view the policy options as they were presented to the President at the time, given the policy priorities and assumptions that prevailed, a case can be advanced on behalf of each of the decisions that was made. It is when the choices are considered in relation to the cumulative pattern of American involvement that the dismal consequences of the commitments that were made becomes evident.

At each critical juncture from 1950 to 1968, the option selected represented an increase in the stakes that the United States had invested in an outcome of the struggle in Vietnam that would be favorable in relation to American goals. In 1968, under great pressure from key advisors such as newly appointed Secretary of Defense Clark Clifford, President Johnson decided to reject the plea of his military advisors for still further increases in the American troop commitment. However, even after 1968, the Nixon administration escalated the bombing of North Vietnam, Laos, and Cambodia, although United States ground forces were gradually withdrawn. It is the pattern of growing involvement, particularly from 1950 to 1968, that led some observers and policy participants in the late 1960s and early 1970s to speak of a Vietnam "quagmire" in which America had become trapped.

Several critics have challenged the accuracy of the quagmire metaphor.[47] The metaphor directs attention away from the accountability of the President and other top officials for their policy decisions, critics argue, by depicting policy makers as having stumbled blindly into the morass until they discovered that they were up to their necks—or perhaps over their heads.

More persuasive, critics argue (and the present author agrees), is a picture of decisions made at each critical juncture by a President who, much of the time, was pessimistic about the prospects of achieving a military victory in Vietnam. The President was constrained from mobilizing the country for an all-out military effort, partly by his own reservations regarding the possible consequences thereof and partly by his reading of what level of military effort would be politically acceptable. Each of a succession of presidents nevertheless persisted in maintaining and gradually escalating the American involvement for reasons that have to do with the President's perceptions of earlier "lessons" for coping with "aggression" (the Munich test) in general and for dealing with Communism in particular.

The Vietnam experience reveals that the "learning" that occurs in the foreign policy process is not simply a matter of a President and his advisors acquiring wisdom and mastering "lessons" from experience. In the first place, such wisdom and mastery may not follow from experience; the "wrong lessons" may be assimilated. The more fundamental analytical point, however, is that the "learning" that occurs in governments is not simply a matter of individual cognition; it is both a bureaucratic and a political process.

Governmental learning is bureaucratic in the sense that it is reflected in the adjustments that are made in organizational doctrine, action, and procedures. Such adjustments condition the response that will be made to future policy experiences. In some instances, governmental organizations may make adjustments that better prepare them for the future. The Defense Department was better prepared to respond to the seizure of the *Mayaguez* in 1975 than it had been to the seizure of the *Pueblo* in 1968, for example— despite intelligence uncertainties that continued to prevail in the *Mayaguez* crisis.

Other events reveal, however, that the "lesson" that is absorbed from policy experiences may reduce the organization's capabilities rather than enhance them. For example, the American experience in the final years of civil war in China, from which the Communist forces of Mao Zedong emerged victorious over the Nationalist forces of Chiang Kai-shek, proved to be an intensely controversial issue in American politics. Several of the American "China hands" who had been serving in diplomatic posts there for years had been warning of the waning support that Chiang enjoyed and of the growing support enjoyed by the Communists. The Truman administration had endeavored futilely to mediate between the warring factions. However, when Chiang and his forces were driven from the mainland in 1949, to establish themselves on Taiwan, critics of the Truman policies alleged that Chiang had been "sold out" by the United States, and that policies reflected the views of "Communist sympathizers" in the Foreign Service.

Beginning in the final months of the Truman administration but continuing with even greater vengeance during the Eisenhower administration, when John Foster Dulles became Secretary of State, the government responded to these allegations by virtually purging the State Department of the "old China hands".[48] As five former State Department officials noted in a letter to the *New York Times* protesting Dulles's policies, "a premium . . . has been put upon reporting and upon recommendations which are ambiguously stated or so cautiously set forth as to be deceiving. When any such tendency begins its insidious work it is not long before accuracy and initiative have been sacrificed to acceptability and conformity."[49]

Because the Communist governing in Beijing (Peking) was denied recognition by the United States, no new crop of "China hands" would be groomed to replace those that had been retired from the service or reassigned. The "lesson" that had been learned from the China controversy of the 1940s and early 1950s was a variation on the ancient practice of slaying the messenger who bears bad tidings. The bureaucratic lesson was to avoid becoming tainted by allegations of being "soft on Communism" by ridding the organization of the sources of controversial views.

The result was that for years thereafter, the expertise readily available to the department on Chinese politics and policies was minimal. As America became more deeply involved in Vietnam in the 1960s, the legacy of the earlier purge was reflected in a tendency of policy makers to substitute simplistic images of a Communist monolith for the more complex and more accurate analyses that might have been available had expertise been retained and refurbished.[50]

The "learning" that occurs in the foreign policy process is political as well as bureaucratic, in the sense that invariably there are differences among participants in the political process regarding the interpretation of policy experience. Which "lesson" will be absorbed from a particular experience, such as the involvement in Vietnam, will be determined by the pattern of influence that prevails in the policy process, not simply by logic.

As Earl Ravenal has noted, in the aftermath of the Vietnam debacle, nearly all Americans agreed that a major "lesson" of that experience was embodied in the slogan, "Never again!" It has become clear, however, that "never again" has a meaning that varies from one group to another. For some, the lesson is to avoid ever again becoming drawn into a conflict that is primarily a civil war or a revolution. For others, the message is that the next time the United States becomes involved in war, the response must be decisive, avoiding the gradualism that characterized strategy in Vietnam. For still others, "never again" means to maintain a focus on America's "real" interests and not get drawn into conflicts in which the investment of American resources and prestige is all out of proportion to the interests.[51]

These and other interpretations of the past become incorporated into the advice and demands of various participants in the political process, both within and outside of the government. Essentially, alternative "lessons" compete with one another for embodiment in foreign policy doctrine and practice in ways that will condition future policy decisions.

It is at this stage of the process, during which existing policies are evaluated and the "lessons" of previous decisions debated, that the Congress as well as the executive branch has an important role to play. The role of the Congress in foreign policy, and the relationship of the Congress to the presidency, are the subject of Chapter 8.

NOTES

1. David Halberstam, *The Best and the Brightest* (New York: Random House, 1972).
2. Steward Alsop, *The Center: People and Power in Political Washington* (New York: Harper & Row, 1968), p. 115.
3. George F. Kennan, *Memoirs 1925–1950*, 2 vols. (Boston: Little, Brown, 1967) I: 325.
4. Kennan, *Memoirs* I: 325.
5. In short, as suggested by a former State Department planner on the basis of a study of planning from the 1940s through the 1970s, there really has been no "golden age"

of planning. There have been successes in every era, but each generation of planners has faced similar pressures for "relevance." Lincoln P. Bloomfield, "Planning Foreign Policy: Can It Be Done?" *Political Science Quarterly* 93 (Fall 1978): 369–391.

6. For more detailed discussions of the budgetary process, with emphasis on the defense budget, see the following. U.S., Office of Management and Budget, *The United States Budget in Brief*, published annually; U.S., Congress, Congressional Budget Office, *Defense Spending and the Economy*, Washington, D.C.: Government Printing Office, Feb. 1983; Lawrence J. Korb, "Military Policy and the Budgetary Process," in *National Security Affairs: Theoretical Perspectives and Contemporary Issues*, ed. B. Thomas Trout and James E. Harf (New Brunswick, NJ: Transaction Books, 1982), pp. 223–248; Arnold Kanter, *Defense Politics: A Budgetary Perspective* (Chicago: University of Chicago Press, 1979); Felix Fabian, "What's All This Fuss about PPBS?", in *American Defense Policy*, 4th ed., ed. John E. Endicott and Roy W. Stafford, Jr. (Baltimore: Johns Hopkins University Press, 1977), pp. 265–275.

7. Estimates in the early 1980s for the B-1 bomber were running $200 million each, for example. The M-1 tank was running $2.7 million a copy; Nimitz-class aircraft carriers were some $3.6 billion apiece.

8. Thus, weapons systems often are a key target of proponents of budgetary cuts. See for example, Jonathan Alter and Phil Keisling, "35 Ways to Cut the Defense Budget," *Washington Monthly* 14 (April 1982): 12–21 ff.

9. Prior to that the fiscal year began on 1 July. The change was made in order to increase the probability that Congress would have had time to act on the budget request received from the President in January.

10. Amos A. Jordan and William J. Taylor, Jr., *American National Security: Policy and Process* (Baltimore: Johns Hopkins University Press, 1981), pp. 191–192.

11. Kanter, *Defense Politics*, pp. 72–75.

12. Aaron Wildavsky, *The Politics of the Budgetary Process* (Boston: Little, Brown, 1964), pp. 135–142.

13. Wildavsky, *Budgetary Process*, pp. 166–167.

14. Kanter, *Defense Politics*, p. 88.

15. The annual deficit was $194 billion even by the end of 1983.

16. David Stockman, quoted in William Greider, "The Education of David Stockman," *Atlantic Monthly* 248 (Dec. 1981): 27ff, 40.

17. Robert Cutler, "The National Security Council under President Eisenhower," testimony delivered 24 May 1960 before the Subcommittee on National Policy Machinery, U.S. Senate Committee on Government Operations, and reprinted in *The National Security Council: Jackson Subcommittee Papers on Policy-Making at the Presidential Level*, ed. Sen. Henry M. Jackson (New York: Praeger, 1965), pp. 111–139.

18. John E. Endicott, "The National Security Council," in *American Defense Policy*, 5th ed., ed. John F. Reichert and Steven R. Sturm (Baltimore: Johns Hopkins University Press, 1982), pp. 521–527.

19. Endicott, in *American Defense Policy*, pp. 521–522.

20. John M. Collins, *U.S. Defense Planning: A Critique* (Boulder, Co: Westview, 1982), p. 32.

21. In a study of the State Department many years ago, Roger Hilsman found important differences in outlook between intelligence analysts and officials in operating roles, although both shared the assumption that future events could be anticipated best simply on the basis of the instincts one acquires from long experience rather than by scholarly analysis and in-depth historical research. Roger Hilsman, Jr., "Intelligence and Policy-Making in Foreign Affairs," *World Politics* 5 (Oct. 1952): 1–25; reprinted in Davis B. Bobrow, ed., *Components of Defense Policy* (Chicago: Rand McNally, 1965), pp. 349–367.

22. Jackson, *The National Security Council*, p. 23.

23. Roberta Wohlstetter, *Pearl Harbor: Warning and Decision* (Stanford, Calif: Stanford University Press, 1962), p. 387.

24. Subsequent wartime activity provided ample additional incentive for strengthening the intelligence capability of the government.

25. This and other aspects of congressional scrutiny of the CIA and other intelligence agencies are discussed in some detail by Cecil V. Crabb and Pat M. Holt, *Invitaiton to Struggle: Congress, the President and Foreign Policy* (Washington, D.C.: Congressional Quarterly, 1980), pp. 137–160. See also Harry Howe Ransom, "Strategic Intelligence and Intermestic Politics," in *Perspectives on American Foreign Policy: Selected Readings*, ed. Charles W. Kegley, Jr. and Eugene R. Wittkopf (New York: St. Martin's, 1983), pp. 299–319.

26. For contrasting answers to these questions, see Stansfield Turner and George Thibault, "Intelligence: The Right Rules," *Foreign Policy*, 48 (Fall 1982): 122–138; Michael M. Uhlmann, "Approaches to Reform of the Intelligence Community," in *Intelligence Requirements for the 1980s: Elements of Intelligence*, ed. Roy Godson (Washington, D.C.: National Strategy Information Center, 1979), pp. 9–19.

27. Key sections of the report of the Long Commission were published on the day that they were made public in the *New York Times*, Dec. 29, 1983, pp. 5–9. The excerpt quoted is at p. 5.

28. A useful analysis is provided by Richard G. Head, Frisco W. Short, and Robert C. McFarlane, *Crisis Resolution: Presidential Decision Making in the Mayaguez and Korean Confrontations* (Boulder, Co: Westview, in cooperation with the National Defense University, 1978).

29. Many reforms already had been made by the time of the *Mayaguez* crisis, in reaction to previous failures. For example, in 1968 the National Military Command Center in Washington, D.C., did not receive the emergency messages sent form the *Pueblo* that the ship was being assaulted by North Korean warships until it was too late for a response to be helpful (a two-and-a-half hour transmission time for one message, and one-and-a-half hours for another). A similar lag in the transmission of crucial messages occurred the following year when an American EC-121 military reconnaissance plane reported that in was being tracked and was in imminent danger off the coast of North Korea. By the time the messages were received in Washington, the plane had been shot down with the loss of all of its crew members. For a discussion of the system, see Head, Short, and McFarlane, *Crisis Resolution*, pp. 85–99.

30. Paul Y. Hammond, testimony May 20, 1982, in U.S., Congress, House Committee on Armed Services, Investigations Subcommittee, *Hearings: Reorganization Proposals for the Joint Chiefs of Staff*, 97th Cong., 2d sess., 1982, p. 597.

31. Evolution of the machinery in response to various problems that were experienced is described in Head et al., *Crisis Resolution*, chap. 4. A discussion of C³I in the Reagan administration is provided in U.S., Department of Defense, *Report to the Congress on the FY 1984 Budget, FY 1985 Authorization Request, and the FY 1984–88 Defense Programs*, Washington, D.C.: Government Printing Office, Feb. 1, 1983, pp. 241–259.

32. See John D. Steinbruner, "Nuclear Decapitation," *Foreign Policy*, 45 (Winter 1981–82): 16–28.

33. The structure of the apparatus, with particular emphasis on national security decision making, is described in several sources: I. M. Destler, *Presidents, Bureaucrats and Foreign Policy: The Politics of Organizational Reform* (Princeton, NJ: Princeton University Press, 1972); Robert H. Trice, "The Structure of the National Security Policy System," in *National Security Affairs: Theoretical Perspectives and Contemporary Issues*, ed. B. Thomas Trout and James E. Harf (New Brunswick, NJ: Transaction Books for the National Strategy Information Center, 1982), pp. 159–183; R. Gordon Hoxie, *Command Decision*

and the Presidency: A Study of National Security Policy and Organization (New York: Crowell for Reader's Digest Press, 1977); Endicott, in *American Defense Policy*; Jackson, *The National Security Council.*

34. Cited in Joseph Kraft, "Kennedy's Working Staff," *Harper's* 225 (Dec. 1962): 33.

35. Louis W. Koenig, *The Chief Executive,* paperback rev. ed. (New York: Harcourt, Brace, 1968), p. 176.

36. Colonel Zane Finkelstein, in videotaped discussion with the author at the U.S. War College, Carlisle Barracks, Pa, July 6, 1979.

37. Theodore Sorensen, *Kennedy* (New York: Harper & Row, 1965), p. 346.

38. Roger Hilsman, *To Move a Nation: The Politics of Foreign policy in the Administration of John F. Kennedy* (New York: Doubleday, 1967); Arthur Schlesinger, Jr., *A Thousand Days* (Boston: Houghton Mifflin, 1965); Sorensen, *Kennedy.*

39. Elie Abel, *The Missile Crisis* (Philadelphia,: J. B. Lippincott, 1966), p. 48.

40. Schlesinger, *A Thousand Days,* p. 297.

41. Ernest R. May, *"Lessons" of the Past: The Use and Misuse of History in the American Foreign Policy* (New York: Oxford University Press, 1973).

42. An incisive analysis of American policies by a man who served as Director of Vietnam Affairs in the State Department in 1963–1964 attaches major importance to the value that civilian as well as military participants in the policy process attached to "toughness and force." Paul M. Kattenburg, *The Vietnam Trauma in American Foreign Policy, 1945–1975* (New Brunswick, NJ: Transaction Books, 1980), pp. 155–164. Richard J. Barnet, who also served in the Kennedy administration, notes the reference among his colleagues in that era to "the hairy chest syndrome." Barnet, *Roots of War: The Men and Institutions Behind U.S. Foreign Policy* (Baltimore: Penguin Books, 1972), p. 109.

43. *The Pentagon Papers: The Defense Department History of United States Decisionmaking on Vietnam,* Senator Gravel edition, 4 vols. (Boston: Beacon Press, 1971) 2: 33–34.

44. *The Pentagon Papers,* 2: 199.

45. In a discussion with Doris Kearns in 1970, Johnson recalled the factors that had influenced his decision in 1965 to increase the American involvement in Vietnam. "Everything I knew about history told me that if I got out of Vietnam and let Ho Chi Minh run through the streets of Saigon, then I'd be doing exactly what Chamberlain did [at Munich] in World War II. . . . I believed that the loss of China had played a large role in the rise of Joe McCarthy. And I knew that all these problems, taken together, were chickenshit compared with what might happen if we lost Vietnam. For this time there would be Robert Kennedy out in front leading the fight against me, telling everyone that I had betrayed John Kennedy's commitment to South Vietnam. That I had let a democracy fall into the hands of the Communists. That I was a coward. An unmanly man. A man without a spine." Doris Kearns, *Lyndon Johnson and the American Dream* (New York: Harper & Row, 1976), pp. 252–253. See also Halberstam, *The Best and the Brightest,* pp. 644–645.

46. Kattenburg discusses ten "fateful decisions" in the years 1961–1975, having previously described several other earlier policy decisions, such as Truman's commitment to the French beginning in 1950 and the series of decisions made by the Eisenhower administration in 1954 and 1955 during and after the seige at Dien Bien Phu. Kattenburg, *The Vietnam Trauma.* See also the detailed treatment by Stanley Karnow, *Vietnam: A History* (New York: Viking, 1983), the basis for a televised documentary series on the war.

47. Such critics most notably include Daniel Ellsberg, *Papers on the War* (New York: Simon & Schuster, 1972), and Leslie H. Gelb with Richard K. Betts, *The Irony of Vietnam: The System Worked* (Washington, D.C.: Brookings Institution, 1979).

48. See especially E. J. Kahn, *The China Hands: America's Foreign Service Officers and What Befell Them* (New York: Viking, 1975). See also Michael Schaller, *The U.S. Crusade*

in China, 1938–1945 (New York: Columbia University Press, 1979); and John King Fairbank, *Chinabound: A Fifty-Year Memoir* (New York: Harper & Row, 1982).

49. Letter published Jan. 17, 1954, cited with comment by Hans J. Morgenthau, "John Foster Dulles," in *An Uncertain Tradition: American Secretaries of State in the Twentieth Century*, ed. Norma A. Graebner (New York: McGraw-Hill, 1961), pp. 289–308, 299.

50. James C. Thomson, Jr., "How Could Vietnam Happen? An Autopsy," *The Atlantic Monthly* 22 (April 1968): 47–53.

51. Earl C. Ravenal, *Never Again: Learning from America's Foreign Policy Failures* (Philadelphia: Temple University Press, 1978).

SUGGESTED ADDITIONAL READING

ALLISON, GRAHAM, and SZANTON, PETER. *Remaking Foreign Policy: The Organizational Connection.* New York: Basic Books, 1976.

BETTS, RICHARD K. "Analysis, War, and Decision: Why Intelligence Failures Are Inevitable." *World Politics* 31 (Oct. 1978): 61–89.

——————— . *Soldiers, Statesmen and Cold War Crises.* Cambridge, MA: Harvard University Press, 1977.

BRACKEN, PAUL. *The Command and Control of Nuclear Forces.* New Haven, CT: Yale University Press, 1983.

CHAN, STEVE. "The Intelligence of Stupidity: Understanding Failures in Strategic Warning." *American Political Science Review* 73 (March 1979): 171–180.

EYSENCK, H. J., and KAMIN, LEON. *The Intelligence Controversy.* New York: John Wiley and Sons, 1981.

GELB, LESLIE H., with BETTS, RICHARD K. *The Irony of Vietnam: The System Worked.* Washington, DC: Brookings, 1979.

GEORGE, ALEXANDER L. *Presidential Decision-Making in Foreign Policy: The Effective Use of Information and Advice.* Boulder, CO: Westview, 1980.

HUNTINGTON, SAMUEL P., ed. "National Security Decision Making in the White House and its Organization." Special issue. *World Affairs* 146 (Fall 1983): 211 pp.

KATTENBURG, PAUL. *The Vietnam Trauma in American Foreign Policy, 1945–1975.* New Brunswick, NJ: Transaction Books, 1980.

KINNARD, DOUGLAS. *The Secretary of Defense.* Lexington, KY: University of Kentucky Press, 1980.

KRONENBERG, PHILIP S. *Planning U.S. Security: Defense Policy in the Eighties.* New York: Pergamon, 1982.

ORMAN, JOHN M. *Presidential Secrecy and Deception: Beyond the Power to Persuade.* Westport, CT: Greenwood Press, 1980.

RANSOM, HARRY H. "Review Essay—Being Intelligent about Secret Intelligence Agencies." *American Political Science Review* 74 (March 1980): 141–148.

RAVENAL, EARL C. *Never Again: Learning From America's Foreign Policy Failures.* Philadelphia, PA: Temple University Press, 1978.

SALISBURY, HARRISON E. *Vietnam Reconsidered: Lessons From a War.* New York: Harper & Row, 1984.

SULLIVAN, WILLIAM H. "Dateline Iran: The Road Not Taken." *Foreign Policy* 40 (Fall 1980): 175–186.

THOMSON, JAMES C., JR. "On the Making of U.S. China Policy, 1961–69: A Study in Bureaucratic Politic." *The China Quarterly* 50 (April/June 1972): 220–243.

CHAPTER 8

᪐

The President and Congress
in the Formulation
of Foreign Policy

"In some ways, Congress is like a dangerous animal that you're trying to make work for you. You push him a little bit and he may go just as you want but you push him too much and he may balk and turn on you. You've got to sense just how much he'll take and what kind of mood he's in every day. For if you don't have a feel for him, he's liable to turn around and go wild. And it all depends on your sense of timing."

> —President (and former Senator) Lyndon B. Johnson

"Unfortunately, many in the Congress seem to believe they're still in the troubled Vietnam era, with their only task to be vocal critics and not responsible partners in developing positive, practical programs to solve real problems."

> —President Ronald Reagan

As emphasized in the previous chapter, if a nation-state is to adapt successfully over time to the demands of a changing world environment and changing domestic circumstances, creative adjustment is required not only in the substance of foreign policy but also in the institutional structure within which demands are processed and policies formulated and executed. It becomes important to examine the foreign policy role of the Congress, especially in relation to the presidency, to see how adequate this important institution of government has proved to be to the demands of the modern era.

The allocation of authority and responsibility among the Congress, the President, and the judicial branch were defined by the framers of the American Constitution nearly 200 years ago. Naturally, those who drafted the Constitution for a largely agrarian society of some 3.9 million people, in a new nation insulated from the major world powers by oceans then difficult to traverse, could not anticipate the needs of an advanced industrial society and world superpower, which as of the 1980 census numbered 227 million persons.

The authority of the presidency in this two-hundred-year evolution has grown to such proportions that critics in the 1970s spoke of an "imperial presidency."[1] Especially in the foreign policy realm, the dominant role of the President is clear. On the other hand, it would be erroneous to depict the growth of presidential power in foreign affairs as having been attained entirely at the expense of congressional authority. In important respects, congressional responsibilities in foreign affairs have increased rather than diminished in the past half-century. The pattern since the outbreak of World War II, in short, is one of a vast increase in foreign policy responsibilities for the government as a whole, but with growth and bureaucratization particularly characteristic of the executive branch.

Although the assumption of increased responsibilities has made severe demands on the Congress and the presidency for cooperation with one another in the foreign policy process, it also has engendered fierce competition. The constitutional allocation of authority among the branches, Edward Corwin perceptively observed many years ago, is "an invitation to struggle."[2]

THE PRESIDENT AND CONGRESS: PHASES IN AN EVOLVING RELATIONSHIP

The role that the Congress plays in the foreign policy process must be understood in relation to the evolution of the struggle with the executive branch. The pattern since the era of Franklin Roosevelt, during which the modern presidency took form, is revealing. The early post-World War II era witnessed a brief and

251

largely unsuccessful effort to reassert congressional prerogatives in foreign policy that had been claimed by the President. Congress in the late 1950s and early 1960s acquiesced to presidential foreign policy initiatives, such as the escalation of the American involvement in Vietnam. Growing disenchantment with the Vietnam war, together with the discrediting of the presidency in the Watergate affair and revelations of abuses in various parts of the executive branch such as the CIA, paved the way for the reassertion of Congress in the late 1960s and 1970s.

During his first year in office following a landslide victory, Ronald Reagan appeared to be on the verge of reestablishing total dominance over the Congress in foreign affairs. However, the Democrats remained in control of the House of Representatives by a substantial margin. After a brief "honeymoon" period, partisan opposition to Reagan's leadership thus revived the traditional pattern of discord and rivalry between the branches.

Such discord and rivalry often seem to the immediate participants as well as to the American public to present a frustrating impediment to the attainment of foreign policy effectiveness and efficiency. Sometimes such perceptions are well founded. At its best, however, the struggle between branches represents a system of checks and balances that not only is vital to the maintenance of democracy but that also can foster adaptation of the nation's foreign policies and institutions to changing domestic needs and a changing world environment.

An examination of the shifting relationship between Congress and the President in the years beginning with the New Deal will help to clarify the importance and the limitations of the role of the Congress in the foreign policy process. Attention is devoted in the last two-thirds of this chapter to the congressional foreign policy role in the 1970s and 1980s, with emphasis on congressional war powers, involvement in the ratification of treaties, the congressional "power of the purse", and general oversight of the executive branch.

DEPRESSION, WAR, AND
THE GROWTH OF PRESIDENTIAL POWER

The Great Depression that followed the stock market crash of 1929 had vast repercussions in America and abroad. The mandate for Franklin Roosevelt when he became president in 1933 was to utilize the federal government as the instrument of relief for persons who were experiencing the greatest distress from the economic collapse and as the instrument for effecting economic recovery. The New Deal programs that were put in place to carry out the mandate represented an unprecedented enlargement of the federal bureaucracy. Moreover, the Democrat-controlled Congress readily granted Roosevelt vast discretionary authority to design and implement programs tailored to meet the urgent needs of the time.

The Supreme Court, however, was unsympathetic to the New Deal expansion of presidential authority. In 1935, the Court ruled on the constitutionality of a major piece of New Deal legislation, the National Industrial Recovery Act. This act had been designed to promote industrial recovery through the creation of a large administrative apparatus in the executive branch to supervise "codes of fair competition." The codes, for regulating prices, wages, and working conditions, were to be drawn up by the industries themselves, with the approval of the President, or by the President in cases where industries were unable to agree upon an acceptable proposal. To the dismay and indignation of the President, the Court declared the act unconstitutional.

Article I, Section I of the Constitution, the Court noted, vests "*all* legislative powers" in the Congress. For the Congress to authorize the President to develop codes was to indulge in an unconstitutional delegation of legislative authority.

THE CURTISS-WRIGHT CASE   In the light of the Court's denial of presidential discretionary authority in domestic affairs, the judicial endorsement of such authority in foreign affairs is particularly interesting. The classic opinion was rendered in 1936 in the case of *U.S. v. Curtiss-Wright Export Corporation.*

The congressional action that was challenged in the case stemmed from congressional concern over allegations that munitions manufacturers encouraged war in the search for profits. The Nye Munitions Hearings, which began in the Senate in 1934, symbolized the concern. In the same year, the Congress passed a joint resolution authorizing the President to prohibit the sale of arms and munitions to certain countries in South America if, in his judgment, such sale would stimulate conflict in the countries concerned. The resolution left it to the discretion of the President to issue an order prohibiting such sale; moreover, having issued the order, he could subsequently revoke it.

Pursuant to the resolution, President Roosevelt ordered the embargo of arms shipments to countries at war in the Chaco (Bolivia and Paraguay). Because the Curtiss-Wright Export Corporation continued to sell guns to Bolivia, the corporation was convicted of violating the executive order. Appealing the conviction all the way to the Supreme Court, the corporation argued that the President had acted through a congressional delegation of authority that was clearly unconstitutional.

In short, in the Curtiss-Wright case, the Court was faced with an institutional arrangement similar to the one it had declared unconstitutional in the cases involving the National Industrial Recovery Act (*Schechter v. United States* and *Panama Refining Company v. Ryan*).

Mr. Justice Sutherland, one of the "nine old men" whom President Roosevelt denounced for "obstruction" of the New Deal, rendered the opinion for the Court in the Curtiss-Wright case. Surprisingly, in light of the previous decisions, the Court upheld the constitutionality of the congressional delegation of authority to the President. The fact that the President was not granted such authority in enumerated form in the Constitution was, in the opinion of the Court, not a barrier to the exercise of such authority in foreign affairs. As Justice Sutherland put it:

> The broad statement that the federal government can exercise no powers except those specifically enumerated in the Constitution, and such implied powers as are necessary and proper to carry into effect the enumerated powers, is categorically true only in respect of our internal affairs. . . . The powers to declare and wage war, to conclude peace, to make treaties, to maintain diplomatic relations with other sovereignties, *if they had never been mentioned in the Constitution*, would have vested in the government as necessary concomitants of nationality. . . .
>
> Not only, as we have shown, is the federal power over external affairs in origin and essential character different from that over internal affairs, but participation in the exercise of the power is significantly limited. In this vast external realm, with its important, complicated, delicate and manifold problems, *the President alone* has the power to speak or listen as a representative of the nation. . . .[3]

THE WARTIME PRESIDENCY   During World War II, President Roosevelt sought a substantial increase in his discretionary authority. In his message to Congress in January 1941, almost a year before the formal entry of the United States into the war, Roosevelt presented the rationale for enabling the President to act without being dependent at every turn upon explicit congressional authorization.

No one can tell the exact character of the emergency situations that we may be called upon to meet. The Nation's hands must not be tied when the Nation's life is in danger. We must all prepare to make the sacrifices that the emergency—as serious as war itself—demands. *Whatever stands in the way of speed and efficiency in defense preparations must give way to the national need.*[4]

Congress responded to the President's plea by granting him broad sanction to exercise emergency powers. For example, he was able to regulate wages, prices, and hours in accord with his estimates of national need; to issue rules rationing food, gasoline, and other goods critical to the war effort; to control the activities of aliens and of citizens of German, Italian, and Japanese descent; and to order government control of mines and factories if strikes or other disturbances threatened, in his judgment, the interruption of war production. In the Lend-Lease Act, passed early in 1941, Congress empowered the President to loan American goods and services to those nation-states whose defense he deemed vital to the preservation of American security.

Moreover, many important and far-reaching foreign policy decisions were made by the President during or on the eve of the war without prior congressional sanction. The most notable of these include the agreement in 1940 to loan fifty American destroyers to Great Britain, in return for a ninety-nine year lease of air and naval bases on British territory in Newfoundland and the Caribbean, and the secret agreements negotiated by President Roosevelt with other heads of state at Casablanca, Cairo, Tehran, and Yalta.

POSTWAR CONGRESSIONAL CONTENTIOUSNESS

As willing as most members of Congress were to yield to the President in response to the appeal of wartime necessity, as the war drew to a close—and especially after Roosevelt's death in April 1945—Congress began to become more assertive. When the Republicans gained control of both houses of Congress following the 1946 elections, the struggle with the presidency intensified.

The role of Senator Arthur Vandenberg, a prewar isolationist and a leading postwar foreign policy spokesman for the Republicans, was described in Chapter 4. Vandenberg's willingness and ability to work with Truman in forging a bipartisan approach to major foreign policy issues was crucial. The point that is pertinent to the present discussion, however, is that Truman felt compelled to consult with congressional leaders such as Vandenberg in foreign policy matters to a far greater degree than Roosevelt had done.

Still, many members of the Congress felt that the balance between the two branches had not been restored to a sufficient degree, not with sufficient assurance that abuses would not recur in the future. Only an amendment to the Constitution could provide such assurance, many believed.

Although it was during the Truman administration that such sentiment crystallized in Congress, Truman was out of office by the time a constitutional amendment was formally introduced into the Senate. This was done on the first day that Congress convened in January 1953 by Republican John W. Bricker of Ohio, together with sixty-two cosponsors. The amendment was designed especially to counter the growing tendency of Presidents to make international commitments on their own, without obtaining the consent of two thirds of the Senate, as the Constitution required in the case of treaties.

Such executive agreements had been used, for instance, in the destroyer-for-bases deal in 1940 and in the controversial agreements signed among the heads of government of the Big Three powers at Yalta and Potsdam. More recent concern stemmed from the fear of some members of Congress that, through American membership in the United Nations, the President might act without congressional involvement to commit the United States to international agreements, such as the Universal Declaration of Human Rights, that might permit the United Nations to interfere in American civil rights problems. Thus, the Bricker Amendment provided (in Section 3) that "Congress shall have the power to regulate all executive and other agreements with any foreign power or international organization. All such agreements shall be subject to the limitations imposed on treaties by this article."[5]

It fell to the popular Republican President, Dwight D. Eisenhower, to cope with the congressional assertiveness that had been unleashed in response to the foreign policy initiatives undertaken by Presidents Roosevelt and Truman. Eisenhower's reaction to the Bricker Amendment is particularly interesting and instructive. Although he had expressed agreement with other Republicans that President Roosevelt had usurped powers from Congress, Eisenhower resisted threats to his own prerogatives. After a few months of trying to conciliate Senator Bricker and his supporters, the President came to regard the Bricker Amendment as "a damn thorn in our side" that would reduce flexibility in the government's capacity to meet the demands of foreign affairs.[6]

The President endorsed vigorous efforts to defeat the Bricker proposal. After more than a year of intense dialogue between the White House and Capitol Hill and heated debate on the floor of the Senate, the amendment was brought to a vote—and fell one vote short of the two-thirds majority essential to its passage.[7]

THE LATE 1950s TO MID-1960s:
QUIESCENT CONGRESS

Congressional efforts to impose formal checks on the President in his conduct of foreign affairs subsided with the defeat of the Bricker Amendment in 1954. However, in spite of the fact that President Eisenhower resisted congressional restraints on his foreign-policy authority, as his successors would resist similar threats of congressionally imposed restraints, neither President Eisenhower nor his successors could prudently ignore the sizeable body of support that the Bricker Amendment had enjoyed even in defeat.

For example, in 1954, in consideration of a French request for American air and naval support of the beleaguered French outpost, Dien Bien Phu, President Eisenhower sought the advice of congressional leaders from both houses and both major parties. Congressional unwillingness to endorse the use of American armed force at Dien Bien Phu, unless multilateral support for the venture could be attained, eventually led to presidential rejection of the plan.[8]

On the other hand, throughout the ensuing years of the Eisenhower administration and into the Kennedy and Johnson administrations, when the President invoked the claim of threats to American vital interests, he was able to elicit congressional support for virtually unfettered presidential action. The Formosa Straits Resolution is illustrative. Since 1949, when Chiang Kai-shek and his Nationalist forces had been driven from the Chinese mainland to the island of Taiwan (then called Formosa) by the Communist Chinese, the Nationalists and Communists had remained in a state of mutual hostility. Chiang had launched a number of harassment attacks on the mainland and had attempted unsuccessfully to persuade the American government during the Korean war to bomb the mainland. The Communist regime, in turn, had been shelling the offshore islands (Pescadores) and had announced their intention to "liberate" Taiwan (Formosa).

In January 1955, Eisenhower asked Congress to approve a resolution that would authorize the President

> to employ the armed forces of the United States as he deems
> necessary for the specific purpose of securing and protecting Formosa
> and the Pescadores against armed attack, this authority to include
> the securing and protecting of such related positions and territories
> of that area now in friendly hands and the taking of such other
> measures as he judges to be required or appropriate in assuring the
> defense of Formosa and the Pescadores.[9]

The House passed the resolution by a 410 to 3 margin within a matter of hours. Passage was more difficult in the Senate, where critics such as maverick Republican Wayne Morse of Oregon complained that the Formosa Straits Resolution would give the President "a predatory authorization" to wage war. After three days of debate, however, the resolution passed the Senate by a vote of 83 to 3.

Senator Morse's fears came to naught during the Formosa Straits crisis. Almost ten years later, however, Congress again gave the President a virtual "blank check" for the deployment of American armed forces. Of 535 members of Congress, only Morse and Senator Ernest Gruening of Alaska dissented. This time Morse had ample justification for his concerns about commitments that were being sanctioned.

In August 1964, following an alleged attack on United States destroyers in the Gulf of Tonkin by four North Vietnamese patrol boats, President Lyndon Johnson sought and obtained from Congress a joint resolution (S J Res. 189) assuring the President of congressional approval and support of "all necessary measures" that the President, as Commander in Chief of United States forces, might take to protect American forces in Southeast Asia. The resolution gave prior sanction to "all necessary steps, including the use of armed forces" to assist any state within the Southeast Asia

Treaty Organization (SEATO) area. The American bombing of targets in North Vietnam began immediately, followed in 1965 by the dispatch of United States ground combat units to South Vietnam.[10]

The Formosa Straits and Tonkin Gulf resolutions provide examples both of the felt presidential need to enlist congressional support for major foreign policy ventures and of the readiness of the Congress of that era to provide such support uncritically. However, as American troop commitments mushroomed in the months and years after the Gulf of Tonkin incident, as casualties mounted, and as the war escalated in other respects, congressional sentiment changed. For many congressional critics, the Tonkin Gulf Resolution became the symbol of presidential trickery and manipulation that had provided the form of congressional participation in the shaping of policy without the substance.

Senator J. William Fulbright, for example, chairman of the Senate Committee on Foreign Relations, had played a leading role in shepherding the Tonkin Gulf Resolution through the Senate. As Senator Albert Gore of Tennessee subsequently complained to Fulbright, "I interpreted that resolution as approving the specific and appropriate response to this attack [by the North Vietnamese patrol boats], and the chairman of this Committee, in presenting such a resolution, stated to the Senate that this was his interpretation."[11] Indeed, the broad terms in which the resolution was cast enabled the administration to claim congressional sanction for a major escalation of the war. Fulbright was embarrassed and angered, feeling that he had been betrayed by the President, his former Senate colleague.

Johnson, in turn, grew increasingly impatient with congressional critics such as Fulbright, whose abandonment of him was seen not only as an act of personal disloyalty but also as a failure to acknowledge the lessons of history. As he put it in a speech in December, 1967, "To look for the easy way out is to appease aggression as others did in the face of Hitler and Mussolini."[12]

THE TRANSITIONAL ERA: 1965–1968

The years 1965–1968 were a transitional era for the Congress in relationship to presidential leadership in foreign policy. On the one hand, despite the growing reservations that many members had about the commitment of American ground forces to Vietnam, the majority of Congress continued to support the commitment. Until late 1967, the majority of the American public (and thus the majority of congressional constituents) remained supportive of administration policies. Even the minority in Congress that had become vocal in their criticism of the Johnson policies tended to feel compelled to vote for appropriations that would continue the support of American combat troops in Southeast Asia.

On the other hand, critics in Congress also sought to increase the pressure on the administration to reassess its policies and to consider the withdrawal of American forces from Vietnam. Senator Fulbright, for example, called the Foreign Relations Committee into session beginning in 1966 for hearings on Vietnam, providing a forum for a critical review of the administration's policies.[13]

By 1968, latent if not overt resistance to the administration's Vietnam policies had grown among Americans to the point that one further setback in the war would suffice to crystallize opposition. The offensive that was launched by Viet Cong (VC) and North Vietnamese forces at the end of January 1968, during Tet, the Buddhist New Year holiday, provided the catalyst.

Ironically, the offensive was unsuccessful in some important respects, relative to objectives stipulated by the Hanoi regime. However, even allowing for the exaggeration of its success by elements of the American mass media,[14] the offensive was important as "the last straw" that broke the back of the administration's claims about the progress that was being made in the war. Repeatedly, top military leaders and other officials from the administration had been quoted as "seeing the light at the end of the tunnel" and other guarded but positive images of success. In November 1967, for example, General William Westmoreland, the commander of American forces in Vietnam, had told a national television audience on "Meet the Press" that American and South Vietnamese forces were now "winning a war of attrition." A few days later he explained to the National Press Club that the war in Vietnam had entered a new phase, "when the end begins to come into view."[15]

With the Tet offensive, however, the North Vietnamese and VC forces managed to attack all major cities throughout South Vietnam, even including an assault on the American embassy in Saigon. Wishful pronouncements about the war from Washington had lost all of their credibility.

Presidential election-year politics added impetus to the significance of the Tet offensive as a symbol of the failure of the Vietnam policies of the Johnson administration. For example, the New Hampshire primary in March 1968, just a few weeks after Tet, was widely interpreted as a defeat for the President and his policies. Johnson supporters had expected to see the President coast to an easy primary victory. Johnson did get 49.6 percent of the Democratic vote. But Eugene McCarthy, senator from Minnesota and outspoken critic of Johnson policies in Vietnam, ran a close second with 41.9 percent.

Johnson could dismiss as but an annoyance the opposition within his party led by McCarthy. But as a biographer of Johnson's has noted, he was "obsessed" by the apprehension that Senator Robert Kennedy, brother of the President's martyred predecessor, would launch a presidential campaign based on his opposition to the policies in Vietnam.[16] Shortly after the New Hampshire primary, Johnson's fears were realized. Kennedy, hitherto hesitant to be the instrument of dividing the party and to be cast in the role of spoiler of Johnson's re-election, announced his presidential candidacy.

The President had been adamant in defense of his policies. In a speech in Dallas at the end of February, for example, Johnson told his audience,

> Persevere in Vietnam we will and we must. . . . Thousands of our courageous sons and millions of brave South Vietnamese have answered aggression's onslaught with one strong voice. "No retreat" they have said. "Free men will never bow to force and abandon their future to tyranny." That must be our answer, too, here at home. . . . I believe that every American will answer now for the future and for his children's future. I believe he will say, "I did not retreat when the going got tough."[17]

In March, however, Johnson received a report from a task force that he had appointed to review a request from General Westmoreland for an additional 206,000 troops in Vietnam. To "stay the course" in Vietnam evidently would require meeting this request. But to honor the request, the task force noted, would involve increasing monthly draft calls, probably calling military reserve units onto active duty, and seeking additional appropriations from the Congress. In evaluating this report, the President had to confront the evidence of growing opposition to his policies not merely within his own party, but even within the ranks of advisors upon whose judgment he was most dependent.[18]

At the end of March, Lyndon Johnson made the dramatic announcement that he had announced a halt to the bombing of North Vietnam except for the demilitarized zone that separated the north from the south, as a signal of his desire to seek a peace agreement with the North Vietnamese. Furthermore, under no circumstances would he seek or accept his party's nomination for reelection to the presidency.

The policy reversal that began with the startling announcement by Johnson at the end of March was a triumph of sorts not only for prominent antiwar candidates such as Senators McCarthy and Kennedy but also for others in the Congress and in the nation at large who had been urging the President to seek to de-escalate the conflict in Vietnam. The success of critics in effecting a change would serve (as Richard Nixon would soon learn) to encourage other challenges to presidential foreign policy leadership. The weakening of the presidency in the Nixon years as a result of the Watergate affair provided further encouragement to congressional activism.

THE 1970s AND 1980s

The more recent period has been one in which the relationship of Congress to the President in foreign policy matters has moved from strident antagonism, in the 1970s, to cautious collaboration interspersed with periodic skirmishes in the 1980s. Congress has sought to reassert and to some extent redefine its foreign policy role. In this effort, Congress has drawn upon the full gamut of constitutional authority at its disposal—war-making power, involvement in the treaty process, control of the "purse-strings," Senate advice and consent to presidential appointments, and the power to conduct investigations. An examination of some of the successes and failures that Congress has experienced in its encounters with the presidency over the past fifteen years reveals the possibilities but also the limits of congressional foreign policy assertiveness.

WAR POWERS

The struggle between the Congress and the presidency that emerged in the late 1960s and early 1970s was particularly intense in regard to war powers for reasons that are explicable not only in terms of the contemporary experience in Southeast Asia but also in terms of the imprecision of constitutional provisions for a sharing of authority between the legislative and executive branches. The framers of the Constitution had emphatically rejected the British precedent of entrusting both the declaration of war and the execution of war to the executive. The Constitution entrusts to the Congress rather than to the President the power to declare war; at the same time, the President is designated commander-in-chief of the armed forces, responsible not only for commanding forces once war is declared but also for enabling the nation to respond to threats.

As the meaning of the Constitution evolved in response to historical experience, the exercise of presidential authority in the role of commander-in-chief of the armed forces posed an increasing challenge to congressional authority by creating situations in which the commitment of armed forces represented a de facto declaration of war. To cite examples that were especially pertinent in congressional debates in the 1970s, both in Korea in 1950 and in Vietnam in 1965 the President committed American armed forces to combat without a declaration of war.

The vast majority of the members of Congress supported the commitment that was made by the President in 1950 and again in 1965. In each instance, however, not only was the early readiness to endorse American military action abroad followed by disillusionment as casualties mounted, but also a gulf of mutual distrust was created between the White House and Capitol Hill. By the onset of the 1970s, the gulf had become enormous.

In April 1970, President Nixon ordered United States troops to strike across the Vietnamese border into Cambodia to destroy or neutralize bases that had been used by North Vietnamese forces as sanctuaries. The decision to launch the attack, which had the effect of expanding the arena of ground combat, was made in secret with no consultation whatever with Congress. To many members of Congress, already in a mood to challenge such exercise of presidential power, the assault into Cambodia was the final demonstration that presidential freedom of action in the use of force had to be curtailed.

Within weeks, several bills designed to limit the President's war powers had been introduced into the Congress. Hearings on the bills provided the occasion for a searching examination of what a House subcommittee termed "the most complex and perplexing problem with which the subcommittee has yet been concerned."[19] The hearings also provided an extended forum for a critical review of the administration's policies in Southeast Asia.

The repeal of the Tonkin Gulf Resolution in December 1970, was a signal to the President of congressional refusal to continue to provide automatic sanction for military commitments by the President in Southeast Asia. Agreement upon the specifics of a war powers resolution that would govern future commitments in any part of the world proved to be more elusive. Congressional debate on alternative bills continued into 1971, 1972, and even into 1973.

In the summer of 1973, a compromise measure was finally passed by an overwhelming vote in the House of Representatives. An amended version of the bill was passed by a large margin in the Senate. In November, the Congress forwarded to the President for his signature the final version of the joint resolution that had been agreed to in conference committee.

President Nixon, arguing that the legislation would restrict the President to a degree that was contrary to the national interest, vetoed the resolution. In December 1973, the Congress sustained the resolution over the President's veto.

THE WAR POWERS RESOLUTION

The resolution imposed three principal types of demands upon the President in circumstances in which the American armed forces were to be introduced into a hostile environment.[20] First, the resolution required consultation with the Congress before the introduction of armed forces "into hostilities or into situations where imminent involvement in hostilities is clearly indicated by the circumstances, and after every such introduction [the President] shall consult regularly with the Congress until United States Armed Forces are no longer engaged in hostilities or have been removed from such situations."

Second, there was a reporting requirement. The President was to render a written report to the Speaker of the House and to the President pro tempore of the Senate within 48 hours of the introduction of armed forces into a hostile environment (as defined above, and in the act). The initial report was to explain the necessity for the commitment that was being made, the constitutional and legislative authority for the President's actions, and the estimated scope and duration of the involvement. Periodically thereafter, the President was to provide reports on the status of the involvement "so long as such armed forces continue to be engaged in such hostilities or situation."

Third, the resolution provided for the termination of the use of armed forces at any time that the Congress would so direct, by concurrent resolution, and in any event within sixty days after the initial presidential report to the Congress of the deployment of armed forces, with the following exceptions: unless Congress had extended the authorized time period by law, had declared war, or was physically unable to meet because of armed attack. If the President were to certify in writing to the Congress that "unavoidable military necessity respecting the safety of the United States Armed Forces requires the continued use of such armed forces in the course of bringing about a prompt removal of such forces," then the time period for the involvement of forces could be extended for not more than an additional thirty days.

The termination provisions proved to be the most controversial feature of the War Powers Resolution. Objections were made on legal grounds that in imposing the threat of a legislative veto over presidential exercise of authority, the Congress had exceeded its constitutional authority. On practical grounds, it was argued that this feature of the resolution imposed negative restrictions in a context of emergency where positive cooperation between branches of government would be most important. As one set of congressmen put it, they were troubled by language in the resolution that "permits the exercise of congressional will through inaction." As a minority report noted, the most important provisions of the resolution

are probably unconstitutional and certainly are unwise. . . . The severe restrictions which this resolution seeks to impose on the authority of the President [are] dangerous. . . . Flexibility—not the exact delimination of powers—is a basic characteristic of the Constitution. . . .

> What is most ironic is that this joint resolution, constructed as it is with an eye to our unfortunate experiences during the mid-1960's, would not have prevented our steadily deepening involvement in Vietnam, had it been on the books 10 years ago. For example, there is no reason to believe that Congress after the Gulf of Tonkin incident would have refused to approve Presidential action through the mechanism provided in this measure. Congress . . . would have declared war, had that been requested, or we would have specifically authorized the use of our Armed Forces.[21]

A decision in June 1983 by the United States Supreme Court in declaring unconstitutional the legislative veto in a case dealing with the immigration laws, had the effect of sustaining the criticisms that had been made by those who dissented from the War Powers Resolution. That is, the 1983 case provided the basis for challenging the constitutionality of similar legislative-veto provisions in some 200 other statutes, including the War Powers Resolution.[22]

Nevertheless, until declared otherwise, the War Powers Resolution as a whole remains the law of the land. In September 1983, for example, legislation that was passed authorizing the President to keep United States Marines in Lebanon for eighteen months explicitly invoked the War Powers Act. In November 1983, Congress again invoked the War Powers Resolution in asserting that American troops in Grenada must be removed within the time period specified by the act.

In neither instance, however, did President Reagan acknowledge the legitimacy of limitations on his powers as commander in chief. The manner in which President Reagan has dealt with provisions of the act is consistent with the behavior of his predecessors. It is instructive to review such behavior briefly, together with the behavior of the Congress, in determining the actual—as contrasted to theoretical—effects that the resolution has had in the influence wielded by the legislative and executive branches over war powers.

LIMITS OF THE WAR POWERS CONSTRAINTS IN PRACTICE

President Gerald Ford acknowledged the reporting provisions of the War Powers Resolution on four different occasions within a matter of weeks during the spring of 1975 in rendering reports to the Congress on actions that were taken in Southeast Asia.[23] The first of these occasions was on 4 April, when the Congress was informed that the President had ordered an amphibious task force to the Vietnamese coast in the vicinity of Da Nang, to rescue U.S. nationals and Vietnamese refugees who were fleeing from the major North Vietnamese assault that was underway.

A week later, Congress was informed that 350 Marines had been rushed by helicopters, with tactical air support, to the Cambodian capital of Phnom Penh to rescue American citizens who were endangered as the capital fell to Khmer Communist forces. At the end of April, the South Vietnamese capital, Saigon, was being overrun by North Vietnamese forces; and the Congress was informed of a military rescue mission similar to the one that had been undertaken at Phnom Penh. Two weeks later, the *Mayaguez* incident, which was discussed in the previous chapter, occurred. The Congress was informed that a Marine assault on the island of Koh Tang had been ordered, supported by naval and air forces, for the purpose of rescuing the ship and the crew.

In none of his reports to the Congress did President Ford concede that the provisions of the War Powers Resolution, which would limit the duration of the commitment of forces, were applicable. In each report, the President was careful to use phrases such as, "In accordance with my desire to keep the Congress fully informed on this matter, and *taking note of the provision* of section 4(a)(2) of the War Powers Resolution . . . I wish to report to you concerning. . . "[24] President Jimmy Carter used almost identical wording in April 1980 in reporting the abortive attempt that had been made to carry out a mission to rescue Americans who were held hostage in Iran.[25]

Moreover, despite their reports to the Congress, neither Ford nor Carter conceded the real applicability of the War Powers Resolution as a restriction on the exercise of presidential power. Carter's White House counsel issued a legal opinion supporting the proposition that the President was fully within his constitutional powers as President and Commander-in-Chief in using armed forces in the rescue mission in Iran and that no prior consultation was required.[26] Similarly, Ford has contended that "in none of those instances did I believe the War Powers Resolution applied, and many members of Congress also questioned its applicability in cases of protection and evacuation of American citizens."[27]

The practical difficulties of the consultation provisions of the resolution also have been emphasized by Ford. When the operation at Da Nang began, for instance, Congress was in Easter recess. Of the individuals holding key leadership positions in the Congress, "two were in Mexico, three were in Greece, one was in the Middle East, one was in Europe, and two were in the People's Republic of China. The rest we found in twelve widely scattered states of the Union."[28]

Although various members of Congress have expressed their indignation at not being consulted in advance of these various military actions, the fact is that the majority of Congress has been content to assert the applicability of the War Powers Resolution without vigorously contesting presidential actions that in a strict sense disregard provisions of the resolution. Indeed, despite casualties that were inflicted within weeks of the deployment of some 1,200 Marines to Lebanon beginning in September 1982, President Reagan was able to maintain the fiction that the War Powers Resolution was not applicable because "there is no intention or expectation that U.S. Armed Forces will become involved in hostilities."[29]

Various members of Congress protested, as some had done previously when Presidents Carter and Ford had refused to be bound by the restrictions of the War Powers Act. Yet, when President Reagan finally agreed to a legislative limitation on the commitment of the Marines to Lebanon, in the wake of an extensive debate of the issue, in September 1983 the Congress gave the President authority to keep the Marines there for eighteen months. Moreover, although the legislation made explicit the applicability of the War Powers Resolution, in signing the act, President Reagan maintained that "I do not and cannot cede any of the authority vested in me under the Constitution as president and as commander in chief of United States armed forces."[30]

The debate flared up with renewed intensity the following month, when a suicide attack on Marine Corps barracks in Beirut claimed 241 lives. However, the Reagan administration's decision to keep an American force in place in Lebanon, in order to avoid the impression of weakness in the face of terrorist action, was supported by most Republicans in Congress, and substantial numbers of Democrats including Speaker of the House Thomas P. "Tip" O'Neill. It was not until February 1984, when the political situation in Lebanon had deteriorated so badly that the rationale for a Marine Corps role as "peacekeepers" had been undermined almost completely that congressional sentiment for withdrawing the Marines swelled to major proportions. In that month, with Lebanon engulfed in conflict verging on civil war, President Reagan ordered the beginning of the evacuation of Marines from Lebanon to American naval vessels offshore.

The appropriate conclusion regarding congressional efforts to assert a role in the foreign policy process through legislation that would restrict presidential commitments of armed forces would seem to be one advanced several years ago by William Lanouette.

The War Powers Resolution is one of those wonderful, uniquely American documents that lets all of us say what we want to while doing as much or as little as we please. It has just enough legal muscle to make those who invoke it think for a few minutes, but not enough to stop anyone dedicated to a course of action.[31]

TREATY MAKING POWERS

Closely related to the congressional concern about limiting the President's power to make military commitments that could lead to war has been a concern for arms control. Congressional desire to be involved in the arms control process was expressed as early as 1961, when the Arms Control and Disarmament Agency (ACDA) was created by statute in fulfillment of a campaign pledge made by John F. Kennedy. The act provided:

That no action shall be taken under this or any other law that will obligate the United States to disarm or to reduce or to limit the Armed Forces or armaments of the United States, except pursuant to the treaty making power of the President under the Constitution or unless authorized by further affirmative legislation by the Congress of the United States.[32]

The act put the Congress on record as reaffirming the Senate's constitutional responsibilities for giving its advice and consent (by a two-thirds majority vote) to treaties, thereby discouraging the reliance on executive agreements to finalize arms control negotiations unless specifically authorized to do so by congressional act.

The White House did work closely with key members of the

Congress in negotiating one of the first major arms control agreements with the Soviet Union, the Limited Test Ban Treaty of 1963. A source of considerable frustration to the Congress, however, was the penchant for secrecy that prevailed in much of the executive branch—especially in the Pentagon. Security classifications were imposed upon information about arms developments and weapon systems, even in instances in which the information was crucial to the evaluation of pending arms control agreements.

As Senator Hubert Humphrey of Minnesota lamented in a speech otherwise supportive of the 1963 Test Ban, much of the information that he had at his disposal that was vital to enable him to persuade skeptics about the merits of the treaty had been labelled "secret," and he had been warned not to disclose it. "I do not know how one can possibly come to an understanding regarding this issue if all the evidence is labelled 'secret'," he observed. Noting that a great deal of supposedly secret information finds its way into the press, he emphasized that "the people of the United States are getting sick and tired about this so-called secrecy."[33]

The complaint was a recurring one. An arms control expert who served as counselor to the ACDA and as a member of the U.S. delegation to the Strategic Arms Limitation Talks (SALT) during the Nixon years has described policy making in the early to mid-1970s as characterized by "obsessive secrecy." One consequence, he notes, was that "the *texts* of the various U.S. proposals submitted to the Soviet Union in SALT I and SALT II have never been shown to the Congress, even in executive session, let alone made available for public comment."[34]

In the case of SALT I, however, which was consummated in Moscow in May 1972 in an agreement signed by President Richard Nixon and Leonid Brezhnev, general secretary of the Central Committee of the Communist Party of the Soviet Union, the Congress already had gathered much of the salient information on its own. The agreement had two components: a treaty, limiting each of the two signatory powers to two sites each for the construction of anti-ballistic missiles (ABMs); and an agreement and protocol committing the signatories for five years, while SALT negotiations continued, to refrain from construction of intercontinental ballistic missiles (ICBMs) and submarine-launched ballistic missiles (SLBMs).

In 1969 and 1970, Congress had held extensive hearings on the

ABM, receiving testimony from a wide array of scientific experts as well as governmental officials. Proposals of the Nixon administration for constructing an elaborate ABM system (thereby implementing plans that had been developed in the Johnson administration) had been challenged severely. Moreover, conflicting testimony from experts on the probable effectiveness of the ABM, as well as differing views of the consequences of ABM construction for United States-Soviet relations, had generated what one observer has called "the bitterest fight over a strategic-weapon system in American history."[35]

Thus, the nearly unanimous vote (88–2) in the Senate in 1972 in support of ratification of the ABM treaty is not accurately describable as signifying congressional docility in response to presidential action. Rather, the treaty was supported because it seemed to represent a retreat by the President from policies that had met congressional opposition. Furthermore, the limitation on ABM construction was consonant with congressional estimates of security requirements in that it would be binding on the Soviets (who were ahead in ABM construction) as well as on the United States.

The interim agreement and protocol, the second component of the 1972 Moscow accords, were reviewed and approved by both houses of Congress in general compliance with the 1961 statute requiring congressional endorsement of arms reduction agreements even when no formal treaty is involved. Like the limitation on ABM sites, the restriction on ICBM and SLBM construction was consistent with prevailing sentiment in the Congress in favor of halting the arms race. Moreover, the agreement could be described as a policy initiative that bridged Democratic and Republican administrations. As the party platform that the Democrats approved at their convention in July 1972 proclaimed, "The last Democratic Administration took the lead in pressing for U.S.-Soviet agreement on strategic arms limitation. The recent SALT agreement is an important and useful first step."[36]

The one major challenge that was posed to the interim agreement came not from the pro-detente Democrats who dominated their party in 1972, but from a group of hardline Cold Warriors headed by Senator Henry "Scoop" Jackson, Democrat from Washington. Jackson warned his fellow senators that the numbers of missile launchers that would become fixed by the interim agreement "confer on the Soviet Union the authority to retain or deploy a number of weapons . . . that exceeds our own in every capacity and by a 50 percent margin."[37]

Jackson was especially concerned about ensuring that the SALT II negotiations, scheduled to begin in October 1972, would not be prejudicial to continuing strategic weapon developments that Jackson regarded as essential to American security. After weeks of heated discussions, the Senate accepted an amendment to the agreement that Jackson had introduced, maintaining that no future SALT agreement should be accepted that limited American strategic forces to levels inferior to those of the Soviets. The White House offered no objections to the amendment, which had the effect of strengthening the hand of the executive branch in subsequent bargaining with the Soviets.

STRATEGIC ARMS LIMITATION TREATY

Negotiations for SALT II, which were begun during the Nixon years, were nearly completed by the administration of Gerald Ford, who signed another interim agreement with Soviet leader Brezhnev, this time at the Soviet eastern port city of Vladivostok. It fell to Jimmy Carter, however, to translate the interim agreement into a finalized SALT II treaty, which was signed by Carter and Brezhnev in Vienna in June 1979.[38]

The domestic politics of SALT II have been described elsewhere.[39] Here we simply note several key factors that contributed to opposition to the treaty in the U.S. Senate, and that, in January 1980, led Carter to ask the Senate to defer consideration of the treaty indefinitely.

Support among Senators for the Jackson hardline approach to arms control negotiations had increased by the time Carter entered the White House in January 1977. After extensive discussion with Jackson and other senators, Carter was persuaded to make major changes in the American proposal for a SALT II treaty in ways that represented a major departure from the guidelines that Ford and Brezhnev had agreed to in Vladivostok. Senator Jackson was supportive of the changes, which would require substantially greater reductions in strategic arms than the Soviets hitherto had been willing to make. Moreover, Carter himself had campaigned on a promise to sharply reduce the world's nuclear arsenals.

Few American specialists on Soviet affairs were surprised, however, when Moscow rejected the new American proposal, which was presented by Secretary of State Cyrus Vance in March 1977. Thereafter, negotiations resumed along lines much closer to the limitations in strategic weapons that had been anticipated at Vladivostok. To American hardliners such as Jackson, it seemed obvious that the Carter administration had capitulated in the face of Soviet intransigence. When Carter left for Vienna in June 1979 to sign the SALT II agreements, Jackson disparagingly compared the trip with that of Neville Chamberlain leaving for Munich in 1938.[40]

The agreement at Vienna represented the results of nearly ten years of negotiations and actually had a number of components: the treaty itself, which consisted of nineteen articles, each typically supplemented by one or more "agreed statements" or "common understandings" between the signatory parties; a protocol (with additional agreed statements and common understandings); a memorandum of understanding on the numbers of strategic offensive arms that each side possessed as of 1 November 1978; a joint statement of principles and guidelines for subsequent SALT negotiations; and a separate statement from the Soviet government providing assurances that the so-called "Backfire" bomber would have only medium-range capabilities and would be produced at a rate not to exceed thirty per year.

On the one hand, the fact that the treaty and protocol had been worked out in tortuous detail over a period of years was reassuring to members of Congress suspicious of Soviet intentions and wary of being tricked into an agreement that might subsequently be revealed to be disadvantageous to the United States. On the other hand, the fact that the agreement imposed qualitative limitations (for example, those on the flight testing of missiles) as well as quantitative ones (for example, the number of launchers for ICBMs and SLBMs) made it particularly important to be sure that adherence to the provisions of the treaty was verifiable.

American officials had assured members of Congress that verification was feasible, particularly through intelligence gathered by photograph and electronic means from satellites and from ground locations near the Soviet borders. However, when key intelligence installations in Iran were denied to the United States early in 1979 in the wake of the revolution in that country, charges that the SALT II agreements were not verifiable became more vociferous.

Similarly, when the Carter administration denied the allegations of congressional critics that the Soviets had placed an entire combat brigade of troops in Cuba, only to retract the denial subsequently, fuel was added to the spark of indignation of members of Congress regarding the adequacy of American intelligence. If intelligence had failed in Cuba, skeptics asked, could we be sure that it would be reliable in monitoring Soviet compliance with the SALT II treaty?

It would be erroneous to imagine that most congressional opposition to the SALT II agreement was attributable to concern about specific provisions contained therein, however. The mood in Congress and among their constituents had changed. Groups such as the Committee on the Present Danger that had been sounding the alarm at least since the mid-1970s were attracting broader audiences. America was lagging in military preparedness, such groups warned, at a time when the Soviets were building their strategic capabilities rapidly. In the absence of further modernization and development of American strategic capabilities, it was argued, an arms control agreement might merely accord legitimacy to a Soviet strategic advantage.

Senator Sam Nunn of Georgia, who, although much newer to the Senate than Jackson, had developed a reputation as being one of the most knowledgeable members in defense matters, took the lead in linking potential Senate support for SALT II to a commitment to greater increases in the American defense buildup than Carter had previously requested. Consistent with an agreement among NATO allies for a five-year program of defense modernization, the Carter administration had asked for a 3 percent increase in the defense budget. Nunn, with strong congressional backing, wanted 5 percent. By the autumn of 1979, Carter had agreed to a 5 percent increase.

Senate consent to ratification of the SALT II treaty was still in doubt, however. Only one third of the Senate plus one were needed to kill the treaty. Ironically, however, it was the Soviets themselves, previously eager to see the treaty implemented, who ensured that it would be repudiated in the Senate. In December 1979, Soviet armies invaded Afghanistan, triggering a wave of shock and indignation in the United States and throughout much of the world. Shortly thereafter, announcing that he had learned more about the Soviet Union in recent days than he had learned in the previous two and a half years, President Carter asked the Senate to suspend consideration of the SALT II treaty.[41]

PANAMA CANAL TREATIES

Carter had been more successful in getting approval previously of two treaties redefining the status of the Panama Canal. On the other hand, even in giving its consent to ratification, the Senate (and the House, which became involved in authorizing various facets of treaty implementation) demonstrated a considerable ability to influence not only specifics of this policy endeavor but to shape the congressional-presidential relationship for future encounters.[42]

Like the SALT II treaty, the Panama Canal treaties were the result of many years of negotiations. The process that culminated in the treaties that were signed in 1977 and ratified in 1978 had been triggered by a clash between Panamanians and American residents of the Canal Zone in 1964, resulting in a temporary break in diplomatic relations between the two countries. The nationalistic desire to reduce dependence upon the United States that surfaced in this incident reflected a vivid awareness among Panamanians of the unusual historical origins of their country and of the canal.

In important respects, Panamanian statehood was the product of diplomatic intrigue in which the administration of Teddy Roosevelt, unsuccessful in persuading the government of Colombia to grant the United States the rights to build a canal across the Panamanian isthmus (then Colombian territory), had encouraged a revolt by an insurgent group eager to cooperate with the United States. Two weeks after the newly independent government of Panama was established in 1903, it concluded a treaty with the United States, granting to the latter the rights to construct a canal across the isthmus and to control in perpetuity the ten-mile-wide canal zone, acting "as if it were sovereign."

Renegotiation of the terms of the treaty in 1936 and again in 1955 merely increased the amount of money paid to Panama annually by the United States for use of the canal zone and provided some other modest concessions to Panamanian demands. It had not fundamentally diminished the control of the canal that the United States exercised. The two treaties that were signed in 1977 after a dozen years of negotiation, in contrast, completely altered the terms of control that were embodied in the 1903 treaty.

The first of the new treaties provided for the full control of the canal and the canal zone by Panama beginning in the year 2000. In the interim, the American-owned Panama Canal Company would be superceded by a nine-member Panama Canal Commission, an agency of the American government, but one that would include four Panamanian members. The United States would retain rights to military bases; in turn, annual payments to the government of Panama would be made not only for base rights but also for shipping through the canal.

The second treaty provided for the perpetual neutrality of the canal (and of any new canal that might be constructed across the isthmus) in wartime as well as in peacetime. Warships of the United States and Panama were to be guaranteed expeditious transit (priority, in the event of ships queuing for access to the canal).

The nationalist sentiment in Panama that had provided impetus to an agreement to alter the status of the canal had been matched in the United States during the final stages of negotiations by critics who demanded continued control by the United States. A resolution that was introduced into the House of Representatives in 1975 by Republican Gene Snyder of Kentucky, for example, provided that no appropriated funds could be used "for the purpose of negotiating the surrender or relinquishment of any U.S. rights in the Panama Canal Zone." The resolution was passed by 246–164 vote, although Senate preference for a more supportive position led ultimately to a compromise "sense of the Congress" expression of sentiment that imposed no restrictions on funding.[43]

Flag-waving opposition to an alteration of the status of the canal was expressed on the campaign trail in 1976, both by presidential aspirants such as Ronald Reagan and by those seeking congressional seats from districts or states in which the Panama Canal had become a burning issue. Perhaps the most widely quoted expression of such sentiment was voiced by S. I. Hayakawa, in campaigning for re-election to the Senate from California. He supported United States retention of the canal, Hayakawa told prospective voters, because "We stole it fair and square."[44]

Once the treaties were signed in 1977, the controversy that continued to surround the prospective change in the status of the canal encouraged those Senators who had not yet committed themselves to delay doing so until they could fully assess the political implications for themselves of lending support or opposition to the treaties. A common political ploy was that of hedging bets by expressing or endorsing reservations. One-hundred forty-five amendments to the treaties, 26 reservations, 18 understandings, and 3 declarations were introduced in the Senate.[45] More than 40 senators made visits to Panama, highly publicized to reveal them carefully assessing the situation, in many instances in direct discussions with Panamanian officials.

Negotiations with the White House were another facet of the strategy of Senators who remained uncommitted. Delay in giving approval to the treaties encouraged presidential concessions designed to elicit support. One of the firm opponents of the treaties, Republican Senator Robert Dole, alluded to the presidential favors that were being exchanged for votes in support of the treaties with the suggestion that "he was holding out for a naval base in Kansas".[46]

The fact is that Jimmy Carter expended a considerable amount of political capital in the process of securing support for the treaties. Presidential concessions were made not only in the form of promises of favors in the future but also in the form of an acceptance of modifications of the treaty language or of caveats to the treaty that various senators favored. At one point, President Carter went so far as to lend support to a legislative amendment by Democratic Senator Dennis DeConcini of Arizona that would have enabled the United States to take measures including the use of military force if necessary in order to keep the canal open, even after control had been relinquished to Panama in 2000. The amendment was endorsed in the Senate by 75–23 vote.

Later, confronted with the outrage that had been expressed in Panama at this evident revival of Yankee interventionism, the White House worked with Senate leadership to have a new resolution introduced which effectively negated the option-for-intervention contained in the DeConcini amendment. Senate leadership played an instrumental role not only on this occasion but also on several others in achieving eventual consent of the required two thirds of the Senate to both treaties.

At least as significant as the role played by Senate majority leader Robert C. Byrd of West Virginia was that assumed by Senate minority leader Howard Baker of Tennessee. Baker refrained from making a commitment either in support of or against the treaties for some weeks. The period of keeping to himself whatever conclusions he may have reached about the treaties included a five-day trip to Panama, during which he dealt directly with the Panamanian President, Brigadier General Omar Torrijos Herrera, about modifications that might make the treaties more acceptable in the Senate. The support that Baker ultimately lent to the treaties not only strengthened his hand for subsequent dealings with the White House but also probably exposed the Senator to sufficiently intense criticism that it contributed to his decision to become an outspoken opponent of ratification of the SALT II treaty.[47]

Indeed, the lesson that many members of Congress learned from the experience of the Panama Canal treaties was that support of a controversial commitment could impose high political costs. Of Senators seeking re-election in 1978, fifteen had voted in support of ratification of the canal treaties; nine had voted in opposition. Eight of the nine opponents of the treaties were re-elected; but eight of the treaty proponents were defeated.[48]

The evidence that the treaties lacked broad support among the American public was not lost upon members of the House of Representatives as they began considering legislation required to implement the treaties. The House had the initiative in drafting laws that would authorize the requisite transfer of property, create the new Panama Canal Commission, provide for the protection of employment rights of U.S. personnel, develop toll schedules, and otherwise enable the treaties to be put into operation.

Concerns about protecting United States interests in the region of the canal were further aroused in July 1979 with a victory by Sandinista insurgents in Nicaragua, producing the downfall of the regime headed by Anastasio Somoza, an authoritarian ruler who had maintained close ties to the United States. The link between consternation about the Sandinista victory and House foot-dragging on legislation to implement the Panama Canal treaties was particularly obvious in the statements and actions of Representative John M. Murphy, Democrat of New York. Murphy was a longtime friend of Somoza's, having graduated from the Military Academy in 1950 only four years after Somoza himself became a West Point graduate. Murphy not only criticized the Carter administration for having failed Somoza in his hour of need but also used his role as Chair of the House Committee on Merchant Marine and Fisheries (which had oversight responsibility for the Panama Canal) to attempt to embarrass the administration for the commitment that had been made to the canal treaties.

A resolution that was introduced by Murphy that effectively would have undercut the Panama Canal treaties by imposing conditions for implementation that the Panamanians would find unacceptable was endorsed by the House in July 1979, 224–202. Only through the drastic modification of the provisions of the resolution in Senate–House negotiations in conference was approval finally forthcoming that autumn for legislation that put the new treaties into effect.

POWER OF THE PURSE

The House of Representatives as well as the Senate had been able to get involved in the treaty ratification process, despite the constitutional provisions that limit advice and consent of treaties to the Senate, because of the power of the purse. Control of the nation's "purse strings" doubtless is the most formidable weapon at the disposal of the Congress in its struggle with the executive branch to assert a role in the foreign policy process. Such control refers particularly to the constitutional authority to levy and collect taxes and to appropriate funds. More broadly, the constitutional roots of congressional authority include related powers such as paying the debts, providing for the common defense and general welfare, borrowing money, regulating commerce with foreign nations (as well as among the states), raising and supporting armies, providing and maintaining a navy, and making "all laws which shall be necessary and proper for carrying into execution the foregoing powers."

However, congressional utilization of the power of the purse to assert a role in the foreign policy process has varied from the 1970s to the 1980s in a pattern similar to that found with the exercise of war powers.

CONGRESSIONAL ACTIVISM IN THE 1970s

In the 1970s, Congress utilized its authority in the realm of funding repeatedly to stifle a number of presidential initiatives and to challenge policy priorities of the President. In every fiscal year of the 1970s, for example, the President's defense budget request was cut in the Congress. In so doing, Congress incurred the wrath of the President but was acting in harmony with the mood of the public at large, which had changed profoundly. Writing in 1961, Samuel Huntington noted that in every year since the end of World War

II, the majority of the American public had been either content to follow the President's lead in terms of the funding for defense or had favored even higher amounts.[49] Such attitudes continued to prevail throughout most of the 1960s. By the end of that decade, however, a profound change was evident. Growing disenchantment with the American involvement in Vietnam was accompanied by growing numbers—well over a majority of voters under the age of 30 and a sizeable minority of those over 30—who believed that American military spending in general must be reduced.[50]

Congress responded to their perception of public sentiment not only by reducing defense expenditures but also by imposing restrictions on particular foreign policy endeavors. All funding for "the involvement of United States military forces in hostilities in or over or from off the shores of North Vietnam, South Vietnam, Laos, or Cambodia" was cut in 1973, for example, over the protestations of the Nixon administration.[51]

In 1974, the Congress cut off military aid to Turkey, despite the pleas of the Ford administration that such action would jeopardize American strategic interests in Turkey (which included military bases and intelligence facilities for monitoring activity in the Soviet Union). Congress was reacting to an invasion of Cyprus by Turkey in support of Turkish Cypriots, who had been engaged in conflict with Greek Cypriots on the island largely controlled by the latter. When American military assistance was denied to them beginning in 1975, Turkey retaliated by demanding that the United States severely cut back its installations in Turkey. Not until the Carter administration in 1978 was Congress persuaded to lift the embargo on military assistance to Turkey, with a resultant improvement in United States-Turkish relations.[52]

Congress also used the power of the purse to attempt to alter administrative policies in dealing with repressive and dictatorial regimes. Congressional concern was triggered by widespread reports in the late 1960s and early 1970s of American foreign aid and security assistance being used by various foreign governments for purposes of internal repression and violation of the rights of their citizens. Such reports came from observers in South Vietnam, for example, in Brazil (to which the United States had provided training in "public safety"), in Chile (where the Congress received evidence of CIA involvement in the overthrow of the Allende regime), in the Philippines, and elsewhere.

In legislation passed in 1974, Congress stipulated that "except in extraordinary circumstances" (which the President was required to specify) no security assistance was to be provided to regimes that the President had determined were engaging in violations of "internationally recognized human rights." Such violations included "torture or cruel, inhuman or degrading treatment or punishment; prolonged detention without charges; or other flagrant denials of the right to life, liberty, and the security of the person."[53]

It was in 1974 also that Congress passed the Hughes-Ryan amendment to the foreign aid bill requiring that all covert actions conducted by the government (typically by the CIA) be reported to the Congress. The concern about covert action led the Congress to thwart policies that the Ford administration was pursuing in Angola, the African country that had just received its independence after many years of guerrilla warfare against its Portuguese colonial rulers. As required by the Hughes-Ryan amendment, the Ford administration briefed pertinent congressional committees in 1975 on its decision to provide clandestine aid to one of the factions that was vying for power in Angola on the grounds that it was important to prevent a victory by a rival faction receiving support from the Soviet Union. Several members of Congress were dubious about the wisdom of the decision. Skepticism gave way to anger in a number of instances in subsequent weeks, as members of Congress concluded that representatives of the CIA and the State Department who were conducting the briefings were providing a distorted picture of events in Angola and of the extent and nature of the American involvement.

Funding of the Angolan operation was concealed in the defense budget. In December 1975, the Senate voted by more than a 2-to-1 margin to amend the defense appropriations bill to prohibit the use of appropriated funds "for any activities involving Angola directly or indirectly."[54] In January 1976 the House of Representatives concurred by an even greater margin. The President and his advisors were furious.[55]

Congressional efforts to dictate foreign policy priorities to the administration were evident also in the wording of the International Development and Food Assistance Act of 1975. The act stipulated that the President (later changed to the Secretary of State) must render an annual report on all aid recipients describing the status of human rights in the recipient countries and identifying steps that had been taken to alter American aid programs in ways that would promote human rights.

Similar restrictions on aid to regimes that engaged in the violation of human rights were enacted by Congress in an Agricultural Trade Development and Assistance Act (P.L. 480) and in legislation stipulating the conditions under which the Inter-American Development Bank and the African Development Fund could extend loans and financial assistance. The emphasis on human rights that President Jimmy Carter would give to American foreign policy beginning in 1977 received much praise from its admirers, although condemnation from critics who charged that the rhetoric was not matched by results. Whatever one's verdict on their merit, the Carter human rights policies are consistent with the foreign policy pattern of the 1970s in providing a case of priorities being influenced although not totally dictated by congressional initiative.

CONGRESSIONAL RESPONSIVENESS TO PRESIDENTIAL LEADERSHIP IN THE 1980s

The change that has occurred in congressional-executive relationships in foreign policy in the 1980s is suggested by the responsiveness of the Congress to the leadership of Ronald Reagan in increasing military spending while cutting domestic programs. Particularly notable was the success that President Reagan enjoyed during his first year in office in persuading the Congress to depict the budget in "guns versus butter" terms and to accept his budgetary priorities.

MORE GUNS, LESS BUTTER   Policy choices are not invariably cast in "guns" (defense) or "butter" (domestic programs) terms.[56] Increases in military expenditures do not invariably require or result in decreases in domestic spending. The soaring commitment to American military involvement in Vietnam during the Johnson years did sap the enthusiasm which the Congress previously had demonstrated for the "Great Society" domestic program. However, during the Kennedy years, military spending and domestic spending both increased. Conversely, reductions in the defense budget do not necessarily demand nor ensure that the government will enlarge its commitment to domestic programs; when defense spending was reduced at the end of the Korean War, domestic spending remained virtually unchanged for several years.

Members of Congress are likely to make clear "guns *or* butter" choices only when they are receiving clear signals from their constituents one way or the other. Particularly if members of Congress sense that constituents want both defense and domestic programs increased—or both decreased—they are likely to resist making a highly visible indication of their own priorities. What is striking about the congressional response to the Reagan budget requests, however, especially during his first year in the White House, is that such a choice was required—and the President's preferences were largely endorsed.

A change of the prevailing congressional attitude toward defense spending already had been evident in the final years of the Carter administration. As Joshua Muravchik had noted, "in one afternoon in September 1979, the Senate voted to put the whole $35 billion back [that they had cut from administration defense budgets over the past decade]."[57] Whereas in the early 1970s Congress had provided fewer resources than Presidents thought necessary to meet defense requirements, in 1979 Congress was urging increases in defense spending of a greater magnitude than President Carter had thought imperative. In that sense, congressional assertiveness remained, although congressional policy views had changed.

In the congressional response to President Reagan's budget, in contrast, one finds a pattern of adherence to White House requests that, although not total, suggests clear executive dominance of the structuring of priorities. A signal of the readiness of the Congress to support Reagan budget initiatives was provided in June 1981. In accordance with procedures that had been followed since 1975, the congressional budget committees had drafted a resolution providing spending targets for fiscal year 1982 designed to reconcile federal expenditures with anticipated revenues. In June 1981, however, within a matter of hours Congress gave approval to a substitute budget reconciliation bill of more than 100 pages. Drafted under the guidance of the President's Director of the Office of Management and Budget, the substitute bill reflected the President's priorities.[58]

At the end of the summer, the President submitted a revised budget, sharply reducing the request that he had made initially for defense funding. Even so, the amount requested was above the substantial increases that the Carter FY1982 budget had called for and was nearly double the increase that the NATO powers had agreed to for each year for a five-year period beginning in 1979. Congress not only approved almost all of the Reagan revised defense budget (roughly $200 billion for FY1982) but also accepted some 83 major cuts in domestic programs.

In subsequent years, congressional cuts of presidential defense budget requests became more severe. However, in the light of concern about the growing federal debt that resulted from expenditures far in excess of revenues, and given the magnitude of the defense budget (approaching $300 billion for FY1985), congressional action in dealing with the Reagan budget requests still seemed generous to many observers. As the *Christian Science Monitor* noted in assessing the first three years of the Reagan defense program, "Congress . . . has just nipped around the edges of the defense budget while approving nearly every controversial new weapons system."[59]

The degree of acquiescence that the Congress displayed to Reagan budget requests, especially in 1981, is the more remarkable considering the continuing control of the House of Representatives by the Democrats and considering the enhanced capabilities that the Congress had developed for critically reviewing the programs and proposals of the executive branch.

CONGRESS'S OWN BUREAUCRACY   One of the chronic weaknesses of the Congress in its dealings with the presidency on foreign policy and defense issues has been the limited expertise at the disposal of the legislative branch in comparison with that available in the executive branch. This weakness has served as an argument in favor of presidential dominance of the foreign policy process, keeping congressional involvement limited.

Simultaneously with the increase in assertiveness of Congress in the foreign policy process in the 1970s, however, there occurred a dramatic expansion of congressional staff capabilities. By 1979, some 23,000 research personnel and other staff assistants served the Congress—20,000 more than the number of the world's next largest legislative staff (Canada).[60] In effect, Congress has created its own bureaucracy.

The reasons for the increases in staffing are many. Not only is such growth a response to congressional frustrations in lacking the capabilities to compete with the executive branch in the foreign policy process, but staff increases also reflect a process of internal power struggle and reform.[61]

Six partially independent trends have reinforced one another in altering the internal dynamics of the Congress and increasing the demand for expansion of staff:[62]

1. As the seniority system that had provided the underpinnings of the internal power structure became eroded, new coalitions within Congress emerged, each seeking to enhance its competitive advantage.
2. The traditional reliance on committees as the hub of congressional activity has been largely replaced by a more decentralized system, with the proliferation of subcommittees.
3. Individual members of Congress have sought to have more specialized assistance available to them not only to meet increasingly complex legislative requirements but also to foster effective relations with the media and constituents.
4. In response to program budgeting, PPBS, and similar developments in the executive branch, the General Accounting Office (which reports to the Congress) was given additional responsibility for program evaluation with the Legislative Reorganization Act of 1970. The same act changed the name of the Legislative Reference Service within the Library of Congress to the Congressional Research Service, providing the basis for a considerable enlargement of its staff in order to meet the research needs of various congressional committees.
5. The importance of technological expertise in the assessment of policy commitments as varied as those of the space program and potential commitments to an international Law of the Sea led the Congress to create an Office of Technology Assessment in 1972, with a staff of several dozen professionals whose work was to be supplemented by research performed on a contract basis by nongovernmental agencies and individuals.
6. A long simmering conflict over budget procedures, which not only pitted the Congress against the executive branch but also pitted various congressional committees against one another, bubbled over in the early 1970s. The compromise used to revise procedures and thereby resolve the conflict was the Congressional Budget and Impoundment Control Act of 1974. Among the innovations of the act was the creation of a Congressional Budget Office (CBO) with a professional staff of over 200 individuals.

Reflecting in 1982 on the pattern of change of the previous decade, one of the mavericks who helped to spark reform in the House of Representatives observed

> House reformers were able to achieve their three goals—decentralization of power, greater openness, and enhanced ability to deal with the executive. . . . In so doing, however, they did nothing to improve the chamber's legislative performance or efficiency. In fact, the House's capacity for rational decision-making has been weakened by its new processes—the power of House leaders has waned, and representatives feel increasingly exposed to, and fearful of, constituent recriminations and have become more likely to make committee and floor votes that limit the possibilities for damage in later elections.[63]

The assessment by former congressman Charles W. Whalen, Jr., of Ohio may be unduly harsh. The various procedural, structural and personnel changes that have been instituted in the Congress can be understood as a form of organizational adaptation to complexity and change internally and in the external environment.[64] Clearly, as Whalen acknowledges, congressional capabilities to deal with the executive have been improved. In the foreign policy realm, for instance, Congress now is able to bring more expertise to bear on issues and programs than ever before.

On the other hand, it is equally clear that the changes that have been effected by the Congress have proved to be a mixed blessing, as the process of bureaucratization proved to be in the executive branch. Paradoxically, members of Congress have more staff resources at their disposal, but in many cases they confront a heavier workload than ever before. The proliferation of subcommittees has been accompanied by increased staffing. By 1979, however, there were 210 jurisdictional units in the House of Representatives alone, with the average representative having assignments on six or more committees and subcommittees.[65]

Not only have many members of Congress become increasingly reliant on staff members for information and advice but also less able to find time for reflection on issues and opportunity to engage in the sustained conversations with congressional colleagues that are an integral component of the deliberative function.[66] The budgetary reforms that Congress has enacted provide a particularly vivid illustration of the mixture of benefits and new difficulties attendant to the changes of the 1970s. The creation of the Congressional Budget Office has provided Congress with valuable analytic support. Through CBO studies, Congress now is able to trace the implications of alternative budget decisions and to make an assessment of the present and future state of the economy independent of the assertions and assumptions contained in the presidential budget request. The budget committees that have been created by the act also provide each house of Congress with a broad overview of the budget, linking appropriation decisions to revenue policies in ways that were not accomplished previously.

The system works imperfectly, however. Rather than completely replacing an old set of budgetary procedures with new ones, the 1974 act created a new layer of committees and staff support on top of the structure that already existed. The Senate Foreign Relations Committee and the House Foreign Affairs Committee continue to be involved in the budgetary process, reviewing the authorization of foreign aid programs, for instance. The armed services committees continue to review defense program authorization. The appropriations committees continue to deal with funding, and the Senate Finance Committee and House Ways and Means Committee deal with taxation.

In short, the battles for turf that were characteristic of the budgetary process before the 1974 act continue to be fought, but with additional participants. As one of the most thorough studies of the congressional budget process has observed, "Congress is not quite sure what it wrought in 1974, nor the extent to which it can abide its new discipline."[67]

The inability of Congress to "abide its new discipline" is part of the explanation of the relative ease with which President Reagan was able to persuade Congress in 1981 to abandon its own guidelines in favor of those emanating from the executive branch. However, the experience should not be interpreted as demonstrating that Congress in the 1980s has reverted to the timidity in confronting the President on foreign affairs that was characteristic a quarter century earlier. President Reagan confronted Congress with a sharply defined agenda, with clearly articulated priorities, and proved to be more skillful in negotiating with the Congress than his immediate predecessor had been. Moreover, as one observer has noted, "an entirely new climate in both houses of Congress" prevailed, one in which members were ready to believe that the

1980 election returns signalled that constituents demanded the priorities that President Reagan's budget reflected.[68]

After the "honeymoon" period with President Reagan, Congress became more disposed to question, modify, or reject presidential budgetary and foreign policy initiatives. On the other hand, because a sizeable portion of the Congress in the early 1980s shared the jingoistic outlook toward world affairs that prevailed in the White House, there was qualified support for some loosening of the restrictions that had been imposed on programs such as covert action in the 1970s.

Congress has not totally abdicated its responsibilities for oversight of such programs. The fiscal 1984 intelligence bill, for example, included a provision requiring the President to report to the Congress by mid-March of 1984 on the results of efforts to achieve peace in Central America, along with recommendations for future policies for the area. A presidential commission headed by former Secretary of State Henry Kissinger provided the required report.

On the other hand, Congress gave approval to a fiscal 1984 defense appropriations bill and an intelligence authorization bill that provided $24 million for the continuation of covert aid to groups engaged in guerrilla warfare against the Sandinista government of Nicaragua. That $24 million was less than President Reagan had requested, but a sizeable minority in Congress had favored total cessation of such aid. As the Congressional Quarterly observed, "if the true nature of a compromise can be measured by the disappointment it produces, the more equal half of the Nicaragua compromise went to Reagan."[69]

OTHER CONGRESSIONAL POWERS

Congress has asserted its prerogatives in the foreign policy process in numerous other ways in addition to its utilization of the war powers, treaty powers, and the power of the purse. For example, hearings have been held to provide a forum for a continuing review of the Reagan administration policies in Central America, others to review policies in Lebanon and the Middle East, others to review the Reagan arms control policies. The Senate has used its mandate for giving its advice and consent to presidential appointees to subject the policy preferences and knowledge of such appointees to critical examination and sometimes to stinging criticism. In the case of

President Reagan's designation of Ernest W. Lefever to serve as Assistant Secretary of State for Human Rights, for example, the adverse criticisms made by various Senators in confirmation hearings and the 13–4 negative vote by the Senate Foreign Relations committee resulted in a White House withdrawal of the nomination for consideration. Senate disapproval of the Lefever appointment was widely interpreted as an expression of criticism of the administration for apparent indifference to human rights abroad.

CONCLUSIONS

In short, Ronald Reagan, like Presidents before him (in varying measure), sometimes has prevailed in his efforts to seek congressional support for his foreign policy endeavors and sometimes has failed. The pattern has been one of alternating presidential dominance of the foreign policy process, congressional assertiveness, intermittent deadlock, and frequent bargaining and compromise. It would be misleading to assess this pattern in terms of a "box score" of presidential versus congressional "wins" and "losses," however. Congress sometimes yields to presidential preferences—and it should. Congress sometimes resists, challenges, or modifies presidential initiatives—and it should.

The President and the Congress play distinct but closely intertwined roles in the foreign policy process. What is at stake is not simply institutional advantage in dominating the process but rather the effects of the interplay between institutions on policy outcomes and practices. Crucial questions are how well do the foreign policy process and the institutions that participate in the process serve the needs of the people, and how adaptive have the institutions and procedures been to changing needs, in the light of changing global and domestic circumstances?

Effectiveness (goal attainment) and efficiency (the prudent use of scarce resources) are criteria that must be applied in making an assessment of the performance of foreign policy institutions. But so also are democratic values. How open is the political system to the expression of diverse viewpoints? How representative are the values and ideas that become embodied in foreign policy of those values and ideas held among the citizenry? How accountable are those who make and execute policy to the public?

To zealots of rapid and efficient decision-making in government, the role of Congress must seem more hindrance than help. A deliberative body tends to move with glacial speed. Even as the instrument of democracy, the congressional role can be paradoxical. On countless occasions, Congress has made an important contribution to holding the President and other executive-branch officials accountable for their policy decisions and actions. Yet as Congressman Les Aspin of Wisconsin, among others, has observed, especially in the realm of foreign and defense policy, members of Congress are "reluctant to meet issues head-on, especially when this involves contravening the executive branch; [they] will, if forced, dispose of issues indirectly." Aspin notes that the indirect approach (for example, legislating procedural requirements for executive decision-making rather than declaring a substantive foreign policy position) "offers them a measure of protection from the conflicting pressures of their constituents."[70]

This is no more than to say that members of Congress, like presidents, are creatures of politics—but it is politics that is the lifeblood of democracy. Without minimizing the limitations that Congress has displayed in exercising a role in the foreign policy process, one may agree with Nelson Polsby's recent assessment that "The U.S. Congress remains a uniquely capable and independent legislature even in the face of the enormous development of the presidency in modern times."[71]

Yet major foreign policy challenges lie ahead for the United States. It is important, not just in relation to an assessment of the congressional role but also more generally in relation to an examination of the foreign policy process, to consider these challenges. This is the task of the concluding chapter.

NOTES

1. Arthur M. Schlesinger, Jr., *The Imperial Presidency* (Boston, Ma: Houghton Mifflin, 1973).

2. Edward S. Corwin, *The President: Office and Powers* (New York: New York University Press, 1940), quoted in Cecil V. Crabb, Jr. and Pat M. Holt, *Invitation to Struggle: Congress, the President and Foreign Policy* (Washington, D.C.: Congressional Quarterly Press, 1980).

3. U.S. v. Curtiss-Wright Export Corporation 299 U.S. 304 (1936). Italics are added. Justice McReynold dissented. Justice Stone took no part in the proceedings.

4. *U.S. Peace and War: United States Foreign Policy, 1931–1941* (Washington: Government Printing Office, 1943), pp. 608–611. Italics are added.

5. Senate Joint Res. 1, U.S., 83d Cong. 1st sess., reproduced with commentary in *Congressional Quarterly Almanac, 1953* (Washington: Congressional Quarterly News Features, 1954), pp. 233–237.

6. President Eisenhower's attitudes toward Congress in general and toward the Bricker Amendment in particular are described colorfully in Emmet John Hughes, *Ordeal of Power: A Political Memoir of the Eisenhower Years*, paperback ed. (New York: Dell, 1964), pp. 107–116, 125–128.

7. Even if a two-thirds majority had been attained, two subsequent hurdles would have remained. The House would have had to approve the amendment by a two-thirds majority, and three fourths of the state legislatures would have had to ratify it before the amendment was effective.

8. See Chalmers M. Roberts, "The Day We Didn't Go to War," *The Reporter* 11 (Sept. 14, 1954): 31–35. See also Melvin Gurtov, *The First Viet Nam Crisis: Chinese Communist Strategy and United States Involvement, 1953–1954* (New York: Columbia University Press, 1967).

9. Quoted with commentary by Dwight D. Eisenhower, *Mandate for Change, 1953–1956*, vol. 1 of *The White House Years* (Garden City, NY: Doubleday, 1963), p. 469.

10. See U.S., Congress, Senate, Committee on Foreign Relations, *Hearings: The Gulf of Tonkin, the 1964 Incidents*, 90th Cong., 2d sess., Feb. 20, 1968; and *Hearings: The Gulf of Tonkin, the 1964 Incidents, Part II*, 90th Cong., 2d sess., Dec. 16, 1968. See also Eugene C. Windchy, *Tonkin Gulf* (Garden City, NY: Doubleday, 1971); Joseph C. Goulden, *Truth is the First Casualty—The Gulf of Tonkin Affair: Illusion and Reality* (Chicago: Rand McNally, 1969).

11. U.S., Congress, Senate, Committee on Foreign Relations, *Hearings on Supplemental Foreign Assistance for Fiscal Year 1966, Vietnam*, 89th Cong., 2d sess., 1966, p. 53.

12. Max Frankel, "A Many-Sided Johnson," *New York Times*, Dec. 6, 1967, sec. 1, p. 17. See also Doris Kearns, *Lyndon Johnson and the American Dream* (New York: Harper & Row, 1976), pp. 95–96.

13. See e.g., the excerpts from 1966 testimony in J. William Fulbright, *The Vietnam Hearings* (New York: Random House, 1966).

14. Peter Braestrop, *Big Story: How the American Press and Television Reported and Interpreted the Crisis of Tet 1968 in Vietnam and Washington*, 2 vols. (Boulder, Co: Westview, 1976).

15. *New York Times*, Nov. 20, 1967, sec. 1, p. 1; Nov. 22, 1967, sec. 1, p. 1.

16. Doris Kearns, *Lyndon Johnson and the American Dream* (New York: Harper & Row, 1976), pp. 199–202, 253, 259, 338–339, 343.

17. Lyndon B. Johnson, quoted in Townsend Hoopes, *The Limits of Intervention* (New York: Mckay, 1969), pp. 156–157.

18. These most notably included Clark Clifford, who had been appointed to replace Robert McNamara as Secretary of Defense. Clifford had been "hawkish" in support of the Johnson policies but became progressively skeptical as he confronted the evidence in assessing the Westmoreland request for additional troops. See Hoopes, *The Limits of Intervention*, chaps. 8–9. See also Herbert Y. Schandler, *Lyndon Johnson and Vietnam: The Unmaking of a President*, paperback ed. (Princeton, NJ: Princeton University Press, 1977, 1983), chaps. 7–15.

19. U.S., Congress, House, Committee on Foreign Affairs, Subcommittee on National Security Policy and Scientific Developments, *Hearings: Congress, The President, and the War Powers*, 91st Cong., 2d sess., 1970, p. v. See also U.S., Congress, Senate, Committee on Foreign Relations, *Hearings: War Powers Legislation*, 92d Cong., 1st sess., March–October 1971; and Senate, Committee on Foreign Relations, *Hearings: War Powers Legislation, 1973*, 93d Cong., 1st sess., April 11–12, 1973.

20. The full text is contained in U.S., Congress, House, Committee on Foreign Affairs, Subcommittee on International Security and Scientific Affairs, *The War Powers Resolution: Relevant Documents, Correspondence, Reports*, 97th Cong., 1st sess., 1981.

21. "Supplemental Views of Representatives Buchanan and Whalen," and "Minority Views of Representatives Felinghuysen, Derwinski, Thompson, and Burke," in *The War Powers Resolution: Relevant Documents*, pp. 33–34.

22. Immigration and Naturalization Service v. Chadha, 103 S. Ct. 2764 (1963). The court ruling and the far-reaching implications of declaring the legislative veto unconstitutional are discussed in the *New York Times*, June 24, 1983, pp. 1, 12, 13.

23. The reports by President Ford are contained in *The War Powers Resolution: Relevant Documents*, pp. 39–46.

24. Report dated April 4, 1975, from President Gerald R. Ford to Hon. Carl Albert, Speaker of the House of Representatives, in *The War Powers Resolution: Relevant Documents*, p. 40. Emphasis is added.

25. Report dated April 26, 1980, from President Jimmy Carter to Hon. Thomas P. O'Neill, Jr., Speaker of the House of Representatives, in *The War Powers Resolution: Relevant Documents*, pp. 47–48.

26. Legal opinion of May 9, 1980, by Lloyd Cutler, the President's Counsel, on war powers consultation relative to the Iran rescue mission, in *The War Powers Resolution: Relevant Documents*, p. 49.

27. Gerald R. Ford, John Sherman Cooper lecture at the University of Kentucky, April 11, 1977, reprinted as *The War Powers Resolution: Striking a Balance between the Executive and Legislative Branches* (Washington, D.C.: American Enterprise Institute, June 1977), p. 3.

28. Ford, *The War Powers Resolution: Striking a Balance.* p. 4.

29. Letter, President Ronald Reagan to the Speaker of the House and the President Pro Tempore of the Senate, August 24, 1982, reprinted in U.S., Office of the Federal Register, *Weekly Compilation of Presidential Documents*, August 30, 1982, p. 1065.

30. Written presidential statement quoted by Steven R. Weisman, New York Times News Service, in the *Louisville Courier-Journal*, Oct. 13, 1983, p. A1.

31. William J. Lanouette, "War Powers Irresolution," *National Journal* 12 (May 3, 1980): 740.

32. Public Law 87–297, 75 Stat. 631.

33. U.S., *Congressional Record*, 88th Cong., 1st sess., March 7, 1963.

34. Lawrence D. Weiler, *The Arms Race, Secret Negotiations and the Congress*, occasional paper no. 12 (Muscatine, Ia: Stanley Foundation, 1976), pp. 2–6.

35. R. James Woolsey, "Chipping Away at the Bargains," in *Arms, Defense Policy, and Arms Control*, eds. Franklin Long and George Rathjens, special issue of *Daedalus* 104 (Summer 1975): 175–185.

36. The complete text of the platform that was adopted by the Democrats at their convention July 11, 1972 at Miami Beach is contained in *Congressional Quarterly* 30 (July 15, 1972): 1726–1747. The arms control discussion is at p. 1743.

37. *Congressional Quarterly* 30 (Aug. 19, 1972): 2109. See also Chalmers M. Roberts, "The Road to Moscow," in *SALT: The Moscow Agreements and Beyond*, edited by Mason Willrich and John B. Rhinelander (New York: Free Press, under the auspices of the American Society of International Law, 1974), chap. 1.

38. U.S., Department of State, publication 8984, selected documents no. 12A, *SALT II Agreement*, Washington, D.C.: Government Printing Office, June 1979.

39. See especially I. M. Destler, "Trade Consensus, SALT Stalemate: Congress and Foreign Policy in the 1970s," in *The New Congress*, eds., Thomas E. Mann and Norman J. Ornstein (Washington, D.C.: American Enterprise Institute for Public Policy Research, 1981), pp. 329–359. See also Stephen J. Flanagan, "The Domestic Politics of SALT II: Implications for the Foreign Policy Process," in *Congress, the Presidency and American Foreign Policy*, eds. John Spanier and Joseph Nogee (New York: Pergamon Press, 1981), pp. 44–76.

40. Flanagan, in *Congress, the Presidency and American Foreign Policy*, p. 60.

41. See *Congressional Quarterly* 38 (Jan. 5, 1980): 3–4 and 38 (Jan. 12, 1980): 51–55. See also the transcript of President Carter's interview with Frank Reynolds of ABC-TV's "World News Tonight," *New York Times*, Jan. 1, 1980, sec. 1, p. 4.

42. Several vivid accounts are available of the politics of the process of negotiating and ratifying the Panama Canal treaties. Crabb and Holt, *Invitation to Struggle*, chap. 3; William L. Furlong, "Negotiation and Ratification of the Panama Canal Treaties," in *Congress, the Presidency and American Foreign Policy*, chap. 4; Thomas M. Franck and Edward Wesiband, *Foreign Policy by Congress* (New York: Oxford University Press, 1979), pp. 275–286.

43. Charles W. Whalen, *The House and Foreign Policy: The Irony of Congressional Reform* (Chapel Hill: University of North Carolina Press, 1982), p. 114.

44. Crabb and Holt, *Invitation to Struggle*, p. 82.

45. Ibid., p. 75.

46. Franck and Weisband, *Foreign Policy by Congress*, p. 278.

47. See Christopher Madison, "Percy Tests His Bipartisan Style at the Foreign Relations Committee," *National Journal* 13 (June 6, 1981): 1008–1012.

48. Crabb and Holt, *Invitation to Struggle*, p. 74.

49. Samuel P. Huntington, *The Common Defense: Strategic Programs in National Politics* (New York: Columbia University Press, 1961), pp. 234–251.

50. Bruce M. Russett, "The Revolt of the Masses: Public Opinion on Military Expenditures," in *New Civil-Military Relations: The Agonies of Adjustment to Post-Vietnam Realities*, eds. John P. Lovell and Philip S. Kronenberg (New Brunswick, NJ: Transaction Books, 1974), pp. 57–88.

51. Public Law 93–126, 87 Stat. 451.

52. For a detailed account, see Keith R. Legg, "Congress as Trojan Horse? The Turkish Embargo Problem," in *Congress, the Presidency and American Foreign Policy*, pp. 107–131.

53. Public Law 93–559, 88 Stat. 1795.

54. The congressional response to the operation in Angola is described in vivid detail by Franck and Wiesband, *Foreign Policy by Congress*, pp. 46–57. For an interpretation by the man who was the CIA operations chief in Angola, see John Stockwell, *In Search of Enemies: A CIA Story* (New York: W. W. Norton, 1978).

55. "[President] Ford said that because of Congress the Soviets had gained 'a stronghold in Africa,' and Henry Kissinger declared, 'We had them defeated in Angola, and then we defeated ourselves." Richard L. Strout, "AWACS—Another Chapter in a US Classic, 'Who Makes Foreign Policy?'" *Christian Science Monitor*, Oct. 26, 1981.

56. For example, see James L. Clayton, *Does Defense Beggar Welfare? Myths Versus Realities*, Agenda Paper no. 9 (New York: National Strategy Information Center, 1979). Clayton notes that it in attempting to calculate the effects of defense spending on social welfare programs, it is important to consider the latter at the state and local as well as at the federal level. For an analysis similar in focus to that which Clayton provides but with attention to some of the subtle "opportunity costs" of major commitments to defense spending, see Bruce M. Russett, *What Price Vigilance? The Burdens of National Defense* (New Haven, Ct: Yale University Press, 1970), chap. 5.

57. Joshua Muravchik, "The Senate and National Security: A New Mood," in *The Growing Power of Congress*, ed. David M. Abshire and Ralph D. Nurnberger (Beverly Hills, Calif: Sage, 1981), pp. 199–282, 199.

58. Anthony King, "A Mile and a Half is a Long Way," in *Both Ends of the Avenue: The Presidency, the Executive Branch, and Congress in the 1980s*, ed. Anthony King (Washington, D.C.: American Enterprise Institute, 1983), pp. 246–273, 262. The substitute budget reconciliation bill was introduced jointly by Democratic Representative Phil Gramm of Texas and Republican Representative Delbert Latta of Ohio. For the close link between Congress and OMB on the bill, see Eric L. Davis, "Congressional Liaison: The People and the Institutions," in King, *Both Ends*, pp. 59–95.

59. Brad Knickerbocker, "US Defense Buildup Marches On," *Christian Science Monitor*, Nov. 18, 1983, p. 1.

60. Michael J. Malbin, "Delegation, Deliberation, and the New Role of Congressional Staff," in *The New Congress*, ed. Mann and Ornstein, pp. 134–177. See also James J. Hogan, "Increasing Executive and Congressional Staff Capabilities in the National Security Arena," in *The Changing World of the American Military*, ed. Franklin D. Margiotta (Boulder, Co: Westview, 1978), pp. 103–118.

61. See the first-hand account by former U.S. Representative Charles W. Whalen, Jr., *The House and Foreign Policy*. See also Richard E. Cohen, with Ralph D. Nurnberger, "Congressional Leadership: Seeking a New Role," in Abshire and Nurnburger, eds. *The Growing Power of Congress*, pp. 117–196.

62. The trends can only be summarized here. For details, see Whalen, *The House and Foreign Policy*; King, *Both Ends of the Avenue*; Abshire and Nurnburger, eds., *The Growing Power of Congress*; Franck and Weisband, *Foreign Policy by Congress*; Allen Schick, *Congress and Money: Budgeting, Spending and Taxing* (Washington, D.C.: The Urban Institute, 1980).

63. Whalen, *The House and Foreign Policy*, p. 171.

64. Roger H. Davidson and Walter J. Oleszek, "Adaptation and Consolidation: Structural Innovation in the U.S. House of Representatives," *Legislative Studies Quarterly* 1 (Feb. 1976): 37–65.

65. Roger H. Davidson, "Subcommittee Government: New Channels for Policy Making," in *The New Congress*, ed. Mann and Ornstein, pp. 99–133. The data cited are from U.S., Congress, House, Select Committee on Committees, *Final Report*, H. Rept. 96–866, 96th Cong., 2d sess., 1980, p. 303.

66. The argument is developed by Malbin in *The New Congress*, pp. 171–177.

67. Schick, *Congress and Money*, pp. 566.

68. King, in *Both Ends of the Avenue*, p. 262. In the same volume Hugh Heclo argues that a key to President Reagan's success with Congress lay in the clarity of focus of his appeal. "The economy was the president's first, second, and third priority; it was here that Ronald Reagan engaged in sustained struggles with Congress, launched his major public appeals, and staked his reputation." Heclo, "One Executive Branch or Many?", pp. 26–58, 43.

69. John Felton, "White House Gets Better Half of a Covert Aid Compromise," *Congressional Quarterly* 41 (Nov. 26, 1983): 2486–2487.

70. Les Aspin, "Why Doesn't Congress Do Something?", *Foreign Policy* 15 (Summer 1974): 70–82.

71. Nelson W. Polsby, "Some Landmarks in Modern Presidential-Congressional Relations," in *Both Ends of the Avenue*, pp. 1–25, 20.

SUGGESTED ADDITIONAL READING

ABSHIRE, DAVID M., and NURNBERGER, RALPH D., editors. *The Growing Power of Congress*. Beverly Hills, CA: Sage Publications, 1981.

CRABB, CECIL V., JR., and HOLT, PAT M. *Invitation to Struggle*. Washington, D.C.: Congressional Quarterly Press, 1980.

DESTLER, I. M., and ALTERMAN, ERIC R. "Congress and Reagan's Foreign Power." *Washington Quarterly* 7 (Winter 1984): 91–101.

DODD, LAWRENCE, and OPPENHEIMER, BRUCE I. *Congress Reconsidered*. 2d ed. Washington, D.C.: Congressional Quarterly Press, 1981.

EDWARDS, GEORGE C., III. *Presidential Influence in Congress*. San Francisco: W. H. Freeman, 1980.

FEUERWERGER, MARVIN C. *Congress and Israel: Foreign Aid Decision-Making in the House of Representatives, 1969–1976*. Westport, CT: Greenwood Press, 1979.

FRANCK, THOMAS F., and WEISBAND, EDWARD. *Foreign Policy by Congress*. New York: Oxford University Press, 1979.

FRANCK, THOMAS M. *The Tethered Presidency*. New York: Columbia University Press, 1981.

HOCKING, BRIAN, and SMITH, MICHAEL. "Reagan, Congress and Foreign Policy: A Troubled Partnership." *This World Today* 40 (May 1984): 188–198.

KING, ANTHONY, ed. *Both Ends of the Avenue: The Presidency, the Executive Branch, and Congress in the 1980s*. Washington, D.C.: American Enterprise Institute, 1983.

PASTOR, ROBERT A. *Congress and the Politics of U.S. Foreign Economic Policy, 1929–1976*. Berkeley: University of California, 1980.

SPANIER, JOHN and NOGEE, JOSEPH L. *Congress, the Presidency and American Foreign Policy*. Elmsford, NY: Pergamon, 1981.

TURNER, ROBERT F. *The War Powers Resolution: Its Implementation in Theory and Practice*. Philadelphia, PA: Foreign Policy Research Institute, 1983.

WHALEN, CHARLES W., JR. *The House and Foreign Policy: The Irony of Congressional Reform*. Chapel Hill: University of North Carolina Press, 1982.

PART FOUR

Conclusions

CHAPTER 9

❦

Meeting the Challenges
of the 1980s and 1990s:
Purpose and Adaptation

"The world and our convictions about the world make up our sense of direction, orient us, give us the compass points which direct our actions. Crisis man has been left without a world, handed over to the chaos of pure circumstance, in a lamentable state of disorientation."

—Jose Ortega y Gasset, *Man and Crisis*,
English translation 1958

". . . What is occurring now is, in all likelihood, bigger, deeper, and more important than the industrial revolution. Indeed, a growing body of reputable opinion asserts that the present moment represents nothing less than the second great divide in human history, comparable in magnitude only with the first great break in historic continuity, the shift from barbarism to civilization."

—Alvin Toffler, *Future Shock*, 1970

American policy makers never have had the luxury of dealing with static global or domestic environments. To a greater or lesser extent, adaptation to change always has been a foreign policy imperative. In some historical epochs, however, the adaptive challenge has been particularly severe. One of these epochs, discussed in Chapter 3, was that of the close of the nineteenth century, when a variety of economic, technological, political, and military trends called into question the fundamental assumptions that underlay the traditional orientation of the United States to world affairs. Another critical turning point occurred with World War II. The pattern of foreign policy response to the challenges posed by the postwar world was examined in Chapter 4.

The world and America now have entered still another era,[1] imposing severe demands upon the wisdom, vision, and tenacity of policy makers and the American people. The pace of required adaptation had quickened from a leisurely stroll in the era of George Washington, to a jog by the 1890s, to a sprint by World War II. By comparison, the adjustments demanded by change in the current period are akin to navigating Niagara Falls in a barrel.[2]

The range, magnitude, and consequences of changes that characterize the modern era have been described in detail by others. The world is said to have entered the "post-industrial age," the "technetronic age," the "information age," the "age of discontinuity," the "third wave" of fundamental transformations of civilization.[3] Alvin Toffler's assessment of the pace of change in the modern world leads him to conclude that a consequence for many Americans has been "future shock."[4] John Naisbitt, considering a series of "megatrends" that are having important effects upon our lives, observes that "we are clinging to the known past in fear of the unknown future."[5]

Here we focus simply on some of the dimensions of change that are most salient for American foreign policy. The objective of the chapter is to encourage you to consider what is required in order for the United States to remain true to its ideals while adapting to a rapidly changing pattern of demands and opportunities.

The record of human experience suggests that even in more stable, unhurried times, a common failing has been that of societies and governments clinging to policies, practices, and beliefs long after they had become outmoded by changing circumstances. At the same time, efforts to probe the future and anticipate its requirements are fraught with the risk of major miscalculation. History is littered with plans and predictions that went awry.

The requisites of successful adaption would seem to include (1) boldness and imagination in reflecting on the nature, magnitude, and direction of changes that are occurring or which may occur, but (2) constant receptivity to evidence of unforeseen developments, and (3) flexibility in programs and actions taken to prepare for future contingencies.

What is needed in foreign policy terms, however, is not merely a capacity for coping with change, but also an ability to define and maintain a sense of purpose and vision. The unity of purpose among Americans that might provide a sure sense of direction for meeting future challenges remains elusive. As noted in Chapter 5, the Cold War consensus that sustained American foreign policy in the 1950s and early 1960s broke down in the era of Vietnam, Watergate, and energy and monetary crises.

Although a continuation of sharp divisions within the polity over foreign policy can impede effectiveness and adaptation, a workable policy consensus should not be confused with the absence of policy debate. Foreign policy in the 1980s remains the object of intense debate, and rightly so. Those who share Jesse Jackson's views of the appropriate United States policy toward Cuba or Central America, for example, cannot be expected to embrace policies forged from a sharply differing perspective such as that of Ronald Reagan or Jeane Kirkpatrick. Nor can devotees of the Committee on the Present Danger or the American Legion be expected to unite the nuclear freeze movement in endorsing arms control pro- posals of the current administration.

A workable policy consensus will be rebuilt neither through ex- tolling the imagined virtues of Cold War consensus-lost nor from glossing over honest differences that are rooted in differing values and differing interests. What is needed and what is feasible, how- ever, are for a full and open examination and discussion of American policy priorities in relation to discernible trends in world affairs, and an exploration of the opportunities and potential costs that these trends pose for American vital interests.

The next step is that of making institutional as well as policy adjustments as needed to cope with present and future challenges.

As suggested in Chapters 6, 7, and 8, adaptation is a process that sometimes demands an alteration of policies to fit changing requirements; but sometimes what is required is policy continuity in the face of facile demands for new departures. Moreover, some- times adaptation requires that institutions be insulated against the buffeting effects of an environment in flux, just as sometimes it becomes imperative to modify and revamp institutions in order to enable them to cope with changing demands and remain responsive to popular needs.

No pat formulae are available for meeting the institutional and policy challenges of purposeful adaptation. An important beginning is the development of a sensitivity to the complexity of the pattern of change in the modern world and an awareness of some of the major foreign policy implications of changes that are occurring or are likely to occur.

THE COMPLEX PATTERN OF CHANGE IN THE MODERN WORLD

The pattern of change has contradictory elements. The world is at once becoming "smaller" and yet more fragmented. Nation-states are becoming more economically and politically interdependent, yet not without vast and in some instances growing disparities in the degree of dependence on more affluent or powerful states and with considerable controversy over the policy implications of an interdependent world. Technological change advances the process of modernizing once-traditional agrarian societies, but a countertrend of resurgent traditionalism, hostile to the effects of modernization, is evident. Finally, the international power configuration has been shifting away from the tight bipolar structure that characterized the first two decades after World War II, but on important issues such as nuclear arms control, the two superpowers continue to dominate world politics.

GLOBAL COMMUNITY AND FRAGMENTATION

A revolution in modes of transportation and communication has thrown geographically and culturally distant societies into contact with one another. Jet aircraft transport tourists and traders from one continent to another within hours. The transistor radio brings news, music, and entertainment into previously isolated villages. Video as well as audio images of other cultures are obtainable by television broadcasts relayed over thousands of miles by satellite. Moreover, vast amounts of information can be shared almost instantaneously through the microchip computer.

Scientific and technological breakthroughs continue to be made at a staggering pace. The United States is at the forefront of research and development that will lead to many future breakthroughs. In such activity, America acts as a profound agent of social, economic, technological, and political change. Although the "status quo" label that often is applied to the United States provides a persuasive description of the characteristic American response to political revolution, the label is misleading as a description of the impact of the United States on world affairs. As a technologically advanced industrial power, the United States promotes change through innovation, through fostering of new markets, through education and training of foreign as well as American personnel, through investment practices, and in countless other ways.

A major challenge for American foreign policy makers is to anticipate, assess, and attempt to accommodate the varied consequences of the changes thereby unleashed, or set in motion by competitors, such as Japan, West Germany, and others. Technological innovations invariably have synergistic and partially unforeseen repercussions. They also have contributed to contradictory trends.

In important respects, developments in transportation and communication such as those described above have contributed to making the world "smaller" than it was a half century or a century ago. We human beings from diverse cultures and regions know more about one another than ever before, and we share more experiences. When John F. Kennedy was assassinated in 1963, for example, shock waves from the tragic event flowed instantly worldwide. The British economist and author, Barbara Ward (Baroness Jackson) was attending a large political gathering in Zambia (then Northern Rhodesia) when news of the assassination was received. The proceedings were halted so that the audience could join in prayer and hymns in tribute to the leader of a nation half way around the globe.[6]

People in various parts of the world also are able through radio and television to be an immediate part of festive occasions, such as a royal wedding in England or (usually but not always festive) the Olympic Games. Greater contact among peoples does not necessarily promote harmony, however, as the history of warfare among neighboring tribes or nations shows. Moreover, in the modern world, access has been facilitated not only for tourism and trade but also for the sudden incursion of armed troops or nuclear-tipped missiles. The world has come to share the risk of war and destruction, but not as a community united against a

303

common threat. Rather, the world remains badly divided along ideological, religious, ethnic, and cultural lines.

Such division is evident even within institutions such as the United Nations that were established to foster global community. Of course, the realities of an organization founded on the principle of the sovereign equality of its members intruded upon idealized images of world harmony from the outset. Discussions and debates in the UN inevitably reflected the differences in outlook and in vested national interests of a diverse membership.

However, the difficulties of achieving a broad consensus among UN members on important issues have been compounded by a dramatic increase in membership. Representatives of fifty nation-states gathered in San Francisco for the founding of the organization in the spring of 1945. More than three times that number are represented today. Moreover, the political center of gravity has shifted. From an organization that was dominated through its first fifteen years by the United States, the UN has become an institutional forum for the expression of Third World discontent. This is true especially in the General Assembly, where all member states are represented.

This altered character of the UN helps to explain the reluctance of the United States to utilize the good offices of the UN as an instrument for resolving major international issues and the annoyance that representatives of the United States sometimes have displayed in recent years at the policy orientation and tenor of discussion in the organization and its subsidiaries. For example, in an acrimonious exchange in a UN committee in September 1983, the Soviet delegate charged that the United States had failed to live up to its obligations as host country in denying rights for the airplane carrying Soviet diplomatic personnel to land at the major commercial air terminals in New York and Newark.[7] The American delegate to the committee, Charles Lichtenstein, replied:

> If in the judicious determination of the members of the U.N., they feel they are not welcome and they are not being treated with the hostly consideration that is their due, then the U.S. strongly encourages such member states seriously to consider removing themselves and this organization from the soil of the United States. . . . We will put no impediment in your way, and we will be at dockside bidding you a fond farewell as you set off into the sunset.[8]

Several weeks later, the American government gave official notice of its intention to withdraw from the 161-member United Nations Educational, Scientific and Cultural Organization (UNESCO) at the end of December 1984. The State Department explained the UNESCO "has extraneously politicized virtually every subject it deals with; has exhibited hostility toward the basic institutions of a free society, especially a free market and a free press, and has demonstrated unrestrained budgetary expansion."[9]

Frictions within the United Nations illustrate in microcosm the fractious international milieu with which American policy makers have not yet fully come to terms. If in one sense the world has been getting "smaller" and more of a community, in another important sense the trend has been toward fragmentation.

Even within national boundaries, efforts of governments to forge unity and common allegiance have been countered in innumerable instances with demands of minority groups or tribes for retention of a distinct indentity and sometimes for the right to secession. The problem of national cohesion is acute throughout most of Africa, for example, where the artificiality of national boundaries established during colonial days competes with rather than complements ethnic and tribal groupings. Countless separatist groups are active elsewhere as well: French-speaking Canadians; the Basques in Spain; Kurds in Iraq and Iran; Latvians, Lithuanians, Estonians, Ukrainians, Uzbeks, and many others in the Soviet Union. Moreover, northern Ireland is divided between antagonistic groups of Protestants and Catholics; Lebanon has virtually collapsed from a combination of external pressures and internal conflict among Christians, Sunni and Shi'ite Moslems, and Druze. Within the United States, perhaps the world's most interesting experiment in attempting to provide a cultural "melting pot," disruptive frictions among diverse ethnic groups continue to serve as obstacles to national cohesion.

In short, although changes in technology and communication are among the factors that contribute to a growing sense of community in the world, there is a disturbing countertrend toward global fragmentation. It is now, in one sense, a "global village," as McLuhan and Fiore put it.[10] But as former presidential advisor Zbigniew Brzezinski has observed, the new reality also is that of a "global city," characterized by "a nervous, agitated, tense, and fragmented web of interdependent relations."[11]

INTERDEPENDENCE, DEPENDENCE, AND INDEPENDENCE

Recent American administrations have differed with one another in the extent to which they were willing to embrace the concept that nations of the world are "interdependent." Officials in the Carter administration displayed some enthusiasm for the idea, at least rhetorically. The Reagan administration was much more loath to acknowledge interdependence, preferring to speak of ways in which the United States could remain master of its own destiny in military, diplomatic, and economic affairs.

The concept has come into currency in international affairs, however, precisely because the evidence, especially in economic relationships such as trade, points to a diminished capacity even of the major powers of the world to exercise autarky. It is also the case that major economic issues in international affairs have become closely intertwined with issues of politics and security. The concept is descriptive also of the complex structure of the modern global system, in which nation-states must deal not only with one another but also with multinational corporations, intergovernmental organizations such as the UN and the World Bank, and private groups and individuals.

Growing interdependence would seem to presage a trend toward multilateral cooperation, but again, the pattern proves to be complex, with contradictory elements. To the extent that institutions such as the European Community (EC) and the Association of Southeast Asian Nations (ASEAN) are flourishing, such a trend is evident. On the other hand, nationalistic pride and suspicion continue to hinder efforts to increase multilateral approaches to economic and political problem-solving.

Such pride and suspicion characterize not only the policy posture of brash newly independent states but also the posture of the superpowers. American nationalism was in evidence, for example, in the decision made to oppose an international treaty governing the use of the oceans and their resources. The treaty was signed by representatives of 117 nations at a seaside resort in Jamaica in December 1982, the culmination of nine years of negotiations in the United Nations Conference on the Law of the Sea. The opposition of the Reagan administration to the treaty was primarily directed to provisions that would create a global authority to regulate deep seabed mining, provisions that American mining firms argued would deny to the more enterprising states the fruits of their initiative and expertise. As the American delegate to the conference in Jamaica observed, "They'll say it's the whole world against the U.S., but we're just looking out for our own national interest."[12]

In most respects, the Law of the Sea treaty reflected a continuing response to the claim of individual states rather than an acceptance of the more idealistic argument that the oceans and the resources contained therein, as with outer space, are part of "the common heritage" of all who inhabit the earth, therefore to be kept free of the claims of individual states for exclusive usage or control.[13] For example, the treaty gave sanction to an "exclusive economic zone" two hundred miles from the shores of every coastal state. Because this results in placing some 40 percent of the world's oceans and their resources under the jurisdiction of coastal states, it has been described by one observer as "the biggest 'land grab' in history."[14]

The growing scarcity of many vital resources makes cooperation more essential even as it makes intense competition more probable. In many parts of the world, demand on scarce resources has been aggravated by population growth. The population explosion introduces an element of change unique to the modern period of history.[15] Conservative projections forecast a doubling of the world population in less than half a century; by comparison, nearly seventeen centuries elapsed before the number of persons on earth at the time of Christ had doubled. The rate of population increase is especially great in some regions, such as Latin America, where the current population is expected to double in less than a quarter century. In already populous countries such as the Peoples Republic of China, India, and Indonesia (which together account for roughly 40 percent of the world's population), continuing population increases hamper the effort that is being made to improve the standard of living through industrialization and the modernization of agriculture.

Where population pressures combine with a heavy reliance on imported technologies and resources, the continuing reality is less interdependence than it is dependence. If interdependence remains a useful concept for describing the pattern of relations in the international system as a whole, an enormous variation among nation-states is apparent in resources and in capability for unilateral action in the world arena.

Amidst the violence and bloodshed of World War II, American Presidential aspirant Wendell Willkie captured the dreams of millions when he spoke of a future in which people in all parts of the globe would recognize their commonality as "one world." However, instead of one world emerging in the postwar era, at least four have come into being, with little realistic prospect that existing links of interdependence among them will promote greater harmony in the years immediately ahead.

Conventional terminology refers to the advanced industrialized societies of the West as the "first world," and Communist societies of the East as the "second world." A third world, less developed industrially than the first two, nevertheless includes dozens of nation-states that have begun the process of technological modernization or aspire to do so, and that have the resource base to make such an aspiration realistic. However, there are still other nation-states—a fourth world—that are currently poor and undeveloped, and that have only remote prospects for being able to alter this condition.

MODERNIZATION AND THE
RESURGENCE OF TRADITIONALISM

In one sense, technological change has served to link the people of the Third and Fourth Worlds to those of the more industrialized First and Second Worlds. The cultural impact of the introduction of advanced technology is widely evident. Even many of the poorest nation-states can boast of skyscrapers in their capital cities and international airports equipped with the paraphernalia of the jet age. More subtle signs of the diffusion of cultures as well as technology are found in the appearance of blue jeans in shops from Seoul to Rio, in the reverberations of rock-and-roll music in cafes from Stockholm to Lagos, and in the Pepsi or Coca Cola advertisements from Hong Kong to Mexico City. Less subtle signs are represented by the advanced military equipment—American, Russian, French, Israeli, and other makes—that is in abundance worldwide.

It is not surprising that the modernization process has been accompanied by secularization and the undermining of traditional value and belief systems. Yet technological diffusion also has unleashed some unanticipated forces of friction and social fragmentation. In his studies in the Middle East a quarter of a century ago, Daniel Lerner was able to detect some of the erosion of traditional social structures that was occurring. Lerner found that the intrusion of modern communications media into previously isolated villages generates "psychic mobility"—an ability for the first time to imagine oneself in social roles other than those to which one had been assigned by traditional practice—as well as physical mobility.[16]

Lerner's discovery of psychic mobility in rural Turkey is akin to the stimulus to social and political change that was identified in Chapter 4 as "the revolution of rising expectations," one of the major challenges emerging from the ashes of the post-World War II world. Such sentiment was evident especially in areas of Asia, Africa, and the Middle East that remained under colonial rule or that were attaining freedom from colonial rule, with sometimes extravagant expectations aroused of the benefits that would follow independence. But it continues to be evident not only among newly independent peoples but also among persons who are engaged in a struggle for dignity, freedom from oppression, and freedom from want. In many instances, such persons have experienced only misery and reason for despair. In other instances, however, modern technology has introduced links to a world that they have never known and has aroused new expectations over what life may hold.

Governments in the Third and Fourth worlds have attempted to cope with rising expectations among their people in a variety of ways; but the spiral of mounting demands frequently has exceeded the capacity of regimes to satisfy them.[17] Symbolic substitutes such as mass rallies, charismatic appeals, or allegations of external threats sometimes succeed in buying time for a regime that is unable to meed demands for economic growth and welfare improvements. Yet chronic instability punctuated by the coup d'etat has been the rule rather than the exception in poor nation-states, the product of expectations rising faster than even adept regimes can meet them.

Regimes throughout Latin America, Asia, Africa, and the Middle East have found it necessary to look either to the industrialized states of the West or to the industrialized Communist states for investment, the development of economic infrastructure, and for economic or military assistance. The resulting penetration of Third and Fourth world economies by foreign governments and enterprise in many instances has contributed to economic distortions, with some sectors becoming developed and dynamic and neglected sectors remaining stagnant. Such distortions tend to aggravate cleavages within the society and to foster a vicious cycle of internal conflict and repression.[18]

Looking to the future, one must anticipate that the quest for change among peoples of the Third and Fourth worlds will remain unsatiated, with repression and violence a continuing feature of the political landscape. The challenge for American foreign policy makers will include not merely short-range assessments of the hostility or friendship demonstrated by regimes in power and by groups agitating for change but also efforts to gauge the long-range implications of American support for or opposition to the quest for change.

In the past, assessments of this sort have been hampered by a fixation on the ideological slogans of the agents of change. The twentieth-century's revolutionary movements have been largely dominated by Marxists—Lenin, Mao, Ho Chi Minh, Castro. Moreover, in the past two decades the Soviet Union has sought to establish a position of prestige and influence in the Third and Fourth worlds as a self-proclaimed champion of "national liberation movements." Thus, it is understandable that American policymakers have been inclined (for example, in Southeast Asia, Central America, and parts of Africa) to fear the consequences of radical change for United States interests.

On the other hand, to explain away the revolution of rising expectations as a phenomenon that can and should be contained within perimeters fully consonant with American economic and political traditions or to explain away the demands for change as a mere contrivance of America's ideological adversaries would be to ignore the endogenous roots of deep-felt grievances and aspirations.

Moreover, to define the challenge for American foreign policy of ferment in the Third and Fourth worlds primarily in terms of the East–West struggle would be to ensure that the United States is cast in a self-defeating counterrevolutionary posture in a revolutionary era. This is not to argue on behalf of blanket U.S. support for insurgent movements nor to deny the reality of having to deal with numerous regimes whose policies are less enlightened than most Americans would like. It is to argue, however, that foreign policy ought to be attuned to the dynamics of social and political change.

Paradoxically, regimes may find themselves engulfed in social and political turmoil not only when they are unable to keep abreast of spiralling demands but also when they move too rapidly. Modernization introduced at a pace and with means that reflect a disregard for the need of a society for cultural continuity has its own

310

pricetag. The 1979 revolution in Iran that led to the ouster of the Shah is a vivid case in point. The Shah's vision of a powerfully modernized Iran that would exert dominance throughout the region, imposed in a short space of time with considerable brutality, aroused a profound backlash. Pride in the Persian and Islamic past was too great to sacrifice on the altar of worship of the future. Revolutionary sentiment in Mexico in an earlier era took a similar form, as Mexican novelist Carlos Fuentes has noted. Comparing the xenophobic intensity of the Iranian revolution to sentiments that he and his fellow Mexicans had felt in the 1930s when his government nationalized American oil holdings, Fuentes observed that "our dignity, our identity, depended in great measure on recovering [our] past."[19]

Despite the threat that it poses to traditional values and to traditional institutions, technological modernization affords the hope that means may become available to Third World and Fourth World countries to enable them to overcome problems such as desperate inadequacies in housing, severe food shortages, and widespread disease. Dramatic recent achievements in fields such as medicine, agriculture, engineering, and computer science have clear applicability to the relief of such problems.

States that are entering the "post-industrial age," however, have demonstrated little enthusiasm for making the commitment that would be required to help the poorer nation-states to break out of the vicious cycle of technological backwardness and poverty. Demands expressed by delegations from Third World and Fourth World states in their call for a "New International Economic Order" at a special session of the UN General Assembly in 1974 were an effort to alter prevailing attitudes and policies in technologically advanced societies. But the demands have largely fallen on deaf ears.[20]

The trend thus continues to be one of the rich getting richer and the poor getting poorer. Frictions between rich and poor states (the "North-South" dispute) increasingly define the agenda of world politics. As noted by former West German Chancellor Willy Brandt in reporting to the UN Secretary General the findings of an independent commission on development issues:

There is a real danger that in the year 2000 a large part of the world's population will still be living in poverty. The world may become overpopulated and will certainly be overurbanized. Mass

starvation and the dangers of destruction may be growing steadily
—if a new major war has not already shaken the foundations of
what we call world civilization.[21]

One must note that the technological revolution carries with it
the potential for solving some of the important North-South problems that the Brandt report identified (the elimination of starvation
on a global scale, for instance). But technological developments
also make the threat of a new major war more ominous.

Shortly after the devastating capabilities of the atomic bomb had
been demonstrated at Hiroshima and at Nagasaki, historian Walter
Millis reflected on the "hypertrophy" of war. The atomic bomb,
Millis saw from his analysis of developments in warfare from the
eighteenth to the twentieth century, represented the culmination
of a process by which entire populations were now placed at risk
in time of war. The notion that war could be used as an instrument
of politics, as the nineteenth-century Prussian strategist Karl von
Clausewitz had maintained, had to give way before the prospect
that a third world war would be a holocaust endangering the entire
planet.[22]

In the years since 1945, the developments in nuclear technology
have been supplemented by developments in the methods of deliv-
ering bombs across continents to a target. The array of instruments
available for such purposes included several "generations" of jet
aircraft that can drop bombs or launch missiles to a target, land-
based ballistic missiles (ICBMs), submarine-launched ballistic
missiles (SLBMs), cruise missiles. The missiles themselves can be
"MIRVed" (multiple, independently targetted re-entry vehicle) and
MaRVed (maneuverable re-entry vehicle), with remarkable improvements in accuracy in recent years.

Awesome developments have been made in the nuclear warheads
themselves, especially with the construction and testing of hydrogen
bombs with yields (measured in the equivalent force of explosion
of tons of TNT) roughly one hundred times greater than those of
the atomic bombs dropped at Hiroshima and Nagasaki. Ironically,
dangerous developments have been made not only in increasing
the destructiveness of nuclear weapons but also in making them
smaller and "cleaner" (less radioactive fallout accompanying detona-
tion). The danger of the latter developments lies in the blurring
of the distinction between nuclear weapons and so-called "conven-

tional" weapons, leading some strategists to contend that the notion of maintaining a "threshold" between conventional and nuclear war has become obsolete. To the extent that such views become widespread and incorporated into the doctrine of the superpowers, the danger that they will become self-fulfilling prophecies obviously increases.

The development of smaller and lighter nuclear weapons also increases the danger that such weapons will fall into the hands of a terrorist group or those of a fanatical regime. One cannot imagine a terrorist group making use of "Little Boy" or "Fat Man," the cumbersome bombs which, before being dropped on Hiroshima and Nagasaki, respectively, had to be hoisted into specially modified B-29 aircraft.[23] A bomb that can be concealed in the trunk of a car or otherwise maneuvered to location is a different matter, however.

BIPOLARITY AND MULTIPOLARITY

The dependence of the rest of the world on mutual restraint by the two superpowers from employing nuclear weapons is the most visible sign that world affairs continue to be characterized by bipolarity in some important respects. Other evidence lies in space exploration, where other states lag far behind the United States and the Soviet Union and remain largely beholden to the superpowers for whatever benefits may be shared from experiments conducted in space, from communication relay equipment and remote sensing by satellite.[24] Similarly, all states stand to suffer the consequences if the superpowers choose to transform outer space into an arena of Cold War or hot war.

In more general terms, however, the trend in the international system clearly has been away from a tight bipolar structure to a multipolar configuration. For example, what once appeared to be a monolithic Communist bloc dominated by Moscow has become an array of Communist regimes with considerable diversity and tension among them. The Sino-Soviet dispute has provided the United States with the opportunity to "play the China card" to the extent of cultivating trade relations with Beijing, thereby providing incentives for the Chinese to avoid being drawn back into the Soviet orbit. The Yugoslav leader Tito's break with Stalin in 1948 had similar results. The United States found it infeasible to respond to subsequent upheavals in Hungary in 1956, in Czechoslovakia in 1968, and in Poland in 1980–1981 with more than rhetorical support when the Soviets forcibly reasserted their control. The fissures that have occurred within Eastern Europe, however, make it obvious that the Soviet Union no longer is able to enjoy automatic compliance on the part of its Warsaw Pact allies.

The rifts in the Eastern bloc are paralleled by changes in the West. The North Atlantic Treaty Organization (NATO), at its 1949 inception a structure in which West European allies as well as Canada took their cues from the United States, has become a partnership that survives only through agreements reached in hard bargaining among relative equals. As former Secretary of State Henry Kissinger has noted, however, in a major statement in 1984 assessing United States policy toward NATO, adjustments have not been made adequately to reflect the changes in the relationship among members.

> Existing arrangements are unbalanced. When one country dominates the alliance on all major issues—when that one country chooses weapons and decides deployments, conducts the arms-control negotiations, sets the tone for East-West diplomacy and creates the framework for relations with the Third World—little incentive remains for a serious joint effort to redefine the requirements of security or to coordinate foreign policies. Such joint efforts entail sacrifices and carry political costs. Leaders are not likely to make the sacrifice or pay the cost unless they feel responsible for the results.[25]

Kissinger advocates giving the European allies the major responsibility for decisions affecting NATO security; for example, European armies should assume the primary responsibility for the conventional defense of NATO, and one of them should become Supreme Allied Commander Europe (SACEUR), a position heretofore held exclusively by American generals. Whether or not Kissinger's recommendations are implemented, it seems clear that the future will require a major readjustment of relationships within the North Atlantic community. Disagreements over economic issues, defense requirements, arms control, and diplomatic priorities have reached a level of severity that will not be easily resolved.

The changes that are occurring in the structure of the international system are evident beyond the strains that have become evident in the Warsaw Pact and NATO alliances. Particularly on issues such as those of international economics and monetary policy, environmental concerns (such as the usage of international waterways, industrial polution, and acid rain), and energy, the policy positions taken by participants in the world arena tend to depart markedly from bipolar affiliations.[26]

The Japanese have become one of the world's strongest economic powers, for instance, thereby emerging from early post-World War II dependence upon the United States to become a major competitor with America, as well as one of its principal trading partners. The Organization of Petroleum Exporting Countries (OPEC) seemed to have become another important independent voice in world affairs following the 1973 energy crisis, in which OPEC engineered massive oil-price increases. However, in the years since then, little semblance remains of the unity that temporarily was attained. As a result, OPEC as an entity remains relatively non-influential, although major oil-producing countries such as Saudi Arabia in the Middle East, Libya in North Africa, Nigeria in West Africa, Venezuela and Mexico in Latin America, and Indonesia in Southeast Asia are able, in varying degrees, to make claims as regional powers.

South Africa will continue to be important both as a major source of the world's gold and other minerals, and as the focal point of hostility among black African states. Countries such as Brazil, which is one of the world's leading sources of iron ore and bauxite (used to produce aluminum) and has become an industrialized power, no doubt will be increasingly prominent in world affairs. Other newly industrialized countries (NICs) such as South Korea, Taiwan, Singapore, and Hong Kong also promise to play an increasing role in world affairs, although distortions in the developmental process that were noted earlier make each country susceptible to political upheaval that could hamper its international influence.

Moreover, the deep indebtedness of states such as Brazil, Mexico, Argentina, India, and Poland places serious obstacles in the way of further development. The United States, as a major source of funding for the World Bank and other institutions with loans in jeopardy, has particular reason for concern about this problem. Several of the heavily indebted states, unable to make interest payments on loans, already have sought and obtained a rescheduling of debt payments. Should multiple defaults occur, there would be devastating global repercussions.

Another important trend that alters the configuration of world politics is that of multinational corporations (MNCs) exercising influence on actions and events.[27] Multinational corporations such as major oil companies, International Business Machines (IBM), General Electric (GE), International Telephone and Telegraph (IT&T), Dupont, most leading automobile manufacturers, aircraft manufacturers such as Boeing, and other companies have important financial holdings in the country where they maintain their head-quarters (the home country) as well as extensive economic in-vestments and business arrangements in countries elsewhere (host countries) where they maintain branches or subsidiaries. Although home and host countries may be able to impose some restrictions and regulations on the MNCs, the pattern of influence is recip-rocal—MNCs increasingly have an impact upon the policies of the governments where they do business. Moreover, the MNCs them-selves are agents of change, through their own investment in science and technology, through the impact produced by the penetration of foreign economies and foreign cultures, and through repercussions on the global monetary system.

FOREIGN POLICY FOR A NEW ERA

The decline in the ability of the United States to wield unfettered control over large numbers of world events reflects economic, technological, and political changes that have been occurring worldwide, with a corresponding increase in the complexity of the global power structure. The challenge of formulating and executing foreign policies that are appropriate to an increasingly complex pattern of demands and opportunities is formidable. No IIMMP will solve the problems that lie ahead. Rather, responsibility for tackling the problems falls to the American people and their leaders, utilizing the political institutions that were described in earlier chapters. In many instances, solutions will require the skills, ener-gies, and commitment from many nations rather than from America alone. The challenge of purposeful adaptation by the United States will be met to the extent that participants in the process are able to see beyond what used to be or what might have been to the world as it is today and as it can be tomorrow, and are able to design American foreign policies accordingly.

NOTES

1. It may well be, as Modelski, Thompson, and others argue, that there is a cyclical dynamic that operates in the global system, and that the current period of change represents the transition from one long cycle to the next. See George Modelski, "The Long Cycle of Global Politics and the Nation-State," *Comparative Studies in Society and History* 20 (April 1978): 214–235. Also William R. Thompson, "Uneven Economic Growth, Systemic Challenges, and Global Wars," *International Studies Quarterly* 27 (1983): 341–355.

2. The metaphor was suggested by Barbara Ward (Lady Jackson), *Spaceship Earth* (New York: Columbia University Press, 1966), p. 3.

3. Edward Corniss, ed., *The Great Transformation: Alternative Futures for Global Society* (Bethesda, Md: World Future Society, 1983); Daniel Bell, "Notes on the Post-Industrial Society," *The Public Interest* 6 and 7 (Winter and Spring 1967): 24–35, 102–118; Zbigniew Brzezinski, *Between Two Ages: America's Role in the Technetronic Era* (New York: Viking, 1971); Peter F. Drucker, *The Age of Discontinuity* (New York: Harper & Row, 1969); Herman Kahn and Anthony J. Wiener, *The Year 2000: A Framework for Speculation on the Next Thirty-Three Years* (New York: Macmillan, 1967). A radically different vision (with a critique of the works of Bell, Kahn, and Wiener) is provided by William Irwin Thompson, *At the Edge of History: Speculations on the Transformation of Culture* (New York: Harper & Row, 1971). See also *The Futurist*, published monthly by the World Future Society: An Association for the Study of Alternative Futures; and *Futures*, the Journal of Forecasting and Planning, published six times a year for the Institute for the Future.

4. Alvin Toffler, *Future Shock* (London: Pan Books, 1970). See also Toffler's more recent commentary on social change, *The Third Wave* (New York: Morrow, 1980).

5. John Naisbitt, *Megatrends: Ten New Directions Transforming Our Lives* (New York: Warner Books, 1982), p. 249.

6. Ward, *Spaceship Earth*, p. 5.

7. The denial had come in the wake of the Soviet destruction of a Korean airliner.

8. *Facts on File* 43 (Sept. 23, 1983): 717. Also see Richard Bernstein, "U.S. Aide Suggests Members Take the U.N. Elsewhere if Dissatisfied," *New York Times*, Sept. 20, 1983, p. 1.

9. Bernard D. Nossiter, "U.S. is Said to be Isolated in its Opposition to Sea-Law Treaty," *New York Times*, Dec. 9, 1982, p. 10; Nossiter, "Sea Law Signed by 117 Nations; U.S. Opposes It," *New York Times*, Dec. 11, 1982, p. 1; *Facts on File* (Dec. 31, 1983): 977.

10. H. Marshall McLuhan and Quentin Fiore, *War and Peace in the Global Village* (New York: Bantam, 1968).

11. Brzezinski, *Between Two Ages*, p. 19.

12. Thomas A. Clingan, Jr., quoted by Bernard D. Nossiter, "U.S. is Said to be Isolated in its Opposition to Sea-Law Treaty," *New York Times*, Dec. 9, 1982, p. 10.

13. The concept that the seas were part of "the common heritage" of humanity was introduced into United Nations discussions in 1970 by the ambassador from Malta, Arvid Pardo. See also Francis X. Cunningham, "The Common Heritage," *Foreign Service Journal* 58 (July/August 1981): 13–15.

14. Roger Revelle, "Law of the Sea," *Bulletin of the Atomic Scientists* 39 (May 1983): 14.

See also John Temple Swing, "Law of the Sea," *Bulletin of the Atomic Scientists* 39 (May 1983): 14–19.

15. Some of the implications of accelerating population growth and limited resources are explored by Robert S. McNamara, "Population and International Security," *International Security* 2 (Fall 1977): 25–55; Paul Ehrlich, Anne Ehrlich, John Holdren *Ecoscience* (San Francisco: Freeman, 1977); Tomas Frejka, *The Future of Population: Alternative Paths to Equilibrium* (New York: John Wiley & Sons, 1973); and Dennis Pirages, *Global Ecopolitics* (North Scituate, Ma: Duxbury, 1978).

16. Daniel Lerner, *The Passing of Traditional Society* (New York: Free Press, 1958).

17. As noted by Deutsch, often there tends to be a gap between the degree of political mobilization of potentially or actually dissident elements of a society and the degree to which such persons are assimilated into the authority structure. The "mobilization-assimilation" gap represents a challenge to the legitimacy of the regime, and thus to the stability of existing political institutions. Karl W. Deutsch, *Nationalism and Social Communication* (Cambridge, Ma: Technology Press, the Massachusetts Institute of Technology and John Wiley & Sons, 1953).

18. Bruce Russett and Harvey Starr cite the experience of Brazil from the early 1960s through the 1970s as a vivid example of the cycle of distorted development, foreign penetration, and internal conflict and coercion. Russett and Starr, *World Politics: The Menu for Choice* (San Francisco: Freeman, 1981), pp. 476–481. For a detailed analysis that is sensitive to the complexities that are associated with the Brazilian experience, see Sylvia Ann Hewlett, *The Cruel Dilemmas of Development: Twentieth-Century Brazil* (New York: Basic Books, 1980). A more general discussion of the current Latin American situation is provided by F. Parkinson, "Latin America, Her Newly Industrialising Countries and the New International Economic Order," *Journal of Latin American Studies* 16 (May 1984): 127–141.

19. Carlos Fuentes, interviewed by Richard Eder. *New York Times,* Jan. 9, 1980, p. A2.

20. See Albert Fishlow, Carlos Diaz-Alejandro, Richard R. Fagen, and Roger D. Hansen, *1980s Project of the Council on Foreign Relations: Rich and Poor Nations in the World Economy* (New York: McGraw-Hill, 1978). See also Geoffrey Barraclough, "Waiting for the New Order," *New York Review* (Oct. 26, 1978), pp. 45–54, and "The Struggle for the Third World," *New York Review* (Nov. 9, 1978), pp. 47–58.

21. Independent Commission on International Development Issues under the Chairmanship of Willy Brandt, *North-South: A Program for Survival* (Cambridge, Ma: MIT Press, 1980), p. 11.

22. Walter Millis, *Arms and Men: A Study in American Military History* (New York: New American Library, 1956), chap. 6. The literature on the threat of nuclear war and its implications for American foreign policy is now vast. Some valuable recent additions to the literature include The Harvard Nuclear Study Group, *Living With Nuclear Weapons* (New York: Bantam Books, 1983), and Richard Smoke, *National Security and the Nuclear Dilemma: An Introduction to the American Experience* (Reading, Ma: Addison-Wesley, 1984).

23. "Little Boy," the uranium bomb that was dropped on Hiroshima, weighed approximately four and a quarter tons and measured 120 inches in length by 28 inches diameter. "Fat Man," a plutonium bomb dropped on Nagasaki, weighed over five tons, and was 128 inches long and 60 inches in diameter. Norman Polmar, *Strategic Weapons: An Introduction,* rev. ed. (New York: Crane Russak for the National Strategy Information Center, 1982), figs. 1-2 and 1-3; John Toland, *The Rising Sun* (New York: Random House, 1970), pp. 869–875, 900.

24. The superpowers, however, have committed themselves to various international agreements regarding the use of outer space. The Limited Test Ban Treaty of 1963 prohibits the testing of nuclear weapons in outer space. The Outer Space Treaty of 1967 precludes

national claims to the moon and other celestial bodies and forbids parties to the treaty (the United States, the Soviet Union, and more than one hundred other states) from placing into earth's orbit "any objects carrying nuclear weapons or any other kinds of weapons of mass destruction" and from installing such weapons in outer space or on celestial bodies in any manner. Moreover, signatory parties have pledged "to be guided by the principle of co-operation and mutual assistance" in their exploration and other activities in outer space, "with due regard to the corresponding interests of all other State Parties to the Treaty." The texts of the treaties and brief histories of negotiations have been published by the United States Arms Control and Disarmament Agency, *Arms Control and Disarmament Agreements*, 1982 ed. (Washington, D.C.: Government Printing Office, 1982). See also Seyom Brown, Nina W. Cornell, Larry L. Fabian, and Edith Brown Weiss, *Regimes for the Ocean, Outer Space, and Weather* (Washington, D.C.: Brookings Institute, 1977).

25. Henry Kissinger, "A Plan to Reshape NATO," *Time* 123 (March 5, 1984): 20–24.
26. See Pirages, *Global Ecopolitics;* Robert O. Keohane and Joseph S. Nye, *Power and Interdependence: World Politics in Transition* (Boston: Little, Brown, 1977); Ole R. Holsti, Randolph M. Siverson, and Alexander L. George, eds., *Change in the International System* (Boulder, Co: Westview, 1980).
27. See e.g., C. Fred Bergsten, Thomas O. Horst, and Theodore H. Moran, *American Multinationals and American Interests* (Washington, D.C.: Brookings Institute, 1978); Richard J. Barnet and Ronald E. Muller, *Global Reach: The Power of the Multinational Corporations* (New York: Simon & Schuster, 1974); Raymond Vernon, *Storm over the Multinationals: The Real Issues* (Cambridge, Ma: Harvard University Press, 1977).

SUGGESTED ADDITIONAL READING

BERES, LOUIS RENE. *Apocalypse: Nuclear Catastrophe in World Politics.* Chicago: University of Chicago Press, 1980.

BERGSTEN, C. FRED, editor. *The Future of the International Economic Order.* Lexington, MA: Heath, 1973.

CHACE, JAMES. *Solvency: The Price of Survival, An Essay on American Foreign Policy.* New York: Random House, 1981.

COHEN, STEPHEN D. *The Making of United States International Economic Policy: Principles, Problems and Proposals for Reform.* New York: Praeger, 1981.

DEUDNEY, DANIEL. *Whole Earth Security: A Geopolitics of Peace.* Worldwatch Paper no. 55. Washington, D.C.: Worldwatch Institute, July 1983.

DUIGNAN, PETER, and RABUSHKA, ALVIN, eds. *The United States in the 1980s.* Abridged edition. Reading, MA: Addison-Wesley by arrangement with the Hoover Institution Press, 1980.

EBINGER, CHARLES K. *The Critical Link: Energy and National Security.* Cambridge, MA: Ballinger Publishing Co., 1981.

ECKES, ALFRED E., JR. *The United States and the Global Struggle for Minerals.* Austin, TX: The University of Texas Press, 1979.

FALK, RICHARD. *The End of World Order.* New York: Holmes and Meier, 1983.

FEINBERG, RICHARD E. *The Intemperate Zone: The Third World Challenge to U.S. Foreign Policy.* New York: Norton, 1983.

GILPIN, ROBERT. *War and Change in World Politics.* New York: Cambridge University Press, 1981.

HARVARD NUCLEAR STUDY GROUP. *Living with Nuclear Weapons.* New York: Bantam Books, 1983.

HOLSTI, OLE R.; SIVERSON, RANDOLPH M.; and GEORGE, ALEXANDER L., eds. *Change in the International System.* Boulder, CO: Westview, 1980.

HOPKINS, RAYMOND F., and PUCHALA, DONALD J. *Global Food Interdependence: Challenge to American Foreign Policy.* New York: Columbia University Press, 1980.

KUPPERMAN, ROBERT H., and TAYLOR, WILLIAM J., Jr. *Strategic Requirements for the Army to the Year 2000.* Lexington, MA: D. C. Heath, 1984.

LEHMAN, JOHN; and WEISS, SEYMOUR. *Beyond the SALT II Failure.* New York: Praeger, 1981.

ODELL, JOHN S. *U.S. International Monetary Policy: Markets, Power, and Ideas as Sources of Change.* Princeton, NJ: Princeton University Press, 1982.

PRANGER, ROBERT J., ed. "Dimensions of U.S. Foreign Policy in the 1980s," special double issues of AEI *Foreign Policy and Defense Review* 4 (1984).

RUSSETT, BRUCE. *Prisoners of Insecurity: Nuclear Deterrence, the Arms Race, and Arms Control.* San Francisco: Freeman, 1983.

SAGAN, CARL. "Nuclear War and Climatic Catastrophe." *Foreign Affairs* 62 (Winter 83/84): 257–292.

SHUE, HENRY. *Basic Rights: Subsistence, Affluence, and American Foreign Policy.* Princeton, NJ: Princeton University Press, 1980.

STEIN, JONATHAN B. *From H-Bomb to Star Wars: The Politics of Strategic Decision Making.* Lexington, MA: Lexington Books, 1984.

THOMPSON, WILLIAM IRWIN. *At the Edge of History: Speculations on the Transformation of Culture.* New York: Harper & Row, 1971.

U.S., PRESIDENT'S COMMISSION FOR A NATIONAL AGENDA FOR THE EIGHTIES, Panel on the United States and the World Community. *The United States and the World Community in the Eighties.* Washington, DC: Government Printing Office, 1980.

Index